Foreword

by Maria Miller MP
Parliamentary Under secretary of State and Minister for Disabled People

Helping disabled people to participate fully in society is at the heart of the Government's work on disability equality. The OpenBritain guide makes a valuable contribution to the lives of disabled people and I am pleased to introduce the 2011 edition.

Providing a wide range of information on accessibility in one place allows disabled visitors to make informed choices about the places that may best suit them.

Not only is this initiative creating a national and comprehensive access information system which

is useful to anyone visiting the UK, it also provides businesses with an additional way to highlight and promote their accessible services.

OpenBritain is playing an important part in incentivising more businesses to improve their own accessibility and provides a challenge to those that aren't listed. With over 10 million disabled people in the UK, it clearly makes good business sense to make services accessible to disabled customers.

The Government is firmly committed to supporting disabled people to participate fully in society and will seek every opportunity to do so.

I am sure that even more businesses will be striving to be listed in this guide in the years to come.

Maa Miller

Welcome

to the new OpenBritain guide to accessible places to stay and visit.

This is the second OpenBritain guide, and we are delighted that the demand for it was such that we are increasing the print run. We must thank Motability for their support in ordering copies to be distributed through their showrooms. We also thank the National Federation of Shopmobility, and RADAR, for their continued support, along with all the advertisers and members who have made this whole enterprise viable.

It has been a momentous year for us, with major new supporters signing up. Thanks to the involvement of British Telecom (BT) we are working hard at creating an OpenBritain opensource open platform, which will launch during 2011, and enable a whole range of innovative projects to work from the access data that we are putting together. Our work has been boosted enormously thanks to the partnership of DisabledGo with OpenBritain. DisabledGo undertake a wide range of access audits which have all been based on very detailed consultation with different disability groups, and have agreed that OpenBritain can use their relevant data, including over 30,000 individual venues or properties. VisitBritain are also offering invaluable support through their national tourism database, NTOP/EnglandNet.

This guide continues to include all the accommodation providers inspected under the National Accessible Scheme operated by VisitEngland, along with those known to the Scottish and Welsh tourism agencies. All the providers listed in the former RADAR guides have been invited to join OpenBritain and be subject to randomized checks of their facilities.

Readers should therefore be aware that there is a distinction between those properties who have been officially inspected, and those who are self-assessed but subject to a random check. OpenBritain cannot take responsibility for information which has been wrongly supplied to us. We are keen to include a wide range of choice for you, the traveller looking for accessible facilities, and as all the schemes in the UK are voluntary rather than statutory, there is no one comprehensive, reliable source.

It is also evident that what will suit one person may not suit another. However, with the new OpenBritain database and open platform, we are working hard to get all the various collections of data under one roof and easily searchable for you. Also our openbritain.net website will be revamped in the Spring, and we hope that you can help us build the level of information available by giving feedback that will help other travellers. We are delighted that BT volunteers will help us collect new data to help 'fill in the gaps' in our coverage. However, we have the most extensive accessible tourism data in the UK on the OpenBritain website and guide.

If you are planning a visit to the UK from overseas, this is the guide for you. You may perhaps be planning a visit to see the London Olympics and Paralympics, and Tourism for All will be there to help.

We are encouraged that the new government has maintained the support that we met from the last one. The Department of Culture Media and Sport, which includes Tourism, have continued to provide us with a small grant, and we have met John Penrose MP, the new Tourism Minister and gained his ongoing interest. The new Disability Minister, Maria Miller MP is kindly providing a foreword for this guide. We thank them both and look forward to a positive year ahead of making sure we are ready to welcome the world – people of all abilities and interests – in 2012.

Thank you for your support

Jenifer Littman

Jenifer Littman, Chief Executive, Tourism for All UK

There's more to life than shopping

There's the beach ▪ park ▪ woods ▪ hills ▪ walks ▪ jogging ▪ canoeing ▪ fishing ▪ sailing

Get out there in style and rise to new challenges in comfort in our lightweight, fun and stylish range of Delta All-Terrain Buggies, or the Hippocampe Amphibious Wheelchair.

To experience new environments, enjoy previously inaccessible places or just hit the beach, call Delichon on **01725 519405**, or visit **www.delichon.co.uk** There **is** more to life than shopping.

Delichon Ltd.
Performance Seating Systems

Kings Yard, Martin, Fordingbridge, Hants SP6 3LB
T: 01725 519405 **E**: info@delichon.co.uk

Foreword

By Sally Davis, Chief Executive, BT Wholesale

Among the many choices we make every day is whether we focus on a person's ability or simply see their disability.

As a company, and as one of the largest employers in country, BT embraces diversity in all its forms. This means investing to create a work environment that is fully accessible and provides the tools to help all BT people contribute fully to the success of our business.

We know that when BT's workforce mirrors the diversity inherent in our customer base, we have a chance to better understand our customers, and what they need.

BT chooses to invest in innovation to create products, services and solutions that help bridge the barriers a

disability can create. By providing access to appropriate telecommunications, we can help everyone participate in and contribute fully to society and the economy overall.

This is not a grand act of corporate altruism. No sensible business would choose to ignore a significant market opportunity. There are over 10 million people in the UK with a disability and if BT doesn't address their needs, someone else will choose to.

Like telecommunications, tourism and leisure is a market. When people with disabilities go on holiday, they want their break to be without barriers. Businesses that recognise and address this need will benefit. It's a choice businesses can make.

BT is proud to support OpenBritain, its goal and the support it offers businesses to enable access and remove barriers for people with disabilities.

When we all get behind it, the UK economy will benefit as well.

Sally Davis

Meeting our Czech and Italian colleagues in Italy at Accessible Tourism in Europe (ATE)

Tourism for all UK

"The world from a disabled person's viewpoint is often very different. I notice the places below waist level that don't get cleaned, for instance. If everyone shared my viewpoint, there would be a lot better service for everyone....."

"It was the first time I had got up courage to book into a hotel. Thanks to Tourism for All, we got all the information we needed, and the hotel really looked after us. "

Tourism for All UK is a national charity dedicated to improving accessible facilities and services, and providing the information that disabled people need in order to make informed decisions about where and how they can travel, stay, visit and take part in the wonderful tourism opportunities the UK offers.

For years disabled people have told us about the problems they encounter, the courage it takes to travel, and the difficulties of finding information located on so many different websites.

This new guide and its associated website OpenBritain.net is our answer to the information problem. Thanks to the support of partners - the **national tourism boards,** access company **DisabledGo,** disability charities, especially

RADAR and the **National Federation of Shopmobility,** and **British Telecom** - we are now close to reaching our dream. This is to be able to provide this information all from one source, encouraging everyone to lodge their relevant data on a single information platform. By making it available to developers who can thus create different applications and imaginative projects, it can reach people in a variety of ways and according to their needs.

We have to thank **British Telecom** and their opensource technology experts **Osmosoft** in particular for undertaking this on our behalf. In addition to the partners mentioned above, who together have a wealth of information, we also have to thank a range of industry organisations from the **British Hospitality Association,** to **English Heritage,** the **Historic Houses Association,** the **Automobile Association** and many more. The **OpenBritain.net** website will continue to develop to reflect the growth of support, with information and offers designed to meet your needs.

You may find a human voice on the phone or someone who can answer your detailed enquiries by email is the only way to gain the level of assurance you need. Tourism for All UK operates the only free helpline and independent information service that provides this. With 30 years of expertise as an organisation, we hope to answer all your questions.

Carrie-Ann Fleming is TFA's Information officer, and works from the Vitalise call centre offices in Kendal, Cumbria.

The free TFA helpline is funded by charitable support, mostly generated from membership fees from those who choose to join us as Friends. We invite all readers of this guide to consider joining TFA as a Friend. This not only helps us to secure the future of this vital service, but also provides you with a range of benefits:

Become a Friend of Tourism for All and enjoy:

- A reservations service with discounted hotel rates – accessible rooms at discounted rates, up to 35% off at participating hotels all over the UK and Europe.

- Regular Newsletters and E-Bulletins – with news, new places to stay and visit, members articles, developments in the law and practices in the tourism sector, and more.

- Up to 5 free Regional and specialist access information guides (worth £3.50 each) online, or in printed information guides.

- Access to members only areas of the TFA website – including a members forum, where you can share stories, post enquiries, and give feedback so that you can benefit from the experiences of others, and play a role in pushing forward the agenda in making change happen.

- Many other time-limited exclusive offers on holidays, places to stay and visit which are published on the TFA Website and in the newsletter.

- NEW! Exclusive members' days at accessible attractions

All this for only £25.00 which you can save in a single hotel booking.

TFA Patron Tanni Grey-Thompson (left) helps launch OpenBritain in Buckinghamshire with partners from BT, Buckinghamshire, and DisabledGo

20 YEARS OF TFA SERVICE

Tourism for All Services is a wholly owned subsidiary of the charity that offers access audits, destination audits, and advice to business and public sector organisations seeking to improve their accessibility or comply with the Disability Discrimination Act. Businesses advised by TFA Services have gone on to win Access Awards:

> "I cannot thank Brian Seaman and Tourism for All enough for all their help and advice – the whole accessible issue was made easy with their guidance and support. Put simply, we could never have done it, or done it so well, without you".
> **Mortons House Hotel, Dorset**

The contact is **Brian Seaman**, on **01293 776225** or **brian@tourismforall.org.uk**

We can also offer online staff training in welcoming disabled guests. The Access for All Training has been developed with the help of people with impairments and industry professionals, and is endorsed by the Institute of Hospitality. The contact for **Access for All Training** is **Tim Gardiner** on **timgardiner@tourismforall. org.uk** All business members of Tourism for All and OpenBritain can access this training free of charge.

Tourism for All Services Limited donates 100% of all profits to the charity Tourism for All UK Registered Charity 279169

A company limited by guarantee Registered in England No 02567422 VAT No: GB 602 6087 66 Registered Office: 16 Swordfish Drive, Christchurch, Dorset BH23 4TP

A good night guaranteed, across the nation.

With over 600 accessible hotels nationwide, it's easy for you to stay away from home with Premier Inn. Our guests tell us they love the value we offer, our clean and comfortable rooms and the warm welcome they receive from our team members. Add to this our unique Good Night Guarantee and you can be assured of a great stay whatever your needs, wherever you stay.

Book now at **premierinn.com**

Everything's Premier but the Price

RADAR is a national network of disability organisations and disabled people. RADAR represent their members by fast-tracking their opinions and concerns to policy-makers and legislators in Westminster and Whitehall, and launching campaigns to promote equality for all disabled people. Registered Charity 273150

Books which open doors to independent living

To help people living with ill-health, injury or disability lead as independent a life as possible. RADAR has published two valuable guides.

If Only I'd Known That A Year Ago

A guide for newly disabled people, their families and friends

A self-help guide signposting to valuable support and specialist information on social and health care, welfare rights and benefits

National Key Scheme Guide (NKS) 2010: accessible toilets for disabled people

A guide to the 8,000+ accessible disabled toilets around the UK fitted with the National Key Scheme lock.

An important part of freedom is having the confidence to go out, knowing that public toilets will be available that are accessible and meet your requirements.

Copies are available from RADAR t 020 7250 3222
e radar@radar.org.uk minicom 020 7250 4119 web www.radar-shop.org.uk

How to use this guide

OpenBritain is the new definitive guide for visitors to the UK with access needs. Packed with easy to use information - where to stay, how to get there, and what to see and do when you arrive. Working with organisations and companies throughout the UK, all offering products and services dedicated to making Britain more accessible.

OpenBritain offers you a wide choice of accommodation, from hotels to B&B's, self catering properties to caravan parks. All the accommodation within this guide must either be accessed under the National Accessible Scheme (NAS) or a member of VisitScotland, Visit Wales, Visit London schemes or self-assessed though **OpenBritain.** Those with NAS inspection are flagged to offer you the highest level of reassurance.

Looking for great places to visit whilst you are there? At the end of each accommodation section you will find attractions for that region. **OpenBritain** members offer you more detailed information on what facilities they provide and look out for the 'AS' symbol, which is your at-a-glance guide to those with an Access Statement.

The restaurants appearing in 'Where to Eat' have been inspected by DisabledGo and assessed in detail for accessibility. The listing is just a small selection for the region, you can find more choice and detail at **www.disabledgo.com**

OpenBritain helps you with 'getting there... and back'. The travel section will give you up-to-date, useful information, hints & tips on travelling in and around the UK. All the information you need on planes, trains and automobiles.

Don't forget, home or away, the UK is accessible. **OpenBritain** members are offering you a whole range of facilities, equipment, services and experiences you might never have considered before. Look inside to find out much more about what is available.

With over a decade of experience in the manufacture of bespoke adjustable beds, we can offer high quality sleeping solutions that have your specific needs in mind. We offer a range of sizes from 2ft 3" to 6ft 0" and a number of different upholstered and wooden base options. However our pride and joy is our selection of mattresses, which offer both fantastic comfort and very high longevity.

We also offer a range of accessories, including full divan bases, storage draws, wireless handsets, and our special "Carer-Assist" bed lifter, which can be fitted to beds from 3ft to 4ft 6".

Contact us for more information on our products!

Website: www.motiontech.co.uk

Telephone: 01636 816455

Ratings

Star ratings are internationally recognisable and give you a guide to the standard of quality for accommodation. Whether rated by VisitEngland, VisitScotland, VisitWales or the AA, these ratings give you information at a glance.

Star ratings made simple

★	No frills, basic facilities
★★	Well maintained with a good level of service
★★★	Friendly, very good quality and well presented
★★★★	Excellent standards, high quality facilities and attentive service
★★★★★	Exceptional service and surroundings. An extra bit of luxury

More detail can be found on

www.theaa.com/travel

www.enjoyengland.com/stay

www.visitscotland.com/guide/where-to-stay

**www.visitwales.co.uk/
holiday-accommodation-in-wales**

Awards

★★★★★ **Gold and Silver Awards -** Highlighted
★★★★★ by gold or silver coloured stars, these colours denote properties offering the highest levels of quality within their star rating (part of the EnjoyEngland scheme).

Accommodation types

The following types of accommodation can be found in this guide:

■ **Hotels**: Hotel, Small Hotel, Country House Hotel, Town House Hotel, Metro Hotel, Budget Hotel, Restaurant with Rooms, Serviced Apartments

Guest Accommodation: Guest Accommodation, Bed & Breakfast, Guest House, Farmhouse, Inn

Hostel Accommodation: Hostel, Group Hostel, Activity Accommodation, Backpacker, Bunkhouse, Camping Barn

■ **Self Catering:** Self Catering, Approved Caravan Holiday Homes, Chalets, Campus Accommodation

■ **Camping & Caravan Parks:** Camping Park, Touring Park, Holiday Park, Holiday Village, Forest Holiday Village

Detailed descriptions of these accommodation types can be found at **openbritain.net**

National Accessible Scheme

England

Accommodation is assessed under VisitEngland's National Accessible Scheme, which includes standards useful for hearing and visually impaired guests in addition to standards useful for guests with mobility impairment.

Accommodation taking part in this scheme will display one or more of the mobility, visual or hearing symbols shown on this page.

When you see one of the symbols, you can be sure that the accommodation and core facilities have been thoroughly assessed against demanding criteria. If you have additional needs or special requirements, we strongly recommend that you make sure these can be met by your chosen establishment before you confirm your booking.

Visual Impairment Symbols

Typically provides key additional services and facilities to meet the needs of visually impaired guests.

Typically provides a higher level of additional services and facilities to meet the needs of visually impaired guests.

Hearing Impairment Symbols

Typically provides key additional services and facilities to meet the needs of guests with hearing impairment.

Typically provides a higher level of additional services and facilities to meet the needs of guests with hearing impairment.

London

This Guide lists hotels in London that have not been assessed under VisitEngland's National Accessible Scheme. These establishments do, however, have bedrooms suitable for wheelchair users and have been audited on behalf of the London Development Agency by Direct Enquiries. For more information go to directenquiries.com/LDAhotels.

Scotland

All kinds of accommodation are assessed by VisitScotland Quality Advisors, based on criteria drawn up with the co-operation of organisations which deal with wheelchair users. This is part of the VisitScotland grading schemes. Criteria can be found on **visitscotland.com/accommodation/accessiblescotland** Accommodation accessibility is checked every three years. Entries show one of three symbols.

 Category 1 - Accessible to a wheelchair user travelling independently.

 Category 2 - Accessible to a wheelchair user travelling with assistance.

 Category 3 - Accessible to a wheelchair user able to walk a few paces and up a maximum of three steps.

Wales

Owners of all types of accommodation in Wales should have a full Access Statement available to visitors.

Mobility Impairment Symbols

 Older and less mobile guests
Typically suitable for a person with sufficient mobility to climb a flight of steps but who would benefit from fixtures and fittings to aid balance.

 Part-time wheelchair users
Typically suitable for a person with restricted walking ability and for those who may need to use a wheelchair some of the time and can negotiate a maximum of three steps.

 Independent wheelchair users
Typically suitable for a person who depends on the use of a wheelchair and transfers unaided to and from the wheelchair in a seated position. This person may be an independent traveller.

 Assisted wheelchair users
Typically suitable for a person who depends on the use of a wheelchair and needs assistance when transferring to and from the wheelchair in a seated position.

  Access Exceptional is awarded to establishments that meet the requirements of independent wheelchair users or assisted wheelchair users shown above and also fulfil more demanding requirements with reference to the British Standards BS8300.

The criteria VisitEngland and national/regional tourism organisations have adopted do not necessarily conform to British Standards or to Building Regulations. They reflect what the organisations understand to be acceptable to meet the practical needs of guests with mobility or sensory impairments and encourage the industry to increase access to all.

Accommodation entries explained

All the establishments featured in this guide must be either inspected under the National Accessible Scheme (NAS), operated by VisitEngland, or under those operated by VisitScotland, VisitLondon or other regional schemes, OR accommodations, attractions, or services who have joined OpenBritain on a self-assessed basis, and are subject to random checks. The former offer a higher level of assurance and are clearly flagged.

1 Locations

Entries are listed alphabetically by town name, by county, within each region. Some properties, where located in a small village may be listed under a nearby town (within 7 miles).

Complete addresses are not given for Self Catering properties for security reasons and the town(s) listed may be a distance from the establishment. Please check the location at time of booking.

2 Map References

Maps can be found starting on page 366 of the guide.

3 Contact Information

Establishment name and booking details including telephone number.

Note: Prices and ratings shown were supplied to us by the proprietors in Summer 2010. These may have been changed after this guide has gone to press and we advise that you check at time of booking.

Prices are shown in pounds sterling and include VAT where applicable.

4 Prices

Bed & Breakfast: Per room for B&B and per person for evening meal (d=Double s=Single)

Hotels: Per room for B&B and per person for half board (d=Double s=Single).

Evening Meal: Prices shown are per person per night.

Self Catering: Prices shown are per unit per week for low and high season (inc. VAT)

Camping and Caravan Parks: Per pitch per night for touring pitches; per unit per week for caravan holiday homes.

5 Opening

Indicates when the establishment is open.

6 Symbols

An at-a-glance view of services and facilities available. The key to these symbols can be found on page 22.

7 Access Statements

'AS' denotes that an Access Statement is available. These can be viewed on openbritain.net

8 Ratings

Quality Rating awarded to the establishment. For more information see pg 17.

9 Travel Directions

Location and brief directions.

Sandringham | Park House Hotel

AS

Enjoy England ★★

Open: All year

Rooms per night:
s: £110.00-£158.00
d: £186.00-£288.00
p/p half board:
d: £108.00-£173.00
Meals: £15.00-£17.50
Shop: 1.5 miles
Pub: 1.5 miles

Sandringham PE35 6EH
t 01485 543000 **e** parkinfo@lcdisability.org
parkhousehotel.org.uk

3B1

Located on the Royal Sandringham Estate, the hotel has 8 single and 8 twin rooms and is adapted for people with mobility difficulties/ disabilities with or without carers/ companions. The hotel is fully accessible and care is available if required.

Location: From King's Lynn, A149 to Hunstanton, follow tourist signs to Sandringham. Hotel is on RHS, just before Sandringham Visitor Centre.

Access:
∴ ♿ abc 📷 🐾 🏢 ☺ ♿
♿

General:
🛏 ✕ 🍸 P♿ ✿ 📧 ♿

Room:
🛏 ♨ 📻 🚾 S ☕

Key to symbols

Information about many of the facilities and services available at attractions, hotels/places to stay and restaurants is given in the form of symbols.

 Fully wheelchair accessible

 Seat Available

 WC WC Standard

 Adapted Changing Rooms

 Changing Places Facilities

 @ **FAX** Contacting the venue

 Home Service

 P ★★★ Car Parking at Venue

 P ★★ Blue Badge Parking Available

 P ★ Public Car Park (200m approx)

 Adapted Accommodation

 Sign Language used

 Disability Awareness Training

 Access trained staff

 Facilities for the visually impaired

 Induction Loop system

 Hearing facilities

 abc Large print information

 ∴ Braille information

 Assistance dogs welcome

 Wheelchair accessible leisure facilities

 Designated wheelchair accessible public toilet

Wheelchair accessible dining area

Wheelchair accessible ground floor

National Accessible Scheme

For information on the National Accessible Scheme, see page 18

Wheelchair accessible bedroom		Chemical toilet disposal point
Children welcome		Motor home waste disposal point
Designated parking		Showers
Ramped or level entrance		Laundry facilities
Staff available to assist by arrangement		Caravans
Licensed bar		Motor caravans
Evening meal by arrangement or restaurant on site		Tents
Special diets by arrangement		Wheelchair accessible gardens
Accessible Lift		Tactile routes
Hoist available		Visual alarm system
Garden/patio		Audible alarm system
Bedroom(s) on ground floor		Typetalk available
Text phone/inductive coupler		TV listening device
TV with subtitles		Adapted kitchen
Tea/coffee facilities in all bedrooms		Embossed kitchen equipment
Accessible shower		Daily servicing of unit
Seating in shower		Weekend/midweek bookings
Toilet seat raiser		Food shop on site
Overnight holding area		Caravan holiday homes
Motor home pitches reserved for day trips off-site		Log cabins/lodges
Electrical hook-up points for caravans and tents		Chalets/villas
Calor Gas/Camping Gaz purchase/exchange service		Virtual tour

Britain's most beautiful

For an altogether more relaxing and inspiring day out, visit an RHS Garden near you.

Enjoy glorious vistas, year-round beauty and ever-changing colour across a wide variety of heavenly garden landscapes.

Each RHS Garden is a scented experience and offers limited pre-booked wheelchair availability, wheelchair routes and free admission for assistance dogs and a carer. Each garden also features a Plant Centre, Gift Shop, Coffee Shop(s) and free parking with disabled bays.

RHS GARDEN HARLOW CARR
North Yorkshire

- Limited pre-booked electric scooters & wheelchairs
- Guided walks available on request
- Large print guides available on request

01423 724 690

RHS GARDEN HYDE HALL
Essex

- Free mobility buggy

01245 400 256

Wheelchair Routes
Free Entry
for Assistance Dogs & Carers

days out

RHS GARDEN ROSEMOOR
Devon

- Guided walks available on request

RHS GARDEN WISLEY
Surrey

- Limited pre-booked electric scooters
- Free mobility buggy

 Royal Horticultural Society

01805 624 067

0845 260 9000

www.rhs.org.uk/gardens
RHS Registered Charity No. 222879/SC038262

Shopmobility
...the freedom to get around

What Is Shopmobility?

Shopmobility is a Scheme which lends manual wheelchairs, powered wheelchairs and powered scooters to members of the public with limited mobility, to shop and to visit leisure and commercial facilities within the town, city or shopping centre. It aims to:

- Enable people with temporarily or permanently impaired mobility to engage or re-engage with their community and travel with confidence, thus enhancing their quality of life, and providing them and their carers with independence

- Set uniform and trustworthy standards of safety and service for Shopmobility users, and encourage good practice and consistency of approach

- Act as a national network helping disabled and older people to travel with ease and enjoy shopping, leisure and other facilities

- Encourage equality of access for disabled and older people to all main towns and city centres

How Much Does It Cost?

All Schemes operate slightly differently; some provide **Shopmobility** as a free service while others make a charge. Most Schemes welcome any donations you wish to make.

Who Can Use Shopmobility?

Shopmobility is for anyone, young or old, whether their disability is temporary or permanent. It is available for those with injuries, long or short-term disabilities – anyone who needs help with mobility.

Shopmobility is about the freedom to get around. You do not need to be registered disabled to use it.

How Do I Use Shopmobility?

Each Scheme varies so it is important to contact the Scheme you wish to visit prior to using the service. A member of staff or volunteer will give you all the information you need.

Most Schemes ask that you bring identification containing your name and address on your first visit; this is so that Schemes can complete a registration form and keep a record of your details. Many Schemes will issue you with a membership card, and on your next visit you can simply show this card.

w **www.shopmobilityuk.org**
e **info@shopmobilityuk.org**   t **08456 442446**

NATIONAL FEDERATION OF
Shopmobility

Deaf visitors using British Sign Language

The Ancient Problem of Access

Ideas on a postcard please – how can we create level, step-free access at a 1000-year old castle, that was built on a steep hill, with winding, narrow stairs and acres of cobbles...otherwise known as the Tower of London?!

Tactile palace model

Historic Royal Palaces is the independent charity that cares for the Tower of London, Hampton Court Palace, the Banqueting House, Kensington Palace and Kew Palace. Each palace has survived for hundreds of years; our oldest building is nearly 1000 years old and our youngest a mere 250.

All our palaces ceased being used regularly for royal court purposes in the 18th century. They were first opened to the public in the 19th century, although the Tower of London was open to selected visitors much earlier.

When it comes to improving access, we are presented with a unique set of challenges as historic buildings generally weren't built with disabled access in mind – and palaces and royal residences even less so. Indeed, the Tower of London was specifically built to keep people out!

That said, visitors with special needs are nothing new; at various times we've accommodated monarchs who required additional assistance. For example, towards the end of his life Henry VIII started using a chair on wheels, called a 'tramme', to get between his chambers at Hampton Court Palace. William III suffered from asthma so the staircases at Hampton Court and Kensington Palace – both of which were remodelled by William III and his

Walking up King's Staircase

wife, Mary II, in the 1690s – are shallow and have several landings. Queen Anne, who spent much of her reign at Kensington, was grateful for this foresight as she had difficulty walking.

Henry, William and Anne had a large number of household servants though. If extra help was needed there were people around to assist. Nowadays, we don't have this massive staff resource so must find practical ways to make the palaces as accessible as possible. Disabled people should be able to visit with the minimum of effort on everyone's part!

However, we are limited on the physical changes we can make. During the rebuilding of Kew Palace, which reopened in 2006, we were able to add a lift to the side of the building – but only because there had originally been a service shaft there. Access points, bricked up by previous residents, could be knocked through easily

without damaging the original fabric of the building. It's no good deciding to install a lift if users can't also get out at the relevant floors!

Kensington Palace is in the middle of a £12 million refurbishment project (donations still welcome!) which includes the installation of a lift so that vertical access will be possible from 2012. However, it has only been achieved thanks to years of creative thinking, meticulous planning and negotiation to find somewhere suitable to put it. But we

Wheelchair user on the Broadwalk

Deaf signing in Great H

won't be giving up. Quite apart from the legal requirements of the Disability Discrimination Act (which doesn't override existing legislation concerning the protection of ancient monuments, listed buildings or the Health & Safety Acts), our work is driven by society's changing attitudes to disabled people and by our desire to open up the palaces and their stories to a new visitor group.

Where access is not possible for various reasons, we strive to provide improved interpretation facilities and alternative services. For example, the magnificent Rubens ceiling in the Banqueting House in Whitehall can now be viewed easily by looking down, not up; mirrored tables give a clear view to those who can't easily look up. There are also some enlarged images of the main canvases in the drawers underneath – useful for anyone who wants to see the detail as well as those who need enlarged versions of print and images.

British Sign Language tours are also available at all our palaces for deaf visitors – either on a regular, scheduled basis or on request – as are descriptive tours for blind and partially sighted visitors. Our three Access Panels (made up of disabled people living near the Tower, Hampton Court and Kensington) are a wonderful source of ideas of those small changes that can make a big difference. For example, while recommending that we provide as much seating as possible they also asked that we don't put benches opposite each other, particularly outside. Visitors in need of frequent rests want to admire the view not other seated people.

Our aim is to help everyone explore the story of how monarchs and people have shaped society, in some of the greatest palaces ever built. Some creative, lateral thinking may be required but a lot can be done to make visiting easier and rewarding for those with additional needs.

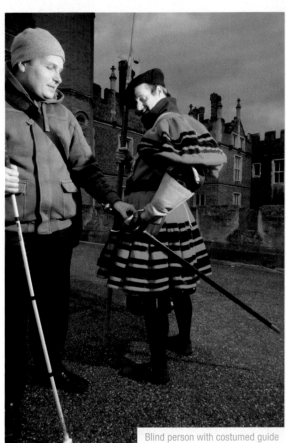
Blind person with costumed guide

For further information about access and visiting any or all of our palaces visit our website
www.hrp.org.uk

Welcome to Accor hotels

Where friendly staff are on hand in over 140 hotels across Britain – whatever your needs, whatever your budget.

SOFITEL
LUXURY HOTELS

Three elegant 5 star French *art de vivre* hotels situated in St James, London, Gatwick and Heathrow T5

4 star hotels with fresh contemporary design. Over 30 across the UK

Mid-market 4 star quality hotels with their own distinct character. Over 30 across the UK

Full-service budget hotels the way you like them. Over 50 across the UK and Ireland

New international budget hotels with distinctive personality and all-inclusive rates. Three London hotels

Low-cost hotels with guaranteed standards. 17 across the UK

For more information and bookings visit
or call 0870 609 0961 / **accor**hotels.com

Motability

it changed our lives!

"

Before joining the Scheme, it was difficult to get around but now I am able to do a lot of things I was struggling to do before.

Namik Ozturk

"

where will yours take you?

use your mobility allowance to get mobile...

Simply exchange it for an all-inclusive worry-free mobility package, including:

- New car, powered wheelchair or scooter
- Insurance
- Servicing and repairs
- Tyres
- Breakdown cover

freephone
0800 093 1000 (MO155B)

or visit **www.motability.co.uk** for further details

Registered Charity No 299745

Make more of every day with Motability

With Motability you can make the most of every day as it gives you the freedom and reassurance of a brand new car, scooter or powered wheelchair simply by using your weekly mobility allowance.

The right mobility solution for you

You can choose from over 4,000 cars from all the major manufacturers, including a range of automatics and lower emission cars. There's a wide range of cars available for no more than your allowance or if you prefer, you can pay a little extra (an Advance Payment) for a more expensive model.

There are also over 200 scooters and powered wheelchairs available, ranging from small, boot scooters to large, road legal (Class 3) scooters and powered wheelchairs. And most of the models available cost less than your weekly mobility allowance.

Adaptations and Wheelchair Accessible Vehicles

If you need adaptations fitted to your car in order to drive, you'll find many of the popular ones add nothing to the cost. There is also a wide range of affordable Wheelchair Accessible Vehicles available.

How Motability could save you money

With Motability, everything is included in your lease, except fuel. And because new cars are usually more fuel-efficient than older ones, you could also save money at the pump.

Worry-free mobility with everything included

When you lease a car through Motability, insurance for two named drivers, servicing and maintenance costs plus RAC breakdown assistance, a 60,000 mileage allowance and replacement tyres and windscreens are all included.

Or, if you choose to lease a scooter or powered wheelchair through Motability, you'll benefit from standard pricing nationwide, insurance, breakdown assistance from Motability Assist, servicing, maintenance, repairs and tyre and battery replacement.

Start your worry-free journey today

With nearly 5,000 dealerships offering Motability across the UK, there's sure to be a Motability Specialist near you. They can answer your questions and provide you with the mobility solution you need. For more information or to find your local car, scooter or powered wheelchair dealer, visit **www.motability.co.uk** or call us on **0800 093 1000** (please quote MO155B).

"Our car is our lifeline to our family and friends, and so much more"

Mr G Mann, Blackpool

"Just knowing the support is ready to help on all those motorways, gives me the confidence I need to do these journeys without anxiety"

Ms R Gunning, Liverpool

"Without Motability I would not be able to run a car and would become almost housebound - it enables me to get to church, go shopping, enjoy holidays and visit places I would not otherwise be able to get to."

Ms J Steel, Bingley

If you, your partner or your child receive either the **Higher Rate Mobility Component of the Disability Living Allowance** or the **War Pensioners' Mobility Supplement** (around £50 a week), you can exchange it for a brand new car, scooter or powered wheelchair through Motability.

Contact us today
Visit: www.motability.co.uk
Call: 0800 093 1000 (lines open daily, 8am-8pm) please quote MO155B

Calvert Trust
Exmoor

Challenging disability through outdoor adventure

Calvert Trust Exmoor provides challenging outdoor adventure for disabled people of all ages and abilities together with their families, friends and carers.

A beautiful Victorian Model Farm conversion is home to this award winning outdoor education centre which has been running for over 13 years, situated next to the **Wistlandpound Reservoir** on the edge of **Exmoor National Park**, close to the stunning **North Devon coast**.

Originally founded in 1978 the Calvert Trust was the inspiration of John Fryer-Spedding, whose vision was to enable people with disabilities to benefit from outdoor activities in the countryside. Since then the Calvert Trust has gone from strength to strength and now operates 3 Centres in Britain welcoming over 11,000 visitors a year, the most southerly being **Exmoor** with other sites in the **Lake District** and the **Kielder Forest**.

At Calvert Trust Exmoor everyone is encouraged to take part; it's what you can do that counts. Multi activity breaks allow guests to try a variety of exciting and stimulating activities in a structured programme, tailored to their

specific needs. The fully accessible centre is registered with the Adventure Activities Licensing Authority and has recently been awarded a prestigious Gold Standard from the Association of Heads of Outdoor Education Centres. All activities are on site, specifically designed and equipped to cater for all ages and abilities, you can even abseil in a wheelchair! The highly experienced, inspirational instructors are qualified by national governing bodies such as the BCU, RYA and BHS and are specially trained to work with people with disabilities. Also on offer are a range of evening activities and free use of the fully accessible swimming pool, Jacuzzi, steam room and sensory room.

'Everyone always notices our beautiful E and ignores her siblings. The staff here talked to our boys. The Instructors were amazing with sensitive thoughtful comments. We have never felt so accepted as a family – we didn't have to explain our daughter's behaviour to anyone. What an amazing experience.'

The Centre caters for all ages and disabilities and has exclusive use of the Wistlandpound Reservoir for sailing, kayaking and canoeing

Accommodation is set around a pretty courtyard within the converted farm buildings

Accommodation is accessible and set around a historic courtyard, which is both secure and pretty. It consists of en-suite single, twin and triple bedded rooms as well as a number of apartments with open plan kitchen and living space for self catering. Mobile hoists, shower chairs, electric beds and other equipment are on offer to make your stay more comfortable. Food is locally sourced and organic wherever possible with fresh meals prepared on site daily. All diets can be catered for by prior arrangement.

Activities provided at Calvert Trust Exmoor include:

- Horse riding (weekday breaks only)
- Carriage driving (indoor & outdoor riding schools)
- Abseiling
- Climbing (indoor & outdoor climbing walls)
- High ropes & challenge course
- Sailing (7 day breaks only)
- Kayaking
- Orienteering
- Bushcrafts
- Canoeing
- Hand crank cycling & KMX bikes
- Archery
- Zipwire

The Centre has exclusive access to the picturesque **Wistlandpound reservoir** for sailing, kayaking and canoeing. There is also an innovative and accessible activity trail that runs around the reservoir which is suitable for wheelchair users, hand crank cycles and KMX bikes.

Indoor and outdoor riding schools allow visitors to improve riding and carriage driving skills

The Whistlandpound Reserv

Throughout the year the Centre runs specialist activities which include Young Carers and Siblings Weekends where young people have the chance to learn skills, have fun and make new friends; indulgent and relaxing Pampering Weekends; horse experience weekends; Active Education for schools including educational field studies and multi activity programmes with the possibility of Corporate Development Challenges, perfect for getting the most out of your team. The Centre also organises Christmas, Easter and various other themed breaks. Keep an eye on the website or contact the Centre for further details.

'This is our third visit as a family. On our first visit, S wouldn't climb on his own, now he has made it to the top of the inside wall and back down again, on his own – Brilliant! Everything has been great, can't wait to come again!'

Calvert Trust Exmoor not only gives its visitors a challenging, fun and rewarding experience but the positive benefits that are ultimately experienced on site are enduring. Why not come and visit for 3, 4 or 7 nights or just come for the day. The centre is conveniently located 2 hours by car from Bristol and Plymouth and just over an hour from Exeter.

For more information, please contact:
Calvert Trust Exmoor, Wistlandpound, Kentisbury, Barnstaple, North Devon EX31 4SJ
Call: 01598 763221
Email: exmoor@calvert-trust.org.uk
Visit: www.calvert-trust.org.uk/emoor

It's what you can do that counts! Climbing, high ropes challenge courses, abseiling and zipwire are all on offer at the Centre

Relaxing
or active breaks
in beautiful coastal and
countryside locations

Life doesn't get much more relaxing than a perfect break by the sea or in the country. Put your feet up and enjoy our warm atmosphere, friendly service and home cooked cuisine at one of our four hotels, all in superb coastal and countryside locations. Choose from a range of leisure activities and entertainment at your chosen hotel.

Vision Hotels offer breaks at prices that won't break the bank. We work hard to ensure we are accessible for all, and each hotel has excellent facilities for guide dogs and pet dogs.

Call us on:
Cliffden Hotel, Teignmouth 01626 770052
Lauriston Hotel, Weston-super-Mare 01934 620758
Russell Hotel, Bognor Regis 01243 871300
Windermere Manor Hotel, Windermere 01539 445801

Or visit:
www.visionhotels.co.uk

Bruce Trust boat Rebecca Holly Lodge

Discover Britain's Inland Waterways

...boating has never been more popular on Britain's canals and rivers, reports Debbie Walker of Drifters, the flagship organisation for narrowboat holidays with over 30 bases across Britain

Caen Locks, Wiltshire

Every year people of all ages and abilities discover something to involve and captivate them on Britain's fascinating 3,000-mile network of navigable canals and rivers. Over 320,000 people go canal boating each year, enjoying a civilised adventure; civilised because you carry all your home comforts with you and an adventure because you are casting off on a waterway journey of discovery. And for those seeking utter relaxation, hotel boats combine all the romance and peace of canals with the services of an experienced guide, caterer and crew.

With Britain's canals in better shape than ever and hundreds of top quality boats available for hire, boating holidays have never been more popular on our peaceful inland waterway network. "The popularity of canal boating has been fuelled by the waterway renaissance which has

Drifters boat entering River Severn

swept across the country in the last decade, with 200 miles of waterway restored and over £1billion invested," explains Sally Ash, British Waterways' head of boating. "The number of boats on our waterways has increased by 35% in the last ten years and there are now more boats than at the height of the Industrial Revolution."

A trip on the waterways can open many doors. For some it can be a way to explore Britain's fascinating industrial heritage, while others will be interested in the wildlife that has colonised the water, the towpaths and the reed fringes of this man-made environment.

The main hire boat season runs from March to October and holiday-makers can choose from day-hire to short breaks or a week or more cruising. Drifters operate over 500 boats from 30 bases across the country. Pets are

welcome on the majority of hire boats, making it a great holiday option for guide dog owners. Self-drive prices start from £9.75 per person per night in low season and from £25 per person per night at the peak of the summer school holidays. Day boat hire starts from £10 per person.

Some holiday boats on the network cater specifically for disabled people. For example the Bruce Trust operates purpose-built, wide-beam canal boats on the beautiful Kennet & Avon Canal. It has a fleet of four boats, two of which offer accommodation for up to 12 people, one for 10 and the fourth for up to six. Three boats operate from Great Bedwyn, near Marlborough and its boat based at Lower Foxhangers Wharf, near Devizes is ideal for cruises to Bath and back. The Trust also offers skippered day trips.

Falkirk Wheel, Scotland

"Each of our broad beam boats offers the flexibility required by people with a wide variety of special needs," explains Danese Rudd, Trust Administrator for The Bruce Trust. "Their extra width - most boats on the network are narrowboats and only 7ft wide - provides excellent space for wheelchair users and special features like hydraulic lifts, boarding ramps, low-level bunks, plus specially fitted showers and toilets, help make it a home from home. Three of the boats have been designed to enable wheelchair users to operate the tiller and steer the boat and two are fitted with a special device that controls the tiller using a joystick, allowing someone with very limited mobility and strength to steer."

In North Wales, the Vale of Llangollen Boat Trust operates two canal boats from Trevor Basin next to the awe-inspiring 126ft high World Heritage Status Pontcysyllte Aqueduct on the beautiful Llangollen Canal. The boats provide skippered day trips and holidays for disabled and disadvantaged people of all ages and are fitted with hydraulic lifts to assist wheelchairs aboard, plus specially designed toilets and washing facilities. For holidays, 'Millie' can take up to six people and for half-day or day trips 'Glas y Dorlan' can take up to 12 people. "We provide day trips, short breaks and holidays for about 1,600 disabled people and their families each year," explains Trust Chairman Gill Thomas.

The Essex-based Canal Boat Project offers self-steer and skippered canal boats with disability access, including double lifts and joy sticks in the stern, enabling the boat to be skippered by wheelchair users. The Project offers boats for day trips or holidays up to two weeks long from its base at Burnt Mill Lane on the River Stort near Harlow.

In Scotland, Seagull Trust Cruises offer free skippered day trip boats for disabled people from bases at Falkirk and Ratho (near Edinburgh) on the Union Canal, Inverness on the Caledonian Canal and at Kirkintolloch on the Forth & Clyde Canal. The Trust also offers a residential canal boat 'Marion Seagull' from its Falkirk base for holidays for families with a member with access needs.

There are other waterways attractions across the country with fully accessible trip boats. In Scotland, the restored Forth & Clyde and Union canals are linked by a breathtaking modern structure: The Falkirk Wheel. This giant rotating boat lift - the first of its kind anywhere in the world – stands at more than 115ft (35m) high (taller than eight stacked double-decker buses) and is now a major visitor attraction in Scotland.

The Falkirk Wheel visitor centre is fully accessible by wheelchair and is fitted with an induction loop for the hearing impaired. The trip boats, which take visitors on an ascent of the wheel, through the 180-metre Roughcastle Tunnel beneath the historic World Heritage site Antonine Wall, also provides wheelchair access.

Narrowboat on Grand Union Canal

Pontcysyllte Aqueduct

Contact details

Standedge Tunnel's visitor centre at Marsden in Yorkshire on the restored Huddersfield Narrow Canal also operates a glass-topped wheelchair accessible boat, taking visitors into the watery heart of the hillside. Cutting through the Pennines, Standedge is not only the longest tunnel on the network (three and a quarter miles!), but it is also the deepest and highest.

The Anderton Boat Lift, near Northwich in Cheshire, otherwise known as 'The Cathedral of the Canals', offers another exciting visitor destination with an access for all trip boat. The Lift was built in 1875 to transport cargo laden boats between the River Weaver and the Trent & Mersey Canal 50ft above. After years of dedicated fund raising and restoration, this extraordinary metal giant, resembling a giant Meccano model, is operating again, providing visitors with a chance to experience the waterways' first ever 'white knuckle ride'.

Improvements to hundreds of miles of towpaths over the last decade mean that there are now plenty of new waterway access points offering disabled people an ideal way to enjoy the waterside environment. For example, The River Stort between Roydon Station and Burnt Mill Lock has a DDA-compliant towpath with a series of access ramps which passes through the beautiful Site of Special Scientific Interest at Hunsdon Mead.

At Ratho, on the Union Canal in Scotland, improvements include specially designed picnic benches, interactive information displays, multi-sensory visitor guides, sensory hedges. The historic Trevor Basin on the Llangollen Canal in North Wales, with its stunning views of the towering Pontcysyllte Aqueduct, was recently awarded a community access award by Wrexham Disability Forum following a series of access improvements, including new paths, seating and interpretation.

Anderton Boat Lift
www.andertonboatlift.co.uk
call: 01606 786777

Britain's inland waterways
www.waterscape.com
call: 01923 201120

Bruce Trust
www.brucetrust.org.uk
call: 01672 515498

Canal Boat Project
www.canalboat.org.uk
call: 01279 424444

Drifters boating holidays
www.drifters.co.uk
call: 0844 984 0322

Falkirk Wheel
www.thefalkirkwheel.co.uk
call: 08700 500 208

Museums on Britain's inland waterways
www.nwm.org.uk

Seagull Trust Cruises
www.seagulltrust.org.uk
email: seagulltrust@btinternet.com

Standedge Tunnel
www.standedge.co.uk
call: 01782 785703

Vale of Llangollen Boat Trust
www.canalboattrust.org.uk
call: 01978 861450

BondAccessibleHolidays

42

'Riverdance Beached' by June Hoyle

Disabled Photographers' Society and OpenBritain 'Accessible Britain' Photographic Competition

Use your imagination, patience and skill to capture, through your camera lens, the images that you believe best reflect "Accessible Britain".

Whether on your doorstep, in your locality or further afield, members and non members from all over the country and from all age groups are invited to take part in this exciting competition!

- **WIN a holiday at one of Britain's finest destinations.**

- **Winners will be announced in October 2011.**

- **The holiday to be taken before 30 September 2012.**

Full terms and conditions of entry are available from the Disabled Photographers' Society website;
www.disabledphotographers.co.uk

The Disabled Photographers' Society is a registered national charity founded in 1968 and has grown steadily since. Run by a group of dedicated unpaid volunteers, there are members from all over the UK and most of the Committee and helpers have physical disabilities so readily appreciate the challenges facing disabled photographers.

The DPS offers individual members adaptations, equipment, support and advice, lending equipment free at the point of need. The society organises exhibitions, holidays for photography, regular competitions, a quarterly magazine "In Focus" and a website with its own forum. Most importantly though, it provides the opportunity to contact like-minded people.

To find out more about the society, including the different membership options, please visit our web site
www.disabledphotographers.co.uk

For general enquiries about us please email
enquiries@disabledphotographers.co.uk

Or write to us at
**The Disabled Photographers' Society
PO Box 85
Longfield,
Kent
DA3 9BA**

Event Mobility Charitable Trust

Whether your choice is the Chelsea Flower Show or something faster at the British Grand Prix... Your Carriage awaits at over seventy fabulous events to ensure you enjoy them to the full, all made possible by Event Mobility Charitable Trust.

Founded in 1998, Event Mobility, staffed primarily by volunteers, provides the short term loan of 250 electric scooters and powered wheelchairs together with 100 manual wheelchairs at countryside events for the benefit of the disabled, elderly and mobility impaired. The scooters give a feeling of independence and freedom to those, who for years, have relied on others to push them around.

1999 brought charitable registration and in the year 2000, the Earl of Shrewsbury agreed to become our Honorary President.

Since registration the charity has grown in experience, achieving widespread recognition throughout the country, gaining awards for its work and that of its volunteers, in particular, twice achieving the Princess Diana of Wales Memorial Award for community service.

A number of grants, including one from the National Lotteries Charity Board, have enabled the charity to purchase a supply of electric scooters and manual wheelchairs all of which are transported in five 40ft trailers establishing a self-sufficient service. Recently, a number of families have been generous enough to donate to the charity, scooters no longer needed and in memory of their loved one. This is not only a very generous act but it ensures that the charity can help even more mobility impaired people enjoy some independence at shows and events. The charity is delighted to accept such gifts.

From providing assistance at a total of 12 shows in 1998/9 the charity has grown and supported 70 events in 2010. It is expected to rise year on year creating an even heavier demand on the services of the charity.

Anyone can use the service. There is no need to be registered disabled or a regular wheelchair user. The service is available to both young and old who are suffering from mobility problems, whether as a result of temporary or permanent disablement, age, accident or illness.

Like most charities, Event Mobility is always seeking financial assistance and sponsorship to continue its work. A number of companies have generously helped out over the years but new sponsors are always welcome.

For further information and for a list of shows and events being attended by Event Mobility visit our website **www.eventmobility.org.uk** phone **01386 725391** or write to **Event Mobility, 8 Bayliss Rd, Kemerton, Tewkesbury, Glos GL20 7JH.**

Understanding the needs of people

Why should a person have to be transferred from their wheelchair when there is equipment available?

How often have lifts broken down and people are unable to move between floors?

How often are steps and uneven terrain a barrier to wheelchair users and the less-able?

We are here to provide the solutions.

Swallow Evacuation & Mobility Products Ltd (Swallow EMP) prides itself on providing a wide range of evacuation / accessibility products to suit most situations. We provide equipment that enables access to most buildings and the ability to have movement, up and down stairs. Hotels, restaurants, holiday homes, schools, universities and public buildings can now all provide access for all without the normal major building disruption and associated expense.

Innovation & Sustainability Awards October 2010

"Goods Mate" winner of 'Best Innovation in Health & Safety' category.
The "Goods Mate" was adapted for our Stair Mate which takes a non powered wheelchair, with the "Goods Mate" roll on roll off platform; the Stair Mate can then be used for moving goods up and down stairs, when not being used for wheelchair users.

EVERYTHING IS POSSIBLE!
Please contact us on 0121 444 3690
or 07789 766632
info@swallowemp.com
www.swallowemp.com

47

Chandelier, Blue Dining Room

Discover the vast and varied treasures at Waddesdon Manor

Waddesdon Manor was built (1874-89), in the style of a 16th century French château, for Baron Ferdinand de Rothschild to entertain his guests and display his vast collection of art treasures. It houses one of the finest collections of French 18th century decorative arts in the world.

The furniture, Savonnerie carpets, and Sèvres porcelain ranks in importance with the Metropolitan Museum in New York and the Louvre in Paris. There is also a fine collection of portraits by Gainsborough and Reynolds and works by Dutch and Flemish Masters of the 17th century. The Rothschild family maintains an active interest in the running of Waddesdon through a family charitable trust under the chairmanship of Lord Rothschild. Since taking over responsibility for the Manor, he has masterminded an extensive programme of building and restoration work. All revenue from admissions, events, the restaurants and shops at Waddesdon go directly towards the upkeep of the House, Collection and Garden.

To ensure less mobile visitors have an inclusive experience all areas of the House, shops and restaurants are accessible to wheelchair users. A lift to the first floor of the House, and stair lift to the second floor are provided to help with your visit. Assistance dogs are allowed into all areas. As we have to ensure the safety of every visitor in the event of an emergency during which we might have to evacuate the building only two wheelchairs are allowed on each floor of the House at any one time. Seats are available throughout the House for visitors to rest. There are induction loops at the Ticket Office, main door of the House, restaurant, shop and lecture room (the Power House). We have Braille guides available on first come first served basis and large type information booklets are available in some rooms. Typetalk is available at Waddesdon Manor. We always recommend that people contact us before their visit so that we can discuss their entire visit in advance – planning your day can make a real difference.

South Front, Waddesdon Manor

For the visually impaired we have objects in the House for handling. In the restaurants we have large print menus and 'easy grip' cutlery. A slip/trip audit has been undertaken to ensure any problem areas have been identified and hazards either eradicated or clearly marked. A buggy service operates between the House and the Stables. There are disabled facilities at the House and the Stables and free wheelchairs provided in the House and the Gardens for visitors' use on a first come first served basis. A drop off facility is available at the front of the House and there is also designated parking.

Waddesdon has one of the finest Victorian gardens in Britain, renowned for its colourful parterre, specimen trees, shady walks and views, fountains and statuary. At its heart is the Aviary, stocked with exotic birds and known for breeding endangered species. As it was in Baron Ferdinand's day, this rococo style building, complete

North Front, Waddesdon Manor

The Dining Roo

with an impressive collection of exotic birds, is a principal feature of the Waddesdon garden. A free map of the Gardens is available from the Ticket Office and shows walks suitable for those in wheelchairs and there is a scented rose garden for sensory stimulation.

The Rothschild name is also synonymous with some of the most coveted wines in the world. The Waddesdon Wine Cellars have been created to house a private collection of these wines – over 15,000 bottles some dating back to 1868 – and to tell something of the story of the Rothschild role in the history of winemaking. Wheelchair access to the Wine Cellars can be arranged by phoning the Booking Office in advance of a visit.

There is also an award winning gift shop, wine shop with a full selection of Rothschild wines and two licensed restaurants. A full programme of events is organised throughout the year including special interest days, wine tastings and family events.

In 2007 The Woodland Playground was created for our younger visitors and in 2008 a nest swing for the less able bodied was added, the Woodland Playground continues to be a popular area for children of all ages.

Waddesdon Manor continues to be committed to making access for visitors with disabilities as fully inclusive as possible, responding where possible to people's needs. It is always wonderful to get feedback from visitors and to know when they have had the experience they had hoped for, and visitors who have required assistance are usually the first ones to take the trouble to write.

Conveniently situated close to London, Oxford and Milton Keynes, Waddesdon offers a fascinating and memorable day out for all the family.

All information is available on the 'Accessibility' page of our website.
www.waddesdon.org.uk
e: info@waddesdon.org.uk
t 01296 653226

Eastshaw Farm House, Sussex

National Trust Cottages

National Trust

The National Trust is well known for its portfolio of over 300 historic houses, gardens and countryside places. However, there are also nearly 400 holiday cottages in the care of the Trust. These cottages provide a variety of accommodation opportunities across England, Wales and Northern Ireland and the number of cottages continues to grow every year.

As with properties which are open to visitors, the Trust takes seriously the responsibility to provide opportunities for disabled people. Over the past few years, there have been programmes of assessing cottages for accessibility and some improvements have been made. However, this year, the Trust has moved forward with a stronger commitment to improving the accessibility of its cottage portfolio. About 10% of the cottages will be assessed in the first phase of this continuing programme. These reviews are supported by the development of a list of basic equipment requirements which it is hoped can be acquired for every cottage.

Alongside access assessments, there has also been training provided for the cottage supervisors to enable them to proactively find opportunities for improvements. The information about the accessibility of each cottage will also be improved on the website with access statements provided. Currently, a symbol is used to identify cottages which may be accessible for some disabled people but, with more details available, it will be much easier to identify the best cottage to book. The access statements will include measurements and images to help explain the exact circumstances at each site. The website itself will be assessed to improve accessibility and the booking office team will have information about the accessibility of each cottage and so will be able to have

Keeper's Cottage, Sussex

more informed discussions with anyone enquiring about booking accommodation.

Eastshaw Cottage is located in the heart of rural Sussex and has already benefitted from this new programme of assessments. This cottage provides a ground floor bedroom and shower room and provides accommodation for 10 people in total. The approach to the cottage is quite a steep slope which may be difficult for some independent wheelchair users. Recommendations to improve accessibility have been identified, including to the kitchen and shower room, but it has been assessed as possible accommodation for ambulant disabled people and accompanied wheelchair users.

Keepers Cottage in Sussex, located close to Eastshaw Cottage, is not as easy to access for wheelchair users. There is no bedroom on the ground floor but people able to manage a staircase for access and egress to bedrooms will be able to consider this as a place to stay. There is a kitchen and shower room available on the ground floor and level entrance is available. Recommendations have been identified for further improvements and it has been identified as possible accommodation for ambulant disabled people.

The Trust is also represented on the DCMS Accessible Tourism Forum. This Forum brings together representatives from tourism organisations and disability organisations to discuss progress in making tourism accessible, including accommodation provisions. The discussions at this Forum, and the business case it has developed, are stimulating organisations to rethink their current provisions and methods of making provisions for accessible tourism.

For more information about National Trust Holiday Cottages, go to **http://www.nationaltrustcottages.co.uk/**

Brochures can be ordered from the website or by calling **0844 8002072**

New challenges
– New solutions

Sheila Sadler shares her life-changing experiences and introduces us to her 'boys' and home-from-home that gives her the freedom of the road.

There comes a point in our lives when, after dedicating most of our waking hours to our profession and our families we take stock and opt for a more leisurely pace with more time for interests and hobbies. In 1990 we exchanged the pressures of living and working in the Thames Valley for more rural Suffolk. I opted only to work part-time, (the youngest offspring was at university) and to widen our scope for walking, exploring different areas and travelling, we bought our first caravan. We replaced children in the home with two Golden Retrievers, one who had been my leaving present from full-time teaching. As a keen gardener, I also had the challenge of a new plot to design, dig, plant out, and maintain. We looked forward to family and friends visiting, joined local societies, and settled into a full and enjoyable agenda.

But, in a split second, all this changed when, in March 1996, travelling in a colleague's car to a meeting, she failed to see a vehicle ahead slowing down, swung her car into the oncoming lane, hit the accelerator instead of the brake and we were head on into an articulated lorry. Tragically she lost her life and I, lucky to survive, but left with limited mobility, reduced upper body strength and pain, lost my independence, with that my self-esteem and self-confidence. Simple tasks such as picking up an article from the floor suddenly required concentration and balance control. It took four years for me to accept my limitations and to prioritise our 'quality of life'. (Four years of, not only physical battles but mental battles with insurance companies, and employers from which we emerged disillusioned with an insecure financial future as,

despite finally receiving a compensation award it would no way ever compensate for our loss of future earnings and pensions.) At this time I probably squandered money on private medical treatments, which would only provide temporary relief, until I accepted there were aids, and adaptations out there (for the asking) to improve my quality of life. Using a motorised wheelchair enabled me to participate for more hours each day without needing a rest break or painkillers. Providing tracks were accessible, we could enjoy longer walks together with our dogs and I could participate more fully in events.

We left Suffolk and moved to Somerset, here no one knew me 'before wheels' I had a new identity. Like our house and our car, the original caravan could not accommodate my needs. I remember the first time we attempted to use it after the accident, the realisation of my reduced capabilities. Assuming our old caravanning routine I tried to re-arrange the seating to make up the bed and couldn't lift the cushions; went automatically down on my knees to get something from a cupboard and couldn't get up.

We spent some of the compensation sum on a caravan with a fixed bed, shopped around to find wide steps with a rail, and had a power mover fitted as I could no longer help physically to position the van.

So, horizons were broadened – the caravan became my travelling bedroom whenever we visited family and friends. We toured different areas on holidays researching beforehand suitable wheelchair friendly walks and sights to visit. It may sound strange, but it was a few years before I would allow myself to open the door to facilities displaying the disabled sign! Overcoming that particular hurdle meant I would avail myself of the excellent facilities provided for disabled on caravan and camping sites (especially the club sites)

In 2006, our horizons had widened but what about independence? I still felt I needed John with me anywhere away from home. So enter a beautiful 12-week-old dark golden retriever puppy we named Juneau. Having researched Assistance Dogs I felt, being retired and with my husband, I could not justify applying to a Charity. I set about training Juneau to help me with tasks around the home such as picking up items from the floor, unloading the washing machine, taking my shoes and socks off etc. He learnt quickly, always anxious to please. I am so grateful that, having met the Staff at Canine Partners at a Roadshow, they generously offered us the opportunity to be assessed, and when successful took Juneau into their training programme. Three months later I joined him on the two-week residential course for new partnerships; very apprehensive, my first time away from home without John, but this was an overwhelming experience. Juneau was my carer 24/7; he never got into his bed at night until I was in mine. I met very special people, dedicated staff, and returned home with new-found confidence, my dog in his purple jacket alongside my chair, I could go anywhere. This began for us as a family, a fulfilling and enjoyable mission to raise awareness and funds for this wonderful charity. We gave talks and demonstrations and attended events as a visual aid.

Tragically and suddenly in 2009 Juneau died of a rare condition and the bottom dropped out of my world. The Charity, like a second family, grieved with us, but also encouraged me forward to continue Juneau's legacy. In October I was invited to Headquarters to meet "a special boy" in advanced training. Who could not bond immediately with Kerly's smiling black face, quirky tan thumbprints above his eyes, and his exuberance? Our residential training was emotional but he has a wonderful temperament, is keen to work and loves everyone. We were once again, in demand and anxious to help fund raise whenever and wherever we could. Unfortunately I had struggled with caravanning in 2009 finding it difficult to negotiate the steps safely plus balance and manoeuvrability inside. We had kept details of a caravan with wheelchair access seen at a road show, so decided to follow this up.

A somewhat hazardous journey to snow-covered Kent in January was well worth it as, having spent the afternoon at Nirvana Sales, inside their Nirvana Esprit 520 model we had found the answer to continuing caravanning, possibly forever!

With its wide door, our particular van has an electric wheelchair lift (but there are other options for access) my chair, Kerly and I are transported easily into the van. The layout has floor space for movement; there are no tripping hazards as the "bathroom" folds flat against the wall with a curtain to draw round when in use. The fixed bed is very comfortable, the cupboards easily accessible and the light and bright interior makes it a special home from home. Therefore not surprisingly, we have spent almost as much time living in our caravan as at our home. Taking advantage of the option to site the van on

locations for shows and other events, we are now able to support Canine Partners whenever required. Arriving a day before, the van provides ample transporting space for merchandise, gazebo etc. For the duration of the event, close at hand, it is there for rest and refreshment breaks, not only for us but also for all our Canine Partners contingent. To date we have been to Brindley Heath Country Show, Sherborne Castle, Royal Bath & West Show, and South West Disability show.

In 2010 we booked 4 sites over 3 weeks, holiday combined with visits to friends, long walks with our boys in the Peak District, Teesdale, and Clumber Park. We feel like ambassadors for both Canine Partners and Nirvana Caravans. Hopefully meeting us will convey a positive scenario to others that whatever challenges face us in life, there are ways and means to find the positive, to push the boundaries and pursue a fulfilling and enjoyable quality of life.

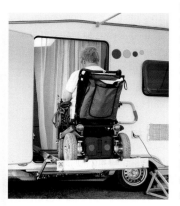

Contact details

Canine Partners
www.caninepartners.co.uk
call 08456 580 480

Nirvina
www.nirvana.com
call 0800 328 1475

Lady with restricted growth going through ticket barriers

Better Than Ever

Britain's rail network is now more accessible than it has ever been.

Most trains now have facilities for customers with disabilities. Information screens and audible announcements have removed the uncertainty once felt by many customers with sensory impairments.

Many stations have been refurbished so that there are step free routes to train services and the Department for Transport is now five years into its 10-year Access for All scheme which will revolutionise access at a further 200 stations. Discount schemes for disabled people, such as the Disabled Persons Railcard, have also helped keep train travel as an affordable alternative to other modes of transport.

Planning your Journey

If you want to make sure that every leg of your journey is accessible there are a number of services available to help you. If you have a computer you can go to the National Rail enquiries website at **www.nationalrail.co.uk** and use its Journey Planner to plan your route. Once you've done this you can state your access needs on the Stations Made Easy page and find the route through each station that best suits your preferences.

For those of you who prefer human contact you can call **National Rail enquiries on 08457 48 49 50** or call your

train company directly. If you're no fan of the phone, you can always visit the nearest staffed station. Travel advice is also available on **www.disabledpersons-railcard.co.uk**.

Assistance

Train companies can also provide you with help using their services. If you need assistance, you should book it at least 24 hours before you travel. This lets the train companies check the accessibility of the stations you will be using and if necessary, arrange alternative transport to or from the nearest accessible station. If you're planning to travel at a time when a station is usually unstaffed, the 24 hour notice period also allows time for staff to be relocated.

Rail staff will help you get on and off of trains but they cannot escort customers throughout the whole of their journey, nor can they provide personal care (for example, help with eating and drinking, taking medication or using the toilet) or carry heavy luggage.

Concourse at London Marylebone

Wheelchairs

There are a limited number of spaces for wheelchair users on each train so, where reservations apply, it is recommended you book your space in advance. Most trains accommodate wheelchairs that are within the dimensions 700mm wide by 1200mm long. The maximum combined weight of a person and their wheelchair that can be conveyed is limited by two things: the capabilities of the member of staff assisting the passenger and the stated maximum safe working load of the ramp (between 230kg and 300kg).

Powered scooters

Because scooters come in a wide variety of shapes and sizes, many have problems on trains, including: tipping backwards on ramps; being heavier than the ramp's safe working load; or being the wrong shape to manoeuvre safely inside a carriage. These problems mean that some companies have trains that cannot carry scooters. If you are

a scooter user you should contact the train company you want to travel with or check its scooter policy on **www.nationalrail.co.uk**.

The Disabled Persons Railcard

If you have a disability that makes travelling by train difficult you might qualify for the Disabled Persons Railcard. The Railcard allows you (and a friend if you're not travelling alone) to get 1/3 off most rail fares throughout Great Britain.

One-year and three-year cards are available. You must provide proof that you are eligible. If you have: a visual impairment, a hearing impairment, epilepsy, or are in receipt of a disability-related benefit you are likely to qualify. Card prices and application forms detailing the evidence you must send in can be downloaded from **www.disabledpersons-railcard.co.uk**, requested by phone from **0845 605 0525** or found in the leaflet Rail Travel Made Easy (available from stations and disability information providers).

Mount Stuart

Discovering Britain's beautiful gardens

As soon as the first buds start to appear, our minds naturally turn to visiting historic gardens. There are so many now with excellent access for disabled people.

First, let me say that it's essential to contact any house or garden before you visit, so that they can advise you about specific access details. It's also important to remember that these are historic places, and their terrain may be difficult, so take a strong companion with you!

Levens Hall

Many garden owners include access information on their websites - just look at those of two we have recently visited – **Cottesbrooke Hall** in Northamptonshire, and **Pashley Manor Gardens** in East Sussex. Both these relatively small gardens are packed full of good things, and care has been taken to devise routes around them to avoid marked changes of level and steps. **Cottesbrooke** has various small gardens, scented flowers and plants, and many water features, including lakes, pools and fountains. **Pashley** has formal flower gardens, lakes and vistas, and fascinating exhibitions of statuary, much of which visually impaired people may touch. Each has a delightful and accessible tea-room.

There are many such gardens around Britain; let me take you on a short tour of some of them:

HISTORIC HOUSES ASSOCIATION

Picton Castle

Newby Hall

seasons, with a collection of garden rooms, formal lawns, seasonal bedding, a statuary collection and an Arboretum with trees from all over the world.

Families should visit **Burton Agnes Hall** in East Yorkshire. The gardens and the ground floor of the house are fully accessible; there is a maze, and a mile-long woodland sculpture walk; some of the sculptures may be enjoyed by touch. If you are unable to climb stairs, ask to see an album of pictures of the upper floors of the house.

Self-drive buggies and manual wheelchairs may be borrowed for a trip around the extensive and beautiful gardens at **Newby Hall**, in North Yorkshire – and a miniature railway is accessible to people able to transfer from their wheelchairs.

A buggy is available to tour the lovely garden at **Sutton Park**, near York. The house has a new lift, greatly improving access for people who find stairs difficult.

The famous topiary garden at **Levens Hall** in Cumbria has gravelled paths. An electric buggy is available for hire. The house is not accessible, but a new DVD gives a tour of the open rooms.

In Scotland, a visit to the magical **Blair Castle** near Pitlochry, Perthshire is rewarding for any visitor unable to climb stairs – the entire ground floor is accessible and an audio visual gives a 25 minute rolling display. There is an electric buggy for hire; the extensive walled garden must be visited. **Mount Stuart** on the Isle of Bute has an audio-visual display, and good access to much of its many acres of gardens.

Two very differing gardens in Wales offer good access to wheelchair users. At **Picton Castle Garden**, near Haverfordwest, Pembrokeshire, the Walled Garden is slightly sloping, accessible and a joy. There are seats of a good height, and a long wall on which to perch and enjoy the pond and fountain. **Dyffryn**, Cardiff is a garden for all

Burton Agnes Hall

The delightful 19th century walled garden of **Leighton Hall**, near Carnforth in north Lancashire has cottage garden flowers and roses on the walls. The house is accessible and there are no roped-off areas, this is a family home, where visitors are welcomed; pianists may play the Concert Steinway piano!

At **Rockingham Castle** in Leicestershire, the formal gardens are generally accessible to those with impaired mobility. A new by-pass path avoids a set of steps in the Rose Garden. There is a large print welcome leaflet and guidebook, and an audio tour.

The house and garden at **Holme Pierrepont Hall** near Nottingham, are accessible; there is a stair lift in the house.

Boughton House, near Kettering, Northamptonshire, has an excellent website which gives comprehensive tours of the house and pictures of the gardens. A great deal of access has been created here, and disabled people are admitted free of charge.

At **Holkham Hall** in Norfolk, the restoration of 6½ acres of 18th century walled gardens is nearing completion. The gardens are open this year for the first time since 1995, and visitors may see how the project is developing.

There is limited parking for disabled people near the gardens. The house has a stair climber - more details, including an Access Statement, are given on Holkham's excellent website.

Much of the 30 acres of gardens at **Sherborne Castle** in Dorset are accessible to wheelchair users and buggy drivers –the paths have a smooth surface, and visitors will enjoy the extensive views of the lake and parkland.

West Dean, near Chichester, West Sussex, has good access to the majority of its gardens, including the Walled

Blair Castle

Garden, but access is restricted to some of the glasshouses. A map is available, showing recommended routes.

The Walled Garden at **Loseley Park**, near Guildford, Surrey is ideal for people with limited mobility, and visually impaired visitors will enjoy the rose, herb and flower gardens.

All these houses and gardens have excellent facilities for disabled people, accessible WCs, shops, and tea-rooms or restaurants. Everything you'll need for a really good day out.

by *Valerie Wenham*
for the Historic Houses Association

For more information on these and hundreds of other historic houses and gardens visit www.hha.org.uk

Vehicle Rental Opens Up Britain

"At AVH we have developed a service that gives disabled and elderly people and their family, friends and carers the ultimate flexibility and convenience for getting around the UK" says Jon Reynolds of specialist adapted vehicle rental provider, AVH.

"Whether they need a wheelchair accessible vehicle that has sufficient space for passengers and luggage, or an adapted vehicle for a disabled driver to get behind the steering wheel themselves. That's also why we are very pleased to be a Premier Supporter of Tourism for All – supporting its goals of improving accessibility right across the UK."

Adapted Vehicle Hire is the UK's leading adapted vehicle and wheelchair accessible vehicle rental provider. Established since 2005 AVH has a clear understanding of the very specialist requirements of disabled drivers and passengers, with extensive experience of providing adapted and wheelchair accessible vehicles on either short or long-term rental.

Personal service: Every booking is discussed direct with the disabled user or driver to ensure that AVH can supply a vehicle that is precisely 'fit for purpose'. A state of the art adaptations workshop ensures that every vehicle is fitted with the appropriate adaptations.

A wealth of vehicle choice: AVH operates an extensive fleet, from compact city cars to larger wheelchair accessible vehicles, offering a wealth of choice. For example, not all disabled drivers want to drive small

or medium sized vehicles. For a greater level of luxury and comfort, as well as more space for passengers and luggage, AVH has the solution. AVH also provides solutions for drivers who need wheelchair accessibility but don't want to drive larger vehicles. Plus it provides greater choice for wheelchair users who want to drive themselves, including a fully adapted Mercedes Sprinter.

Location no barrier: AVH drivers, trained to provide detailed handovers, can deliver vehicles anywhere in the UK.

"We have built a strong reputation for high quality customer service, including delivery and collections of vehicles around the country" concludes Jon Reynolds. "So whatever vehicles disabled drivers and passengers need, we can help, providing them with the freedom to get out and about."

Disabled and elderly travellers and their family and friends can call the AVH customer helpline to discuss their specific vehicle requirements to ensure they can rent the vehicle they need, when they need it.

wwww.adaptedvehiclehire.com
Tel: 0845 257 1670

Enjoy England

England is a country of impressive diversity and variety, divided into nine distinct regions – each with its own unique personality. From the rolling hills of the Cotswolds and bustling city life of Manchester, to the charms of sleepy Cornish villages and the dramatic coastal splendour of the North East.

Home to 21 of Britain's UNESCO World Heritage Sites, including **Hadrian's Wall** in the North East, **Stonehenge** in the South West, **Canterbury Cathedral** in the South East and the **Tower of London** and **Maritime Greenwich** in London, you can also find all seven of Britain's Heritage Cities in England.

In every region of England there are hundreds of fantastic attractions to enjoy. As well as London's world-famous attractions, you'll find historical sites like **Stonehenge**, ecological attractions such as the **Eden Project** and great family attractions ranging from zoos and safari parks to picnic spots and beaches.

So whether you're visiting a quaint market town or charming cathedral city, shopping in a vibrant city centre or exploring its rugged coastline, England has an impressive range of things to do and places to see.

Accessible England

Tourism businesses are working hard to make their facilities and services more accessible to everyone.

So whether **The Great North Museum** (Newcastle-upon-Tyne) takes your fancy, **The National Theatre** (London), **Imperial War Museum** (Duxford), **Windsor Castle** (Berkshire) or **Bosworth Battlefield** (Leicestershire), you are sure of a warm welcome.

Accommodation providers may have introduced a large print menu, which will be of great use to those who forget their reading glasses, and attractions may have added low level interpretation boards for children to read. All of these little improvements will help you and your family to have a better holiday in England.

National Accessible Scheme

VisitEngland runs a scheme to highlight those accommodation businesses which have improved their accessibility. The National Accessible Scheme (NAS) is great if you have a visual, hearing or mobility impairment giving you the confidence to book somewhere which suits your specific needs. A trained assessor has checked it out before you have checked in. So remember - next time you book your accommodation in England look out for the NAS logos. You can also search for NAS accredited accommodation at **www.enjoyengland. com/access.** See page 18 for more information.

Stonehenge © Britain on View

Tower of London © Britain on View

England

South West	72	Heart of England	202
South East	118	Yorkshire & Humber	216
London	146	Northwest	234
East of England	158	North East	256
East Midlands	184		

Information is key

All VisitEngland star rated accommodation and quality assured attractions are now required to provide information on their facilities and services to help you 'know before you go'. This information is presented as an Access Statement, which is simply a document that tells you lots of useful details about the premises and its surroundings. Typical information may include, for example, the frequency of buses, useful telephone numbers, the number of steps to the front door and the availability of subtitles on televisions. So, when you are next researching which accommodation to stay at and attractions to visit, ask to see their access statements.

EnjoyEngland.com now has a dedicated information section for people with physical or sensory needs. Whether you're travelling on foot, by car, bus, taxi or train, in fact whatever type of transport you're using, there's a section containing all you need to know about travelling around England. To make your travels around England easier and more enjoyable for you, we've put together some practical information we hope you'll find useful. So if you need to use accessible toilets, information on the RADAR National Key Scheme and Changing Places is available. Find out more at **www.enjoyengland.com/access**.

enjoy**England**®

Further information

Travel and tourism information for people with physical and sensory needs:

www.enjoyengland.com/access

The incredible South West

The South West's beautiful and undulating landscapes include Bournemouth and Poole, Dorset, Wiltshire, Somerset, the Cotswolds and Forest of Dean, Bristol, Bath, Devon, Cornwall and the Isles of Scilly. Each destination provides the visitor with an array of attractions, gorgeous gardens, beautiful beaches, fantastic festivals and the chance to indulge in some mouth-watering local produce.

The natural environment is one of the biggest draws for vistors; rolling hills, rugged coast, quaint villages, beautiful gardens, dramatic wind swept moor-land and sandy beaches are all waiting to be discovered. The impressive **South West Coast Path** surrounds 630 miles of coastline offering inspiring views and every stretch of the path is graded online in terms of its difficulty of terrain, with many sections wheelchair accessible - see **southwestcoastpath.com**

There are no limits when exploring the South West with many of the regions well known beaches offering a high level of accessibility, this includes **Hayle's Bay** beach near the stunning **Polzeath** in Cornwall and the charming **Poole Harbour** in Dorset. Some of our famous attractions also have good access such as **Bristol Zoo**, **Castle Drogo** in Devon and **Longleat** in Wiltshire.

The South West is also home to picturesque villages, charming towns and historical cities. **Bath**, **Bristol** and **Exeter** are amongst the historical and vibrant cities with some beautiful architecture. The many museums and art galleries give visitors a glimpse into the background of each city and its respective county.

Food is something the population of the South West is extremely passionate about. Whatever part of the region you visit there'll be plenty of opportunities to taste the local delights on offer, organic meats, delicious ciders, creamy desserts and fresh seafood can be devoured. For those of

Clifftop above Durdle Door on the Jurrassic coast of Dorset.

Salisbury Cathedral

South West

Cornwall, Isles of Scilly, Devon, Dorset, Gloucestershire, Somerset, Wiltshire

you who take your cheese seriously there's plenty to choose from that are unique to the South West such as Gloucestershire's Stinking Bishop or Dorset's Blue Vinney. What's more, our farmer's markets and farm shops give visitors a chance to take our unique culinary delights home with them.

The South West is full of myths and legends from the mysteries that surround **Stonehenge** in Wiltshire, to the **King Arthur** connections in Somerset and Cornwall.

Additionally there's **Bodmin Moor**, Cornwall where the dramatic landscapes provide the perfect inspiration for writers and poets alike.

There is an abundance of award winning accommodation available to suit all budgets, including family farm stays, luxury lodges and tree houses, bed and breakfast, campsites and hotels so whatever kind of experience you desire, the South West is able to provide.

Come and see for yourself the wonderful range of destinations, attractions and beautiful locations waiting to be explored by all.

Find out more
www.visitsouthwest.co.uk

Ellwood Cottages, Dorset.

Tourist Information Centres

Tourist Information Centres are a mine of information about local and regional accommodation, attractions and events. Visit them when you arrive at your destination or contact them before you go:

Avebury	Avebury Chapel Centre	01672 539425	all.tic's@kennet.gov.uk
Bath	Abbey Chambers	0906 711 2000	tourism@bathtourism.co.uk
Bodmin	Shire Hall	01208 76616	bodmintic@visit.org.uk
Bourton- On-The-Water	Victoria Street	01451 820211	bourtonvic@btconnect.com
Bridport	47 South Street	01308 424901	bridport.tic@westdorset-dc.gov.uk
Bristol: Harbourside	Wildwalk @Bristol	0906 711 2191	ticharbourside@destinationbristol.co.uk
Brixham	The Old Market House	01803 211 211	holiday@torbay.gov.uk
Bude	Bude Visitor Centre	01288 354240	budetic@visitbude.info
Burnham-On-Sea	South Esplanade	01278 787852	burnham.tic@sedgemoor.gov.uk
Camelford	North Cornwall Museum	01840 212954	manager@camelfordtic.eclipse.co.uk
Cartgate	South Somerset TIC	01935 829333	cartgate.tic@southsomerset.gov.uk
Cheddar	The Gorge	01934 744071	cheddar.tic@sedgemoor.gov.uk
Cheltenham	Municipal Offices	01242 522878	info@cheltenham.gov.uk
Chippenham	Yelde Hall	01249 665970	tourism@chippenham.gov.uk
Chipping Campden	The Old Police Station	01386 841206	information@visitchippingcampden.com
Christchurch	49 High Street	01202 471780	enquiries@christchurchtourism.info
Cirencester	Corn Hall	01285 654180	cirencestervic@cotswold.gov.uk
Coleford	High Street	01594 812388	tourism@fdean.gov.uk
Corsham	Arnold House	01249 714660	enquiries@corshamheritage.org.uk
Devizes	Cromwell House	01380 729408	all.tic's@kennet.gov.uk
Dorchester	11 Antelope Walk	01305 267992	dorchester.tic@westdorset-dc.gov.uk
Falmouth	11 Market Strand	01326 312300	info@falmouthtic.co.uk
Fowey	5 South Street	01726 833616	info@fowey.co.uk
Frome	The Round Tower	01373 467271	frome.tic@ukonline.co.uk
Glastonbury	The Tribunal	01458 832954	glastonbury.tic@ukonline.co.uk
Gloucester	28 Southgate Street	01452 396572	tourism@gloucester.gov.uk

Looe	The Guildhall	01503 262072	looetic@btconnect.com
Lyme Regis	Guildhall Cottage	01297 442138	lymeregis.tic@westdorset-dc.gov.uk
Malmesbury	Town Hall	01666 823748	tic@malmesbury.gov.uk
Moreton-In-Marsh	High Street	01608 650881	moreton@cotswold.gov.uk
Padstow & Wadebridge	Red Brick Building	01841 533449	padstowtic@btconnect.com
Paignton	The Esplanade	01803 211 211	holiday@torbay.gov.uk
Penzance	Station Road	01736 362207	pztic@penwith.gov.uk
Plymouth	Plymouth Mayflower Centre	01752 306330	barbicantic@plymouth.gov.uk
Salisbury	Fish Row	01722 334956	visitorinfo@salisbury.gov.uk
Shepton Mallet	70 High Street	01749 345258	sheptonmallet.tic@ukonline.co.uk
Sherborne	3 Tilton Court	01935 815341	sherborne.tic@westdorset-dc.gov.uk
Somerset Visitor Centre	Sedgemoor Services	01934 750833	somersetvisitorcentre@somerset.gov.uk
St Austell	Southbourne Road	01726 879 500	tic@cornish-riviera.co.uk
St Ives	The Guildhall	01736 796297	ivtic@penwith.gov.uk
Stow-On-The-Wold	Hollis House	01451 831082	stowvic@cotswold.gov.uk
Street	Clarks Village	01458 447384	street.tic@ukonline.co.uk
Stroud	Subscription Rooms	01453 760960	tic@stroud.gov.uk
Swanage	The White House	01929 422885	mail@swanage.gov.uk
Swindon	37 Regent Street	01793 530328	infocentre@swindon.gov.uk
Taunton	The Library	01823 336344	tauntontic@tauntondeane.gov.uk
Tetbury	33 Church Street	01666 503552	tourism@tetbury.org
Tewkesbury	100 Church Street	01684 855043	tewkesburytic@tewkesburybc.gov.uk
Torquay	Vaughan Parade	01803 211 211	holiday@torbay.gov.uk
Truro	Municipal Building	01872 274555	tic@truro.gov.uk
Wareham	Holy Trinity Church	01929 552740	tic@purbeck-dc.gov.uk
Warminster	Central Car Park	01985 218548	visitwarminster@btconnect.com
Wells	Town Hall	01749 672552	touristinfo@wells.gov.uk
Weston-Super-Mare	Beach Lawns	01934 888800	westontouristinfo@n-somerset.gov.uk
Weymouth	The King's Statue	01305 785747	tic@weymouth.gov.uk
Winchcombe	Town Hall	01242 602925	winchcombetic@tewkesbury.gov.uk
Yeovil	Hendford	01935 845946/7	yeoviltic@southsomerset.gov.uk

Where to Stay

Bodmin | **Vitalise Churchtown** `AS`

Lanlivery, Bodmin, Cornwall PL30 5BT
t 0845 345 1970 **e** bookings@vitalise.org.uk
vitalise.org.uk

Access: 🅰 🐾 🏢 😊 ♿ ♿ General: 🐎 🛏 ✕ 🍷 🅿 ❀ ♿ Room: 🛏 ☀

Callington | **The Olive Tree**

Open: All year except Xmas and New Year	
Rooms per night:	
s:	£30.00
d:	£55.00
Meals:	£6.50-£12.50

Maders, Nr Callington, Cornwall PL17 7LL
t 01579 384392 **e** kindredspirits@blueyonder.co.uk
theolivetreebandb.co.uk

1C2

Peaceful countryside location, yet centrally situated for exploring all that Cornwall has to offer.

Access: 🐾 🏢 ♿ General: 🐎 🛏 ✕ 🅿 ❀ ♿ Room: 🛏 🆂 ☕

Falmouth | **Rosemullion**

Gyllyngvase Hill, Falmouth, Cornwall TR11 4DF
t 01326 314690 **e** gail@rosemullionhotel.demon.co.uk
rosemullionhotel.co.uk

Access: 📷 😊 General: 🛏 🅿 Room: 🛏 ☀ wc 🆂 ☕

Goohaven | **Silver Bow Park**

Goohaven, Nr Truro, Cornwall TR4 9NX
t 01872 572347
chycor.co.uk/silverbow

Access: 🐾 🏢 😊 ♿ General: 🔲 🔌 🛒 🔥 🚿 🚻 🍴 🅦🅟 Pitch: 🚐 🚎 �'

©Britain on View/Tony Pleavin

OPEN BRITAIN **PLANNING A DAY OUT? WHY NOT MAKE IT A SHORT- BREAK?**
Fabulous 'Places to Stay' in every region

Hayle | Atlantic Coast Caravan Park

AS

Enjoy England ★★★★

🛏 (15)

🚐 (15)

⛺ (15)

🏠 (19)

15 touring pitches
Open: 1st March until
beginning January

53 Upton Towans, Hayle, Cornwall TR27 5BL
t 01736 75071 **e** enquiries@atlanticcoastpark.co.uk
atlanticcoastpark.co.uk

1B3

The park is situated alongside the sand dunes of St Ives bay, bordering gwithian beach, a fantastic quiet beach ideal for families & surfers. The park is also is also pet friendly.

Location: Leave A30 Hayle exit, Turn right to B3301, Approx 1 mile on left is where we are situated

Access:
🔌 🐕 🏧 ☺ ♿ ♿
General:
📖 🛎 📷 🧺 📞 WP
Pitch:
🛏 🏠 🚐 ⛺

Helston | Elm Cottage

Cadgwith, Ruan Minor, nr. Helston, Cornwall
t 0844 800 2070 **e** cottages@nationaltrust.org.uk
nationaltrustcottages.co.uk

Helston | Lower Pentire Barn

National Trust Booking Office, Degibna, Helston, Cornwall TR12 2PR
t 0844 800 2070 **e** cottages@nationaltrust.org.uk
nationaltrustcottages.co.uk

Access: ☺ General: 🐴P⑤ Unit: 🛏♿♿

Launceston | Forget-me-not Farm Holidays

Enjoy England ★★★★

Units: 4 Sleeps: 2-6
Open: All year

Low season p/w:
£280.00
High season p/w:
£980.00

Mrs Sheila Kempthorne, Forget-me-not Farm Holidays, Trefranck, St Clether, Launceston, Cornwall PL15 8QN **t** 01566 86284
e holidays@trefranck.co.uk
forget-me-not-farm-holidays.co.uk

1C2

Experience life on a family farm, nestled between Bodmin Moor and the spectacular Cornwall coast.

Access: 🏧 General: 🐴📖P⑤ Unit: 🛏🏧♿🛏📺⑤♿🍴❀

Looe | Bocaddon Holiday Cottages

Enjoy England	★★★★
Units: 3	Sleeps: 4
Open: All year	

Low season p/w:
£220.00
High season p/w:
£720.00

Mrs Alison Maiklem, Bocaddon Holiday Cottages, Bocaddon Farm, Lanreath, Looe PL13 2PG **t** 01503 220192 **e** holidays@bocaddon.com
bocaddon.com

1C2

Bocaddon Holiday Cottages consist of three barn conversions, situated in the centre of our farm.

Access: 🅷 ♿ General: 🎠 P S Unit: 🛁 ⬆ ♿ ⬛ ♿ ✿

Looe | Tudor Lodges

 **AS**

Enjoy England	★★★★
Units: 6	Sleeps: 2-6
Open: All year	

Low season p/w:
£215.00
High season p/w:
£830.00
Shop: 2 miles

Mr & Mrs M Tudor, Tudor Lodges, Morval, Looe, Cornwall PL13 1PR
t 01579 320344 **e** mollytudor@aol.com
tudorlodges.co.uk

1C2

Six 2007/08 individual award winning accessible countryside lodges. Sleeps 2 to 6 persons. (Two person discount). Three double bedrooms. Balconies front/rear. Profiling beds. Electric hoists, rise/recline chairs. Large level entry wheelchair accessible shower. Ideal touring base. Eden Project.

Location: Looe 3 miles, sandy beaches/fishing port. Polperro 8 miles. Fowey via ferry 11 miles. Eden Project 22 miles.

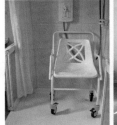

Access:
🅷 ✳ ⬛ ♿
General:
🎠 P S
Unit:
🛁 ⬆ ♿ ⬛ ♿ S ♿ ✿

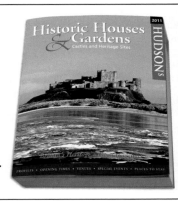

Lostwithiel | **Brean Park**

Enjoy England ★★★★★
Units: 1   Sleeps: 1-8
Open: All year

Low season p/w:
£850.00
High season p/w:
£2195.00
Shop: 5 miles
Pub: 5 miles

General:
🐾🗓️P⑤
Unit:
⚗️🔥🏠♨️♿🌿

Mrs Janet Hoskin, Brean Park Farm, Lostwithiel, Cornwall PL22 0LP
t 01208 872184 **e** breanpark@btconnect.com
breanpark.co.uk

1B2

Spectacular views of Lanhydrock House and parkland, this single storey luxury barn offers accommodation of the highest standard in Cornwall. Spacious and easily accessible throughout. All bedrooms are en suite. Relax and enjoy the countryside and nature at its best.

Location: Accessible from A30 and A38. A few minutes drive from Eden Project. Convenient for North and South coast beaches.

Lostwithiel Fowey | **Hartswheal Stables**

Enjoy England ★★★★
Units: 1   Sleeps: 1-4
Open: All year

Low season p/w:
£380.00
High season p/w:
£720.00

Mrs Wendy Jordan, Hartswell Farm, Saint Winnow, Lostwithiel Fowey
PL22 0RB   **t** 01208 873419 **e** hartswheal@connexions.co.uk
connexions.co.uk/hartswell

1B3

Converted granary with garden and friendly livestock, electric bed and ceiling hoist, tracking to bathroom.

Access: 🅰️ 🐎 ☺ General: 🐾₆🗓️P Unit: ⚗️🖼️🏠♿♨️🚾♿🌿

OPEN BRITAIN **DECIDED WHERE TO GO? SEE ATTRACTIONS FOR WHAT TO DO**
Ideas and information at the end of each regional section

Mount Hawke | Ropers Walk Barns

 AS

Enjoy England ★★★★

Units: 1   Sleeps: 4

Open: All year

Low season p/w:
£365.00

High season p/w:
£890.00

Shop: <0.5 miles

Pub: 1.5 miles

Mrs Liz Pollard, Ropers Walk Farm, Rope Walk, Mount Hawke, Truro
TR4 8DW   t 01209 891632   e peterandliz@roperswalkbarns.co.uk

roperswalkbarns.co.uk

1B3

Situated in small working farm, on
the fringe of friendly village; perfect
for accessing many Cornish
attractions; 8 miles from Truro and
2 miles to the coast.
Accommodation is wheelchair
accessible; awarded mark 3 by the
National Accessible Scheme.

Location: See website for details
(http://www.roperswalkbarns.co.uk/
directions.shtml)

General:
🐾 ⓘ P Ⓢ

Unit:
♨ ♿ 🧹 ♿ 📻 Ⓢ ♿ 🌸

Newquay | Dewolf Guest House

AS

AA   ★★★★   100 Henver Road, Newquay, Cornwall TR7 3BL
    t 01637 874746   e holidays@dewolfguesthouse.com

dewolfguesthouse.com/

Access: 🐾 🗑 ♿   General: 🐾 🍴 ✕ 🍷 🌸   Room: ♨ 🚾 ☕

Padstow | **Seafood Restaurant**

AA ★★★

Open: All year except Xmas

Rooms per night:
s: £97.00-£310.00
d: £97.00-£310.00
Shop: <0.5 miles
Pub: <0.5 miles

Riverside, Padstow, Cornwall PL28 8BY
t 01841 532 700 **e** reservations@rickstein.com
rickstein.com

1B2

Our 40 rooms are smart but relaxed, and friendly too. We think of somewhere we'd like to stay and what we like; good powerful showers, fresh crisp linen, beautiful bathrooms for indulgent soaking, pure white towels. Double or twins available.

Location: Road: M5 to Exeter, A30 to Bodmin, follow the road to Padstow. Rail: Bodmin Parkway Station. Plane: Newquay International Airport.

Access:
abc ✕ 🐾 🏠 😊 ♿ 🦽

General:
🛋 🍽 ✕ 🍷 P♿ ✿ 📧 ♿

Room:
♿ 🛏 🛗 🚾 S 🍵

Padstow | **Yellow Sands Cottages**

 AS

Enjoy England ★★★-★★★★★

Units: 1 Sleeps: 1-6
Open: All year

Low season p/w:
£320.00
High season p/w:
£790.00

Mrs Sharon Keast, Yellow Sands Cottages, Harlyn Bay, Padstow, Cornwall PL28 8SE **t** 01637 881548 **e** keast3@btinternet.com
yellowsands.co.uk

1B2

4* Gold Award Cottage, within 250m of Harlyn Bays Sandy Shore and Padstow 2.5 miles.

General: 🛋 📷 P S Unit: ♿ 🛏 ♿ 🛗 🚾 S 🦽 ✿

Pillaton | **Kernock Cottages**

 AS

Enjoy England
★★★★-★★★★★

Units: 4   Sleeps: 2-6
Open: All year

Low season p/w:
£350.00
High season p/w:
£1450.00
Shop: 4 miles
Pub: 0.5 miles

Mrs Beth Bailey, Pillaton, Saltash, Cornwall PL12 6RY
t 01579 350435 **e** hughbeth@kernockcottages.com
kernockcottages.com

1C3

Heather Barn is a beautifully converted 5* (Gold Award) NAS M3a single level barn conversion in a private orchard garden in our 25-acre estate. 2 Double (or twin) bedrooms, one with level-entry shower, large parking area, private terrace & BBQ.

Location: Just outside the village of Pillaton, only 10 miles from Plymouth; ideally placed for exploring SE Cornwall and South Devon.

General:

Unit:

Porthtowan | **Rosehill Lodges**

AS

Enjoy England   ★★★★★

Units: 10   Sleeps: 1-6
Open: All year

Low season p/w:
£530.00
High season p/w:
£1660.00
Shop: 0.5 miles
Pub: 0.5 miles

Mr John Barrow, Rosehill Lodges, Porthtowan, Cornwall TR4 8AR
t 01209 891920 **e** reception@rosehilllodges.com
rosehilllodges.com

1B3

Luxury lodges on the Cornish coast. Pamper yourself. King size beds, log burners, your own personal hot tub spa. Level access throughout. Glass covered decking for dining alfresco and those stargazing nights. Easy level access from car to lodge.

Location: Rosehill is located within the coastal village of Porthtowan on the North coast of Cornwall, just 100yds past beach road.

Access:

General:

Unit:

Port Isaac | **Carnweather**

National Trust Booking Office, Doyden House, Port Quinn, Port Isaac, Cornwall PL29 3SU **t** 0844 800 2070 **e** cottages@nationaltrust.org.uk
nationaltrustcottages.co.uk

Access: General: P Unit:

Port Isaac | **Tolraggott Farm Cottages**

Enjoy England ★★★★

Units: 3 Sleeps: 2-8
Open: All year

Low season p/w:
£275.00
High season p/w:
£1400.00

Mrs Harris, Tolraggott Farm Cottages, Tolraggott Farm, St Endellion, Port Isaac PL29 3TP **t** 01208 880927 **e** email@rock-wadebridge.co.uk
rock-wadebridge.co.uk **1B2**

Disabled friendly cottages, wet rooms with bars and shower seats. All living areas wheelchair accessable.

General: P Unit:

Portreath | **Tehidy Holiday Park**

AS

AA ★★★
Enjoy England ★★★★

Units: 24 Sleeps: 1-6
Open: All year

Low season p/w:
£210.00
High season p/w:
£690.00
Shop: <0.5 miles
Pub: <0.5 miles

Access:
General:
P
Unit:

Mr and Mrs Richard and Julia Barnes, Tehidy Holiday Park, Harris Mill, Illogan, Portreath, Cornwall TR16 4JQ **t** 01209 216489
e holiday@tehidy.co.uk
tehidy.co.uk **1B3**

Cottages, Holiday Caravans and Camping/Touring on our multi-award winning park. Tehidy Holiday Park, its accommodation and facilities are beautifully kept and sit comfortably in our wooded valley. Only 2 miles from one of our many local beaches.

Location: A30 towards Redruth. Exit Porthtowan and Portreath. On roundabout right to Portreath. Left at cross roads. Over next cross roads.

Ruan High Lanes | Trenona Farm Holidays

AS

Enjoy England ★★★★

Units: 2 Sleeps: 2-6
Open: All year

Low season p/w:
£350.00
High season p/w:
£975.00

Mrs Pamela Carbis, Trenona Farm Holidays, Trenona Farm, Ruan High Lanes, Truro TR2 5JS **t** 01872 501339
e pam@trenonafarmholidays.co.uk
trenonafarmholidays.co.uk

1B3

Two single storey cottages - 2/3 accessible en suite bedrooms own garden/patio. Level 2 mobility.

Access: ⚐ General: ⮐P⑤ Unit: 🔥♨️♿🛏️🚾⑤♿✿

St Just | Swallow's End

Enjoy England ★★★★

Units: 1   Sleeps: 4
Open: All year

Low season p/w:
£200.00
High season p/w:
£595.00

Mr David Beer, Swallow's End, Kelynack Moor Farmhouse, Bosworlas, Penzance TR19 7RQ **t** 01234 871731 **e** beerdav@gmail.com
westcornwalllets.co.uk

1A3

Swallow's End is an attractive self-catering annexe to the lovely Kelynack Moor Farmhouse.

Access: ⓗ abc General: ⮐⓪P⑤ Unit: 🔥♨️♿🛏️🚾⑤♿✿

Tintagel | Trewethett Farm Caravan Club Site

AS

Enjoy England ★★★★★

🚐 (142)
            £14.90-£27.20
🚚 (142)
            £14.90-£27.20
142 touring pitches
Open: 25 March - 7 November

Shop: 2.5 miles
Pub: 2.5 miles

Trethevy, Tintagel, Cornwall PL34 0BQ
t 01840 770222
caravanclub.co.uk

1B2

The site boasts a cliff top setting, with breathtaking views over Bossiney Cove with its safe and sandy beach. The coastal path borders the site and there are spectacular walks. Tintagel is a popular resort with shops and restaurants aplenty.

Location: A30, A395 (Camelford), A39 (Bude), left before transmitter, B3266 (Boscastle), B3263. Site on right in 2 miles.

Access:
ⓗ ⚐ 🚻 ☺ ♿
General:
⑤🚐🏕️🔥💡🚿🚾
Pitch:
🚐🚚

Tresmeer/Launceston | **An-Skyber**

Enjoy England ★★★

Units: 1   Sleeps: 4-6
Open: All year

Low season p/w:
£200.00
High season p/w:
£755.00
Shop: 6 miles
Pub: 2 miles

Access:
⊞ ♿ wc
General:
⌂ ⊟ P
Unit:
▦ ♿ ▦ wc ♿ ✿

Mr & Mrs Harold & Julie Walters, An-Skyber, Tresmeer, Launceston,
Cornwall PL15 8QT   **t** 01566 781339 **e** juliewalters@uwclub.net
an-skyber-holidays.co.uk

1C2

Converted barn suitable for severe
disabilities requiring full assistance,
to less disabled. Wheelchair users &
carers. Accessibility is important,
providing comfort and security.
Sleeps 4. Quiet rural area, close to
towns, beaches, moorland. Profiling
bed, Portable hoist. Shower
wheelchair.

Location: From A30, A395 Kennards
House junction. Through Pipers Pool.
Road right to Tresmeer. End turn
right. Bus shelter, turn right.

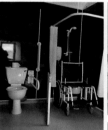

Truro | **The Captain's Quarter**

National Trust, The Captain's Quarter, St Anthony-in-Roseland, Truro,
Cornwall TR2 5HA   **t** 0844 800 2070 **e** cottages@nationaltrust.org.uk
nationaltrustcottages.co.uk

Access: ☺ General: ⊟⑤ Unit: ▦ ♿ ▦ ♿ ✿

Truro | **Engine House**

National Trust, Engine House, Trelissick, Feock, Truro TR3 6QL
t 0844 800 2070 **e** cottages@nationaltrust.org.uk
nationaltrustcottages.co.uk

Access: ☺ General: ⌂P⑤ Unit: ▦ ♿ ▦ ♿ ✿

Truro | **The Major's Quarter**

National Trust, The Major's Quarter, St Anthony-in-Roseland, Truro,
Cornwall TR2 5HA   **t** 0844 800 2070 **e** cottages@nationaltrust.org.uk
nationaltrustcottages.co.uk

Access: ☺ General: ⊟P⑤ Unit: ▦ ♿ ▦ ♿ ✿

Truro | **Tregoninny Farm** `AS`

Open: All year

Rooms per night:
s: £30.00-£45.00
d: £50.00-£80.00
p/p half board:
d: £40.00-£55.00
Meals: £8.00-£15.00

Tresillian, Truro, Cornwall TR2 4AR
t 01872 520145
tregoninny.com

1B3

Four ground floor fully accessible rooms. Wheel-in showers, mobile hoist, level entry to ground floor.

Access: ♿ abc ⚲ ♨ ♿ ♿   General: ☎ ⛱ ✕ P ❀ ♿   Room: ♿ ♨ ♿ ♿ ☕

Veryan | **Dairy Cottage**

National Trust, Gwendra, Veryan, Truro, Cornwall TR2 5PF
t 0844 800 2070 **e** cottages@nationaltrust.org.uk
nationaltrustcottages.co.uk

Access: ☺ General: ▣ P ⓢ Unit: ♿ ♿ ♿ ❀

Jersey | **Maison Des Landes Hotel**

p/p half board:
d: £65.00-£75.00
Shop: 2 miles
Pub: 2 miles

St Ouen, Jersey, Channel Islands JE3 2AA
t 01534 481683 **e** contact@maisondeslandes.co.uk
maisondeslandes.co.uk

1D3

Established for more than 40 years, this specialist hotel provides carefree full board holidays for the disabled and their families in single, twin and family rooms. Nine miles from St. Helier with free daily minibus tours for sightseeing and shopping.

Location: Flights to Jersey from most UK Airports and Ferries from Weymouth, Poole, Portsmouth and Saint Malo.

Access:
♿ abc ⚲ ♨ ☺ ♿ ♿
General:
☎ ⛱ ✕ ♟ P ❀ ♿
Room:
♿ ♨ ♿ ♿ ⓢ ☕

St Helier | **Jersey Cheshire Home**

Open: All year

Rooms per night:

s: £75.00-£150.00

p/p half board:

d: £75.00-£150.00

Shop: 0.5 miles

Pub: 1 mile

Eric Young House, Rope Walk, St Helier, Jersey JE2 4UU
t 01534 285858 **e** david@jerseycheshirehome.je
jerseycheshirehome.je

1D3

Respite Suite available on the Ground Floor of the Home, accessible directly from outside or through the home emprises a bedroom designed for disabled users, totally accessible bathroom; seperate lounge area.

Access:

 ✶ 🐾 🏠 😊 ♿ ♿

General:

🍳 ✗ P♿ ❀ ⬆ ♿

Room:

🛏 🔥 ♿ wc 📷 S ☕

Barnstaple | **Calvert Trust Exmoor**

Wistlandpound, Kentisbury, Barnstaple, Devon EX31 4SJ
t 01598 763221 **e** exmoor@calvert-trust.org.uk
calvert-trust.org.uk/exmoor

Access: 🅰 abc ✶🐾 😊 ♿ General: 🐾 🔘 S Unit: 🛏 ♿ 🏠 ♿ ♿ wc ♿ ♿ ✏

OPEN BRITAIN **DECIDED WHERE TO GO? SEE ATTRACTIONS FOR WHAT TO DO**
Ideas and information at the end of each regional section

Brixham | **Hillhead Caravan Club Site** THE CARAVAN CLUB

AS

Enjoy England ★★★★★

🚐 (239)
£15.40–£35.50

🚍 (239)
£15.40–£35.50

⚊ (12)

239 touring pitches
Open: 25 March - 2 January 2012

Hillhead, Brixham, Devon TQ5 0HH
t 01803 853204
caravanclub.co.uk

1D2

Set in 22 acres of Devon countryside near Brixham, with many pitches affording stunning views. There's plenty of entertainment on site - an outdoor heated swimming pool, skateboard ramp and entertainment complex housing a games room, shop, restaurant and bar.

Access:
⚠ 🐕 🏠 ☺ ♿ 🚻
General:
🔲 📶 🍴 📮 🚿 ☕ 📤 🚰 🚐
✖
Pitch:
🚐 🚍 ⚊

Location: A380 (Newton Abbot) onto A3022 (Brixham). Right onto A379. Two miles keep left onto B3025. Site entrance on left.

Budeigh Salterton | **Ladram Bay Holiday Park**

AS

Enjoy England ★★★★

🚐 (144)
£15.00–£30.00

🚍 (144)
£15.00–£30.00

⚊ (41)
£15.00–£30.00

🏠 (540)
£185.00–£1080.00

250 touring pitches
Open: Mid March to the end of October

Shop: 3 miles
Pub: 1 mile

Otterton, Budleigh Salterton, Devon EX9 7BX
t 01395 568398 **e** welcome@ladrambay.co.uk
ladrambay.co.uk

1D2

Nestled in the Devon Hills overlooking the Jurassic Coast, Ladram Bay is the Holiday Park in Devon that has something to offer everyone. We have all the amenities on site that you'll ever need with our own private sheltered beach.

Location: Off M5 junction 30, head towards Sidmouth, we are signposted from Newton Poppleford taking you through Colaton Raleigh and Otterton.

Access:
📷 🐕 ♿ 🚻 🚲
General:
🔲 🍴 📶 ☕ 📤 🚰 ☕ ✖
Pitch:
🚐 🏠 🚍 ⚊

Exeter | Hue's Piece

Enjoy England	★★★★
Units: 1	Sleeps: 4
Open: From April 2011	

Low season p/w:
£340.00
High season p/w:
£775.00
Shop: 1 mile
Pub: 1 mile

Mrs Anna Hamlyn, Hue's Piece, Paynes Farm, Broadclyst, Exeter EX5 3BJ
t 01392 466720 **e** annahamlyn@paynes-farm.co.uk
paynes-farm.co.uk

1D2

Welcoming converted barn on friendly family-run National Trust farm. VisitEngland 4 stars. South West Tourism Gold Award winner for Access for All. One double bedroom and two singles. Private parking and pretty cottage garden with lovely open views across farmland.

Location: M5 Junction 30. First exit to Sowton and Rockbeare. Left to Broadclyst. Right opposite school. Right to Elbury. 2nd left.

Access:
abc 🐾 🏛

General:
🐴 📷 P S

Unit:
⚲ 🛏 🔥 ♿ 📶 🚾 S 🦽 ✿

Honiton | Combe House

AA ★★★
Enjoy England ☆☆☆

Gittisham, Honiton, Devon EX14 3AD
t 01404 540400 **e** stay@combehousedevon.com
combehousedevon.com

Access: abc 🐾 🏛 ☺ 🚾 General: 🐴 🍽 ✕ 🍷 P ✿ 🐴

Modbury | **Broad Park Caravan Club Site**

AS

Enjoy England ★★★★

🚐 (112)
£13.10–£25.40

�caravan (112)
£13.10–£25.40

112 touring pitches
Open: 25 March - 7 November

Shop: 1 mile
Pub: 1 mile

Higher East Leigh, Modbury, Ivybridge, Devon PL21 0SH
t 01548 830714
caravanclub.co.uk

1C3

Situated between moor and sea, this makes a splendid base from which to explore South Devon. Head for Dartmoor, or seek out the small villages of the South Hams.

Location: From B3027 (signposted Modbury), site on left after 1 mile.

Access:
🅰♿🐾🚿🚾😊♿
General:
📷🚐📮🚜🔌🚪🚰🚿 WP
Pitch:
🚐🚍

Plymouth | **Holiday Inn Plymouth**

disabled Ⓖⓒ

AA ★★★★

Armada Way, Plymouth, Devon PL1 2HJ
t 01752 639988 **e** hiplymouth@qmh-hotels.com
holidayinn.co.uk

Access: abc 🖼🐾🚿😊♿♿ General: 🛏🍴✖🍷P♿🔼♿ Room: 🛏Ⓖ🚾⌂S☕

GETTING THERE IS NOT A PROBLEM!
OPEN See Getting there….. and back section (p314)
BRITAIN Everything you need for a hassle-free journey

Sidbury | **Putts Corner Caravan Club Site** THE CARAVAN CLUB

AS

Enjoy England ★★★★

(117) £13.10–£25.40

(117) £13.10–£25.40

117 touring pitches

Open: 25 March - 7 November

Shop: 2.5 miles

Pub: 1 mile

Putts Corner, Sidbury, Sidmouth, Devon EX10 0QQ

t 01404 42875

caravanclub.co.uk **1D2**

A quiet site in pretty surroundings, with a private path to the local pub. Bluebells create a sea of blue in spring, followed by foxgloves.

Location: M5 jct 25 onto A375 (Sidmouth). Turn right onto B3174. In about 0.25 miles turn right into site entrance.

Access:

General:

Pitch:

South Molton | **Stable Cottage**

AA ★★★★★

Enjoy England ★★★★★

Units: 1 Sleeps: 6

Open: All year

Low season p/w: £390.00

High season p/w: £835.00

Mrs V Huxtable, Stable Cottage, Stitchpool Fm, Sth Molton EX36 3EZ

t 01598 740130 **e** stitchpoolcottage@hotmail.co.uk

stitchpoolfarm.co.uk **2C1**

Peaceful countryside setting on farm, 5 star M3A barn conversion, 3 bedroom, Jacuzzi bath, Gardens.

Access: General: P Unit:

Tiverton | **West Pitt Farm**

AS

Enjoy England ★★★-★★★★★

Units: 6 Sleeps: 2-18

Open: All year

Low season p/w: £300.00

High season p/w: £1600.00

Ms Susanne Westgate, West Pitt Farm, Whitnage, Tiverton EX16 7DU

t 01884 820296 **e** susannewestgate@yahoo.com

westpittfarm.co.uk **1D2**

Willow Tree 5 Star accessible cottage with excellent facilities set in glorious Devonshire countryside.

Access: abc General: P Unit:

Torquay | Atlantis Holiday Apartments

   AS

Enjoy England ★★★★
Units: 6 Sleeps: 2-4
Open: All year

Low season p/w:
£220.00
High season p/w:
£700.00

Mrs Pauline Roberts, Atlantis Holiday Apartments, Solsbro Road, Chelston, Torquay TQ2 6PF   **t** 01803 607929 **e** enquiry@atlantistorquay.co.uk
atlantistorquay.co.uk   **1D3**

4 Star Gold Award. Near seafront, shops, railway station and attractions. No meters. Wi-fi access.

Access: ᵃᵇᶜ 🏃 ☺ General: ⛵📷**P**Ⓢ Unit: 🔥♨️♿📶WCⓈ♿❄

Woolacombe | Sunnymeade

AS

Enjoy England ★★★
Open: All year

Rooms per night:
s: £25.00-£32.00
d: £64.00-£74.00
p/p half board:
d: £50.00-£53.00
Meals: £17.50

Dean Cross, West Down, Nr. Woolacombe, Devon EX34 8NT
t 01271 863668 **e** info@sunnymeade.co.uk
sunnymeade.co.uk   **1C1**

3* VisitBritain wheelchair-friendly ground floor en suite rooms, wheel-in showers. Accessible lounge, bar, dining room.

Access: ♿ General: ⛵🍴✕♟️P♿❄♿ Room: 🔥♨️📶WCⓈ🍵

Yelverton | Overcombe House

AS

Enjoy England ★★★★
Open: All year

Rooms per night:
s: £60.00-£70.00
d: £75.00-£90.00

Old Station Road, Horrabridge, Yelverton PL20 7RA
t 01822 853501 **e** enquiries@overcombehotel.co.uk
overcombehotel.co.uk   **1C2**

Comfortable, fully En Suite, guest accommodation, situated in Dartmoor National Park between Tavistock and Plymouth.

Access: ᵃᵇᶜ 🏃♿ General: 🍴❄♿ Room: 🔥♨️📶WCⓈ🍵

Alton Pancras | Bookham Court

 **AS**

Enjoy England
★★★★-★★★★★
Units: 4 Sleeps: 4-8
Open: All year

Low season p/w:
£235.00
High season p/w:
£1160.00

Mr & Mrs Andrew Foot, Whiteways, Bookham, Dorchester DT2 7RP
t 01300 345511 **e** andy.foot1@btinternet.com
bookhamcourt.co.uk   **2B3**

Luxury barn conversions with panoramic views, games room, wildlife hide, fishing walks. Sea 30 minutes.

Access: 🐕 General: ⛵📷**P**Ⓢ Unit: 🔥♨️♿📶♿❄

Bournemouth | **BOD** AS

Units: 1 Sleeps: 2-6 Open: All year	Anna Stanger, Access for All Seaside Holidays Ltd, 69 Boscombe Overcliff Drive, Bournemouth, Dorset BH5 2EJ **t** 01202 423046 **e** admin@afash.co.uk
Low season p/w: £450.00 High season p/w: £950.00	afash.co.uk **2B3**

Comfortable, family friendly flat overlooking sea. Entirely accessible, wet-rooms, profiling bed, broadband. Garden, beach hut.

Access: ᵃᵇᶜ ⊁ General: ⯑⯑P Unit: ⯑⯑⯑⯑⯑⯑⯑⯑ ✽

Bridport | **Lancombes House**  AS

Enjoy England ★★★★ Units: 4 Sleeps: 4-12 Open: All year	Mr Adrian Semmence, Lancombes House & Cottages, West Milton, Bridport DT6 3TN **t** 01308 485375 **e** info@lancombes-house.co.uk lancombes-house.co.uk **2A3**
Low season p/w: £400.00 High season p/w: £2100.00	200 year old converted barn/farm buildings set in 9 acres within the Dorset AONB.

Access: ᵃᵇᶜ ⊁ General: ⯑⯑PⓈ Unit: ⯑⯑⯑⯑ ✽

Corfe Castle | **Isolation Hospital 2**

National Trust, Isolation Hospital 2, Corfe Castle, Dorset BH20 5DU
t 0844 800 2070   **e** cottages@nationaltrust.org.uk
nationaltrustcottages.co.uk

Access: ☺ General: PⓈ Unit: ⯑⯑⯑⯑⯑ ✽

Ferndown, Nr Bournemouth | **Birchcroft**  AS

Enjoy England ★★★★ Units: 1 Sleeps: 1-8 Open: All year	HolidayInDorset, 32 Dunkeld Road, Bournemouth BH3 7EW **t** 01202 766774 **e** holidayindorset@btinternet.com holidayindorset.org **2B3**
Low season p/w: £420.00 High season p/w: £1200.00	Nature lover's secret hideaway 4 Star. Rhododrendron woods. Stunning views of countryside and wildlife.

Access: ⯑ General: ⯑⯑PⓈ Unit: ⯑⯑⯑⯑⯑⯑⯑ ✽

Isle of Purbeck | **The Farmhouse**

National Trust, The Farmhouse, Middlebere Farm, Isle of Purbeck, Dorset BH20 5BJ   **t** 0844 8002070   **e** cottages@nationaltrust.org.uk
nationaltrustcottages.co.uk

Access: ☺ General: ⯑⯑PⓈ Unit: ⯑⯑⯑ ✽

Poole | Holton Lee - Gateway & Woodland Cottages

Enjoy England ★★★
Units: 2   Sleeps: 8-10
Open: All year

Low season p/w:
£390.00
High season p/w:
£1558.00

Mrs Louise Vaughan, Holton Lee, East Holton, Holton Heath, Poole, Dorset
BH16 6JN   t 01202 631063   e facilities@holtonlee.co.uk
holtonlee.co.uk

2B3

On 350 acre nature reserve, both have twin and
double rooms and are fully accessible.

Access: ♿ 🐾 ♿ General: 🎠 P Ⓢ Unit: 🛋 🔥 🛋 📺 WC 🖥 Ⓢ ♿ ✿

Portland | Portland Lodge

Beds: 5 double, 2 twin

Open: All year except Xmas
and New Year

Rooms per night:
s: £45.00-£57.00
d: £62.00-£74.00

Easton Lane, Portland, Dorset DT5 1BW
t 01305 820265   e info@portlandlodge.com
portlandlodge.com

2B3

We have 30 en suite rooms with 7 designed for
physically disabled on the ground-floor.

Access: ♿ ♿ General: 🎠 🍽 P Room: 🛋 🔥 🛋 ♨

Swanage | Haycraft Caravan Club Site   THE CARAVAN CLUB

AS

Enjoy England ★★★★★
🚐 (53)
        £15.30-£27.20
🚍 (53)
        £15.30-£27.20
53 touring pitches
Open: 18 March - 7
November

Shop: 0.5 miles
Pub: 1.5 miles

Haycrafts Lane, Swanage, Dorset BH19 3EB
t 01929 480572
caravanclub.co.uk

2B3

Peaceful site located five miles from
Swanage, with its safe, sandy
beach. Spectacular cliff-top walks,
Corfe Castle, Lulworth Cove and
Durdle Door are within easy reach.
The Swanage Railway is a favourite
with young and old alike.

Location: Take A351 from Wareham
to Swanage, at Harmans Cross turn
right into Haycrafts Lane, site 0.5
miles on the left.

Access:
♿ 🐾 🚶 ☺ ♿
General:
🖥 🐾 🚗 😊 💧 ☎ 🚐
Pitch:
🚐 🚍

Weymouth | **Breakwaters**

Enjoy England ★★★★	Joy Sangster, Breakwaters, 4 & 5 Hope Square, Weymouth DT4 8TR
Units: 8 Sleeps: 2-8	**t** 01305 789000 **e** admin@dream-cottages.co.uk
Open: All year	dream-cottages.co.uk

2B3

Low season p/w: £610.00	Breakwaters has sea views over Portland and Weymouth, Sandsfoot beach is a short walk away.
High season p/w: £1270.00	

General: 🛏️🗄️**P**⑤ Unit: 🧹♿⑤✿

Weymouth | **Character Farm Cottages**

 **AS**

Enjoy England ★★★★	Mrs Ann Mayo, Higher Farm, Rodden, Weymouth DT3 4JE
Units: 7 Sleeps: 2-9	**t** 01305 871347 **e** ann@characterfarmcottages.co.uk
Open: All year	characterfarmcottages.co.uk

2A3

Low season p/w: £235.00	Beautifully converted barn, high quality facilities. Heritage coast. Also smaller properties, downstairs bedrooms and showers.
High season p/w: £1050.00	

Access: 🐾🏛️ General: 🛏️🗄️**P**⑤ Unit: G🧹🏢🚽⑤♿✿

Weymouth | **Millspring**

 **AS**

Enjoy England ★★★★	Joy Sangster, Millspring, 4 & 5 Hope Square, Weymouth DT4 8TR
Units: 2 Sleeps: 2-4	**t** 01305 789000 **e** admin@dream-cottages.co.uk
Open: All year	dream-cottages.co.uk/

2B3

Low season p/w: £320.00	Millspring has a beautiful pond and features a conservatory with lovely views over the garden.
High season p/w: £770.00	

Access: 🐾 General: 🛏️🗄️**P**⑤ Unit: G🧹✿

Weymouth | **Tidmoor Cottages**

Enjoy England ★★★★	Mrs Sarah Townsend, Tidmoor Cottages, 431 Chickerell Road, Chickerell,
Units: 2 Sleeps: 1-4	Weymouth DT3 4DG **t** 01305 787867 **e** sarah@tidmoorstables.co.uk
Open: All year	tidmoorstables.co.uk

2B3

Low season p/w: £300.00	4 star, M1, M11 graded, two great cottages just off the coastal footpath.
High season p/w: £795.00	

General: 🛏️🗄️**P**⑤ Unit: G🧹♿🏢🚽⑤♿✿

Woolland | Ellwood Cottages

AS

Enjoy England	★★★★

Units: 3 Sleeps: 3-6
Open: All year

Low season p/w:
£300.00
High season p/w:
£900.00
Shop: 4 miles
Pub: 1 mile

Mr & Mrs John & Ann Heath, Ellwood Cottages, Woolland, Blandford Forum, Dorset DT11 0ES   t 01258 818196
e admin@ellwoodcottages.co.uk
EllwoodCottages.co.uk

2B3

Superbly equipped cottages where comfort and relaxation are top priorities. Wet-rooms, indoor heated splash pool, therapy room with visiting therapists, and recreation room with free Broadband access. Guest garden with stunning views.

Location: Located in the beautiful North Dorset countryside, near Blandford, and within easy reach of Weymouth and the stunning Jurassic Coast.

Access:
🅰 abc ✈ 🔔 ☺
General:
🐎 ⊡ P Ⓢ
Unit:
♿ 🛁 ♨ ♿ 🛏 🖼 ☕ Ⓢ
♿ ❀

Bristol | Holiday Inn Bristol Filton

AS

Filton Road, Hambrook, Bristol BS16 1QX
t 0870 400 9014 e Bristol@ihg.com
holidayinn.co.uk

Access: ⠿ abc ▢ ✈ 🔔 ☺ ♿ ❀ General: 🐎 ☷ ✕ ♟ P ❄ ▣ ⤓ Room: ♿ Ⓢ ☕

Bristol | **Winford Manor**

 AS

Enjoy England ★★★

Open: All year

Rooms per night:
s: £75.00-£85.00
d: £95.00-£165.00
p/p half board:
d: £70.00-£100.00
Meals: £12.50-£35.00
Shop: 1 mile
Pub: 1 mile

Old Hill, Bristol BS40 8DW
t 01275 472292 **e** reservations@winfordmanor.co.uk
winfordmanor.co.uk

2A2

Set in the Chew Valley not far from Bristol Airport, Winford Manor offers accommodation to suit every budget. Fabulous, accessible services, complimented by friendly professional service. The hotel's Labyrinth restaurant caters for all dietary requirements with delicious simplicity.

Location: Just off A38, near Bristol Airport, see website for full directions.

Access:
abc ☑ ✷ 🐾 ☺ ⚫ ♿
General:
🛋 ╫ ✕ 🍷 P☕ ✿ 🎁 ♿
Room:
♿ ♨ 🛏 📺 🖨 S 🍵

Cheltenham | **Cheltenham Racecourse Caravan Club Site**

AS

Enjoy England ★★★

Open: April to October

Prestbury Park, Evesham Road, Prestbury, Cheltenham GL50 4SH
t 01242 523102
caravanclub.co.uk

Access: ✷ 🐾 ☺ ♿ General: 🖨 🎁 🐾 🚙 💀 🎁 ♿ ⓦ Pitch: 🚐 🚏

Chipping Campden | **Cotswold Charm**

 AS

Enjoy England ★★★★

Units: 1 Sleeps: 5-2
Open: All year

Low season p/w:
£490.00
High season p/w:
£900.00

Mr Michael, Stephen & Shirley Haines, Cotswold Charm, Blind Lane, Westington, Chipping Campden GL55 6ED   **t** 1386 841883
e info@cotswoldcharm.co.uk
cotswoldcharm.co.uk

2B1

Top Farm and Chipping Campden central to Cotswolds, Vale Evesham, Stratford-upon-Avon, Oxfordshire Downs.

Access: abc ✷ 🐾 ♿ General: 🛋 P S Unit: ♿ 🎁 ♨ ♿ 🛏 🖨 ✿

Gloucester | **Holiday Inn Gloucester-Cheltenham**

AS

Crest Way, Barnwood, Gloucester, Gloucestershire GL4 3RX
t 0871 942 9034 **e** reservations-gloucester@ihg.com
holidayinn.co.uk

Access: abc ☑ ✷ ☺ ♿ ♿ General: 🛋 ╫ 🍷 P☕ ✿ 🎁 ♿ Room: ♿ 🛏 🖨 📺 S 🍵

Moreton-in-Marsh | Moreton-in-Marsh Caravan Club Site

AS

Enjoy England ★★★★★

🚐 (183)
£15.90–£29.30

🚎 (183)
£15.90–£29.30

183 touring pitches
Open: All year

Shop: <0.5 miles
Pub: <0.5 miles

Bourton Road, Moreton-in-Marsh, Gloucestershire GL56 0BT
t 01608 650519
caravanclub.co.uk

2B1

An attractive, well-wooded site within easy walking distance of the market town of Moreton-in-Marsh. On-site facilities include crazy golf, volleyball and boules. Large dog-walking area.

Location: From Moreton-in-Marsh on A44 the site entrance is on right 250yds past end of the speed limit sign.

Access:
🅗 🐾 🏛 ☺ ♿
General:
◻ 🚗 🔌 🚰 💧 🛖 ⓦⓟ
Pitch:
🚐 🚎

Tewkesbury | Croft Farm Water Park

Mr Alan Newell, Croft Farm Water Park, Bredons Hardwick, Tewkesbury, Gloucs GL20 7EE **t** 01684 772321 **e** alan@croftfarmleisure.co.uk
croftfarmleisure.co.uk

Access: ♿ General: 🛋 ◻ P S Unit: 🛁 🏛 ♿ 💺

Yorkley | 2 Danby Cottages

♿ AS

Enjoy England ★★★

Units: 1 Sleeps: 1-6
Open: All year

Low season p/w:
£300.00
High season p/w:
£850.00

Gareth Lawes, 23 Cotham Road South, Bristol BS6 5TZ
t 0117 942 2301 **e** glawes@talktalk.net
2danbycottages.co.uk

2B1

Comprehensively equipped six person, two bathroom cottage: heart of forest, pets, children welcome, walks, views.

Access: 🐾 ♿ General: 🛋 ◻ P S Unit: 🛁 🔲 🏛 ♿ 💺 🚿 S ♿ ✿

Bath | **Carfax Hotel**

 AS

Enjoy England   ★★

Open: All year except Xmas

Rooms per night:
s: £85.00-£176.00
d: £120.00-£180.00
p/p half board:
d: £74.50-£104.50
Meals: £10.95-£14.50

13-15 Great Pulteney Street, Bath BA2 4BS
t 01225 462089 **e** reservations@carfaxhotel.co.uk
carfaxhotel.co.uk

2B2

A trio of Georgian town houses in the centre of Bath. Lifts, lounge and carpark.

Access: abc    General: Room:

Bath | **Lime Kiln Farm**

Enjoy England   ★★★★★

Ms Judy Hallam, Lime Kiln Farm, Faulkland, Radstock BA3 5XE
t 01373 834305 **e** limekilnfarm@live.co.uk
limekilnfarm.co.uk

Access: abc   General: Unit:

Beetham | **Five Acres Caravan Club Site** THE CARAVAN CLUB

AS

Open: March to October

Beetham, Chard TA20 3QA
t 01460 234519
caravanclub.co.uk

Access: General: Pitch:

Blue Anchor | **Primrose Hill Holidays**

AS

Enjoy England   ★★★★
Units: 4   Sleeps: 1-5
Open: March to November,

Low season p/w:
£340.00
High season p/w:
£590.00

Mrs Jo Halliday, Wood Lane, Blue Anchor, West Somerset TA24 6LA
t 01643 821200 **e** info@primrosehillholidays.co.uk
primrosehillholidays.co.uk

1D1

Winner Accessible Somerset 2008/9. Four 2 bedroomed bungalows. Level access. Wheel-in wet rooms.

Access: abc   General: Unit:

Bridgwater | **Ash-Wembdon Farm Cottages**

AA   ★★★★
Units: 2   Sleeps: 4
Open: All year

Low season p/w:
£235.00
High season p/w:
£520.00

Mr Clarence Rowe, Ash-Wembdon Farm Cottages, Ash-Wembdon Farm, Hollow Lane, Bridgwater TA5 2BD
t 01278 453097 **e** c.a.rowe@btinternet.com
farmstayuk.com

1D1

Escape and enjoy yourselves at our luxury farm cottages, fully equipped to very high standard.

General: Unit:

Burnham on Sea | **Wall Eden Farm** — AS

Enjoy England ★★★

Units: 4 Sleeps: 5-7
Open: All year

Low season p/w:
£335.00
High season p/w:
£852.00
Shop: 1.5 miles
Pub: 1.5 miles

Mr Andrew Wall, Manager, Wall Eden Farm, New Road, East Huntspill, Highbridge, Somerset TA9 3PU
t 01278 786488 **e** walleden@btinternet.com
walledenfarm.co.uk

1D1

All luxury log cabins are easily accessible. Can sleep up to 6 people in each with 1 double room and 2 twins, walk in wet room and seperate bathroom.

Location: Junction 22 M5, head for Highbridge A38, enter the village of West Huntspill, turn left signposted for Secret World.

Access:
abc 🐕 🏛 ♿

General:
🐾 🖸 P Ⓢ

Unit:
♨ 🏖 ♿ 🏚 🖸 ♿ ❀

Chard | **Tamarack Lodge** — AS

Enjoy England ★★★★

Units: 1   Sleeps: 12
Open: All year

Low season p/w:
£420.00
High season p/w:
£950.00

Matthew Sparks, Fyfett Farm, Otterford, Nr. Chard, Somerset TA20 3QP
t 01823 601270 **e** matthew.sparks@tamaracklodge.co.uk
tamaracklodge.co.uk

1D2

Hand crafted log cabin, suitable for wheelchairs, beautiful views on family livestock farm, Blackdown, Somerset.

Access: 🅷 🐕 ♿ General: 🐾 🖸 P Ⓢ Unit: ♨ 🍴 🏖 ♿ 🏚 ♿ ❀

Godney | **Swallow Barn** — AS

Enjoy England ★★★★

Units: 1 Sleeps: 2-8
Open: All year

Low season p/w:
£350.00
High season p/w:
£785.00

Mrs Hilary Millard, Swallow Barn, Double Gate Farm, Godney, Nr Wells BA5 1RX **t** 01458 832217 **e** doublegatefarm@aol.com
doublegatefarm.com and doublegatefarm.co.uk

2A2

Breakfast available. Fishing. Welcome tray/homemade cake. Park 5 mins. 10% meal deal with www.panboroughinn.co.uk

Access: .: abc 🐕 General: 🐾 🖸 P Ⓢ Unit: ♨ 🍴 🏖 ♿ 🏚 ♿ Ⓢ ❀

High Littleton | Greyfield Farm Cottages

Enjoy England
★★★★-★★★★★

Units: 5   Sleeps: 2-4
Open: All year

Low season p/w:
£261.00
High season p/w:
£639.00
Shop: 0.5 miles
Pub: 0.5 miles

Mrs June Merry, Greyfield Farm Cottages, The Gug, High Littleton
BS39 6YQ   **t** 01761 471132   **e** june@greyfieldfarm.com
greyfieldfarm.com

2B2

Close to Bath, Bristol & Wells. Edge of village, peaceful private hillside, good views, ideal touring centre. Spacious, Cosy Cottages. Double-Glazing, Central Heating. Ideal for Short Breaks & Winter Visits.

Access:

General:

Unit:

Horsington | Half Moon Inn

Enjoy England   ★★★

Open: All year except Xmas

Rooms per night:
s: £45.00-£65.00
d: £65.00-£85.00

Off Higher Road, Templecombe BA8 0EF
t 01963 370140   **e** halfmoon@horsington.co.uk
horsington.co.uk

2B3

Quiet village location. Level access accommodation with a slope from car park to main bar.

Access: General: Room:

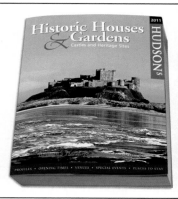

Lower Godney | Double-Gate Farm

   AS

AA	★★★★
Enjoy England	★★★★

Open: All year except Xmas and New Year

Rooms per night:
s:	£60.00-£80.00
d:	£70.00-£110.00

Shop: 3 miles

Double-Gate Farm, Godney, Nr Wells BA5 1RX
t 01458 832217 **e** doublegatefarm@aol.com
doublegatefarm.com

2A2

Lovely Georgian farmhouse on working farm. Farmhouse bedrooms: first floor en suite. Four riverside suites: ground floor, double wheelchair turning space, wet rooms, patio doors to riverside terrace. Three x double/single bed. One x double/2 single beds; all movable.

Location: From Wells A39 south to Polham. Turn right, continue 3 miles. Farm on left after Inn.

Access:
.: abc 🐾 ♿ ⚷ ⚹

General:
🐎 P♿ ✿ ♿

Room:
🛏 ♨ 📺 🚾 🅂 🍵 ♿

Lympsham, Weston-super-Mare | Hope Farm Cottages

Enjoy England	★★★★
Units: 4	Sleeps: 1
Open: All year	

Low season p/w:
£200.00
High season p/w:
£680.00

Malcolm & Aline Bennett, Brean Road, Lympsham, Weston-super-Mare, Somerset BS24 0HA   **t** 01934 750506 **e** hopefarmcottages@gmail.com
hopefarmcottages.co.uk

1D1

4 x 4* ground floor cottages - beautifully converted, set in a peaceful location.

Access: 🏃🚾 General: 🐎📺P🅂 Unit: 🛏♿📺🚾🅂♿✿

Minehead | **The Promenade**

Enjoy England ★★★

Open: All year

Rooms per night:

s:	£40.00-£50.00
d:	£80.00-£100.00

p/p half board:

d:	£55.00-£70.00
Meals:	£14.99

Shop: 0.5 miles
Pub: <0.5 miles

The Esplanade, Minehead, Somerset TA24 5QS
t 01643 702572 **e** promenade@livability.org.uk
livability.org.uk

1D1

The Promenade is accessible by wheelchair users travelling independently and has TFA NAS category-1 status.

Location: Minehead is on the edge of Exmoor National Park. With good road links to the county of Somerset and beyond.

Access:

General:

Room:

Minehead | **Woodcombe Lodges**

AS

Enjoy England ★★★★

Units: 8   Sleeps: 2-10
Open: All year

Low season p/w:
£195.00
High season p/w:
£1395.00

Mrs Nicola Hanson, Woodcombe Lodges, Bratton Lane, Minehead,
Somerset TA24 8SQ   **t** 01643 702789 **e** nicola@woodcombelodge.co.uk
woodcombelodge.co.uk

1D1

4 star lodges and cottages sleep 2-10 persons in 3 acre gardens. Rural near sea/shops.

General: 🛋️◻️**P**ⓢ Unit: 🛏️♨️♿🖥️♿✿

Stogumber, Taunton, Somerset. | **Wick House**

AS

Enjoy England ★★★★

Open: All year

Rooms per night:

s:	£35.00-£50.00
d:	£70.00-£80.00

p/p half board:

d:	£53.00-£72.00
Meals:	£18.00-£22.00

Brook Street, Stogumber, Taunton, Somerset TA4 3SZ
t 01984656422 **e** sheila@wickhouse.co.uk
wickhouse.co.uk

1D1

Relax in 4 star, friendly family B&B. Lovely village setting. Quantock Hills and Exmoor NP.

Access: ♿ General: 🛋️🍴✕♟️**P**✿♿ Room: 🛏️♨️🖥️☕

Taunton | Holiday Inn Taunton M5 J25

AA   ★★★   Deane Gate Avenue, Taunton, Somerset TA1 2UA
t 0871 942 9080
holidayinn.com/tauntonm5

Access: abc ☑ ☺ 🚾&&   General: ☎ ⛄✖ ⛾P& ⊡   Room: &🚾♨

Wells | Saint Marys Lodge

Enjoy England ★★★★	Mrs Jane Hughes, St Mary Mead, Coombe Cottages, Croscombe, Wells, Somerset BA5 3QU t 01749 342157 e jane@st-marys-lodge.co.uk
Units: 1 Sleeps: 7	st-marys-lodge.co.uk **2A2**
Open: All year	

Low season p/w:
£450.00

High season p/w:
£900.00

4*(NAS M3A) Luxurious detached 4 bedroom house. South facing patio. Parking. Central heating. Double glazed.

Access: Ⓗ ⚘ 🚾&   General: ☎ 📷P Ⓢ   Unit: & ⊞♨&🚾 🚾Ⓢ&✿

Wells | Manor Farm Bed and Breakfast

Open: All year

Rooms per night:	
s:	£40.00-£60.00
d:	£70.00-£90.00
Meals:	£7.50-£10.00

Manor Farm, Dulcote, Wells, Somerset BA5 3PZ
t 01749 672125   e rosalind.bufton@talktalk.net
wells-accommodation.co.uk   **2A2**

Lovely farmhouse, close Wells, beautiful views, friendly animals, caring owner, gardens, conservatory, recommended by Sawdays.

Access: ⚘ ♦🚾&   General: 📷✖P&✿&   Room: &♨🚾Ⓢ♨

Weston-Super-Mare | **The Royal Hotel**

AS

Enjoy England ★★★

Open: All year

Rooms per night:

s:	£69.00
d:	£99.00-£140.00

p/p half board:

d:	£69.50-£90.00
Meals:	£15.00-£25.00

1 South Parade, Weston-super-Mare, North Somerset BS23 1JP
t 01934 423100 **e** reservations@royalhotelweston.com
royalhotelweston.com

1D1

Sea Front Location, Restaurant & Bars, Lift, Carpark, Shopping Centre 200 Yards, Entertainment, Disabled Friendly.

Location: We are situated on the Seafront just past the Grand Pier next door to the Winter Gardens Pavillion.

Access:
abc 🗐 🏢 ☺ ♿ 🚻

General:
🐎 🍽 ✕ 🍷 P♿ ❀ ⊞ ♿

Room:
🔥 ♨ Ⓢ ☕

Worle | **Villa Ryall**

Units: 1 Sleeps: 8

Open: All year

Low season p/w:
£280.00

High season p/w:
£530.00

Livability Self Catering Holidays, PO Box 36, Cowbridge, Vale of Glamorgan CF71 7TN **t** 08456 584478 **f** 01446 775060
e selfcatering@livability.org.uk
livability.org.uk

1D1

Beautiful four-bedroom bungalow with 2 ground floor accessible bedrooms. Weston-Super-Mare 3 miles.

Access: 🅰 ☺ 🚻 General: 🐎 P Ⓢ Unit: ♿🖼🔥♿♨🚻Ⓢ♿❀

Swindon | **Holiday Inn Express Swindon City Centre**

Bridge Street, Swindon, Wiltshire SN1 1BT
t 01793 602000 **e** reservations@exhiswindon.com
exhiswindon.co.uk

Access: abc 🗐 🐕 🏢 ☺ 🚻♿ General: 🐎 ✕ 🍷 ⊞ ♿ Room: 🔥♨🚻Ⓢ☕

Warminster | **Longleat Caravan Club Site** CARAVAN CLUB

AS

Enjoy England ★★★★★

🚐 (165)
£16.40–£29.30

🚍 (165)
£16.40–£29.30

165 touring pitches
Open: 25 March - 7 November

Shop: 3 miles
Pub: 1 mile

Warminster, Wiltshire BA12 7NL
t 01985 844663
caravanclub.co.uk

2B2

Close to Longleat House, this is the only site where you can hear lions roar at night! Cafés, pubs and restaurants within walking distance.

Location: A362 (Frome), at roundabout 1st exit into Longleat Estate. Through toll booths, follow caravan and camping signs for 1 mile.

Access:
🅗 🐾 🧴 😊 ♿

General:
▫️🚐📶🚿💡🚰🚻🚽 WP

Pitch:
🚐🚍

Cornwall

ALBASTON

Todsworthy Farm Holidays
Mr Pellow, Todsworthy Farm Holidays, Albaston, Gunnislake PL18 9AW
t 01822 834744 **e** jon@todsworthyfarmholidays.co.uk
w todsworthyfarmholidays.co.uk

ALVERTON

Penzance Youth Hostel
Castle Horneck, Alverton, Penzance TR18 4LP
t 01736 362666 **e** penzance@yha.org.uk

BODMIN

Chark Country Holidays
Mrs Jenny Littleton, Chark Country Holidays, Redmoor, Bodmin PL30 5AR
t 01208 871118 **e** charkholidays@tiscali.co.uk
w charkcountryholidays.co.uk

Lanhydrock Hotel & Golf Club
Lostwithiel Road, Lanhydrock, Bodmin PL30 5AQ
t 01208 262570 **e** info@lanhydrockhotel.com
w lanhydrockhotel.com

BOSCASTLE

The Old Coach House
Tintagel Road, Boscastle PL35 0AS
t 01840 250398 **e** stay@old-coach.co.uk
w old-coach.co.uk

Reddivallen Farm
Boscastle PL35 0EE
t 01840 250854 **e** liz@redboscastle.com
w redboscastle.com

CALLINGTON

Berrio Mill Holiday Cottages
Mr & Mrs Ivan Callanan, Berrio Mill Holiday Cottages, Berrio Mill, Golberdon, Callington PL17 7NL
t 01579 363252 **e** enquiries@berriomill.co.uk
w berriomill.co.uk

DAVIDSTOW

Pendragon Country House
Davidstow, Camelford PL32 9XR
e enquiries@pendragoncountryhouse.com

FALMOUTH

The Lerryn Hotel
De Pass Road, Falmouth TR11 4BJ
t 01326 312489 **e** lerrynhotel@btconnect.com
w thelerrynhotel.co.uk

FOWEY

South Torfrey Farm
Mr & Mrs Andrews, South Torfrey Farm, Golant, Fowey PL23 1LA
t 01726 833126
e debbie.andrews@southtorfreyfarm.com
w southtorfreyfarm.com

GOLANT, FOWEY

Penquite Farm Holidays
Mrs Ruth Varco, Penquite Farm Holidays, Penquite Farm, Golant, Fowey PL23 1LB
t 01726 833319 **e** ruth@penquitefarm.co.uk
w penquitefarm.co.uk

HAYLE

Rowan Barn
Bosworgy Road, Townshend, Hayle TR27 6ES
t 01736 851223 **e** info@rowanbarn.co.uk
w rowanbarn.co.uk

KERRIER

Gwel an Mor Lodges
Owner, Gwel an Mor Lodges, Portreath TR16 4PE

KILKHAMPTON

Forda Lodges & Cottages
Mr & Mrs Jim Chibbett, Kilkhampton, Bude EX23 9RZ
t 01288 321413 **e** info@forda.co.uk
w forda.co.uk

LAUNCESTON

Ta Mill
Miss Helen Shopland, Ta Mill, St Clether, Launceston PL15 8PS
t 01840 261797 **e** helen@tamill.co.uk
w tamill.co.uk

LOOE

Bucklawren Farm
Mrs Jean Henly, Bucklawren Farm, St. Martin, Looe PL13 1NZ
t 01503 240738 **e** bucklawren@btopenworld.com
w bucklawren.com

LOSTWITHIEL

A little bit of heaven Manelly Fleming
Mrs Daphne Rolling, A Little Bit Of Heaven, Manelly Fleming Farm, St Veep, Lostwithiel PL22 0NS
t 01208 872564 **e** daphne@alittlebitofheaven.co.uk
w alittlebitofheaven.co.uk

MARAZION

Ocean Studios
Mrs Heather Wenn, Mounts Bay House, Turnpike Hill, Marazion TR17 0AY
t 01736 711040 **e** enquiries@mountsbayhouse.co.uk
w mountsbayhouse.co.uk

MAWGAN PORTH

The Park
Mrs Charmian Licsauer, Mawgan Porth, nr. Torquay TR8 4BD
t 01637 860322 **e** charmian@mawganporth.co.uk
w mawganporth.co.uk

NEWQUAY

No. 3 Atlantic Reach
Ms Lynne Campbell, No. 3 Atlantic Reach, 213 Penmere Drive, Newquay TR7 1RY
t 01637 870578 **e** lynne.campbell786@btinternet.com
w atlantic-reach-newquay-no3.co.uk

PADSTOW

Arum House Bed and Breakfast
3 Grenville Road, Padstow PL28 8EX
t 01841 532364 **e** emmathompson@talktalk.net
w padstow-bed-and-breakfast.com

PENZANCE

Hotel Penzance
Britons Hill, Penzance TR18 3AE
t 01736 363117 **e** reception@hotelpenzance.com
w hotelpenzance.com

POLZEATH

Manna Place
Mrs Ann Jones, 14 Trenant Close, Polzeath PL27 6SW
t 01208 863258 **e** anniepolzeath@hotmail.com
w mannaplace.co.uk

REDRUTH

Higher Laity Farm
Mrs Lynne Drew, Higher Laity Farm, Portreath Road,
Redruth TR16 4HY
t 01209 842317 **e** info@higherlaityfarm.co.uk
w higherlaityfarm.co.uk

Trengove Farm Cottages
Mrs Lindsey Richards, Trengove Farm Cottages, Trengove
Farm, Cot Road, Illogan TR16 4PU
t 01209 843008 **e** richards@farming.co.uk
w trengovefarm.co.uk

ROCHE

Owls Reach
Mrs Diana Pride, Owls Reach, Colbiggan Farm, Roche, St
Austell PL26 8LJ
t 01208 831597 **e** info@owlsreach.co.uk
w owlsreach.co.uk

SITHNEY

Tregoose Farmhouse
Mrs Hazel Bergin, Tregoose Farmhouse, Trelo, Southern
Cross, Boundervean Lane, Camborne TR14 0QB
t 01209 714314 **e** hazel.bergin@dsl.pipex.com
w tregooselet.co.uk

ST MAWES

Pollaughan Farm
Mrs Valerie Penny, Pollaughan Farm, Portscatho, Truro
TR2 5EH
t 01872 580150 **e** holidays@pollaughan.co.uk
w pollaughan.co.uk

THE LIZARD

Lizard Point Youth Hostel
Lizard TR12 7NT
t 0870 770 6120

TOWAN CROSS, PORTHTOWAN

Arvor Holidays
Mrs Pat Williams, Pentowan Farm, Towan Cross,
Porthtowan, Truro TR4 8BZ
t 01209 891611 **e** pat@arvorholidays.com
w arvorholidays.com

TREATOR

Woodlands Country House
Treator, Padstow, Cornwall PL28 8RU
t 01841 532426 **e** enquiries@woodlands-padstow.co.uk
w woodlands-padstow.co.uk

TRURO

Trelagossick Farm
Mrs Rachel Carbis, Trelagossick Farm, Ruan High Lanes,
Truro TR2 5JU
t 01872 501338 **e** enquiries@trelagossickfarm.co.uk
w trelagossickfarm.co.uk

Isles of Scilly

ST MARY'S

Atlantic Hotel
Hugh Street, St Mary's TR21 0PL
t 01720 422417 **e** atlantichotel@staustellbrewery.co.uk
w atlantichotelscilly.co.uk

Isles of Scilly Country Guest House
Sage House, High Lanes, St Mary's TR21 0NW
t 01720 422440 **e** scillyguesthouse@hotmail.com
w scillyguesthouse.co.uk

Devon

ASHBURTON

Wooder Manor Holiday Homes
Mrs Angela Bell, Widecombe-in-the-Moor, Newton Abbot,
Devon TQ13 7TR
t 01364 621391 **w** woodermanor.com

BEESANDS

Beeson Farm Holiday Cottages
Mr & Mrs Robin Cross, Beeson Farm, Beeson, Kingsbridge
TQ7 2HW
t 01548 581270 **e** info@beesonhols.co.uk
w beesonhols.co.uk

BRAUNTON

Phoenix Retreat
Mrs Carol Earner, Phoenix Retreat, Phoenix Care at Home
Ltd., Unit B Chivenor Business Park, Barnstaple EX31 4AY
t 01271 816577 **f** 01271 816577
w phoenixholidayretreat.co.uk

BUCKLAND BREWER

West Hele
Mrs Lorna Hicks, West Hele, Buckland Brewer, Bideford
EX39 5LZ
t 01237 451044 **e** lorna.hicks@virgin.net
w westhele.co.uk

BUDLEIGH SALTERTON

Badgers Den
Leo & Mandy Dickinson, Badgers Den, Dalditch Lane,
Knowle, Budleigh Salterton EX9 7AH
t 01395 443282 **e** mandydickinson3@btinternet.com
w holidaycottagedevon.com

HIGH BICKINGTON

Country Ways
Mrs Kate Price, Country Ways, Little Knowle Farm, High
Bickington, Umberleigh EX37 9BJ
t 01769 560503 **e** kate@country-ways.net
w country-ways.net

HOLCOMBE ROGUS

Old Lime Kiln Cottages
Mrs Sue Gallagher, Old Lime Kiln Cottages, Holcombe
Rogus, Wellington TA21 0NA
t 01823 672339
e bookings@oldlimekiln.freeserve.co.uk
w oldlimekilncottages.co.uk

LONG BARN

Creedy Manor
Mrs Sandra Turner, Creedy Manor, Long Barn Farm,
Crediton EX17 4AB
t 01363 772684 **e** sandra@creedymanor.com
w creedymanor.com

MORETONHAMPSTEAD

Budleigh Farm
Mr Arthur Harvey, Budleigh Farm, Moretonhampstead,
Newton Abbot TQ13 8SB
t 01647 440835 **e** harvey@budleighfarm.co.uk
w budleighfarm.co.uk

NORTHLEIGH

Smallcombe Farm
Northleigh, Colyton EX24 6BU
t 01404 831310 **e** maggie_todd@yahoo.com
w smallcombe.co.uk

Smallcombe Farm Self Catering
Mrs Maggie Todd, Smallcombe Farm Self Catering,
Northleigh, Colyton EX24 6BU
t 01404 831310 **e** maggie_todd@yahoo.com
w smallcombe.co.uk

OKEHAMPTON

Beer Farm
Mr & Mrs Annear, Beer Farm, Okehampton EX20 1SG
t 01837 840265 **e** info@beerfarm.co.uk
w beerfarm.co.uk

PLYMOUTH

Haddington House Apartments
Mr & Mrs Luxmoore, 42 Haddington Road, Stoke Damerel,
Plymouth PL2 1RR
t 07966 256984 **e** luxmoore@btinternet.com
w plymouth-self-catering.co.uk

SANDFORD

Ashridge Farm
Ashridge Farm, Sandford, Crediton EX17 4EN
t 01363 774292 **e** info@ashdridgefarm.com
w ashridgefarm.co.uk/

TORQUAY

Crown Lodge
83 Avenue Road, Torquay TQ2 5LH
t 01803 298772 **e** stay@crownlodgehotel.com
w crownlodgehotel.co.uk

South Sands Apartments
Mr & Mrs Paul & Deborah Moorhouse, South Sands
Apartments, Torbay Road, Livermead, Torquay TQ2 6RG
t 01803 293521 **e** info@southsands.co.uk
w southsands.co.uk

UGBOROUGH

Venn Farm
Mrs Stephens, Venn Farm, Ugborough, Ivybridge PL21 0PE
t 01364 73240

YEALMPTON

Kitley House Hotel and Restaurant
Kitley Estate, Yealmpton, Plymouth PL8 2NW
t 01752 881555 **e** sales@kitleyhousehotel.com
w kitleyhousehotel.com

Dorset

ABBOTSBURY

Gorwell Farm Cottages
Mrs Mary Pengelly, Gorwell Farm Cottages, Gorwell,
Abbotsbury, Weymouth DT3 4JX
t 01305 871401 **e** mary@gorwellfarm.co.uk
w gorwellfarm.co.uk

BEAMINSTER

Stable Cottage
Mrs Diana Clarke, Stable Cottage, Meerhay Manor,
Beaminster, Dorset DT8 3SB
t 01308 862305 **e** meerhay@aol.com
w meerhay.co.uk

BRIDPORT

Tamarisk Farm Holiday Cottages
Mrs Josephine Pearse, Tamarisk Farm, West Bexington,
Dorchester, Dorset DT2 9DF
t 01308 897784 **e** holidays@tamariskfarm.com
w tamariskfarm.com/holidays

CHARMOUTH

The Poplars
Mrs Jane Bremner, Wood Farm Caravan and Camping Park,
Axminster Road, Charmouth, Bridport DT6 6BT
t 01297 560697 **e** holidays@woodfarm.co.uk
w woodfarm.co.uk

CORFE CASTLE

Mortons House Hotel
45 East Street, Corfe Castle, Dorset BH20 5EE
t 01929 480988 **e** stay@mortonshouse.co.uk
w mortonshouse.co.uk

DORCHESTER

Aquila Heights Guest House
44 Maiden Castle Road, Dorchester DT1 2ES
t 01305 267145 **e** aquila.heights@tiscali.co.uk
w aquilaheights.co.uk

FIFEHEAD MAGDALEN

Top Stall
Mrs Kathleen Jeanes, Top Stall, Factory Farm, Fifehead
Magdalen, Gillingham SP8 5RS
t 01258 820022 **e** kath@topstallcottage.co.uk
w topstallcottage.co.uk

LONG BREDY

Stables Cottage
Ms Margarette Stuart-Brown, Long Bredy, Dorchester
DT2 9HN
t 01305 789000 **e** admin@dream-cottages.co.uk
w dream-cottages.co.uk

LYTCHETT MINSTER

**South Lytchett Manor Touring Caravan &
Camping Park**
Dorchester Road, Lytchett Minster, Poole BH16 6JB
t 01202 622577 **e** info@southlytchettmanor.co.uk
w southlytchettmanor.co.uk

POOLE

The New Beehive Hotel
Cliff Drive, Canford Cliffs, Poole BH13 7JF
t 01202 701531 **e** info@thenewbeehive.co.uk
w thenewbeehive.co.uk

STOKE ABBOTT

Lewesdon Farm Holidays
Mr & Mrs Micheal & Linda Smith, Lewesdon Farm Holidays,
Lewesdon Farm, Stoke Abbott, Beaminster DT8 3JZ
t 01308 868270
e lewesdonfarmholiday@tinyonline.co.uk
w lewesdonfarmholidays.co.uk

SWANAGE

9 Quayside Court
Mr Graham Hogg, 9 Quayside Court, Lilliput Avenue,
Chipping Sodbury, Bristol BS37 6HX
t 01454 311178 **e** graham.hogg@blueyonder.co.uk
w bythequayholidays.co.uk

TINCLETON

Tincleton Lodge and Clyffe Dairy Cottage
Mrs Jane Coleman, Tincleton Lodge and Clyffe Dairy
Cottage, Eweleaze Farm, Tincleton, Dorchester DT2 8QR
t 01305 848391   **e** enquiries@dorsetholidaycottages.net
w dorsetholidaycottages.net

WEYMOUTH

Jubilee View Apartment
Mrs Jennifer Deagle, Jubilee View Apartment, 41 Melrose
Road, Southampton SO15 7PG
t 023 078 0301   **e** jubileeview@googlemail.com
w jubileeview.com

WINTERBORNE HOUGHTON

Houghton Lodge
Mrs Clarice Fiander-Norman, Houghton Lodge, Winterborne
Houghton, Blandford Forum DT11 0PE
t 01258 882170   **e** enquiries@houghtonlodge.com
w houghtonlodge.com

Gloucestershire

AWRE

The Priory Cottages
Ian Cowan, The Priory Cottages, Awre, Newnham GL14 1EQ
t 07919 407128   **e** rigc@onetel.com
w thepriorycottages.co.uk

CHELTENHAM

Prestbury House
The Burgage, Prestbury, Cheltenham GL52 3DN
t 01242 529533   **e** enquiries@prestburyhouse.co.uk
w prestburyhouse.co.uk

GLOUCESTER

The Lodge
Mr Brian C Morgan, Little Allaston farm, Driffield Road,
Lydney, Gloucester GL1 4EU
t 01594 843745

LITTLE LARKHILL

Stable Cottage
Ms Gaye Mitchell, Stable Cottage, Larkhill Grange, Little
Larkhill, Tetbury GL8 8RU
t 01666 500063   **e** gayephysio@btinternet.com

NEAR TEWKESBURY

Deerhurst Cottages
Mrs Nicole Samuel, Deerhurst Cottages, Abbots Court Farm,
Deerhurst, Tewkesbury GL19 4BX
t 01684 275845   **e** nic_samuel@hotmail.com
w deerhurstcottages.co.uk

NEWENT

Drews Farm Barn
Mr Alan Brace, Brookside, Much Marcle, Ledbury HR8 2LX
t 01531 660362   **e** alan@muchmarcle.f9.co.uk

PARKEND

The Fountain Inn
Parkend, Lydney GL15 4JD
t 01594 562189   **e** thefountaininn@aol.com

Somerset

BISHOPS LYDEARD

Redlands
Trebles Holford, Taunton TA4 3HA
t 01823 433159   **e** redlandshouse@hotmail.com
w escapetothecountry.co.uk

BRIDGWATER

Buzzard Heights B&B
Aethandune, Tower Hill Road, Bridgwater TA7 9AJ
t 01278 722743   **e** teresa@buzzardheights.co.uk
w buzzardheights.co.uk

CANNINGTON

Blackmore Farm
Blackmore Lane, Nr Bridgwater TA5 2NE
t 01278 653442   **e** dyerfarm@aol.com
w dyerfarm.co.uk

CASTLE CARY

Clanville Manor Tallet and Lone Oak Cottage
Mrs Snook, Clanville Manor Tallet and Lone Oak Cottage,
Clanville Manor, Clanville, Nr Castle Cary BA7 7PJ
t 01963 350124   **e** info@clanvillemanor.co.uk
w clanvillemanor.co.uk

CHEDDAR

Cheddar YHA
Hillfield, Cheddar BS27 3HN
t 01934 742494   **e** cheddar@yha.org.uk
w yha.org.uk

CHEWTON MENDIP

The Garden House
Ms Jane Clayton, Owner, The Garden House, Lilycombe
Farm, Chewton Mendip, Somerset BA3 4NZ
t 01761 241080   **e** jclayton@janeclayton.co.uk
w lilycombe.co.uk

CLAVERTON DOWN

University of Bath
The Avenue, Claverton Down, Bath BA2 7AY
t 01225 386622   **e** acc-bathtourism@rt.bath.ac.uk
w haatbath.com

EXFORD

Westermill Farm
Mr Oliver Edwards, Westermill Farm, Exford, Exmoor,
Minehead TA24 7NJ
t 01643 831238   **e** swt@westermill.com
w westermill.com

FITZHEAD

Linnets
Mrs Patricia Grabham, Linnets, Church Road, Nr
Wivliscombe TA4 3JX
t 01823 400658   **e** patricia.grabham@onetel.net
w linnetsfitzhead.co.uk

STATHE

Walkers Farm Cottages
Mr & Mrs William Tilley, Walkers Farm Cottages, Walkers
Farm, Stathe, Burrowbridge, Bridgwater TA7 0JL
t 01823 698229   **e** info@walkersfarmcottages.co.uk
w walkersfarmcottages.co.uk

TAUNTON

Holly Farm Cottages
Mr & Mrs Robert & Liz Hembrow, Holly Farm Cottages, Holly
Farm House, Meare Green, Stoke St Gregory, Nr Taunton
TA3 6HS
t 01823 490828   **e** robhembrow@btinternet.com
w holly-farm.com

TYTHERINGTON

Lighthouse Guest House
The Grange, Tytherington, Frome BA11 5BW
t 01373 453585   **e** contact@lighthouse-uk.com

WESTON-SUPER-MARE

Beverley Guest House
11 Whitecross Road, Weston-super-Mare BS23 1EP
t 01934 622956   **e** beverley11@hushmail.com
w beverleyguesthouse.co.uk

Milton Lodge Guest House
15 Milton Road, Weston-super-Mare BS23 2SH
t 01934 623161   **e** info@milton-lodge.co.uk
w milton-lodge.co.uk

Spreyton Guest House
72 Locking Road, Weston-super-Mare BS23 3EN
t 01934 416887   **e** info@spreytonguesthouse.com
w spreytonguesthouse.com

Wiltshire

BRADFORD-ON-AVON

Church Farm Country Cottages
Mrs Trish Bowles, Church Farm Country Cottages, Church
Farm, Winsley, Bradford-on-Avon BA15 2JH
t 01225 722246   **e** stay@churchfarmcottages.com
w churchfarmcottages.com

SALISBURY

The Old Stables
Mr Giles Gould, The Old Stables, Bridge Farm, Lower Road,
Salisbury SP5 4DY
t 01722 349002   **e** mail@old-stables.co.uk
w old-stables.co.uk

Where to Go

Falmouth | **Pendennis Castle**

Open: For opening hours and prices, please call 0870 333 1181 or visit www.english-heritage.org.uk/properties

Pendennis Headland, Falmouth, Cornwall TR11 4LP
t 0870 333 1181 **e** customers@english-heritage.org.uk
english-heritage.org.uk/pendennis

The perfect day out for families as there is so much to see and do!

Access: abc 🐾 ☺ &wc &x 🐾 🗊 🔢 & &G   General: P& 🗊 &

St Mawes | **St Mawes Castle**

Open: For opening hours and prices, please call 0870 333 1181 or visit www.english-heritage.org.uk/properties

St. Mawes, Nr. Truro, Cornwall TR2 5DE
t 0870 333 1181 **e** customers@english-heritage.org.uk
english-heritage.org.uk/stmawes

Sat overlooking the Sea, the elaborately decorated Castle offers families a great day out.

Access: abc 🐾 ☺ &wc &x 🐾 🗊   General: P& 🗊

Summercourt | **Dairyland Farm World**

Nr. Newquay, Cornwall TR8 5AA
t 01872 510349 / 01872 510246 **e** info@dairylandfarmworld.co.uk
dairylandfarmworld.com

Okehampton | **Okehampton Castle**

Open: For opening hours and prices, please call 0870 333 1181 or visit www.english-heritage.org.uk/properties

Castle Lodge, Okehampton, Devon EX20 1JA
t 0870 333 1181 **e** customers@english-heritage.org.uk
english-heritage.org.uk/okehampton

Let our free audio tour bring this romantic ruin to life. There's plenty to explore!

Access: 🐾 &wc 🐾 🗊   General: P&

Great Torrington | **RHS Garden Rosemoor**

Great Torrington, Devon EX38 8PH

t 01805 624067 **e** rosemooradmin@rhs.org.uk

rhs.org.uk/rosemoor

Access: ✖ ♿ ♿ ✖ ♿ ♿ ♿ General: ♿ ♿ ✿ ♿ ♿

Plymouth | **Plymouth Mayflower Visitor Centre**

3-5 The Barbican, Plymouth, Devon PL1 2LR

t 01752 306330 **e** barbicantic@plymouth.gov.uk

visitplymouth.info/attractions

Portland | **Portland Castle**

Open: For opening hours and prices, please call 0870 333 1181 or visit www.english-heritage.org.uk/properties

Liberty Road, Castletown, Portland, Dorset DT5 1AZ

t 0870 333 1181 **e** customers@english-heritage.org.uk

english-heritage.org.uk/portland

Discover one of Henry VIII's finest coastal forts and enjoy a great family day out.

Access: ∴ ☺ ♿ ♿ ✖ ♿ ♿ ♿ ♿ General: ♿ ♿ ♿

Bristol | **Bristol Hippodrome**

Saint Augustines Parade, Bristol BS1 4UZ

t 0117 302 3310 **e** steve.jones@livenation.co.uk

Bristolhippodrome.org.uk

Access: abc ✖ ☺ ♿ ✖ ♿ ✖ ♿ General: ♿ ♿

Gloucester | **Gloucester Cathedral**

12 College Green, Gloucester, Gloucestershire GL1 2LX

t 01452 528095

gloucestercathedral.org.uk

Winchcombe | **Hailes Abbey**

Open: For opening hours and prices, please call 0870 333 1181 or visit www.english-heritage.org.uk/properties

Nr. Winchcombe, Cheltenham, Gloucestershire GL54 5PB

t 0870 333 1181 **e** customers@english-heritage.org.uk

english-heritage.org.uk/hailesabbey

Enjoy a fascinating day out, take the audio tour and discover the history.

Access: abc ✖ ☺ ♿ ♿ ✖ ♿ ♿ General: ♿ ♿ ♿

Bath | **St Michaels Without**

Broad Street, Bath BA1 5LJ

t 01225 447103 **e** office@stmichaelsbath.org.uk

stmichaelsbath.org.uk

Nr Amesbury | **Stonehenge**

Open: For opening hours and prices, please call 0870 333 1181 or visit www.english-heritage.org.uk/properties

Nr. Amesbury, Wiltshire SP4 7DE

t 0870 333 1181 **e** customers@english-heritage.org.uk

english-heritage.org.uk/stonehenge

Britain's most intriguing prehistoric monument. Uncover the mysteries guided by a complimentary audio tour.

Access: .: abc ✖ ☺ ⓦⓒ ⓧ ⚘ ▣ ▦ ⓖ General: P ▣ ⟓

Salisbury | **Old Sarum**

Open: For opening hours and prices, please call 0870 333 1181 or visit www.english-heritage.org.uk/properties

Castle Road, Salisbury, Wiltshire SP1 3SD

t 0870 333 1181 **e** customers@english-heritage.org.uk

english-heritage.org.uk/oldsarum

With 5,000 years of history, the iron age hill fort is an impressive site.

Access: abc ✖ ☺ ⓦⓒ ⓧ ⚘ ▣ ⓖ General: P ▣ ⟓

Warminster | **Longleat**

Longleat, Warminster, Wiltshire BA12 7NW

t 01985 844400 **e** enquiries@longleat.co.uk

longleat.co.uk

Access: ✖ ⓦⓒ ⓧ ⚘ ⓖ ⓖ General: P ▣ ✿ ⟓

For more information on
accommodation **attractions**
activities **events** and holidays
contact the **Tourist Information Centres**
see regional listings for the nearest one.

Where to Eat

Brixham | **Bistro 46**

46 Middle Street, Brixham, Devon TQ5 8EJ
t 01803 858936 **e** info@bistro46.com
bistro46.com

General: 🖘 @FAX 🧍🦽 🅿️

Devon | **McDonald's**

Brixham Road, Paignton, Devon TQ4 7PE
t 01803 558672
mcdonalds.co.uk

General: 🖘 🚲 🧍🦽 wc ♿ 🦽 🅿️⋆⋆⋆

Paignton | **Cilantro**

75 Torquay Road, Paignton, Devon TQ3 2SE
t 01803 551392 **e** cilantroonline@gmail.com
cilantroonline.co.uk

General: 🖘 @FAX 🚲 🧍🦽 🦽 🅿️

Plymouth | **Bella Italia**

Unit 4 Derrys Cross, Plymouth, Devon PL1 2SW
t 01752 662143
bellaitalia.co.uk

General: 🖘 🚲 🧍🦽 wc ♿ 🦽 .: abc 🅿️

Plymouth | **Morgan's Brasserie and Bar**

Princess Street, Plymouth, Devon PL1 2EU
t 01752 255579
morgansbrasserie.co.uk

General: 🖘 🧍🦽 wc 🦽 🅿️

Torquay | **Pier Point Restaurant and Bar**

Torbay Road, Torquay, Devon TQ2 5HA
t 01803 299935 **e** info@pier-point.co.uk
pier-point.co.uk

General: 🖘 @FAX 🚲 🧍🦽 ♿ 🅿️

Torquay | **Treasury Bar and Restaurant**

1 Palk Street, Harbourside, Torquay, Devon TQ2 5EL
t 01803 298002 **e** info@thetreasurybartorquay.co.uk
thetreasurybartorquay.co.uk

General: 🖘 @FAX 🚲 🧍🦽 ♿ abc 🅿️

113

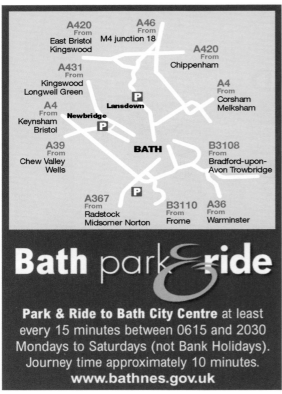

SOUTH SOMERSET
A GUIDE FOR VISITORS WITH DISABILITIES

Picturesque villages, country walks, historic houses and gardens—South Somerset has so much to offer for all abilities.

Please contact Yeovil Tourist Information on **01935 845 946** for our updated guide.

www.visitsouthsomerset.com

Beacon Authority

Adding to Life
pluss

SHOP MOBILITY in Taunton

Taunton's Shopmobility Centre

Shopmobility is a **free** loan service of manual and powered wheelchairs and electric scooters to **anyone** with temporary or permanent limited disability.

Shopmobility is at **Paul Street Orchard Shoppers Car Park**

To book your vehicle Tel: Taunton (01823) 327900

Makes Shopping Easier!

NATIONAL FEDERATION OF
Shopmobility
2011

The directory of Shopmobility Schemes in the UK, Channel Islands & ROI

Get trained - Get out - Get independent
The Shopmobility experience is not just about shopping!

www.shopmobilityuk.org

St Michael's WITHOUT

Welcome to St. Michael's Without

Come and visit us in our beautiful church. All are welcome; find a peaceful spot away from the bustle of the city, enjoy our café, explore our building or find out about forthcoming concerts and events.

St. Michael's Without, Broad Street, Bath BA1 5LJ
(Next to the main post office and Podium shopping centre)

Open 10.00am - 4.00pm Monday to Saturday
Sunday services at 9.00am and 10.30am

www.stmichaelsbath.org.uk   Tel: 01225 447103

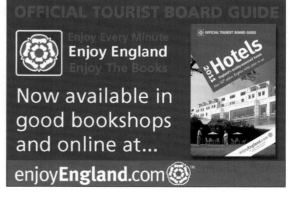

Great days out in the South East

The South East is your quintessential slice of England. Meander around an English country garden, explore outstanding castles, enjoy colourful festivals and savour English wine. From 400 miles of glorious coastline, to the dreaming spires of Oxford, there's so much to discover.

History in the making

Relive the **1066 Battle of Hastings** and take the interactive audio tour at the **Abbey and Battlefield**. Board the world-famous **HMS Victory at Portsmouth Historic Dockyard**. Explore one of the many breathtaking castles, including **Windsor**, **Arundel** and **Leeds (Kent)**. Admire elegant cathedrals and hear gentle sounds of evensong at **Oxford**, **Canterbury** or **Chichester**. Behold 'the finest view in England' according to Winston Churchill's mother, at **World Heritage Site Blenheim Palace, Oxfordshire**.

Full-on fun

Ride the Jungle Coaster at **Legoland, Windsor**, meet colourful characters at **Dickens World, Kent**, delight in the fantabulous award-winning **Roald Dahl Museum and Story Centre, Buckinghamshire** or discover over 250 exotic and endangered species at **Marwell Wildlife, Hampshire**.

Shore pleasures

Unwind on our own unspoilt island; the **Isle of Wight**, home to **Queen Victoria's Osborne House**. Visit the charming beaches of **Brighton**, **Eastbourne** and **Margate**, all popular Victorian playgrounds. Save your small change for the slot machines on the pier or tasty fish and chips. Wander the sand dunes at **West Wittering**, watch kite surfers at **Pevensey Bay**, see the spectacular **White Cliffs of Dover**, or sample an unrivalled number of water-sports at **Calshot Activities Centre, Hampshire**.

Denbies vineyard, Surrey

HMS Victory at the Portsmouth Historic Dockyard

South East

**Berkshire, Buckinghamshire, Hampshire,
Isle of Wight, Kent, Oxfordshire, Surrey, Sussex**

Tourist Information Centres	121	Where to Go	137
Where to Stay	122	Where to Eat	140

At one with nature

Savour a picnic in **Kent**, the 'Garden of England', home to the iconic **Sissinghurst Castle Garden**. Explore the **RHS's flagship garden at Wisley, Surrey**, or international gardens at **Paradise Park, East Sussex**. Devour a tasty pub lunch then traverse the tracks of the **South Downs Way**, or **Ridgeway and Thames Path** then explore the vibrant **River Thames**. If its escapism you crave, retreat to the **New Forest National Park** for ancient woodland and picturesque villages, wild deer, ponies and cattle.

Festival fever

Be inspired by a true celebration of the arts, at the hip **Brighton festival** every May. Dress up for **Glyndebourne's opera** for the epitome of elegance. Revel with jolly folks in Victorian costumes during the **Broadstairs Dickens Festival**. Enjoy rock, pop and hip hop mixed with a liberal dose of mud at August's **Reading Festival**. Don't forget the **Henley Royal Regatta**, where rowers demonstrate their sporting prowess, or fill your lungs with invigorating sea air at the internationally acclaimed **Cowes Week**.

The Needles

Roald Dahl Museum

Welcoming all to South East England

South East England offers an increasing range of accessible accommodation to meet the needs of all visitors. Sample the culinary delights of the '**Nurse's Cottage Restaurant with Rooms**' in the **New Forest**, stay on a working farm at **Heath Farm Self Catering Cottages**, **Sussex**, get away from it all at **Borthwood Cottages**, **West Bay Club** or **Sunny Bay Apartments** on the **Isle of Wight** or indulge in luxury leisure facilities at the **Holiday Inn Windsor/Maidenhead**. Escape to the seaside at **Seaspray Victorian Guest House**, **Hastings**, explore **Oxford** from **Abbey Guest House** or stay in the **Garden of England** at **Little Silver Country Hotel**, **Kent**.

Many attractions across the region offer excellent accessibility, including **Waddesdon Manor, Buckinghamshire**, **Blenheim Palace**, **Oxfordshire**, **the Abbey and Battlefield at Hastings, Sussex** and **Pallant House Gallery, Chichester**, winner of numerous accessibility awards.

Enjoy accessible outdoor attractions including **Marwell Wildlife**, **Hampshire** and **Legoland, Windsor**. Savour hot doughnuts at **Brighton Pier,** marvel at the 7th century **Winchester Cathedral**, or shop 'til you drop at **West Quay, Southampton**. Wheelchair users can access the flying areas, bird hides and picnic areas

at the **Hawk Conservancy Trust, Andover**, which also boasts interactive sessions and large print.

For something completely different, visit **Dickens World, Kent, Denbies Wine Estate, Surrey, Paradise Park, East Sussex** or the **Roald Dahl Museum and Story Centre, Buckinghamshire**.

Historic properties, gardens, eateries, shops, family attractions and entire towns and cities are going the extra mile to welcome all visitors. Investment in staff disability awareness training, facilities, adaptations and building work is increasing in an effort to become the most accessible region in the UK.

Brighton, **Winchester**, **Windsor** and major towns in Buckinghamshire have undertaken full access audits. Buckinghamshire boasts the unique position of being the birthplace of the **Paralympics at Stoke Mandeville in 1948** and hosts the **Olympic rowing at Dorney Lake in 2012**.

An accessibility audit is also being carried out in **Kent**, focusing on **Medway**, **Dover**, **Canterbury** and **Tunbridge Wells**.

Find out more
www.visitsoutheastengland.com

Tourist Information Centres

Tourist Information Centres are a mine of information about local and regional accommodation, attractions and events. Visit them when you arrive at your destination or contact them before you go:

Aylesbury	The Kings Head	01296 330559	tic@aylesburyvaledc.gov.uk
Banbury	Spiceball Park Road	01295 259855	banbury.tic@cherwell-dc.gov.uk
Bicester	Bicester Village	01869 369055	bicester.vc@cherwell-dc.gov.uk
Brighton	Royal Pavilion Shop	0906 711 2255	brighton-tourism@brighton-hove.gov.uk
Burford	The Brewery	01993 823558	burford.vic@westoxon.gov.uk
Canterbury	12/13 Sun Street	01227 378100	canterburyinformation@canterbury.gov.uk
Chichester	29a South Street	01243 775888	chitic@chichester.gov.uk
Cowes	9 The Arcade	01983 813818	info@islandbreaks.co.uk
Croydon	Croydon Clocktower	020 8253 1009	tic@croydon.gov.uk
Dover	The Old Town Gaol	01304 205108	tic@doveruk.com
Gravesend	Towncentric	01474 337600	info@towncentric.co.uk
Hastings	Queens Square	01424 781111	hic@hastings.gov.uk
Lewes	187 High Street	01273 483448	lewes.tic@lewes.gov.uk
Maidstone	Town Hall, Middle Row	01622 602169	tourism@maidstone.gov.uk
Margate	12-13 The Parade	0870 2646111	margate.tic@visitor-centre.net
Marlow	31 High Street	01628 483597	tourism_enquiries@wycombe.gov.uk
Newbury	The Wharf	01635 30267	tourism@westberks.gov.uk
Newport	The Guildhall	01983 813818	info@islandbreaks.co.uk
Oxford	15/16 Broad Street	01865 726871	tic@oxford.gov.uk
Portsmouth	Clarence Esplanade	023 9282 6722	vis@portsmouthcc.gov.uk
Portsmouth	The Hard	023 9282 6722	vis@portsmouthcc.gov.uk
Ramsgate	17 Albert Court	0870 2646111	ramsgate.tic@visitor-centre.net
Rochester	95 High Street	01634 843666	visitor.centre@medway.gov.uk
Romsey	Heritage & Visitor Centre	01794 512987	romseytic@testvalley.gov.uk
Royal Tunbridge Wells	The Old Fish Market	01892 515675	touristinformationcentre@tunbridgewells.gov.uk
Ryde	81-83 Union Street	01983 813818	info@islandbreaks.co.uk
Rye	The Heritage Centre	01797 226696	ryetic@rother.gov.uk
Sandown	8 High Street	01983 813818	info@islandbreaks.co.uk
Shanklin	67 High Street	01983 813818	info@islandbreaks.co.uk
Southampton	9 Civic Centre Road	023 8083 3333	tourist.information@southampton.gov.uk
Winchester	Guildhall	01962 840500	tourism@winchester.gov.uk
Windsor	Royal Windsor Shopping Centre	01753 743900	windsor.tic@rbwm.gov.uk
Witney	26A Market Square	01993 775802	witney.vic@westoxon.gov.uk
Woodstock	Oxfordshire Museum	01993 813276	woodstock.vic@westoxon.gov.uk
Worthing	Marine Parade	01903 221066	tic@worthing.gov.uk
Yarmouth	The Quay	01983 813818	info@islandbreaks.co.uk

Where to Stay

Reading | **Holiday Inn Reading - South M4, Jct.11**

Basingstoke Road, Reading, Berkshire RG2 0SL
t 0871 702 9067 **e** reservations-reading@ihg.com
holidayinn.com/reading-south

Access: abc 🔲 ✝ 🏢 ☺ 🚾 ♿ General: 🛏 🍴 ✕ 🍷 P♿ ❄ 🔼 ♿ Room: 🛏 🔲 🅂 ♨

Reading | **Holiday Inn Reading M4, Jct.10**

Wharfedale Road, Winnersh Triangle, Reading RG41 5TS
t 0118 944 0444 **e** reservations@hireadinghotel.com
meridianleisure.com/reading

Access: abc 🔲 ✝ 🏢 ☺ 🚾 ♿ General: 🛏 🍴 ✕ 🍷 P♿ ❄ 🔼 ♿ Room: 🛏 🔲 🅂 ♨

Aylesbury | **Holiday Inn Aylesbury**

AA ★★★

New Road, Weston Turville, Aylesbury, Bucks HP22 5QT
t 01296 734000 **e** aylesbury@ihg.com
holiday-inn.co.uk

Access: abc 🔲 ✝ 🏢 ☺ 🚾 ♿ General: 🛏 🍴 ✕ 🍷 P♿ ❄ ♿ Room: 🛏 🚾 🔲 🅂 ♨

Aylesbury | **Olympic Lodge**

Enjoy England ★★★

Open: 2C1

Rooms per night:
s:	£55.95-£68.95
d:	£55.95-£68.95
Meals:	£8.53-£10.40
Shop: 1 mile	
Pub: 1 mile	

Guttmann Road, Stoke Mandeville, Aylesbury, Buckinghamshire HP21 9PP
t 01296 461120 **e** bdmstokemandeville@leisureconnection.co.uk
olympic-lodge.co.uk

2C1

The Olympic Lodge Hotel offers some of the best value and accessible hotel accommodation in Buckinghamshire. Conference rooms are situated directly next to the Olympic Lodge Hotel. There are 50 fully accessible twin bedded rooms.

Location: http://www.stokemande villestadium.co.uk/location/

Access:
🅰 🏢 ☺ 🚾 ♿
General:
🛏 🍴 ✕ 🍷 P♿ ❄ 🔼 ♿
Room:
🛏 🔲 📶 ♨

Milton Keynes | **Holiday Inn Milton Keynes**

AA ★★★★ 500 Saxon Gate West, Milton Keynes MK9 2HQ
t 01908 698508 **e** reservations-miltonkeynes@ihg.com
holiday-inn.co.uk

Access: abc 🗓 ⚡ 🔋 ☺ ♿ ♿ General: 🛋 ⛄ ✕ 🍷 P♿ ⛲ ♿ Room: 📺 ☕

Fareham | **Holiday Inn Fareham**

Cartwright Drive, Titchfield, Fareham PO15 5RJ
t 0871 942 9028 **e** reservations-fareham@ihg.com
holiday-inn.co.uk

Access: .: abc 🗓 ☺ ♿ General: 🛋 ⛄ 🍷 P♿ ✿ ♿ Room: 📺 ☕

Farnborough | **Holiday Inn Farnborough**

Lynchford Road, Farnborough, Hampshire GU14 6AZ
t 0871 942 9029 **e** reservations-farnborough@ihg.com
holidayinn.co.uk/farnborough

Access: 🗓 ⚡ ☺ ♿ ♿ General: 🛋 ⛄ ✕ 🍷 P♿ ✿ ♿ Room: 📺 ☕

Lymington | **Bench Cottage and Little Bench**   AS

Units: 2   Sleeps: 2-4
Open: All year

Low season p/w:
£250.00
High season p/w:
£785.00
Shop: 0.5 miles
Pub: 0.5 miles

Mrs Mary Lewis, Lodge Road, Pennington, Lymington, Hampshire
SO41 8HH   **t** 01590 673141   **e** enquiries@ourbench.co.uk
ourbench.co.uk   **2C3**

Our fully accessible purpose built self catering cottages sleep up to four guests, and offer a range of specialist equipment for your use. We are an ideal base to enjoy the delights of Hampshire and the New Forest National Park.

Location: From the A337 to Lymington turn off at Pennington Village and through village centre. Turn off opposite Pennington Common.

Access:
🅗 abc
General:
🛋 📠 P 📺
Unit:
♿ ♿ 🧹 ♿ 🚾 📺 ♿ ✿

Lymington | The Nurse's Cottage Restaurant with Rooms

   AS

AA ★★★★
Enjoy England ★★★★

Open: Closed 3 weeks March and November/ December

p/p half board:
d: £97.50-£107.50

Station Road, Sway, New Forest National Park SO41 6BA
t 01590 683402 **e** stay@nursescottage.co.uk
nursescottage.co.uk

2C3

Award-winning ground-floor single, twin and double accommodation in District Nurses' cosy former home: all rates include Afternoon Tea on arrival, Three-Course Dinner, Full English Breakfast and daily newspaper. Bargain Breaks for 3+ nights. Restaurant fully accessible and open to non-residents.

Location: Situated in centre of Sway village near shops. Easy access from mainline London Waterloo to Weymouth railway.

Access:
abc 😊 &wc

General:
🍴✗ 🍷 🌼 ᵹ

Room:
♿🏨📶📺wc 🍵📱 S 🍵

Southampton | Holiday Inn Express Southampton M27 Jct 7

Botley Road, West End, Southampton SO30 3XA
t 02380 606060 **e** reservations@expressbyholidayinn.uk.net
meridianleisure.com/southampton

Access: abc 😊 &wc ᵹ General: 🛏🍴✗🍷P ᵹ 📧 ᵹ Room: ♿🏨📶 S 🍵

Southampton | Holiday Inn Southampton

AA ★★★
Open: All year

Herbert Walker Avenue, Southampton SO15 1HJ
t 08719429073
holiday-inn.co.uk

Access: ∴ 🗐 🐾 🏨 &wc ᵹ General: 🛏🍴🍷P ᵹ 📧 ᵹ Room: S 🍵

Southampton | Vitalise Netley Waterside House

AS

Abbey Hill, Netley Abbey, Southampton SO31 5FA
t 0845 345 1970 **e** bookings@vitalise.org.uk
vitalise.org.uk

Access: 🅰 🏨 😊 &wc ᵹ General: 🍴✗🍷P ᵹ 🌼📧ᵹ Room: ♿🏨📶 S 🍵

Southampton, Eastleigh | Holiday Inn Southampton - Eastleigh M3, Jct.13

AS

Leigh Road, Eastleigh SO50 9PG
t 0871 942 9075
holiday-inn.co.uk

Access: ∴ abc 🗐 🐾 😊 &wc ᵹ General: 🛏🍴✗🍷P ᵹ 🌼📧ᵹ Room: ♿ 🍵

Winchester | **Morn Hill Caravan Club Site** AS

Enjoy England ★★★

(120) £11.40–£23.90

(120) £11.40–£23.90

(1)

120 touring pitches
Open: 25 March to 7 November

Access:

General:

Pitch:

Alresford Road, Winchester SO21 1HL
t 01962 869877
caravanclub.co.uk

2C3

A large site divided into two areas, well separated by good trees and shrubs. Convenient for the ferries or for exploring the area. Winchester is an old cathedral city of considerable charm with many of its ancient buildings.

Location: M3 to J9 (from North), J10 (from South) onto A31; roundabout continue towards Easton; right at pub. Site in 100yds.

St Helen's | **The Old Club House**

National Trust, The Old Club House, St Helen's, Isle of Wight PO33 1XY
t 0844 8002070 **e** cottages@nationaltrust.org.uk
nationaltrustcottages.co.uk

Access: General: Unit:

OPEN BRITAIN
DECIDED WHERE TO GO? SEE ATTRACTIONS FOR WHAT TO DO
Ideas and information at the end of each regional section

Yarmouth | **West Bay Country Club & Spa**

Enjoy England ★★★★

Units: 2   Sleeps: 1-4
Open: All year

Low season p/w:
£280.00
High season p/w:
£1110.00

Sarah Craft, West Bay Country Club & Spa, Halletts Shute, Yarmouth, Isle of Wight PO41 0RJ   **t** 01983 760355   **e** info@westbayclub.co.uk
westbayclub.co.uk

2C3

West Bay is a four star, self-catering village set in 28 acres of gated, landscaped grounds. Its two accessible cottages have adjacent parking, two twin bedrooms, spacious wet rooms and kitchens that are suitable for a wheelchair user.

Location: Less than a mile from the Yarmouth ferry terminal in West Wight - an area of outstanding natural beauty.

Access:
🅰 abc 🦻 ✗ 🎒 ☺ ♿

General:
🐴 📷 P Ⓢ

Unit:
♨ 🎛 🪜 ♿ 🛏 📺 Ⓢ ♿ ❀

Faversham | **Sandhurst Farm Forge**

Seed Road, Newnham, Sittingbourne, Kent ME9 0NE
t 01795 886854   **e** rooms.forge@btinternet.com
sandhurstfarmforge.co.uk

Room: ♨ ☕

Folkestone | Black Horse Farm Caravan Club Site  AS

Enjoy England ★★★★★

🚐 (140)
£13.10–£25.40

🚎 (140)
£13.10–£25.40

⛺ (20)

140 touring pitches
Open: All year

Shop: <0.5 miles
Pub: <0.5 miles

Access:
🐾🛗☺♿

General:
📷🚿😊🛒☕🚐

Pitch:
🚐🚎⛺

385 Canterbury Road, Densole, Folkestone, Kent CT18 7BG
t 01303 892665
caravanclub.co.uk

3B4

Set in the heart of farming country in the Kentish village of Densole on the Downs. This is a quiet, relaxed country site, ideally for families wishing to visit the many interesting local attractions including the historic city of Canterbury.

Location: M20 jct 13 onto A260 to Canterbury, 2 miles from junction with A20, site on left 200yds past Black Horse.

Hollingbourne | Bearsted Caravan Club Site AS

Enjoy England ★★★★★

Ashford Road, Hollingbourne, Maidstone ME17 1XH
t 01622 730018
caravanclub.co.uk

Access: 🐾🛗☺♿ General: 📷🚿😊🛒☕🚐 Pitch: 🚐🚎

Margate | Smiths Court Hotel

disabled

Enjoy England ★★★

Open: All year except Xmas

Rooms per night:
s: £50.00–£60.00
d: £75.00–£85.00
p/p half board:
d: £64.75–£76.75
Meals: £14.75–£16.75

21-27 Eastern Esplanade, Cliftonville, Margate, Kent CT9 2HL
t 01843 222310 **e** info@smithscourt.co.uk
smithscourt.co.uk

3C3

The Smiths Court is set on the clifftops with 43 individually decorated rooms and suites.

Access: abc 🐾🛗♿ General: 🛏️🍴✕🍷♿✳️ Room: 🛁☕ 📺📶

Sevenoaks | **Hay Barn & Straw Barn**

AS

Enjoy England ★★★★

Units: 2 Sleeps: 1-6
Open: All year

Low season p/w:
£340.00
High season p/w:
£525.00
Shop: 1.2 miles
Pub: 0.8 miles

Access:
abc 🐕🚶

General:
🐎 📶 P S

Unit:
🛁🧹♿📺 S ♿ ❀

Mr J Piers Quirk, Watstock Farm, Wellers Town Road, Chiddingstone,
Edenbridge TN8 7BH **t** 07770 762076 **e** info@watstockbarns.co.uk
watstockbarns.co.uk

2D2

Converted 2007 on family farm, all
ground-floor, self-catering. Two-
person Hay Barn has wetroom/
shower, four-person Straw Barn has
Aquability bath with sidedoor &
handshower. Share common hall so
can rent together.

Location: Full map on our website.
Sevenoaks & Royal Tunbridge Wells
8 & 9 miles. M25-J5 9 miles.

St Michaels | **Little Silver Country Hotel**

Enjoy England ★★★

Open: All year

Rooms per night:
s: £60.00-£75.00
d: £95.00-£135.00
p/p half board:
d: £62.00-£80.00
Meals: £14.50-£27.00

Ashford Road, Tenterden TN30 6SP
t 01233 850321 **e** enquiries@little-silver.co.uk
little-silver.co.uk

3B3

Luxury accommodation with whirlpool baths.
Accessible restaurant serving local foods. Licensed
for wedding ceremonies.

Access: abc 🐕🚶♿♿ **General:** 🐎🍽✕♟ P♿ ❀♿ **Room:** 🛁🧹📺♿

Burford | **Burford Caravan Club Site** 🦢 THE CARAVAN CLUB

Enjoy England ★★★★

🚐 (119)

£14.90–£27.20

🚎 (119)

£14.90–£27.20

119 touring pitches
Open: 25 March - 7
November

Shop: 3 miles
Pub: 1.8 miles

Bradwell Grove, Burford, Oxfordshire OX18 4JJ
t 01993 823080
caravanclub.co.uk

2B1

Attractive, spacious site opposite
Cotswold Wildlife Park. Burford has
superb Tudor houses, a museum
and historic inns. A great base from
which to explore the Cotswolds.

Location: From roundabout at A40/
A361 junction in Burford, take A361
signposted Lechlade. Site on right
after 2.5 miles.

Access:
🅰 ✸ 🐴 🛢 ☺ ♿

General:
🗄 📠 🚬 💀 🪣 🚿 🍴

Pitch:
🚐 🚎

Cogges | **Swallows Nest**

♿ | AS

Enjoy England ★★★★

Units: 1 Sleeps: 1-4
Open: All year

Low season p/w:
£275.00

High season p/w:
£450.00

Mrs Jan Strainge, Swallows Nest, Cogges, Witney OX29 6UL
t 01993 704919 **e** jan@strainge.fsnet.co.uk
swallowsnest.co.uk

2C1

Cosy country barn conversion, one mile from Witney.
Oxford, Blenheim and Cotswolds within easy reach.

Access: abc 🛢 ☺ General: ⊁ 🗄 P Unit: 🍳 ♨ 📺 💺 S ♿ ❀

©Britain on View/Tony Pleavin

Oxford | Abbey Guest House

AS

Enjoy England ★★★★

Open: All year

Rooms per night:
s: £45.00–£50.00
d: £70.00–£78.00
Meals: £6.50–£9.50
Shop: <0.5 miles
Pub: <0.5 miles

136 Oxford Road, Abingdon, Oxford OX14 2AG
t +44 0 1235 537020 or +44 0 7976 627252 **e** info@abbeyguest.com
abbeyguest.com   **2C1**

Friendly, homely, non-smoking 5 bedroom guesthouse close to Oxford and Abingdon. 'Easy access' room, with en suite wet-room on ground floor. More information on website, or telephone and we will be pleased to discuss how we can accommodate your requirements.

Location: By car: via A34 (North Abingdon exit) or the A415. By bus: from Oxford/Didcot, stop outside the door.

Access:
abc 🖉 ⚡ 🏰 ☺ ⚡
General:
🐴 🍴 ✕ P 🌸 ⚡
Room:
🛏 🔥 🕯 🔲 ⓢ ☕

Oxford | Holiday Inn Oxford

AS

Peartree Roundabout, Woodstock Road, Oxford OX2 8JD
t 0871 942 9086 **e** Oxford@ihg.com
holidayinn.co.uk

Access: abc 🖉 ⚡ 🏰 ☺ ⚡ ⚡ General: 🐴 🍴 ✕ ⚡ P 🌸 ⊞ ⚡ Room: 🛏 🕯 ☕

Farnham | High Wray

AS

Enjoy England ★★★

Units: 2 Sleeps: 2-4
Open: All year

Low season p/w:
£220.00
High season p/w:
£350.00

Mrs Alexine Crawford, High Wray, 73 Lodge Hill Road, Lower Bourne, Farnham GU10 3RB **t** 01252 715589 **e** alexine@highwray73.co.uk
highwray73.co.uk   **2C2**

Within 2-acre garden of own home is a disabled-friendly garden flat, and Studio.

General: 🐴 📻 P Unit: 🛏 🖊 🔥 🕯 📺 ⚡ 🌸

Gatwick | Holiday Inn Gatwick Airport

Open: All year

Provey Cross Road, Horley, Surrey RH6 0BA
t 0871 9429030 **e** reservations-gatwick@ihg.com
holiday-inn.co.uk

Access: ∴ abc 🖉 ⚡ ⚡ General: 🐴 🍴 ✕ ⚡ P 🌸 ⊞ ⚡ Room: 🛏 ☕

Guildford | **Holiday Inn Guildford**

Open: All year

Egerton Road, Guildford, Surrey GU2 7XZ
t 0871 9429036 **e** daniel.hollett@ihg.com
holiday-inn.co.uk

Access: ⬛😊♿ General: ⛺🍽️P♣ Room: ♨💧

Redhill | **Alderstead Heath Caravan Club Site** THE CARAVAN CLUB

AS

Enjoy England ★★★★

🚐 (150)
£13.10–£25.40

🚏 (150)
£13.10–£25.40

🏕️ (10)

150 touring pitches
Open: All year

Shop: 2.5 miles
Pub: 2.5 miles

Dean Lane, Merstham, Redhill, Surrey RH1 3AH
t 01737 644629
caravanclub.co.uk

2D2

A quiet site with views over the North Downs. Denbies Wine Estate is nearby. For day trips try Chessington and Thorpe Park and the lively city of Brighton. Non-members welcome.

Location: M25 jct 8, A217 Reigate, left to Merstham, left - A23, right - Shepherds Hill (B2031), left - Dean Lane.

Access:
🅰️ 🐾 🧴 😊
General:
🗄️📶🚿🛢️📞🕐☎️ WP
Pitch:
🚐🚏🏕️

Woking | **Holiday Inn Woking**

Victoria Way, Woking, Surrey GU21 8EW
t 01483 221000 **e** info@hiwoking.co.uk
hiwoking.co.uk

Access: 🚶😊♿ General: ⛺🍽️✖🍽️P⬆️ Room: ♨📺S💧

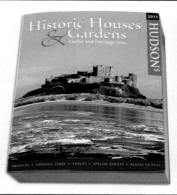

Battle | **Normanhurst Court Caravan Club Site**

Enjoy England ★★★★★

🚐 (149)
£13.10–£25.40

🚎 (149)
£13.10–£25.40

149 touring pitches
Open: 18 March - 3 October

Shop: 1.5 miles
Pub: 1.5 miles

Access:
🅰️ Ⓗ 🐾 🛁 😊 ♿

General:
🔳 ♿ 🏠 🚐 🔌 🔋 🛒 📶

Pitch:
🚐 🚎

Stevens Crouch, Battle, East Sussex TN33 9LR
t 01424 773808
caravanclub.co.uk

3B4

Situated in former gardens with magnificent specimen trees, and colourful rhododendrons in spring. Located close to the 1066 Trail, great for walkers, nature lovers and families. The seaside towns of Eastbourne and Hastings are just a short drive away.

Location: From Battle, turn left onto A271. Site is 3 miles on left.

Brighton & Hove | **Holiday Inn Brighton Seafront**

137 Kings Road, Brighton, East Sussex BN1 2JF
t 01273 828250 **e** reservations@hibrighton.com
hibrighton.com

Access: abc 📷 🐾 😊 ♿ ♿ General: 🪑 🍳 ✕ 🍷 🅿️ ❀ ⬆️ ♿ Room: 🛏️ 📺 ♨️

Brighton & Hove | **Sheepcote Valley Caravan Club Site** CARAVAN CLUB

Enjoy England ★★★★★

🚐 (169)
     £15.70–£29.30

🚍 (169)
     £15.70–£29.30

⛺ (80)

169 touring pitches
Open: All year

Shop: 0.5 miles
Pub: 0.5 miles

Access:
🅷 ⚐ 🐾 🏧 ☺ ♿
General:
🗑 📶 📻 🚮 🔌 ☎ 🚾
Pitch:
🚐 🚍 ⛺

East Brighton Park, Brighton, East Sussex BN2 5TS
t 01273 626546
caravanclub.co.uk

2D3

Located on the South Downs, just two miles from Brighton. Visit the Marina, with its shops, pubs and restaurants, and tour the exotic Royal Pavilion. Brighton is a lively town with all the attractions of a seaside holiday resort.

Location: M23/A23, join A27 (Lewes). B2123 (Falmer/ Rottingdean). Right B2123 (Woodingdean). Right at traffic lights (Warren Road). Left (Wilson Avenue).

Eastbourne | **Glyndley Manor Cottage**

Mrs J Woodley, Glyndley Manor Cottages, Hailsham Road, Stone Cross, E Sussex BN24 5BS **t** 01323 843481 **e** enquiries@glyndleycottages.co.uk
glyndleycottages.co.uk

Access: abc ⚐ 🏧 ♿ General: 🛋 🔳 P S Unit: 🍳 🔥 🏧 ⛷ 📺 🚾 ♿ ❀

Glynde | **Caburn Cottages**

Enjoy England ★★★★
Units: 9 Sleeps: 2-6
Open: All year

Low season p/w:
£280.00
High season p/w:
£600.00

Rosemary Norris, Ranscombe Farm, Glynde, Nr. Lewes, East Sussex BN8 6AA **t** 01273 858062 **e** rosemary.norris@hotmail.com
caburncottages.co.uk

2D3

A group of flint/brick cottages, very comfortable, well equipped. Bed linen and towels provided.

Access: 🏧 General: 🛋 🔳 P Unit: 🍳 🏧 ⛷ ♿ ❀

Hastings | **Grand Hotel**

Enjoy England ★★★★★
Open: All year

1 Grand Parade, St. Leonards, Hastings, East Sussex TN37 6AQ
t 01424 428510 **e** info@grandhotelhastings.co.uk
grandhotelhastings.co.uk

Access: ⚐ 🏧 ☺ ♿ General: 🛋 🍴 ✕ 🍷 P ♿ ⛷ Room: 🍳 🏧 📺 🚼

Lewes | Heath Farm

AS

Enjoy England ★★★★

Units: 2   Sleeps: 4-6
Open: All year

Low season p/w:
£450.00
High season p/w:
£700.00
Shop: 1 mile
Pub: <0.5 miles

Mrs Marilyn Hanbury, South Road, Plumpton Green, Lewes, East Sussex
BN8 4EA   **t** 01273 890712 **e** hanbury@heath-farm.com
  heath-farm.com

2D3

Two luxury self-catering cottages on small family working farm in beautiful countryside, close to South Downs, coast and easy access to London. Parlour cottage sleeps 4, Stable cottage 5/6.

Location: A272 through Haywards Heath, follow B2112, left into Wivelsfield Green, right into South Road, left at roundabout, mile on left.

General:
🛏️ ⓞ P Ⓢ
Unit:
♨️ 🪑 ♿ 🦽 📺 ⛹️ ❀

Dulverton | Exmoor House Caravan Club Site THE CARAVAN CLUB

AS

Enjoy England ★★★★

Open: March to November

Oldberry, Dulverton TA22 9HL
t 01398 323268
  caravanclub.co.uk

Access: 🏃😊♿ General: ⓞ🪑🚿👤🍴🚰 Pitch: 🚐🚗

Bognor Regis | Farrell House

Units: 1   Sleeps: 8
Open: All year

Low season p/w:
£280.00
High season p/w:
£550.00

Livability Self Catering Holidays, PO Box 36, Cowbridge, Vale of Glamorgan
CF71 7TN   **t** 08456 584478 **f** 01446 775060
e selfcatering@livability.org.uk
  livability.org.uk

2C3

This property sleeps up to 8 people with an accessible twin and single bedrooms downstairs.

Access: 🄷😊♿ General: 🛏️P Ⓢ Unit: ♨️🛏️🪑♿🦽📺🚰Ⓢ⛹️❀

Bognor Regis | **Rowan Park Caravan Club Site** CARAVAN CLUB

Enjoy England ★★★★★

🚐 (94)
    £13.10–£25.40

🚚 (94)
    £13.10–£25.40

⛺ (6)

94 touring pitches
Open: 25 March - 7 November

Shop: <0.5 miles
Pub: 0.5 miles

Access:
🔥 ✖ 🐕 📷 ☺ ♿wc

General:
🔋 🍳 📻 🚿 🔌 🚰 ☎ WP

Pitch:
🚐 🚚 ⛺

Rowan Way, Bognor Regis, West Sussex PO22 9RP
t 01243 828515
caravanclub.co.uk

2C3

Conveniently situated about 2 miles from the beach, and close to the traditional seaside resort of Bognor Regis. For the theatre goer you are not far from the Chichester Festival Theatre, or from Arundel Castle.

Location: Turn left into Rowan Way at roundabout on A29 (1 mile north of Bognor). Site 100yds on right, opposite Halfords.

Bracklesham Bay | **Tamarisk**

Units: 1   Sleeps: 6
Open: All year

Low season p/w:
£280.00
High season p/w:
£540.00

Livability Self Catering Holidays, PO Box 36, Cowbridge, Vale of Glamorgan CF71 7TN   t 08456 584478 f 01446 775060
e selfcatering@livability.org.uk
  livability.org.uk

2C3

Fully accessible 3 bedroom bungalow only a few minutes walk from the sea.

Access: 🔥 ☺ General: 🐴 Ⓢ Unit: 🛏 🧺 ♿ 📺 wc Ⓢ ♿ ❀

Compton | **The Barn**

🧗 🚵 ♿ AS

Enjoy England ★★★★

Units: 2 Sleeps: 2-6
Open: All year

Low season p/w:
£250.00
High season p/w:
£750.00

Robin Bray, Compton Farmhouse, Compton, Chichester, Sussex PO18 9HB
t 02392 631597/631022 f 02392 631022
e robin.bray4@btopenworld.com
  cottages4you.co.uk

2C3

Listed barn adapted for ground floor disabled access. Twin bedroom, en suite level entry shower.

General: 🐴 P Ⓢ Unit: 🛏 🧺 ♿ 📺 ♿ ❀

Felpham | Beach Lodge

Units: 1   Sleeps: 9
Open: All year

Low season p/w:
£330.00
High season p/w:
£550.00

Livability Self Catering Holidays, PO Box 36, Cowbridge, Vale of Glamorgan CF71 7TN   t 08456 584478 f 01446 775060
e selfcatering@livability.org.uk
livability.org.uk

2D3

Beach Lodge is a large property adapted for wheelchair users, suitable for groups or families.

Access: 🅗 ☺ ♿ General: 🐎 P Ⓢ Unit: ♨ 📠 🛏 ⚱ 🚿 wc Ⓢ 🛁 ✿

Littlehampton | Littlehampton Caravan Club Site

AS

Enjoy England   ★★★★★
Open: April 2011 to January 2012

Mill Lane, Wick, Littlehampton BN17 7PH
t 01903 716176
caravanclub.co.uk

Access: 🐕 🏛 ☺ ♿ General: 🖥 📠 📷 🚗 🔌 🚻 🍴 wp Pitch: 🚐 🚙

Selsey Bill | Seagulls

Units: 1   Sleeps: 6
Open: All year

Low season p/w:
£280.00
High season p/w:
£540.00

Livability Self Catering Holidays, PO Box 36, Cowbridge, Vale of Glamorgan CF71 7TN   t 08456 584478 f 01446 775060
e selfcatering@livability.org.uk
livability.org.uk

2C3

Fully accessible bungalow is right on the Coastal Walk. It sleeps six in 3 bedrooms.

Access: 🅗 ☺ General: 🐎 P Ⓢ Unit: ♨ 📠 🛏 🚿 wc Ⓢ 🛁 ✿

Berkshire
MAIDENHEAD

Holiday Inn Maidenhead-Windsor
Manor Lane, Maidenhead SL6 2RA
t 0871 942 9053   e reservations-maidenhead@ihg.com
w holiday-inn.co.uk/maidenheaduk

Buckinghamshire
LECKHAMPSTEAD

Weatherhead Farm
Leckhampstead, Buckingham MK18 5NP
t 01280 860502   e weatherheadfarm@aol.com

MARLOW

Granny Anne's
Granny Anne's, 54 Seymour Park Road, Marlow SL7 3EP
t 01628 473086   e roger@grannyannes.com
w marlowbedbreakfast.co.uk

Isle of Wight
BRIGHSTONE

Yafford Mill Barn (Island Cottage Holidays)
Ms Honor Vass, Yafford Mill Barn (Island Cottage Holidays),
C/O The Old Vicarage, Kingston, Wareham BH20 5LH
t 01929 481555   f 01929 481070
e enq@islandcottageholidays.com
w slandcottageholidays.com

COWES

The Blue House
Mr Tim Thompson, The Blue House, 88 Chester Square,
London SW1W 9HJ
e tim@housebleu.eu
w housebleu.eu

NEWCHURCH

Mulberry Rest
Mrs Donna Dempsey, Mulberry Rest, Hill Farm, Newchurch
PO36 0NU
t 01983 400096

Southland Camping Park
Winford Road, Newchurch PO36 0LZ
t 01983 865385   e info@southland.co.uk
w southland.co.uk

SANDOWN

Borthwood Cottages
Mrs Anne Finch, Borthwood Cottages, Sandlin, Borthwood
Lane, Sandown PO36 0HH
t 01983 403967   e anne@borthwoodcottages.co.uk
w borthwoodcottages.co.uk

Fort Holiday Park
Avenue Road, Sandown PO36 8BD
t 01983 402858   e bookings@fortholidaypark.co.uk
w fortholidaypark.co.uk

SHANKLIN

Laramie
Mrs Sally Ranson, Laramie, Howard Road, Shanklin
PO37 6HD
t 01983 862905   e sally.ranson@tiscali.co.uk
w laramieholidayhome.co.uk

The Marine Villa
Mr Adrian Primavesi, The Marine Villa, C/O 57 High Street,
Green Street Green, Orpington BR6 6BQ
t 01689 606060   e mowe@totalise.co.uk
w greentiles.co.uk

Sunny Bay Apartments
Mrs Julia Nash, Sunny Bay Apartments, Alexandra Road,
Shanklin PO37 6AF
t 01983 866379   e info@sunnybayapartments.com
w sunnybayapartments.com

Kent
BETTESHANGER

Updown Park Farm
Mrs J R Mongomery, Updown Park Farm, Little Brooksend
Farm, Birchington CT7 0JW
t 01843 841656   e info@montgomery-cottages.co.uk
w montgomery-cottages.co.uk

BIDDENDEN

Heron Cottage
Biddenden, Ashford TN27 8HH
t 01580 291358   e susantwort@hotmail.com
w heroncottage.info

DENSOLE

Garden Lodge Guest House & Restaurant
324 Canterbury Road, Densole, Folkestone CT18 7BB
t 01303 893147   e stay@garden-lodge.com
w garden-lodge.com

GOLDEN GREEN

Goldhill Mill Cottages
Mr & Mrs Cole, Goldhill Mill Cottages, Goldhill Mill, Three
Elm Lane, Tonbridge TN11 0BA
t 01732 851626   f 01732 851881
e vernon.cole@virgin.net
w goldhillmillcottages.com

HEADCORN

Honywood At Curtis Farm
Miss Marion Ray, Curtis Farm, Curtis Farm, Waterman Quarter, Headcorn, Ashford TN27 9JJ
t 01622 890393   e curtis.farm@btopenworld.com
w curtis-farm-kent.co.uk

TUNBRIDGE WELLS

The Brew House Hotel
1 Warwick Park, Royal Tunbridge Wells TN2 5TA
t 01892 520587   e info@brewhousehotel.com
w brewhousehotel.net

Oxfordshire

HIGH COGGES

Springhill Farm Bed & Breakfast
Cogges, Witney OX29 6UL
t 01993 704919   e jan@strainge.fsnet.co.uk

OXFORD

YHA Oxford
2A Botley Road, Oxford OX2 0AB
t 01865 727275   e oxford@yha.org.uk
w yha.org.uk

Surrey

HOLMBURY ST MARY

Bulmer Farm
Mrs Sue Walker, Bulmer Farm Self-catering, Holmbury St. Mary, Dorking RH5 6LG
t 01306 731871   e enquiries@bulmerfarm.co.uk
w bulmerfarm.co.uk

East Sussex

BRIGHTON

myhotel Brighton
17 Jubilee Street, Brighton BN1 1GE
t 01273 900300   e brighton@myhotels.com
w myhotels.com

EASTBOURNE

Hydro Hotel
Mount Road, Eastbourne BN20 7HZ
t 01323 720643   e sales@hydrohotel.com
w hydrohotel.com

EAST DEAN

Beachy Head Holiday Cottages
Ms Michelle Hilton, Estate Office, The Green, East Dean BN20 0BY
t 01323 423878   e michelle@beachyhead.org.uk
w beachyhead.org.uk

ST LEONARDS-ON-SEA

Seaspray
54 Eversfield Place, St Leonards-on-Sea TN37 6DB
t 01424 436583   e jo@seaspraybb.co.uk
w seaspraybb.co.uk

West Sussex

CHICHESTER

George Bell House
4 Canon Lane, Chichester PO19 1PX
t 01243 813586   e bookings@chichestercathedral.org.uk
w chichestercathedral.org.uk

COLDWALTHAM

The Labouring Man
Old London Road, Coldwaltham, Pulborough RH20 1LF
t 01798 872215   e philip.beckett@btconnect.com
w thelabouringman.co.uk

COMPTON

The Bull Pen
Mr Robin Bray, Compton Farmhouse, Compton, Chichester, Sussex PO18 9HB
t 02392 631597/631022   f 02392 631022
e robin.bray4@btopenworld.com
w bookcottages.com

HILL BROW

The Jolly Drover
London Road, Hill Brow, Liss GU33 7QL
t 01730 893137   e thejollydrover@googlemail.com
w thejollydrover.co.uk

HORSHAM

The Springfields Hotel
Springfield Road, Horsham RH12 2PG
t 01403 246770   e bookings@springfieldshotel.co.uk
w springfieldshotel.co.uk

RUNCTON

Cornerstones
Viv & Roland Higgins, Corner Cottages, Greenacre, Goodwood Gardens, Runcton PO20 1SP
t 01243 839096   e v.r.higgins@dsl.pipex.com
w cornercottages.com

Where to Go

Tilbury | **Tilbury Fort**

Open: For opening hours and prices, please call 0870 333 1181 or visit www.english-heritage.org.uk/properties

No 2 Office Block, The Fort, Tilbury, Essex RM18 7NR
t 0870 333 1181   e customers@english-heritage.org.uk
english-heritage.org.uk/tilburyfort

Fascinating for war enthusiasts. View WWI & II gun emplacements and explore the extensive site.

Access: 🚻♿🧑‍🦽   General: 📷

Cowes | **Osborne House**

Open: For opening hours and prices, please call 0870 333 1181 or visit www.english-heritage.org.uk/properties

East Cowes, Isle of Wight PO32 6JX
t 0870 333 1181   e customers@english-heritage.org.uk
english-heritage.org.uk/osbornehouse

Osborne House is one of the Isle of Wight's top attractions, a great day out.

Access: 🚻♿🧑‍🦽   General: 📷✿🏛

Isle of Wight | **Carisbrooke Castle**

Open: For opening hours and prices, please call 0870 333 1181 or visit www.english-heritage.org.uk/properties

Newport, Isle of Wight PO30 1XY
t 0870 333 1181 **e** customers@english-heritage.org.uk
english-heritage.org.uk/carisbrookecastle

March the battlements and meet the famous donkeys on a day out to remember.

Access: &wc & &G General: ☑ ❀ ⌨

Deal | **Walmer Castle & Gardens**

Open: For opening hours and prices, please call 0870 333 1181 or visit www.english-heritage.org.uk/properties

Walmer, Nr Deal, Kent CT14 7LJ
t 0870 333 1181 **e** customers@english-heritage.org.uk
english-heritage.org.uk/walmercastle

Surrounded by beautiful gardens, with a rich history and a charm all of it own.

Access: abc &wc ☑ General: P& ☑ ❀ ⌨

Dover | **Dover Castle**

Open: For opening hours and prices, please call 0870 333 1181 or visit www.english-heritage.org.uk/properties

Dover, Kent CT16 1HU
t 0870 333 1181 **e** customers@english-heritage.org.uk
english-heritage.org.uk/dovercastle

Explore the medieval world of Henry II's royal court and discover the secret WWII tunnels.

Access: ∴ &wc &x ☑ & General: P& ☑ ❀ ⌨

Downe | **The Home of Charles Darwin, Down House**

Open: For opening hours and prices, please call 0870 333 1181 or visit www.english-heritage.org.uk/properties

Downe, Kent BR6 7JT
t 0870 333 1181 **e** customers@english-heritage.org.uk
english-heritage.org.uk/darwin

A fascinating day out, discover the home of Darwin, with new exhibits and audiovisual tours.

Access: ∴ &wc &x ❄ & &G General: P& ☑ ❀ & ⌨

Eynsford | **Lullingstone Roman Villa**

Open: For opening hours and prices, please call 0870 333 1181 or visit www.english-heritage.org.uk/properties

Eynsford, Kent DA4 0JA
t 0870 333 1181 **e** customers@english-heritage.org.uk
english-heritage.org.uk/lullingstoneromanvilla

Become Tony Robinson for a few hours at one of England's most exciting archaeological finds.

Access: ♿🚻 General: ❀♿

Battle | **1066 Battle of Hastings, Abbey & Battlefield**

Open: For opening hours and prices, please call 0870 333 1181 or visit www.english-heritage.org.uk/properties

Battle, East Sussex TN33 0AD
t 0870 333 1181 **e** customers@english-heritage.org.uk
english-heritage.org.uk/battleabbeyandbattlefield

From interactive exhibits to a themed play area it's perfect for all ages!

Access: ⠿ 🐾 ♿🚻

Pevensey | **Pevensey Castle**

Open: For opening hours and prices, please call 0870 333 1181 or visit www.english-heritage.org.uk/properties

Pevensey, East Sussex BN24 5LE
t 0870 333 1181 **e** customers@english-heritage.org.uk
english-heritage.org.uk/pevenseycastle

Towering ruins, dark dungeons and fascinating exhibition, a fun day out for the whole family.

Access: ♿🚻 ♿ 🚻 ♿ General: 🚻

GETTING THERE IS NOT A PROBLEM!
OPEN See Getting there..... and back section (p314)
BRITAIN Everything you need for a hassle-free journey

Where to Eat

Aylesbury | Eamayl

35 New Street, Aylesbury, Bucks HP20 2NL
t 01296 422191 **e** info@eamayl.co.uk
eamayl.co.uk

General: FAX ☃ ⚲ ⚲ WC ⚲ ⚲

Long Crendon | Angel Restaurant

47 Bicester Road, Long Crendon, Bucks HP18 9EE
t 01844 208268 **e** info@angelrestaurant.co.uk
angelrestaurant.co.uk

General: ⚲ FAX ⚲ ⚲

Canterbury | Deeson's

25-26 Sun Street, Canterbury, Kent CT1 2HX
t 01227 767854 **e** info@deesonrestaurant.co.uk
deesonsrestaurant.co.uk/

General: ⚲ FAX ⚲ ⚲ WC ⚲ ⚲ abc

Whitstable | Crab & Winkle

South Quay Harbour, Whitstable, Kent CT5 1AB
t 01227 779377 **e** cnwr@hotmail.co.uk

General: ⚲ FAX ☃ ⚲ ⚲ WC ⚲

Richmond Upon Thames | Carluccio's

31-33 Kew Road, Richmond Upon Thames, Surrey TW9 2NQ
t 020 8940 5037 **e** richmond@carluccios.com
carluccios.com

General: ⚲ FAX ⚲ ⚲ WC ⚲ ⚲

Chichester | Woodies Wine Bar & Brasserie

10-13 St Pancras, Chichester, West Sussex PO19 7SJ
t 01243 779895 **e** matt@woodiesbrasserie.com
woodiesbrasserie.com

General: ⚲ FAX ☃ ⚲ ⚲ ⚲ P

Littlehampton | Oystercatcher

Yapton Road, Climping, Littlehampton, West Sussex BN17 5RU
t 01903 726354
vintageinn.co.uk/theoystercatcherclimping

General: ⚲ ⚲ ⚲ WC ⚲ P

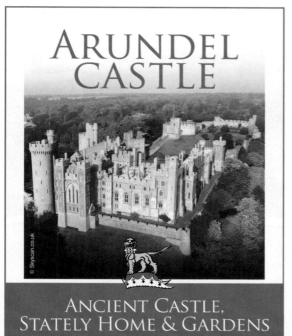

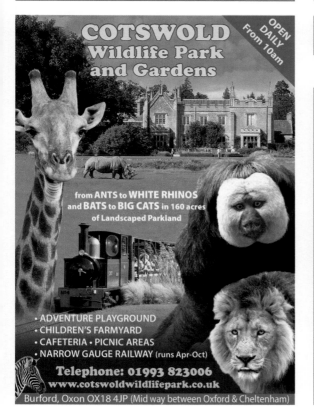

'The award-winning museum is a genuine joy to visit' - Time Out

THE ROALD DAHL MUSEUM AND STORY CENTRE

Great Missenden HP16 0AL | 01494 892192
45 minutes direct from London Marylebone

www.roalddahlmuseum.org

The Look Out Discovery Centre

THE LOOK OUT DISCOVERY CENTRE

A Great Family Day Out, whatever the weather!

Hands on Science and Nature Exhibition - over 80 Exhibits

Open Daily
10am – 5pm

The Look Out Discovery Centre
(Opposite Coral Reef)
Nine Mile Ride, Bracknell
Berks RG12 7QW
Junction 3 off M3 or Junction 10 off M4

- Children' Adventure Playground
- Coffee Shop
- 1,000 Hectares of Crown Estate Woodland
- Gift Shop
- Free Car Parking

Call 01344 354400
for more information

Email: thelookout@bracknell-forest.gov.uk
www.bracknell-forest.gov.uk/be

  Bracknell Forest Council **Be** LEISURE

Winchester City Council

Public toilets are provided in the City Centre and surrounding area. All have facilities for disabled people.

The RADAR key scheme is in use and keys are available for loan or purchase from the Tourist Information Centre or the City Council's Offices, Colebrook Street.

For further information visit the Winchester City Council website
www.winchester.gov.uk.

OPEN LONDON

OpenLondon is the definitive guide for visitors to London with access needs. The guide contains everything required to enjoy London to the full.

 VISIT LONDON VISITLONDON.COM tourismforall

London - World-Class Sights & Hidden Gems

Whatever your interests, you'll be spoilt for choice in London. From fascinating museums and galleries, to West End theatres and top sporting venues, there's plenty to keep you entertained.

See the Sights

London has an extensive travel network allowing you to get around easily. All public buses (except heritage Routemasters) and Docklands Light Railway trains plus many of London's tours are accessible to wheelchair users. **The Merlin Entertainments London Eye** will take you graciously up into the sky giving dramatic views of the many landmarks on the River Thames and beyond.

Take a cruise down the Thames to get a different perspective. **City Cruises** and **Thames Clippers** are wheelchair accessible and provide a hassle-free way to soak up the atmosphere and navigate between the sites. Join **Original London Sightseeing Tours** open-top buses for an entertaining guide through the city past and present (a third of vehicles are wheelchair accessible - contact in advance). For hidden gems and unique experiences that are only in London, see **visitlondon.com**

Soak Up The Culture

London is a true culture capital with 70 large museums and over 30 major art galleries — with a good number providing enhanced access facilities, plus the national museums and galleries offer free entry to the permanent collections (there may be charges for special exhibitions).

The **British Museum** offers sound guides and sign language interpreted tours giving you an insight into hundreds of years of world art and artefacts. Audio guides, Touch Tours and BSL interpreted events are all provided at **Tate Modern's** extensive modern art collection and **Tate Britain's** collection of pieces from 16th century to the present. Visit the huge collection at the **Natural History Museum** including the magnificent Darwin Centre where you can see world-leading scientists at work and incredible specimens. The **Science Museum** offers hundreds of interactive exhibits and an IMAX 3D Cinema. Take an adventure through seafaring history at the **National Maritime Museum** in Greenwich. The **National Theatre**, Gold Award Winner of the Visit London Accessible Tourism Award 2008, produces theatre of international acclaim from classics to newly commissioned works. You can visit the reconstruction of Shakespeare's **Globe Theatre** for performances May to September, or the Exhibition is open year-round.

Sporting Triumphs & Musical Legends

How about a tour of the home of your sporting legends? Many clubs provide guided visits. Try the

London at twilight

British Museum Great Court

London

VISIT
LONDON
VISITLONDON.COM

Arsenal Emirates Stadium which is fully wheelchair accessible or walk in the footsteps of your sporting heroes on the accessible **Wembley Stadium** tour.

If it's musical entertainment that you're after, **The O$_2$** is a world class entertainment venue in the iconic Greenwich dome and home of The O$_2$ arena which plays host to big name musical acts and sporting events throughout the year.

Shopping, Restaurants & Relaxation

Westfield London is the largest in-town shopping centre and restaurants in Europe with over 265 shops and varied dining facilities. Shopmobility motorised scooters can be booked in advance and wheelchairs are available on site. Also, opening in 2011 is Westfield Stratford City. In the West End, visit **Hamleys** on Regent Street – every child's dream with seven floors of toys and delights accessed by lift or escalator.

London has over 6,000 restaurants serving 70 different cuisines, from Michelin star-rated venues to value eats. See **visitlondon.com** for features and listings.

Finally, if you need time to relax after your hectic schedule, why not take some time in one of the Royal Parks such as **St James's** or **Regent's Park**. Take in the views and enjoy the cultivated gardens.

Get in touch

For general information and advice on accommodation:

Visit London
t: 08701 566366
e: visitorinfo@visitlondon.com
web: visitlondon.com

For information on accommodation and useful accessibility maps see visitlondon.com/access

Travel Information Centres

Euston Railway Station
Opposite platform 8

Heathrow Airport

King's Cross Tube Station
Western Ticket Hall

Liverpool Street Tube Station

Piccadilly Circus Tube Station

Victoria Railway Station

View across the River Thames towards the London Eye dominating the skyline on the South Bank

Regent's Pa

Tourist Information Centres

Tourist Information Centres are a mine of information about local and regional accommodation, attractions and events. Visit them when you arrive at your destination or contact them before you go. For more information see **visitlondon.com/welcome**

Bexley Hall Place	Bourne Road	01322 558676	touristinfo@bexleyheritagetrust.co.uk
Britain & London Visitor Centre	1 Regent Street	0870 1 566366	visitorinfo@visitlondon.com
City of London	St Paul's Churchyard	020 7332 1456	
Greenwich	2 Cutty Sark Gardens	0870 608 2000	
Harrow	Gayton Library	020 8427 6012	info@harrow.gov.uk
Holborn	Opp. Holborn tube station	020 7808 3807	
Lewisham	Lewisham Library	020 8297 8317	tic@lewisham.gov.uk
Swanley	Swanley Library & Information Centre	01322 614660	touristinfo@swanley.org.uk
Richmond	Old Town Hall, Whittaker Avenue	020 8734 3363	info@visitrichmond.co.uk
Twickenham	Civic Centre	020 8891 7272	info@visitrichmond.co.uk

Where to Stay

London E16 | Crowne Plaza London - Docklands   AS

Royal Victoria Dock, Western Gateway, London E16 1AL
t 0207 055 2000   **e** sales@crowneplazadocklands.co.uk
crowneplazadocklands.co.uk

Access: 🅿 🐾 👶 ☺ 🚾 ♿   General: 🛋 🍴 ✕ 🍷 P♿ ❀ 🔲 🔲 ♿   Room: 🔌 📺 🍵

London EC4 | Crowne Plaza London - The City

19 New Bridge Street, London EC4V 6DB
t 0871 942 9190   **e** Loncy.Info@ihg.com
crowneplaza.com/Londonthecity

Access: 🐾 👶 ☺ 🚾 ♿   General: 🛋 🍴 ✕ 🍷 ❀ 🔲 🔲 ♿   Room: 🚾 📺 📺 Ⓢ 🍵

London SE2 | Abbey Wood Caravan Club Site   THE CARAVAN CLUB   AS

Enjoy England   ★★★★★

🚐 (210)
      £15.70–£29.30
🚍 (210)
      £15.70–£29.30
⛺ (100)

210 touring pitches
Open: All year

Shop: <0.5 miles
Pub: 3 miles

Access:
🅰 🐾 👶 ☺ ♿
General:
🔲 🔲 🔥 🚮 💀 🔌 ☎ WP
Pitch:
🚐 🚍 ⛺

Federation Road, Abbey Wood, London SE2 0LS
t 0208 311 7708
caravanclub.co.uk

2D2

It feels positively rural when you reach this verdant, gently sloping site with its mature trees and spacious grounds. This site is the ideal base for exploring the capital or nearby Greenwich, which offers its own blend of fascinating attractions.

Location: Turn off M2 at A221. Turn right into McLeod Road, right into Knee Hill. Site 2nd turning on right.

London SW7 | Holiday Inn London Kensington Forum Hotel

97 Cromwell Road, London SW7 4DN
t 0207 341 3098   **e** jay.sharma@ihg.com
holidayinnkensingtonforum.co.uk

Access: ∴ abc 👶 ☺ 🚾 ♿   General: 🛋 🍴 ✕ 🍷 P♿ 🔲 ♿   Room: 🔌 🚾 📺 Ⓢ 🍵

London SW19 | Holiday Inn Express London Wimbledon South

200 High Street, Colliers Wood, Wimbledon, London SW19 2BH
t 0208 545 7300 **e** reservations@exhiwimbledon.co.uk
exhiwimbledon.co.uk

Access: ✦ abc 🛏 ⚓ 🏰 ☺ ♿ ♿ General: 🐴 ♥ P ⊞ ♿ Room: 🛁 ♨ 🛏 wc ⓢ ☕

London W1 | Holiday Inn London - Regents Park

AS

AA ★★★★ Carburton Street, London W1W 5EE
t 0871 942 9111 **e** reservations-Londonregentspark@ihg.com
holidayinn.co.uk

Access: ✦ abc 🛏 ⚓ 🏰 ☺ ♿ ♿ General: 🐴 ♨ ✕ ♥ P ⊞ ♿ Room: 🔢 abc wc 🖃 ⓢ ☕

London W1 | Holiday Inn London Mayfair

3 Berkeley Street, London W1J 8NE
t 0871 9429110 **e** himayfair-reservations@ihg.com
holiday-inn.co.uk

Access: ✦ abc 🛏 🏰 ☺ ♿ ♿ General: 🐴 ♨ ✕ ♥ P ⊞ ♿ Room: 🛏 ☕

London WC1 | Holiday Inn London - Bloomsbury

AS

Coram Street, London WC1N 1HT
t +44 0 871 942 9222 **e** bloomsbury@ihg.com
holidayinn.com/bloomsbury

Access: ✦ 🅷 abc 🛏 ⚓ ☺ ♿ ♿ General: 🐴 ♨ ✕ ♥ P ⊞ ♿ Room: 🛏 ☕

Heathrow | Crowne Plaza Heathrow

AA ★★★★ Stockley Road, West Drayton, Middlesex UB7 9NA
t 01871 9429140 **e** LONHA.reservations@ihg.com
crowneplaza.co.uk/lon-heathrow

Access: 🅷 abc 🛏 ⚓ 🏰 ☺ ♿ ♿ General: 🐴 ♨ ✕ ♥ P ✿ ⊞ ♿ Room: 🛁 ♨ wc ☕

Heathrow | Holiday Inn London Heathrow Ariel

118 Bath Road, Hayes, Middlesex UB3 5AJ
t 44-871-942 9040
holidayinn.com

Access: abc 🛏 ⚓ 🏰 ☺ ♿ ♿ General: 🐴 ♨ ✕ ♥ P ✿ ⊞ ♿ Room: 🛏 ☕

Heathrow | Holiday Inn London Heathrow M4 Jct. 4

AS

Sipson Road, West Drayton, Middlesex UB7 0JU
t 0871 942 9095 **e** steve.shipley@ihg.com
holidayinn.co.uk

Access: abc 🛏 ⚓ 🏰 ☺ ♿ ♿ General: 🐴 ♨ ✕ ♥ P ✿ ⊞ ♿ Room: ♨ 🛏 ☕

Hounslow | Renaissance London Heathrow Hotel

AA ★★★★ Bath Road, Hounslow, Middlesex TW6 2AQ
Open: All year **t** 020 8897 6363 **e** rhi.lhrbr.sales.reservations@renaissancehotels.com
renaissanceLondonheathrow.co.uk

Access: ✦ abc ⚓ 🏰 ☺ ♿ ♿ ♿ General: 🐴 ♨ ✕ ♥ P ✿ ⊞ ♿ Room: 🛁 ♨ 🛏 wc ⓢ ☕

London | **Holiday Inn London Sutton**

Gibson Road, Sutton, Surrey SM1 2RF
t 0871 972 9113 **e** jill.scarlett@ihg.com
holidayinn.co.uk/lon-sutton

Access: .: abc 🔲 ✳ ☺ 🚻 ♿   General: 🛏🍴✕♟P♿🔁♿   Room: 🚾🅂☕

London, Ilford | **Holiday Inn Express - Newbury Park, London**

713 Eastern Avenue, London IG2 7RH
t 0208 709 2200 **e** reservations'express-newburypark.com
hiexpress.co.uk

Access: abc 🔲 🏰 ☺ ♿&   General: 🛏🍴✕♟P♿🔁♿   Room: ▦🅛🚾☕

London NW2 | **Holiday Inn Brent Cross**

AA   ★★★   Tilling Road, Brent Cross, London NW2 1LP
t 0870 400 9112 **e** bregc.reservations@ihg.com
holiday-inn.co.uk

Access: abc 🔲 ✳ 🏰 ☺ ♿&   General: 🛏🍴✕♟P♿🔁♿   Room: 🅛🅂☕

London SE19 | **Crystal Palace Caravan Club Site** THE CARAVAN CLUB   **AS**

Enjoy England ★★★★★	Crystal Palace Parade, London SE19 1UF
🚐 (126)	**t** 0208 778 7155
£15.90–£29.30	caravanclub.co.uk **2D2**
🚚 (126)	
£15.90–£29.30	
🛆 (30)	

A busy but friendly site on the edge of a pleasant park with many attractions for children. In close proximity to all of London's attractions, Tower Bridge, Imperial War Museum, London Eye and Lords Tour to name but a few.

126 touring pitches
Open: 18 March - 2 January 2012

Shop: 0.5 miles
Pub: 0.5 miles

Location: Turn off A205 South Circular at West Dulwich into Croxted Road. The site is adjacent to television mast.

Access:
🅰 ✳ 🏰 ☺ ♿
General:
🔲🚐🎣🚿🚮🚰☕🅦🅟
Pitch:
🚐🚚🛆

Shepperton | **Holiday Inn London Shepperton**

AA   ★★★★   Felix Lane, Shepperton, Middlesex TW17 8NP
t 01932 899988 **e** hishepperton@qmh-hotels.com
holidayinn.co.uk

Access: .: abc 🔲 ✳ 🏰 ☺ ♿&   General: 🛏🍴✕♟P♿❄🔁♿   Room: 🍳🚾🅂☕

Inner London

LONDON E14

Radisson Edwardian Providence Wharf
Radisson Edwardian Providence Wharf, London E14 9PG
t 020 7987 2050 **e** resnpw@radisson.com
w radissonedwardian.com/Londonuk_canarywharf

LONDON W1

YHA London Central
104-108 Bolsover Street, London W1W 6AB

LONDON SE16

YHA London Thameside
20 Salter Road, London SE16 5PR
t 0870 770 6010 **e** thameside@yha.org.uk
w yha.org.uk

LONDON SW7

Meininger City Hostel & Hotel London
65-67 Queen's Gate, London SW7 5JS
t 020 3051 8173 **e** welcome@meininger-hostels.com
w meininger-hostels.com

Outer London

BROMLEY

Best Western Bromley Court Hotel
Coniston Road, Bromley BR1 4JD
t 020 8461 8600 **e** enquiries@bromleycourthotel.co.uk
w bestwestern.co.uk/bromleycourthotel

Where to Go

London - Chiswick | **Chiswick House & Gardens**

Open: For opening hours and prices, please call 0870 333 1181 or visit www.english-heritage.org.uk/properties

Burlington Lane, Chiswick, London W4 2RP
t 0870 333 1181 **e** customers@english-heritage.org.uk
  english-heritage.org.uk/chiswickhouse

A family friendly day out in London? A day trip to Chiswick House is perfect.

Access: 🚻♿ General: ♿

London - Eltham | **Eltham Palace**

Open: For opening hours and prices, please call 0870 333 1181 or visit www.english-heritage.org.uk/properties

Court Yard, Eltham, London SE9 5QE
t 0870 333 1181 **e** customers@english-heritage.org.uk
  english-heritage.org.uk/elthampalace

A perfect day out for anyone interested in art, stylish interiors and grand gardens.

Access: 🚻♿ General: ♿

London - Twickenham | **Marble Hill House**

Open: For opening hours and prices, please call 0870 333 1181 or visit www.english-heritage.org.uk/properties

Richmond Road, Twickenham, London TW1 2NL
t 0870 333 1181 **e** customers@english-heritage.org.uk
  english-heritage.org.uk/marblehillhouse

Built as a retreat from the hustle and bustle, the perfect spot for afternoon tea.

Access: abc 🚻♿ General: ♿

Where to Eat

London E1 | Lanes Restaurant & Bar

East India House, 109-117 Middlesex Street, London E1 7JF
t 020 7247 5050 **e** info@lanesrestaurant.co.uk
lanesrestaurant.co.uk

General: 🐕 @FAX 🚲 🚶 ♿ WC ♿ 🚶♿

London EC2 | Corney And Barrow

1 Ropemaker Street, London EC2Y 9HT
t 020 7382 0606 **e** citypoint@winebar-corbar.co.uk
corney-barrow.co.uk

General: 🐕 @FAX 🚲 🚶 ♿ WC ♿ 🚶♿ abc

London N1 | Glassworks

N1 Centre, Upper Street, London N1 0PS
t 020 7354 6100 **e** P4015@jdwetherspoon.co.uk
LloydsNo1.co.uk

General: 🐕 @FAX 🚶 ♿ WC ♿ 🚶♿ abc

London NW6 | North London Tavern

375 Kilburn High Road, Kilburn, London NW6 7QB
t 020 7625 6634 **e** northLondontavern@realpubs.co.uk

General: 🐕 @FAX 🚶 ♿ WC ♿ 🚶♿

London SE13 | Maggie's Cafe & Restaurant

320-322 Lewisham Road, Lewisham, London SE13 7PA
t 020 8244 0339 **e** info@maggiesrestaurant.co.uk
maggiesrestaurant.co.uk

General: 🐕 @FAX 🚲 🚶 ♿ P

London SW1 | Bamford & Sons

31 Sloane Square, London SW1W 8AQ
t 020 7881 8010
bamfordandsons.com

General: 🐕 @FAX 🚲 🚶 ♿ WC ♿ 🚶♿

London W8 | Kensington Wine Rooms

127-129 Kensington Church Street, London W8 7LP
t 020 7727 8142 **e** richard@greatwinesbytheglass.com
greatwinesbytheglass.com

General: 🐕 @FAX 🚶 ♿ ♿ 🚶♿

RENAISSANCE. A NEW WAY TO SAY 'HELLO'

At the Renaissance London Heathrow Hotel, we understand it's the small things that make a big difference. With the lobby, concierge, restaurant, bar, reception and Starbucks, specially designed disabled bedrooms and bathrooms, and allocated parking all on one level; your stay is bound to be comfortable and enjoyable with us.

For each disabled room booked and stayed in on a Friday, Saturday or Sunday until 31st December 2011 you will receive a complimentary bottle of house wine in your room when you quote OBG11.

To take advantage of this offer please call **020 8897 6363** and ask for Internal Reservations quoting **OBG11**. Alternatively you can email the hotel's Internal Reservations department on **rhi.lhrbr.sales.reservations@renaissancehotels.com** please remember to quote **OBG11**.

RENAISSANCE LONDON HEATHROW HOTEL
Bath Road Hounslow Middlesex
TW6 2AQ United Kingdom
t: +44 (0)20 8897 6363   f: +44 (0)20 8897 1113
RenaissanceLondonHeathrow.co.uk

HOSPITALITY AWARDS
AA
2010 - 2011
AA Hotel Group of the Year
2010 - 2011

R
RENAISSANCE®
LONDON HEATHROW HOTEL

Guildhall Art Gallery

An historic collection in a modern building, purpose-built for disability access.

Re-opened in 1999, Guildhall Art Gallery displays London subjects and portraits from the 17th century to the present day and a fine collection of Victorian paintings including works by Constable, Landseer, Tissot and the Pre-Raphaelites. In addition there is a programme of temporary exhibitions. The remains of Roman London's amphitheatre are also on view.

Guildhall Art Gallery
Guildhall Yard London EC2V 5AE

Open Monday-Saturday 10am-5pm (last admission 4.30pm)
Sunday noon-4pm (last admission 3.45pm)

Telephone: 020 7332 3700
Textphone: 020 7332 3803
Fax: 020 7332 2242
email: guildhall.artgallery@cityoflondon.gov.uk
website: www.guildhall-art-gallery.org.uk

CITY
OF
LONDON

Dante Gabriel Rossetti *La Ghirlandata*, 1873

Historic Royal PALACES

Access for all

We are the independent charity that cares for the Tower of London, Hampton Court Palace, the Banqueting House, Kensington Palace and Kew Palace.

We encourage everyone, whatever their needs, to discover the stories of how monarchs and people have shaped society in five of the greatest palaces ever built.

For further information about access and visiting any or all of our palaces, call us on 0844 482 7777 (textphone: 18001 0844 482 7777) or visit our website www.hrp.org.uk

National Theatre

The National Theatre is at the centre of the cultural life of the country, housing three auditoriums on London's South Bank presenting over 1,000 performances every year.

Visitors can also enjoy free exhibitions and live music, outdoor summer events and more. We aim to be accessible and welcoming to all and are committed to making your visit as easy and enjoyable as possible.

Backstage Tours

Go backstage at Britain's largest theatre complex and discover the secrets behind bringing our productions to the stage.

Eating & Drinking

Restaurants, cafés and bars can be found throughout the building, most with al fresco seating overlooking the vibrant South Bank.

For details of captioned and audio-described performances visit the website, or for access information call 020 7452 3400.

VISIT LONDON AWARDS 2008 ★★★★★ GOLD WINNER

enjoyEngland Awards for Excellence 2009 SILVER WINNER

Tickets £15 plus companion at same price
Join our free mailing list to receive updates access@nationaltheatre.org.uk

Supported by
ARTS COUNCIL ENGLAND

020 7452 3000 • nationaltheatre.org.uk/access

©Britain on View

OPEN BRITAIN **PLANNING A DAY OUT? WHY NOT MAKE IT A SHORT- BREAK?**
Fabulous 'Places to Stay' in every region

Come and enjoy the wide open spaces of the East of England

Visit Britain's Magical Waterland, the Broads, ideal for boating holidays and a haven for birds and wildlife. Or try taking a punt along the manicured lawns and medieval colleges of historic Cambridge. Stroll from castle to ancient churches along the cobbled streets of Norwich.

Glimpse the fascinating 'off-duty' life of Her Majesty the Queen at her country retreat at **Royal Sandringham** or see the treasures of a mystery Saxon King in the burial ship at **Sutton Hoo**.

Step into an 18th century landscape painting in **Constable Country**. The water meadows, river and mill are all there, just as the Great Master painted them. Follow in the footsteps of those magnificent men in the flying machines with a visit to the **Imperial War Museum Duxford**. Whatever your interest you will find something to fascinate you in this unspoilt and very special corner of England.

Beautiful coastline, glorious countryside, historic cities and fascinating heritage, the East of England has it all, plus a unique and charmingly quirky character which is all its own. Just a short train ride from the bright lights and frenetic twenty first century life of London into another more serene and peaceful world, a world where time takes a breather.

The East coast offers something for everyone from the excitement of the popular resorts like **Southend-on-Sea** and **Great Yarmouth** to the salt marshes of North Norfolk and Suffolk. Childhood memories spring into life in the old-fashioned seaside havens like **Sheringham** and **Southwold**, while sleek yachts and sturdy fishing smacks jostle for position in picturesque ports.

Discover the almost car-free roads; stop off to explore little towns and villages. Rest in the cool stillness of medieval churches and revel in the kaleidoscopic colours of country gardens. Follow in the footsteps

Sailing on Barton Broad, Norfolk

Norwich Cathedral

East of England

Bedfordshire, Cambridgeshire, Essex, Hertfordshire, Norfolk, Suffolk

Tourist Information Centres	160	Where to Go	178
Where to Stay	162	Where to Eat	179

of Kings and Queens to sumptuous stately homes, places like **Woburn Abbey**, **Hatfield House** and **Knebworth House**.

Take a few days out for a city break and enjoy shopping and sightseeing in one of the cities of the East, they seem to have a more relaxed atmosphere than some in others parts of England. **Norwich** is a treat with its Norman castle, cathedral and its medieval market place – plus it is in the top ten shopping destinations in the UK. **Cambridge** is a treasure house with its unique academic ambience and medieval architecture; little **Ely**, a delightful, undiscovered gem, sitting demurely beneath its triumphant cathedral.

Wherever you go, keep an eye out for the East of England's magic ingredient – a quirky individuality that has been around for centuries. It crops up unexpectedly in different forms, an extravagant folly, an eccentric tradition or a weird and wonderful tale. This all adds to the experience of a visit to the East of England.

Find out more
www.visiteastofengland.com

Punting on the river Cam

Holkham Beach, Norfol

Tourist Information Centres

Tourist Information Centres are a mine of information about local and regional accommodation, attractions and events. Visit them when you arrive at your destination or contact them before you go:

Aldeburgh	152 High Street	01728 453637	atic@suffolkcoastal.gov.uk
Aylsham	Bure Valley Railway	01263 733903	aylsham.tic@broadland.gov.uk
Beccles	The Quay	01502 713196	becclesinfo@broads-authority.gov.uk
Bedford	Old Town Hall	01234 221712	touristInfo@bedford.gov.uk
Bishop's Stortford	2 Market Square	01279 655831	tic@bishopsstortford.org
Braintree	Town Hall Centre	01376 550066	tic@braintree.gov.uk
Brentwood	Pepperell House	01277 200300	michelle.constable@brentwood.gov.uk
Burnham on Crouch	1 High Street	01621 784962	burnhamtic@one-place.org.uk
Bury St Edmunds	6 Angel Hill	01284 764667	tic@stedsbc.gov.uk
Cambridge	Peas Hill	01223 457577	info@visitcambridge.co.uk
Chelmsford	8 Dukes Walk	01245 283400	chelmsfordvisitor.information@firstgroup.com
Clacton	Town Hall	01255 686633	clactontic@tendring.gov.uk
Colchester	1 Queen Street	01206 282920	vic@colchester.gov.uk
Cromer	Louden Road	0871 200 3071	cromerinfo@north-norfolk.gov.uk
Deepdale Information	Deepdale Farm	01485 210256	info@deepdalefarm.co.uk
Diss	Meres Mouth	01379 650523	dtic@s-norfolk.gov.uk

Downham Market	The Priory Centre	01366 383287	downham-market.tic@west-norfolk.gov.uk
Dunstable	Priory House	01582 890270	tic@dunstable.gov.uk
Ely	Oliver Cromwell's House	01353 662062	tic@eastcambs.gov.uk
Felixstowe	91 Undercliff Road West	01394 276770	ftic@suffolkcoastal.gov.uk
Flatford	Flatford Lane	01206 299460	flatfordvic@babergh.gov.uk
Great Yarmouth	Maritime House	01493 846346	tourism@great-yarmouth.gov.uk
Harwich	Iconfield Park	01255 506139	harwichtic@btconnect.com
Hertford	10 Market Place	01992 584322	tic@hertford.gov.uk
Holt	3 Pound House	0871 200 3071	holtinfo@north-norfolk.gov.uk
Hoveton	Station Road	01603 782281	hoveton.info@broads-authority.gov.uk
Hunstanton	Town Hall	01485 532610	hunstanton.tic@west-norfolk.gov.uk
Ipswich	St Stephen's Church	01473 258070	tourist@ipswich.gov.uk
King's Lynn	The Custom House	01553 763044	kings-lynn.tic@west-norfolk.gov.uk
Lavenham	Lady Street	01787 248207	lavenhamtic@babergh.gov.uk
Letchworth Garden City	33-35 Station Road	01462 487868	tic@letchworth.com
Lowestoft	East Point Pavilion	01502 533600	touristinfo@waveney.gov.uk
Luton	Luton Central Library	01582 401579	touristinformation@luton.gov.uk
Maldon	Wenlock Way	01621 856503	tic@maldon.gov.uk
Newmarket	Palace House	01638 667200	tic.newmarket@forest-heath.gov.uk
Norwich	The Forum	01603 213999	tourism@norwich.gov.uk
Peterborough	3-5 Minster Precincts	01733 452336	tic@peterborough.gov.uk
Saffron Walden	1 Market Place	01799 524002	tourism@saffronwalden.gov.uk
Sandy	10 Cambridge Road	01767 682728	tourism@sandytowncouncil.gov.uk
Sheringham	Station Approach	0871 200 3071	sheringhaminfo@north-norfolk.gov.uk
Southend-On-Sea	Pier Entrance	01702 215620	vic@southend.gov.uk
Southwold	69 High Street	01502 724729	southwold.tic@waveney.gov.uk
St Albans	Town Hall	01727 864511	tic@stalbans.gov.uk
St Neots	The Old Court	01480 388788	stneots.tic@huntsdc.gov.uk
Mid Suffolk	Museum of East Anglian Life	01449 676800	tic@midsuffolk.gov.uk
Sudbury	Town Hall	01787 881320	sudburytic@babergh.gov.uk
Waltham Abbey	2-4 Highbridge Street	01992 652295	tic@walthamabbey-tc.gov.uk
Wells-next-the-Sea	Staithe Street	0871 200 3071	wellsinfo@north-norfolk.gov.uk
Wisbech	2-3 Bridge Street	01945 583263	tourism@fenland.gov.uk
Witham	Town Hall	01376 502674	ticwitham@braintree.gov.uk
Woodbridge	Station Buildings	01394 382240	wtic@suffolkcoastal.gov.uk
Wymondham	Market Cross	01953 604721	wymondhamtic@btconnect.com

Where to Stay

Sandy | **Acorn Cottage**

  AS

Enjoy England ★★★★

Units: 4 Sleeps: 2-8
Open: All year

Mrs Margaret Codd, Highfield Farm, Tempsford Road, Sandy SG19 2AQ
t 01767 682332 **e** margaret@highfield-farm.co.uk
highfield-farm.co.uk

2D1

Low season p/w:
£250.00
High season p/w:
£800.00

Converted barn in courtyard on a working arable
farm. Wooden floors on one level throughout.

General: ⬥🗖P🅂 Unit: 🛋🖼🧹🛁🧺🚿❀

Cambridge | **Cherry Hinton Caravan Club Site** THE CARAVAN CLUB

AS

Enjoy England ★★★★★

🚐 (60)
£15.30–£27.20

🚚 (60)
£15.30–£27.20

⛺ (6)

60 touring pitches
Open: All year

Shop: 0.8 miles
Pub: <0.5 miles

Lime Kiln Road, Cherry Hinton, Cambridge CB1 8NQ
t 01223 244088
caravanclub.co.uk

2D1

Imaginatively landscaped site set in
old quarry, bordered by nature trail
and set within an area of SSI. It's a
ten minute bus journey from site
into the city centre. Take a guided
walk or punt along the River Cam.

Location: Head to Fulbourn on A11.
At roundabout in Fulbourn head to
Cambridge. Left at trafficlights. Left
into Lime Kiln Road.

Access:
🅰♿❌🏧☺♿
General:
🗖🖼📷♿🔌♿🚻☕🆆🅿
Pitch:
🚐🚚⛺

Cambridge | **Crowne Plaza Cambridge**

AA
★★★★

Downing Street, Cambridge, Cambridgeshire CB2 3DT
t 0871 942 9180 **e** reservations-cpcambridge@ihg.com
crowneplaza.com/cambridgeuk

Access: 📷🏧☺♿♿ General: ⬥🍽♿🔌🛁 Room: 🧺🆆🅂🚿

Huntingdon | **Grafham Water Caravan Club Site** THE CARAVAN CLUB

Enjoy England ★★★★★ Church Road, Grafham, Huntingdon PE28 0BB
t 01480 810264
caravanclub.co.uk

Access: 🏠 ☺ ♿ General: 📦 📶 🚿 🔌 ☕ ☎ 📶 Pitch: 🚐 🚑

Huntingdon | **Houghton Mill Caravan Club Site** THE CARAVAN CLUB

Enjoy England ★★★★

🚐 (65)

£14.90–£27.20

🚑 (65)

£14.90–£27.20

Ⅰ (8)

65 touring pitches
Open: 25 March - 7
November

Shop: 0.5 miles
Pub: 0.5 miles

Access:
🏠 🐾 🏠 ☺ ♿
General:
📦 🔌 📶 🚿 🔌 ☕ ☎
Pitch:
🚐 🚑 Ⅰ

Mill Street, Houghton, Huntingdon, Cambridgeshire PE28 2AZ
t 01480 466716
caravanclub.co.uk

3A2

Situated on the banks of the Great Ouse with spectacular views across to the National Trust's Houghton Mill with milling demonstrations every Sunday. There's an abundance of footpaths and bridleways for walkers, horse riders and cyclists.

Location: Continue through market square of Houghton Village into Mill Street, church on right. Site entrance on left before last house.

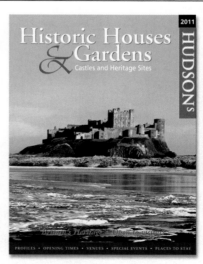

Peterborough | **Ferry Meadows Caravan Club Site**

AS

Enjoy England ★★★★★

🚐 (252)
£14.70–£27.20

🚙 (252)
£14.70–£27.20

⛺ (6)

252 touring pitches
Open: All year

Shop: 1 mile
Pub: <0.5 miles

Access:
🅰 ⚡ 🎠 ☺ 🚻♿

General:
▯ ▤ ▨ ⚙ 🔌 🚰 🚿 ⚓

Pitch:
🚐 🚙 ⛺

Ham Lane, Peterborough, Cambridgeshire PE2 5UU
t 01733 233526
caravanclub.co.uk

3A1

The perfect family holiday site, ideally located in a country park with steam trains, lake, cycle and walking trails and many sporting facilities. Enjoy sailing, windsurfing and fishing or head to Peterborough for ice skating, bowling, shopping and theatre.

Location: From any direction, on approaching Peterborough, follow the brown signs to Nene Park and Ferry Meadows.

Quiet Waters caravan Park | **Quiet Waters Caravan Park**

AS

Enjoy England ★★★★
AA ★★★

Access: 🚻♿ General: ▯ ▨ 🔌 🚰 🚿 Pitch: 🚐 ▢ 🚙 ⛺

Hemingford Abbots, Huntingdon, Cambridgeshire PE28 9AJ
t 01480 463405 **e** quietwaters.park@btopenworld.com
quietwaterscaravanpark.co.uk

OPEN BRITAIN **DECIDED WHERE TO GO? SEE ATTRACTIONS FOR WHAT TO DO**
Ideas and information at the end of each regional section

Bradfield | **Curlews**

 AS

Enjoy England ★★★★

Open: All year

Rooms per night:
s: £60.00-£70.00
d: £70.00-£95.00
Shop: 1 mile
Pub: <0.5 miles

Station Road, Bradfield, Manningtree CO11 2UP
t 01255 870890 **e** margherita@curlewsaccommodation.co.uk
curlewsaccommodation.co.uk   **3C2**

Experience accommodation at its best. Luxury double and twin B&B rooms plus customised self-catering disabled suite to NAS M2 standard. Most rooms with views over the Stour estuary and farmland.

Location: Take A120 towards Harwich turning left at Horsley Cross onto B1035. Turn right at TV mast $1\frac{1}{2}$ miles to Curlews.

Access:
🅷 ⚒ ♿
General:
🐴 🍳 P♿ ✿ ♿
Room:
♿ 🛏 📺 📺 S ☕

Brentwood | **Holiday Inn Brentwood**

AA   ★★★

Brook Street, Brentwood, Essex CM14 5NF
t 0871 942 9012 **e** reservations-brentwoodm25@ihg.com
holiday-inn.co.uk

Access: abc ⚒ ♿ ☺ ♿♿ General: 🐴 🍳 ✕ 🍷 P♿ ✿ ⊡ ♿ Room: ♿ S ☕

Clacton-on-Sea | **Comfort Hotel**

6-8 Marine Parade West, Clacton-on-Sea, Essex CO15 1RD
t 01255 422716
choicehotelseurope.com

Clacton-On-Sea | **Groomhill**

Units: 1   Sleeps: 7
Open: All year

Low season p/w:
£240.00
High season p/w:
£540.00

Livability Self Catering Holidays, PO Box 36, Cowbridge, Vale of Glamorgan CF71 7TN   **t** 08456 584478 **f** 01446 775060
e selfcatering@livability.org.uk
livability.org.uk   **3B3**

Our adapted 3 bedroom bungalow is set in a quiet part of Clacton-on-Sea.

Access: 🅷 ☺ General: 🐴 S Unit: ♿ 🏊 🛏 ♿ 📺 📺 S ♿ ✿

Mersea Island | **Waldegraves Holiday Park**

AA ★★★★
Enjoy England ★★★★

Units: 22   Sleeps: 1-6
Open: March - November

Low season p/w:
£220.00
High season p/w:
£450.00
Shop: <0.5 miles
Pub: <0.5 miles

Mersea Island, Colchester, Essex CO5 8SE
t 01206 382898 **e** holidays@waldegraves.co.uk
waldegraves.co.uk

3B3

22 luxury holiday homes, wheelchair friendly, available to hire for week, midweek and weekend breaks. This is fully self catering consisting of 2 bedrooms, sleeps 5, lounge, dining area, wc & shower. Level grassed camping and caravan pitches available.

Location: B1025 to Mersea, take left towards East Mersea. Take second turning on right follow tourist board signs to Waldegraves.

Access:
🖨 ✕ ♿
General:
🛏 📠 P S
Unit:
♿ 🛁 ♿ ♿ ♿

Hemel Hempstead | **Holiday Inn Hemel Hempstead**   **AS**

AA ★★★
Breakspear Way, Hemel Hempstead, Hertfordshire HP2 4UA
t 0871 942 9041 **e** hemelhempsteadm1@ihg.com
holidayinn.co.uk

Access: ∴ abc 🖨 🏃 ☺ ♿ General: 🛏 🍴 ✕ ♟ P ✿ ☒ ♿ Room: ♿ 🍵

St Albans | **Holiday Inn Luton South**

London Road, Markyate, Nr Luton, AL3 8HH
t 01582 449988 **e** hiluton@qmh-hotels.com
holidayinn.com/luton-sthm1j9

Access: 🖨 ☺ ♿ General: 🛏 🍴 ✕ ♟ P ✿ ☒ ♿ Room: ♿ 🍵

Bacton | **Primrose Cottage**

Enjoy England ★★★

Units: 1   Sleeps: 6

Low season p/w:
£374.00
High season p/w:
£622.00

Mr & Mrs Allan Epton, Primrose Cottage, Cable Gap Holiday Park, Coast Road, Bacton, Norfolk NR12 0EW
t 01692 650667 **e** holiday@cablegap.co.uk
cablegap.co.uk

3C1

2 bedroom bungalow in Bacton. Double glazed, centrally heated. Open plan living area. Wet Room.

Access: ♿ General: 🛏 📠 P S Unit: ♿ 🏃 ♿ ♿ S ♿

Beeston | **Holmdene Farm**

Enjoy England ★★★

Units: 1   Sleeps: 1-8

Low season p/w:
£300.00
High season p/w:
£650.00

Mrs Gaye Davidson, Holmdene Farm, Syers Lane, Beeston, King's Lynn PE32 2NJ   **t** 01328 701284   **e** holmdenefarm@farmersweekly.net

holmdenefarm.co.uk   **3B1**

Our two cottages, Stables and Oat Store, are both converted from traditional farm buildings.

Access: ✶✶ ♿ General: ⬦P Ⓢ Unit: ♨ 🛏 ♿ 📺 ▯ ♿ ✿

Bircham Newton | **Norfolk Disabled Friendly Cottages**

Units: 8   Sleeps: 4-10
Open: All year

Low season p/w:
£528.00
High season p/w:
£980.00

Mr & Mrs William Bennion, Church Farm, Bircham Newton PE31 6QZ
t 01485 578603   **e** bennion@paston.co.uk

norfolkdisabled-friendlycottages.co.uk/   **3B1**

We provide self catering cottages designed to accommodate both disabled & able-bodied familes and friends.

Access: Ⓗ abc ✶✶ 🚽 ♿ General: ⬦📺P Ⓢ Unit: ♨ 📺 🛏 ♿ 📺 📺 Ⓢ ♿ ✿

Cromer | **Seacroft Caravan Club Site** ᴛʜᴇ CARAVAN CLUB

Enjoy England ★★★★★

🚐 (130)
               £15.90–£31.20
🚐 (130)
               £15.90–£31.20
⛺ (30)

130 touring pitches
Open: 25 March - 2 January 2012

Shop: 1 mile

Access:
Ⓗ ✶✶ 🚽 😊 ♿
General:
📺 📺 🔥 🚗 ☺ 🍴 ♿ ✕

Pitch:
🚐 🚐 ⛺

Runton Road, Cromer, Norfolk NR27 9NJ
t 01263 514938

caravanclub.co.uk   **3C1**

Ideal site for a family holiday with leisure complex including bar, restaurant, entertainment plus an outdoor heated swimming pool. The surrounding area offers plenty to attract all ages, including golf, sea and fresh water fishing and birdwatching.

Location: Turn left off A149 (Cromer-Sheringham). Site entrance on left in 1 mile.

Diss | Ivy House Farm Cottages (Owl Cottage)

Enjoy England ★★★★
Units: 1 Sleeps: 1-7
Open: All year

Low season p/w:
£605.00
High season p/w:
£1100.00

Mr. Paul Bradley, Wortham, Diss, Norfolk IP22 1RD
t 01379 898395 **e** prjsbrad@aol.com
ivyhousefarmcottages.co.uk

3B2

The lounge and bedroom open by french windows onto the garden that surrounds Owl Cottage.

Access: 🚶 General: 🐴📻P⑤ Unit: ♨♨♿📺🚾♿❀

Diss | Norfolk Cottages (Bluebell Cottage)

Enjoy England ★★★★
Units: 4 Sleeps: 2-8
Open: All year

Low season p/w:
£446.00
High season p/w:
£767.00

Mrs Cathy Smith, Malthouse Farm, Malthouse Lane, Gissing, Norfolk IP22 5UT **t** 01379 658021 **e** bookings@norfolkcottages.net
norfolkcottages.net

3B2

Converted from the original dairy Bluebell offers light and spacious accommodation throughout and is one of four cottages and leisure building set around a courtyard. Can be hired together with Primrose to create a larger cottage via an interconnecting door.

Access:
🅰🐾☺🚾
General:
🐴📻P⑤
Unit:
♨♨♿📺🚾♿❀

Diss | **Norfolk Cottages (Honeysuckle Cottage)**

 AS

Enjoy England ★★★★
Units: 4   Sleeps: 2-8
Open: All year

Low season p/w:
£793.00
High season p/w:
£1346.00

Mrs Cathy Smith, Malthouse Farm, Malthouse Lane, Gissing, Norfolk
IP22 5UT   **t** 01379 658021   **e** bookings@norfolkcottages.net
norfolkcottages.net   **3B2**

Converted two storey old granary. Honeysuckle offers spacious family accommodation and is one of four cottages and leisure building set around a courtyard. A tracked hoist and steps give full access to both pool and spa in the leisure building.

Access:
🅗 🐾 ☺ ♿
General:
☼ 🗄 P Ⓢ
Unit:
🛏 🏠 ♿ 🖥 📺 🚿 ✿

Diss | **Norfolk Cottages (Primrose Cottage)**

AS

Enjoy England ★★★★
Units: 4   Sleeps: 2-8
Open: All year

Low season p/w:
£446.00
High season p/w:
£767.00

Mrs Cathy Smith, Malthouse Farm, Malthouse Lane, Gissing, Norfolk
IP22 5UT   **t** 01379 658021   **e** bookings@norfolkcottages.net
norfolkcottages.net   **3B2**

Converted from the original dairy Primrose offers light and spacious accommodation throughout and is one of four cottages and leisure building set around a courtyard. Can be hired together with Bluebell to create a larger cottage via an interconnecting door.

Access:
🅗 🐾 ☺ ♿
General:
☼ 🗄 P Ⓢ
Unit:
🛏 🏠 ♿ 🖥 📺 🚿 ✿

Diss | Norfolk Cottages (Rose Cottage)

Enjoy England ★★★★
Units: 4 Sleeps: 2-8
Open: All year

Low season p/w:
£793.00
High season p/w:
£1346.00

Mrs Cathy Smith, Malthouse Farm, Malthouse Lane, Gissing, Norfolk
IP22 5UT **t** 01379 658021 **e** bookings@norfolkcottages.net
norfolkcottages.net   **3B2**

Sensitively restored oak barn Rose offers light and spacious accommodation and is one of four cottages and leisure building set around a courtyard. The leisure building has a tracked hoist and steps giving full access to the pool and spa.

Access:

General:

Unit:

East Harling | Berwick Cottage

Enjoy England ★★★★
Units: 1 Sleeps: 2-6
Open: All year

Low season p/w:
£550.00
High season p/w:
£820.00

Mrs Miriam Toosey, The Lin Berwick Trust, Eastgate House, Upper East Street,
Sudbury CO10 1UB **t** 01787 372343 **e** info@thelinberwicktrust.org.uk
thelinberwicktrust.org.uk   **3B2**

Berwick Cottage offers exceptional self-catering accommodation for the severely disabled, their families and carers.

Access: .: ⓗ abc   General: Unit:

Edgefield, (Near Holt) | Wood Farm Cottages

Enjoy England ★★★★
Units: 8 Sleeps: 2-6
Open: All year

Low season p/w:
£200.00
High season p/w:
£815.00

Mrs Diana Jacob, Wood Farm Cottages, Wood Farm, Plumstead Road, Edgefield,
Melton Constable NR24 2AQ **t** 01263 587347 **e** info@wood-farm.com
wood-farm.com   **3B1**

Near Holt, well equipped converted barns and stables, original features. Internet access. Graded 4 Star.

Access: abc General: Unit:

Great Snoring | Vine Park Cottage B & B

Enjoy England ★★★★

Open: All year except Xmas and New Year

Rooms per night:
s: £40.00-£50.00
d: £60.00-£70.00

Thursford Road, Great Snoring, Fakenham, Norfolk NR21 0PF
t 01328 821016 **e** rita@vineparkcottagebandb.co.uk
vineparkcottagebandb.co.uk

3B1

Set on an arable farm, 4 star silver award Bed & Breakfast accommodation.

Access: ✺ ♿ General: ⛖ **P** ♿ ✿ ♿ Room: ♿ ♨ ♨ 📺 WC ⑤ ♨

Happisburgh | Boundary Stables

Enjoy England ★★★★

Units: 4   Sleeps: 1-6
Open: All year

Low season p/w:
£230.00
High season p/w:
£771.00

Mr & Mrs Julian & Elizabeth Burns, Boundary Stables, Grub Street, Happisburgh, Mundesley NR12 0RX   **t** 01692 650171
e bookings@boundarystables.co.uk
boundarystables.co.uk

3C1

Recently converted stables provide excellent accommodation in a rural setting. All are single storey.

General: 🐴 **P** ⑤ Unit: ♿ ♨ ♿ 📺 WC ♿ ✿

Horning, Norfolk Broads. | King Line Cottages

Enjoy England ★★★-★★★★

Units: 5   Sleeps: 4-9
Open: All year except Xmas and New Year

Low season p/w:
£315.00
High season p/w:
£1897.00
Shop: 0.5 miles

Mr Robert King, Ferry Road, Horning, Norfolk NR12 8PS
t 01692 630297 **e** info@norfolk-broads.co.uk
norfolk-broads.co.uk

3C1

King Line Cottages, English Tourist Board 4 star rated, consists of six holiday homes, overlooking one of the most picturesque parts of the River Bure at Horning Ferry. These cottages have been awarded an English Tourist Board accessibility rating 1&2.

Location: Norwich ringroad A1042, left A1151 through Wroxham, right turn onto A1062 to Horning. Right into Lower Street, right Ferry Road.

Access:
♨ ☺
General:
🐴 **P**
Unit:
♿ ♨ ♿ 📺 WC ♿ ✿

Hunstanton | Caley Hall Hotel

 **AS**

AA	★★★
Enjoy England	★★★

Open: Not Xmas & New Year

Rooms per night:
s: £50.00-£200.00
d: £80.00-£200.00
p/p half board:
d: £75.00-£125.00
Meals: £20.00-£30.00

Old Hunstanton Road, Old Hunstanton, Hunstanton PE36 6HH
t 01485 533486 **e** mail@caleyhallhotel.co.uk
caleyhallhotel.co.uk

3B1

The bar, restaurant and chalet style rooms have been converted from 17thC farm buildings.

Access: abc ⚐ 🐾 🏛 ♿ General: 🛋 🍴 ✕ ♟ P♿ ❀ ♿ Room: 🛏 🎷 📺 wc 🅂 ☕

Norwich | Holiday Inn Express Norwich

AS

Drayton High Road, Hellesdon, Norwich NR6 5DU
t 01603 780 010 **e** sales@exhinorwich.co.uk
exhinorwich.co.uk

Access: abc ⚐ 🐾 🏛 ☺ ♿ wc ♿ General: 🛋 ✕ ♟ P♿ ❀ ➕ ♿ Room: 🛏 🎷 📺 🅂 ☕ ♨

Norwich | Holiday Inn Norwich

AS

AA ★★★

Ipswich Road, Norwich, Norfolk NR4 6EP
t 0871 942 9060 **e** reservations-norwich@ichotelsgroup.com
holiday-inn.co.uk

Access: abc ⚐ ☺ ♿ wc ♿ General: 🛋 🎷 ✕ ♟ P♿ ❀ ♿ Room: 🛏 🅂 ☕ ♨

Norwich | Spixworth Hall Cottages

AS

Enjoy England ★★★★

Units: 8 Sleeps: 4-12
Open: All year

Low season p/w:
£200.00
High season p/w:
£1250.00

Mrs Sheelah Cook, Spixworth Hall Cottages, Grange Farm, Buxton Road, Spixworth, Norwich, Norfolk NR10 3PR **t** 01603 898190
e hallcottages@btinternet.com
hallcottages.co.uk

3C1

Quality cottages near Norwich and Broads with log fires and space to relax and unwind.

Access: abc 🏛 ☺ General: 🛋 🖥 P 🅂 Unit: 🛏 🖥 🎷 ♿ 📺 wc 🅂 ☕ ♿ ❀

Sandringham | **Park House Hotel** ♿ AS

Enjoy England ★★

Open: All year

Rooms per night:
s: £110.00–£158.00
d: £186.00–£288.00
p/p half board:
d: £108.00–£173.00
Meals: £15.00–£17.50
Shop: 1.5 miles
Pub: 1.5 miles

Access:
.: 🅷 abc ▨ ✯ 🛆 ☺ ♿ ⓦⒸ
⅘

General:
🍳 ✕ ⚱ 🄿 ✿ 🖭 ♿

Room:
🛏 🔥 📻 📺 🅂 ☕

Sandringham PE35 6EH
t 01485 543000 **e** parkinfo@lcdisability.org
parkhousehotel.org.uk   **3B1**

Located on the Royal Sandringham Estate, the hotel has 8 single and 8 twin rooms and is adapted for people with mobility difficulties/ disabilities with or without carers/ companions. The hotel is fully accessible and care is available if required.

Location: From King's Lynn, A149 to Hunstanton, follow tourist signs to Sandringham. Hotel is on RHS, just before Sandringham Visitor Centre.

Sandringham | **The Sandringham Estate Caravan Club Site** THE CARAVAN CLUB AS

Enjoy England ★★★★★

🚐 (136)
        £16.40–£29.30
�caravan (136)
        £16.40–£29.30
136 touring pitches
Open: All year

Shop: 1 mile
Pub: 1 mile

Access:
🅰 ✯ 🛆 ☺ ♿ⓦⒸ

General:
🔲 🔳 🔈 🚗 ⊕ 🔶 ⚑ 🆆🅿

Pitch:
🚐 �caravan

Glucksburg Woods, Sandringham, Norfolk PE35 6EZ
t 01553 631614
caravanclub.co.uk   **3B1**

Set in the heart of the Royal Estate. Take a walk to Sandringham House, the famous residence of the Royal Family and enjoy the Country Park – kids will love the nature trails, land train ride and adventure playground.

Location: A149 from King's Lynn (Hunstanton). Right onto B1439 (West Newton). Site on left after 0.5 miles.

Thetford | **Next Door at Magdalen House**

Enjoy England ★★★★

Units: 1   Sleeps: 1-2
Open: All year

Low season p/w:
£300.00
High season p/w:
£450.00

Keith & Lorna Cootes, Magdalen House, 18 Buntings Lane, Methwold,
Thetford, Norfolk IP26 4PR   **t** 01366 727255   **e** k.cootes@btconnect.com
magdalenhouse.co.uk   **3B2**

Luxury apartment for two in peaceful surroundings. 4
star rated, access level 2, see website.

Access: ✖ ⬛ General: ⬛P⬛ Unit: ⬛⬛⬛⬛⬛⬛⬛⬛⬛

Wendling | **Greenbanks**

 **AS**

Enjoy England ★★★★

Open: All year except Xmas
and New Year

Rooms per night:
s: £89.00-£109.00
d: £120.00-£200.00
p/p half board:
d: £84.00-£124.00
Meals: £23.00-£30.00

Greenbanks, Wendling, Dereham NR19 2NA
t 01362 687742   **e** info@greenbankshotel.co.uk
greenbankshotel.co.uk   **3B1**

Spacious, ground floor suites 2-6
guests in serviced and self-catering
accommodation, overlooking lakes.
Free view TV, level wet-room, onsite
restaurant using local produce, and
hydrotherapy pool. Exceptional
central location for Norwich, Coast
or the Broads. Family and Pet
friendly.

Location: Greenbanks is equidistant
Dereham and Swaffham, just off the
A47,the Wendling turn off. Satellite
navigation use the postcode: NR19
2NA.

Access:
✖⬛⬛
General:
⬛⬛✖⬛P⬛⬛⬛
Room:
⬛⬛⬛⬛⬛

Wroxham | **Meadow Brown Cottage**

AS

Units: 1   Sleeps: 1-5
Open: All year

Low season p/w:
£300.00
High season p/w:
£600.00

Mr Alfred Levy, Meadow Brown Cottage, 6 Ruston Reaches, Chapel Road,
East Ruston, Norwich NR12 9AA   **t** 07785273763   **e** sue@levy1.plus.com
meadowbrowncottage.com   **3C1**

Delightful, totally refurbished end of terrace cottage
with beautiful views over garden and fishing lake.

General: ⬛⬛P⬛ Unit: ⬛⬛

Beccles | **The Lodge**

Enjoy England ★★★★

Units: 1 Sleeps: 1-3
Open: All year

Low season p/w:
£375.00
High season p/w:
£495.00
Shop: <0.5 miles
Pub: <0.5 miles

Mrs Karen Renilson, Catherine House, 2 Ringsfield Road, Suffolk, Beccles NR34 9PQ **t** 01502 716428 **e** karenrenilson@hotmail.com
catherinehouse.net

3C1

A self catering property. The interior has been designed for wheelchair users and the less mobile. Accessibility rating Level M31. Self Catering Enjoy England 4 Star Gold Award. There is one bedroom with a King Size Bed.

Location: Located on Ringsfield Road, Beccles, Suffolk. 5 minutes walk from Town Centre, 18 miles on the A146 miles from Norwich.

Access:
abc
General:
🐕P⑤
Unit:
🛏🪜♿📺🚾♿ ☘

Ipswich | **Holiday Inn Ipswich**

Open: All year

London Road, Ipswich, Suffolk IP2 0UA
t 0871 942 9045 **e** reservations.ipswich@ihg.com
holidayinn.co.uk

Access: abc 🖉 🐕🪑♿ | General: 🐕🍽✕🍷P♿ ❄⊞♿ | Room: 🛏☕

Join today!

Lowestoft | Pakefield Caravan Park

Enjoy England ★★★★

🚐 (361)

🚐 (12)
£17.00–£20.00

🏠 (12)
£125.00–£535.00

385 touring pitches
Open: 1st March - 30th November

Shop: <0.5 miles
Pub: 0.5 miles

Access:
🅰 H abc 🎨 🐾 🛢 ☺ 🚾 ♿

General:
🔲 ⛏ 🕯 🔌 📂 ♀ WP ✕

Pitch:
🚐 🏠 🚐

Arbor Lane, Pakefield, Lowestoft NR33 7BQ
t 01502 561136 **e** enquiries@pakefieldpark.co.uk
pakefieldpark.co.uk

3C1

Pakefield Caravan Park is a level and accessible site situated within close proximity of the beach and the local shops. The park offers comfortable holiday accommodation with a layout suitable for some disabled customers. Further details available on request.

Location: 2 miles south of Lowestoft off main A12. Look out for main brown tourist signs.

Nayland | Gladwins Farm Self Catering Cottages

Enjoy England
★★★★-★★★★★

Units: 8   Sleeps: 2-8
Open: All year

Low season p/w:
£290.00
High season p/w:
£1995.00

Mrs Susie Bradshaw, Harpers Hill, Nayland, Colchester CO6 4NU
t 01206 262261 **e** contact@gladwinsfarm.co.uk
gladwinsfarm.co.uk

3B2

In Suffolk's Constable Country with marvellous views and fishing. Not far from the sea.

Access: 🐾🛢☺ **General:** 🛏🖥P⑤ **Unit:** 🛏⚫🚾⑤♿❀

Wattisfield | Jayes Holiday Cottages

Enjoy England ★★★

Units: 2   Sleeps: 2-4
Open: All year

Low season p/w:
£205.00
High season p/w:
£400.00

Mrs Denise Williams, Walsham Road, Wattisfield, Diss IP22 1NZ
t 01359 251255 **e** info@jayesholidaycottages.co.uk
jayesholidaycottages.co.uk

3B2

Set in quiet countryside, our specially adapted cottages overlook a large pond with fishing facilities.

Access: 🐾 **General:** 🛏P⑤ **Unit:** 🛏🖥🔥⚫📶🚾⑤♿❀

Cambridgeshire

LITTLE DOWNHAM

Wood Fen Lodge
Wood Fen Lodge, 6 Black Bank Road, Little Downham, Ely
CB6 2UA
t 01353 862495   **e** info@woodfenlodge.co.uk
w woodfenlodge.co.uk

WISBECH ST. MARY

Common Right Barns
Mrs Teresa Fowler, Common Right Barns, Plash Drove,
Tholomas Drove, Peterborough PE13 4SP
t 01945 410424   **e** teresa@commonrightbarns.co.uk
w commonrightbarns.co.uk

Essex

ASHDON

Hill Farm Holiday Cottages
Mrs Annette Bel, Hill Farm Holiday Cottages, Radwinter
Road, Ashdon, Saffron Walden CB10 2ET
t 01799 584881
e hillfarm-holiday-cottages@hotmail.co.uk
w hillfarm-holiday-cottages.co.uk

CHELMSFORD

Boswell House Hotel
118/120 Springfield Road, Chelmsford CM2 6LF
t 01245 287587   **e** boswell118@aol.com
w boswellhousehotel.co.uk

HALSTEAD

The White Hart
15 High Street, Halstead CO9 2AA
t 01787 475657   **w** innpubs.co.uk

ST OSYTH

The Cartlodge at Lee Wick Farm
Mr Robert Clarke, The Cartlodge, The Barn, Lee Wick Lane,
St Osyth, Clacton-on-Sea CO16 8ES
t 01255 823031   **e** info@leewickfarm.co.uk
w leewickfarm.co.uk

WALTON-ON-THE-NAZE

Bufo Villae Guest House
31 Beatrice Road, Walton-on-the-Naze, Frinton-on-Sea
CO14 8HJ
t 01255 672644   **e** bufovillae@btinternet.com
w bufovillae.co.uk

Hertfordshire

CHESHUNT

YHA Lee Valley Village
Windmill Lane, Cheshunt, Waltham Cross EN8 9AJ
t 01992 628392   **e** leevalley@yha.org.uk
w yha.org.uk

Norfolk

AYLMERTON

Roman Camp Inn
Holt Road, Aylmerton, Sheringham NR11 8QD
t 01263 838291   **e** enquiries@romancampinn.co.uk
w romancampinn.co.uk

BACTON

Castaways Holiday Park
Paston Road, Bacton-on-Sea, North Walsham NR12 0JB
t 01692 650436   **e** castaways.bacton@hotmail.co.uk

BURGH ST. PETER

Waveney River Centre
Staithe Road, Burgh St. Peter, Beccles NR34 0BT
t 01502 677343   **e** info@waveneyrivercentre.co.uk
w waveneyrivercentre.co.uk

DEREHAM

Moor Farm Stable Cottages
Paul Davis, Moor Farm Stable Cottages, Moor Farm, Foxley,
Fakenham NR20 4QP
t 01362 688523   **e** mail@moorfarmstablecottages.co.uk
w moorfarmstablecottages.co.uk

EAST RUNTON

Incleborough House
Lower Common, East Runton, Cromer NR27 9PG
t 01263 515939   **e** enquiries@incleboroughhouse.co.uk
w incleboroughhouse.co.uk

FRITTON

Fritton Lake Woodland Lodge Holiday Park
Mr Brian Humphrey, Fritton Lake Country World, Beccles
Road, Fritton, Great Yarmouth NR31 9HA
t 01493 488208   **w** great-yarmouth.angle.uk.com/attra
ctions/frittonlake.cgi

GISSING

Norfolk Cottages
Mrs Cathy Smith, Norfolk Cottages, 17 Owen Road, Diss
IP22 4ER
t 01379 658021   **e** bookings@norfolkcottages.net
w norfolkcottages.net

HAPPISBURGH

Church Farm Barns
Norfolk Country Cottages, Carlton House, Market Place,
Reepham, Norwich NR10 4JJ
t 01603 871872   **e** info@norfolkcottages.co.uk
w norfolkcottages.co.uk

HEACHAM

Oakhill
Mrs Sandra Hohol, Birds Norfolk Holiday Homes, 62
Westgate, Hunstanton PE36 5EL
t 01485 534267   **f** 01485 535230
e shohol@birdsnorfolkholidayhomes.co.uk
w norfolkholidayhomes-birds.co.uk

HUNSTANTON

Foxgloves Cottage
Terry & Lesley Heade, Foxgloves Cottage, 29 Avenue Road,
Hunstanton PE36 5BW
t 01485 532460   **e** deepdenehouse@btopenworld.com
w foxglovescottage.co.uk

KELLING

The Pheasant Hotel
Coast Road, Kelling, Blakeney NR25 7EG
t 01263 588382
e enquiries@pheasanthotelnorfolk.co.uk
w pheasanthotelnorfolk.co.uk

LITTLE SNORING

Jex's Farm Barn
Stephen & Lynn Harvey, Jex's Farm Barn, Jex Farm, Little
Snoring, Fakenham NR21 0JJ
t 01328 878257
e farmerstephen@jexfarm.wanadoo.co.uk
w jexfarm.co.uk

MUNDESLEY

Overcliff Lodge
46 Cromer Road, Mundesley NR11 8DB
t 01263 720016   **e** enquiries@overclifflodge.co.uk
w overclifflodge.co.uk

SANDRINGHAM (6 MILES)

Oyster House
Lynn Road, West Rudham PE31 8RW
t 01485 528327   **e** oyster-house@tiscali.co.uk
w oysterhouse.co.uk

SHERINGHAM

Sheringham YHA
1 Cremers Drift, Sheringham NR26 8HX
t 0870 770 6024   **e** sheringham@yha.org.uk
w yha.org.uk

TITCHWELL

Titchwell Manor Hotel
Titchwell, King's Lynn PE31 8BB
t 01485 210221   **e** margaret@titchwellmanor.com
w titchwellmanor.com

TRIMINGHAM

Woodland Leisure Park
Church Street, Trimingham, Norwich NR11 8AL
t 01263 579208   **e** info@woodland-park.co.uk
w woodland-park.co.uk

WELLS-NEXT-THE-SEA

Wells-next-the-Sea YHA
Church Plain, Wells-next-the-Sea NR23 1EQ
t 01328 711748   **e** wellsnorfolk@yha.org.uk
w yha.org.uk

Suffolk

ALDEBURGH

Brudenell Hotel
The Parade, Aldeburgh IP15 5BU
t 01728 452071   **e** info@brudenellhotel.co.uk
w brudenellhotel.co.uk

BLAXHALL

Blaxhall YHA
Heath Walk, Blaxhall, Woodbridge IP12 2EA
t 01728 688206   **e** blaxhall@yha.org.uk
w yha.org.uk

CARLTON COLVILLE

Ivy House Country Hotel
Ivy Lane, Beccles Road, Lowestoft NR33 8HY
t 01502 501353
e reception@ivyhousecountryhotel.co.uk
w ivyhousecountryhotel.co.uk

COMBS

Jackbridge Cottage
Ian & Teresa Pemberton, Jackbridge Cottage, Jacks Lane,
Great Finborough, Stowmarket IP14 2NQ
t 01449 672177
e pembertons@jackbridgefarm.plus.com

COTTON

Coda Cottages
Mrs Kate Sida-Nicholls, 2 Park Farm, Dandy Corner
IP14 4QX
t 01449 780076   **e** codacottages@dandycorner.co.uk
w codacottages.co.uk

CRATFIELD

School Farm Cottages
Mrs Claire Sillett, School Farm Cottages, Church Road,
Cratfield, Halesworth IP19 0HU
t 01986 798844   **e** schoolfarmcotts@aol.com
w schoolfarmcottages.com

EDWARDSTONE

Sherbourne Farm Lodge Cottages
Mrs Anne Suckling, Sherbourne Farm Lodge Cottages,
Sherbourne House Farm, Edwardstone, Sudbury CO10 5PD
t 01787 210885
e enquiries@sherbournelodgecottages.co.uk
w sherbournelodgecottages.co.uk

HALESWORTH

Old Stables
Mr Geoffrey Kiddy, A E Kiddy & Son, Wissett Lodge, Lodge
Lane, Halesworth IP19 0JQ
t 01986 873173   **f** 01986 873173
e mail@wissettlodge.co.uk
w wissettlodge.co.uk

HAUGHLEY

Red House Farm Cottages
Mrs Mary Noy, Red House Farm, Station Road, Haughley,
Stowmarket IP14 3QP
t 01449 673323

HENLEY

Damerons Farm Holidays
Mr & Mrs Wayne & Sue Leggett, Damerons Farm Holidays,
Main Road, Henley, Ipswich IP6 0RU
t 01473 832454   **e** info@dameronsfarmholidays.co.uk
w dameronsfarmholidays.co.uk

HITCHAM

The White Horse Inn
The Street, Hitcham, Ipswich IP7 7NQ
t 01449 740981   **e** lewis@thewhitehorse.wanadoo.co.uk
w thewhitehorsehitcham.co.uk

LOWESTOFT

Hotel Victoria
Kirkley Cliff, Lowestoft NR33 0BY
t 01502 574433   **e** info@thehotelvictoria.co.uk
w thehotelvictoria.co.uk

MICKFIELD

Read Hall Cottage
Mr & Mrs Andrew & Andrea Stewart, Read Hall Cottage,
Read Hall, Mickfield, Stowmarket IP14 5LU
t 01449 711366   **e** info@readhall.co.uk
w readhall.co.uk

MIDDLEWOOD GREEN

Leys Farmhouse Annexe
Mrs Heather Trevorrow, Blacksmith's Lane, Middlewood
Green, Earl Stonham, Stowmarket IP14 5EU
t 01449 711750   **e** leysfarmhouse@btinternet.com
w leysfarmhouseannexe.co.uk

SAXMUNDHAM

Bluebell, Bonny, Buttercup & Bertie
Mrs Margaret Gray, Park Farm, Sibton, Saxmundham
IP17 2LZ
t 01728 668324   **e** mail@sibtonparkfarm.co.uk
w sibtonparkfarm.co.uk

SOUTHWOLD

Newlands Country House
72 Halesworth Road, Reydon, Southwold IP18 6NS
t 01502 722164   **e** info@newlandsofsouthwold.co.uk
w newlandsofsouthwold.co.uk

The Plough Inn
London Road, Wangford, Southwold NR34 8AZ
t 01502 578239

SWILLAND

Swilland Mill
Mr J Wright, Swilland Mill, High Road, Swilland IP6 9LW
t 01473 785122

Suffolk

WALBERSWICK

Cranborne
Mrs Rebecca Meo, Acanthus Property Letting Services, 9 Trinity St, Southwold IP18 6JA
t 01502 724033   **e** websales@southwold-holidays.co.uk
w southwold-holidays.co.uk

WATTISHAM

Wattisham Hall Holiday Cottages
Mr & Mrs Jeremy & Jo Squirrell, Wattisham Hall Holiday Cottages, Wattisham Hall, Wattisham, Ipswich IP7 7JX
t 01449 740240   **e** enquiries@wattishamhall.co.uk
w wattishamhall.co.uk

WICKHAM SKEITH

Netus Barn
Ms Joy Homan, Netus Barn, Street Farm, Wickham Skeith, Eye IP23 8LP
t 01449 766275   **e** joygeoff@homansf.freeserve.co.uk
w netusbarn.co.uk

Where to Go

Luton | **Wrest Park**

Open: For opening hours and prices, please call 0870 333 1181 or visit www.english-heritage.org.uk/properties

Silsoe, Luton, Bedfordshire MK45 4HS
t 0870 333 1181   **e** customers@english-heritage.org.uk
english-heritage.org.uk/wrestpark

With acres of breathtaking landscape, take a stroll, let the children play or simply relax.

Access: ◻ ᕵ General: ₽ᕵ ◻ ✿

Saffron Walden | **Audley End House & Gardens**

Open: For opening hours and prices, please call 0870 333 1181 or visit www.english-heritage.org.uk/properties

Audley End, Saffron Walden, Essex CB11 4JF
t 0870 333 1181   **e** customers@english-heritage.org.uk
english-heritage.org.uk/audleyend

Experience working kitchens and a fantastic day out, in one of England's grandest country homes.

Access: ᕵ^{wc} ᕵ ᕵ ᕵ^G General: ₽ᕵ ◻ ✿

Framlingham | **Framlingham Castle**

Open: For opening hours and prices, please call 0870 333 1181 or visit www.english-heritage.org.uk/properties

Framlingham, Suffolk IP13 9BP
t 0870 333 1181   **e** customers@english-heritage.org.uk
english-heritage.org.uk/framlinghamcastle

Get active, take the wall walk, see breathtaking views, relax and picnic in the grounds.

Access: ∴ ◻ ᕵ^G General: ◻ ✿

Where to Eat

Clacton-on-Sea | **Pizza Express**

2 Marine Parade West, Clacton-on-Sea, Essex CO15 1RH
t 01255 423248
pizzaexpress.com

General: 🐕 @FAX 🚶 👤 WC ♿ 🚶♿ P⭐ .:🎵

Clacton-on-Sea | **Prezzo**

4 Marine Parade West, Clacton-on-Sea, Essex CO15 1QZ
t 01255 223894 **e** prezzo289@prezzoplc.co.uk
prezzoplc.co.uk

General: 🐕 @FAX 🚲 👤 P⭐

Harwich | **Pier at Harwich**

The Quay, Harwich, Essex CO12 3HH
t 01255 241212 **e** nick@milsomhotels.com
milsomhotels.com

General: 🐕 @FAX 🚲 🚶 👤 WC ♿ 🚶♿ P⭐⭐⭐

St Albans | **Darcy's**

2 Hatfield Road, St Albans, Hertfordshire AL1 3RP
t 01727 730777 **e** info@darcysrestaurant.co.uk
darcysrestaurant.co.uk

General: 🐕 @FAX 🚲 🚶 👤 WC ♿ 🚶♿

Wheathampstead | **Wicked Lady**

15 Nomansland, Wheathampstead, Hertfordshire AL4 8EL
t 01582 832128
thewickedladypub.co.uk

General: 🐕 🚲 🚶 👤 WC 🚶♿ P⭐⭐⭐

Norwich | **Ha! Ha! Bar & Canteen**

29 Tomband, Norwich, Norfolk NR3 1RE
t 01603 621223 **e** haha.norwich@arestaurantgroup.com
hahaonline.co.uk

General: 🐕 @FAX 🚶 👤 WC 🚶♿ abc

Norwich | **Rocco's**

86-88 Prince of Wales Road, Norwich, Norfolk NR1 1NJ
t 01603 624000
roccosnorwich.com

General: 🐕 @FAX 🚶 👤 WC ♿ 🚶

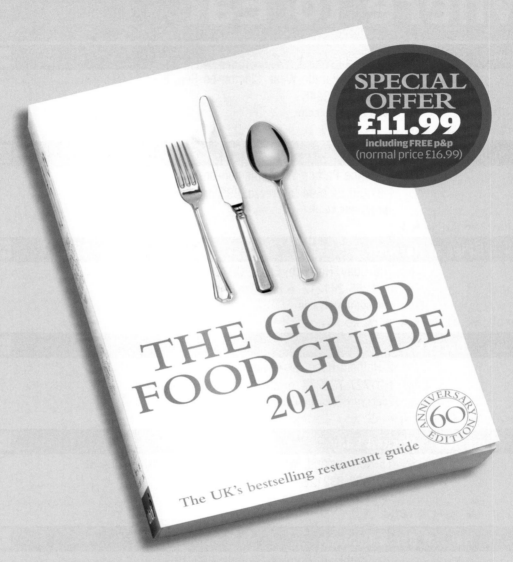

SPECIAL
OFFER
£11.99
including FREE p&p
(normal price £16.99)

THE GOOD
FOOD GUIDE
2011

60 ANNIVERSARY EDITION

The UK's bestselling restaurant guide

**To order your copy of *The Good Food Guide 2011* at
the special offer price of £11.99 including FREE p&p
(normal price £16.99), please call 01992 822800
and quote GFGV11.**

Offer is valid to 31 December 2011.

ISBN: 978 1 84490 195 1 | 624 pages | Full colour, including maps for each region

Park House

Located on the Royal Sandringham estate near King's Lynn in West Norfolk and operated by the charity Leonard Cheshire Disability.

The hotel offers a holiday experience for people with mobility difficulties or disabilities, with or without their carer or companion. The hotel's in-house care team, headed by a registered nurse, ensures that everyone has a break.

Park House is an impressive Victorian country house set in its own grounds amidst the soaring trees and rolling parklands of the Estate. The main house itself was the birthplace of Princess Diana and was made available to the charity by Her Majesty the Queen in 1987.

Experienced nurses and care staff are on hand, if required, 24 hours a day. Whether it is a helping hand getting in and out of bed, 'peace of mind' or full nursing care, the hotel is able to accommodate most requirements.

Equipped to the very highest of standards, all 16 bedrooms (8 single and 8 twins) are en-suite and most are provided with a digital TV, radio, a direct dial telephone and tea & coffee making facilities. The main reception rooms and all of the bedrooms have been refurbished to a very high standard and the spacious conservatory provides a social meeting place at the very heart of the building.

Lifts, ramps and automatic doors provide easy wheelchair access and all bedrooms and bathrooms have been specially equipped, some with overhead hoists and electronic controls to doors.

Facilities within the hotel include a shop, a well-stocked library with talking/large print books, complimentary broadband enabled computer system. Most evenings there is some form of optional entertainment.

The picturesque grounds at Park House are fully accessible and a heated outdoor swimming pool with Arjo hoist is also available between May and September

A fully optional program of escorted excursions are organised to the un-spoilt local countryside, coastline, nature reserves and stately homes that surround Park House.

The Royal residence at Sandringham House is adjacent to the hotel and is also a popular destination, along with the myriad other stately homes within the local area such as Oxborough and Blickling.

All in all, Park House is the ideal country house destination for people with mobility difficulties or disabilities, providing peace of mind and a holiday for everyone.

**Park House Hotel, Sandringham,
King's Lynn, Norfolk PE35 6EH
t 01485 543000 e parkinfo@LCDisability.org
www.parkhousehotel.org.uk**

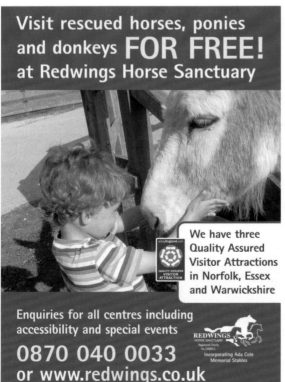

Something for everyone!

Providing a diverse mix of elegant countryside, historic houses, urban cities and modern culture the East Midlands has something for everyone. The region which is made up of six counties – Derbyshire, Leicestershire, Lincolnshire, Northamptonshire, Nottinghamshire and Rutland, is located in the heart of the country and is supported by excellent transport links.

Opened in 2009 **Nottingham Contemporary** is housed in a brand new landmark building designed to reflect Nottingham's lace industry heritage and offers free entry to the four spacious galleries. Just a stones throw away is the **Galleries of Justice**, based in Nottingham's old court house, it offers a range of tours including one of the surrounding Lace Market area that incorporates a number of signposts specifically designed for those with visual impairments.

The regions inspiring landscapes and stately homes which have become a favourite with film makers are also a favourite with visitors. **Chatsworth**, in Derbyshire, which has featured in a number of films including Pride and Prejudice and more recently Wolfman, now offers greater access for all with a new lift and easier entry into the house. Other film locations in the region include **Burghley House**, **Hardwick Hall** and **Lincoln Cathedral.**

Another historic house worth a visit is Lincolnshire's **Doddington Hall and Gardens**. Home to the same family since 1595, the house offers visual tours for those unable to reach the upper floors and a sensory tour of both the house and gardens which includes the opportunity to taste the herbs in the gardens.

Other places of interest include **78 Derngate** in Northampton, an award winning historic house which was remodelled by the world-famous designer and architect, Charles Rennie Mackintosh, and **Bosworth Battlefield Heritage Centre and Country Park**, which relives a famous turning point in British history.

For those visitors who are more interested in adventure, **Sailability** in Northamptonshire provides sailing opportunities for people of all abilities including specially adapted boats for people with limited mobility. While for those looking for something more sedate a visit to **Foxton Locks** in Leicestershire provides the opportunity to view colourful narrowboats as they navigate their way through the famous staircase of locks from the comfort of dry land.

The National Forest in Leicestershire provides the perfect landscape for an adventure. Visitors can explore the forest in a number of ways including via the specially designed walks, such as the **Sence Valley walk** which incorporates audio and visual information boards. And at **Barnsdale Gardens** in Rutland, garden lovers can

Peak District

Chatsworth House

East Midlands

Derbyshire, Leicestershire, Lincolnshire, Northamptonshire, Nottinghamshire

see Britain's largest collection of individually designed gardens, created by television presenters, Geoff Hamilton, for BBC's Gardner's World.

Accommodation

To make the most of a visit to the East Midlands the region offers a selection of accommodation to meet all requirements. For larger groups **imago**, **Burleigh Court,** Loughborough is fully adapted to cater for all guests and recently won gold for 'Access for All' at the National Excellence Awards.

For a secluded break **Elms Farm Cottages** located in the Lincolnshire countryside provides the perfect escape for families or couples and provides easy access to a number of local attractions.

Set in the heart of the **Peak District,** and within easy reach of Chatsworth, **East Lodge Hotel**, which boasts beautiful grounds and an award winning restaurant, offers a luxurious break.

Find out more
www.discovereastmidlands.com

Winnats Pass

Tourist Information Centres

Tourist Information Centres are a mine of information about local and regional accommodation, attractions and events. Visit them when you arrive at your destination or contact them before you go:

Ashbourne	13 Market Place	01335 343666	ashbourneinfo@derbyshiredales.gov.uk
Ashby-De-La-Zouch	North Street	01530 411767	ashby.tic@nwleicestershire.gov.uk
Bakewell	Old Market Hall	01629 813227	bakewell@peakdistrict-npa.gov.uk
Brackley	2 Bridge Street	01280 700111	tic@southnorthants.gov.uk
Brigg	The Buttercross	01652 657053	brigg.tic@northlincs.gov.uk
Buxton	The Crescent	01298 25106	tourism@highpeak.gov.uk
Castleton	Buxton Road	01433 620679	castleton@peakdistrict-npa.gov.uk
Chesterfield	Rykneld Square	01246 345777	tourism@chesterfield.gov.uk
Cleethorpes	42-43 Alexandra Road	01472 323111	cleetic@nelincs.gov.uk
Derby	Assembly Rooms	01332 255802	tourism@derby.gov.uk
Hornsea	120 Newbegin	01964 536404	hornsea.tic@eastriding.gov.uk
Leicester	7/9 Every Street	0906 294 1113	info@goleicestershire.com
Lincoln	9 Castle Hill	01522 873213	tourism@lincoln.gov.uk
Matlock	Crown Square	01629 583388	matlockinfo@derbyshiredales.gov.uk
Northampton	Guildhall Road	01604 838800	northampton.tic@ northamptonshireenterprise.ltd.uk
Nottingham City	1-4 Smithy Row	08444 775 678	tourist.information@nottinghamcity.gov.uk
Ollerton	Sherwood Heath	01623 824545	sherwoodheath@nsdc.info
Oundle	14 West Street	01832 274333	oundletic@east-northamptonshire.gov.uk
Ripley	Town Hall	01773 841488	touristinformation@ambervalley.gov.uk
Sleaford	Advice Centre, Money's Yard	01529 414294	tic@n-kesteven.gov.uk
Swadlincote	Sharpe's Pottery Museum	01283 222848	Jo@sharpespotterymuseum.org.uk

Where to Stay

Ambergate | The Firs Caravan Club Site `THE CARAVAN CLUB` **AS**

Enjoy England ★★★★★	Crich Lane, Belper DE56 2JH
Open: April to November	**t** 01773 852913
	caravanclub.co.uk

Access: 🏛😊♿ General: 🖥📶🚐😀🍴☕🏪 Pitch: 🚐🚙

Ashbourne | Blackwall Plantation Caravan Club Site `THE CARAVAN CLUB` **AS**

Enjoy England ★★★★	Kirk Ireton, Ashbourne DE6 3JL
Open: March to November	**t** 01335 370903
	caravanclub.co.uk

Access: 🏛😊 General: 🖥🛒📶😀☕🍴🏪 Pitch: 🚐🚙

Bakewell | Chatsworth Park Caravan Club Site `THE CARAVAN CLUB` **AS**

Enjoy England ★★★★★

🚐 (120)
　　　£16.00–£32.80

🚐 (120)
　　　£16.00–£32.80

120 touring pitches
Open: All year

Shop: 1 mile
Pub: 1 mile

Baslow, Bakewell, Derbyshire DE45 1PN
t 01246 582226
caravanclub.co.uk

4B2

Breathtaking setting in walled garden on the Estate, with views of the rolling countryside to the west. Children will love the farmyard and adventure playground. Visit the house with its beautifully proportioned rooms, paintings and formal gardens.

Location: From Bakewell onto A619. In 3.75 miles turn right at roundabout (signposted Sheffield). Site entrance on right 150yds.

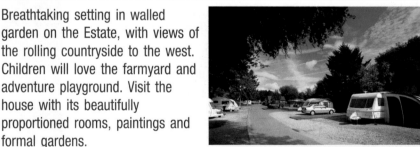
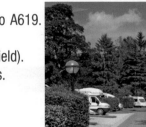

Access:
⚠ 🐾🏛😊♿
General:
🖥📶🚐😀☕🍴🏪
Pitch:
🚐🚙

Bakewell & Matlock | **East Lodge Hotel and Restaurant**   **AS**

Open: All year

Rooms per night:
s: £80.00-£168.00
d: £80.00-£365.00
p/p half board:
d: £120.00-£205.00
Meals: £32.00-£37.50

Rowsley, Nr. Bakewell, Matlock, Derbyshire DE4 2EF
t 01629 734474 **e** info@eastlodge.com
eastlodge.com   **4B2**

Multi-award winning Peak District hotel, nationally renowned for outstanding customer service; exceptional dining; stunning gardens.

Access: abc 🦮 🐾 🏢 ☺ 🚾 ♿ General: 🍽️✕ 🍷 P ⚘ ♿ Room: 🛏️ 🧺 🛁 abc 🚾 S ☕

Buxton | **Grin Low Caravan Club Site** THE CARAVAN CLUB   **AS**

Enjoy England   ★★★★★

🚐 (117)
          £13.90-£25.40
🚙 (117)
          £13.90-£25.40
⛺ (12)

117 touring pitches
Open: 18 March - 7 November

Shop: 1.8 miles
Pub: 0.5 miles

Access:
🅗 🐾 🏢 ☺ 🚾
General:
🗄️ 🐾 🚐 😊 💧 ☕ WP
Pitch:
🚐 🚙 ⛺

Grin Low Road, Ladmanlow, Buxton, Derbyshire SK17 6UJ
t 01298 77735
caravanclub.co.uk   **4B2**

Conveniently placed for exploring the Peak District. Buxton, with its colourful Pavilion Gardens and Opera House offering a wide range of events, makes a great day or evening out. The Peak District National Park is ideal for walkers and cyclists.

Location: Turn left off A53 (Buxton to Leek) at Grin Low signpost, left in 300yds into site approach road.

Chesterfield | **High Hazels**

National Trust, High Hazels, Hardwick Hall, Chesterfield, Derbyshire
S44 5QJ   **t** 0844 800 2070 **e** cottages@nationaltrust.org.uk
nationaltrustcottages.co.uk

Access: ☺ General: 🐴 P S Unit: 🏢 ♿ 🛏️ 🍳 ⚘

Derby | Oaklands Country Lodges

Enjoy England ★★★★

Units: 3 Sleeps: 2-8
Open: All year

Low season p/w:
£380.00
High season p/w:
£1000.00

Claire Redfern, Oaklands Farm, Mount Pleasant, Sutton Road, Church Broughton, Derbyshire DE65 5DE   **t** 01283 730283
e info@oaklandscountrylodges.co.uk
oaklandscountrylodges.co.uk

4B2

Three beautiful timber lodges offering a relaxing holiday with own verandah and Jacuzzi hot tub.

Access: abc ☆☆ ♣ ♿ General: ☎ 🖨 P Ⓢ Unit: ♨ ♨ ♿ 📺 Ⓢ ♿ ✿

Fenny Bentley (Ashbourne) | Homestead Cottage

Enjoy England ★★★★

Units: 1 Sleeps: 1-6
Open: All year

Low season p/w:
£345.00
High season p/w:
£650.00
Shop: 2.5 miles
Pub: 1 mile

Mr and Mrs David and Sandra Snow, Ravenscliffe Farm Holidays, Bradbourne Road, Fenny Bentley, Asbourne, Derbyshire DE6 1LF
t 0787 231 5888 **e** info@ravenscliffefarm.co.uk
ravenscliffefarm.co.uk

4B2

Homestead Cottage has one twin and two double bedrooms, one on ground floor with vanity and direct outside access. The cottage has split levels. Downstairs cloakroom with toilet Bathroom upstairs. Kitchen/dining. A downstairs shower room available by arrangement.

Location: Take A515 Ashbourne to Buxton. After 2 miles, turn right onto the B5056. Ravenscliffe is one mile on the right.

Access:
☆☆
General:
☎ 🖨 P Ⓢ
Unit:
♨ ♿ 📺 Ⓢ ♿ ✿

Matlock | Cuckoostone Cottage

Enjoy England ★★★★

Units: 1 Sleeps: 1-6
Open: All year

Low season p/w:
£315.00
High season p/w:
£700.00

Mrs. Cobb, Cuckoostone Cottage, Cuckoostone House Farm, Sandy Lane, Matlock, Derbyshire DE4 5LD   **t** 01629 580036
e nancy.cobb@btinternet.com

This lovely & comfortable single-storey converted shippen lies at the end of a secluded lane.

Access: ☆☆ ♣ ☺ General: ☎ 🖨 P Ⓢ Unit: ♨ 📺 ✿

Matlock | Hoe Grange Holidays

Enjoy England ★★★★

Units: 3   Sleeps: 2-8
Open: All year

Low season p/w:
£395.00
High season p/w:
£825.00
Shop: 4 miles
Pub: 2 miles

Mrs Felicity Brown, Hoe Grange Holidays, Brassington, Matlock DE4 4HP
t 01629 540262 **e** info@hoegrangeholidays.co.uk
hoegrangeholidays.co.uk   **4B2**

Three award winning log cabins: a real 'home from home', fully equipped kitchen, open plan lounge, spacious bedrooms and luxurious whirlpool bath. Excellent disabled facilities including wet-room shower, mobile hoist and profile bed. Service dogs welcome. Short breaks available.

Location: Working farm, close to Carsington Water, Chatsworth, Dovedale, market towns of Ashbourne, Bakewell, and Matlock.

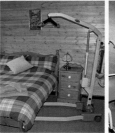
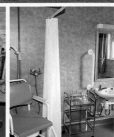

Access:

General:

Unit:

Milford | Ebenezer Chapel

Enjoy England ★★★

Units: 1   Sleeps: 2-22
Open: All year

Low season p/w:
£1000.00
High season p/w:
£1795.00
Shop: <0.5 miles
Pub: <0.5 miles

Mrs Ann Wayne, Director, Derbyshire Holidays, PO Box 7649, Belper, Derbyshire DE56 9DT
t 01332 840564 **e** ann.wayne@derbyshire-holidays.com
derbyshire-holidays.com   **4B2**

An 1846 riverside stone chapel, situated in the village of Milford Derbyshire in the Derwent Valley. There are two lounges, stairlifts, large dining room for 22 people, and sauna suite, 8 bedrooms and a sofa bed in the second lounge.

Location: Milford Derbyshire

General:

Unit:

Nr Hartington | Old House Farm Cottages AS

Enjoy England ★★★★	Mrs Sue Flower, Old House Farm Cottages, Old House Farm, Newhaven, Buxton SK17 0DY **t** 01629 636268 **e** s.flower1@virgin.net
Units: 1 Sleeps: 2-4 Open: All year	oldhousefarm.com **4B2**
Low season p/w: £235.00 High season p/w: £495.00	Charming traditional limestone cottages. Piggery Place, welcomes all including those in wheelchairs. Come and Relax.

General: ⮑🖥P⑤ **Unit:** 🛏♨️♿🛁⛽❀

Staveley | Poolsbrook Country Park Caravan Club Site  AS

Enjoy England ★★★★★

🚐 (86)
£15.30–£27.20

🚚 (86)
£15.30–£27.20

86 touring pitches
Open: 25 March to 7 November

Pavilion Drive, Staveley, Chesterfield S43 3LS
t 01246 470659
caravanclub.co.uk   **4B2**

Set in an extensive country park, including a children's adventure play area, visitor centre, cafe for refreshments and many well stocked lakes for fishing. Site uses a number of sustainable resource and energy features.

Location: M1 j29a; roundabout 2nd exit; 2nd roundabout 1st exit; left into Meadows Drive, left into Pavilion Dr. Site on right.

Access:
🚶☺️♿
General:
🖥🚐🐾♨️🔊🌡️♿📶
Pitch:
🚐🚚

Leicester | Holiday Inn Leicester AS

129 St Nicholas Circle, Leicester, Leicestershire LE1 5LX
t 0871 942 9048 **e** leicestercity.reservations@ihg.com
holiday-inn.com/leicester

Access: 📄🏃🚶☺️♿🚿 **General:** ⮑🍴✕🍷P♿🖥♿ **Room:** 🚿

Leicester | Leicester Marriott — AS

AA ★★★★
Open: All year

Rooms per night:
s: £85.00-£159.00
d: £95.00-£169.00
p/p half board:
d: £106.45-£211.90
Meals: £21.45-£36.00
Shop: 0.5 miles
Pub: 0.5 miles

Smith Way, Grove Park, Enderby, Leicester LE19 1SW
t 01162 820100 e cork.regional.reservations@marriott.com
leicestermarriott.co.uk 4C3

The Leicester Marriott Hotel has 12 accessible king rooms, two of which have roll in showers. All areas in the hotel are accessible including Mixx Restaurant, Tanners Bar, Atrium, Leisure Club and all the bedrooms.

Location: Conveniently located minutes from M1 J21 with easy access to M6/M69/A14 and 4 miles from Leicester city centre.

Access:
General:
Room:

Loughborough | imago at Burleigh Court — AS

Enjoy England ★★★★
Open: All year except Xmas and New Year

Rooms per night:
s: £79.00-£107.00
d: £99.00-£129.00
p/p half board:
d: £100.00-£128.00
Meals: £21.00-£26.00
Shop: 2 miles
Pub: 2 miles

Loughborough University, Loughborough, Leicestershire LE11 3TD
t 08450 364624 e info@welcometoimago.com
welcometoimago.com 4C3

imago at Burleigh Court is one of the Midlands largest 4 star accredited residential conference centres and hotel offering accommodation ranging from the last word in luxury to unmatched quality and value.

Location: Leave jct23 of the M1, taking the A512 Ashby Road to Loughborough. Turn right at first roundabout, into Holywell Way.

Access:
General:
Room:

Market Harborough | **Best Western Three Swans Hotel**

AA ★★★
Open: All year

21 High Street, Market Harborough, Leicestershire LE16 7NJ
t 01858 466644 **e** sales@threeswans.co.uk
bw-threeswanshotel.co.uk

Access: .: abc 🐕 🏛 ⛉ 🚻 ♿ General: 🐕 🍴 ✕ 🍷 P♿ ✽ ⬆ ♿ Room: ♿ 🚻 🍵

Boston | **Elms Farm Cottages**

Enjoy England
★★★★-★★★★★

Units: 8 Sleeps: 2-32
Open: All year

Low season p/w:
£340.00
High season p/w:
£525.00
Shop: 2 miles
Pub: <0.5 miles

Carol Emerson, The Elms, Hubberts Bridge, Boston PE20 3QP
t 01205 290840 **e** carol@elmsfarmcottages.co.uk
elmsfarmcottages.co.uk

3A1

Relax and enjoy the Lincolnshire countryside from our 4 & 5 Star Award Winning Cottages. Elm Farm Cottages are all fully equipped and furnished to a high standard with level floor access. Five cottages with shower rooms for wheelchairs.

Location: 2 miles from Historic Market town of Boston on the A1121 at Hubberts Bridge. Ideally situated for Skegness, Spalding, Lincoln.

Access:
abc 🐕 ☺ ♿
General:
🐕 🖥 P S
Unit:
♿ 🏛 ♿ 🧹 🚻 S ♿ ✽

Boston | **Lincolnshire Special Needs Accommodation Centre**

Helen Banks, 9-14 Croppers Way, Freiston, Boston, Lincolnshire PE22 0QT
t 01205 761373 **e** helen.banks@snac.org.uk
snac.org.uk

General: 🐕 🖥 P S Unit: ♿ 🏛 ♿ ♿ ✽

Hogsthorpe | **Helsey House Cottages**

Enjoy England ★★★★

Units: 2 Sleeps: 4-5
Open: All year

Low season p/w:
£310.00
High season p/w:
£450.00

Mrs Elizabeth Elvidge, Helsey, Hogsthorpe, Nr. Skegness, Lincolnshire
PE24 5PE **t** 01754 872927 **e** eaepcs@yahoo.co.uk
helseycottages.co.uk

4D2

Rural location close to beaches. Special needs/autistic families welcome. Ring to discuss your needs.

Access: 🐕 🏛 ☺ General: 🐕 🖥 P S Unit: ♿ 🏛 ♿ 🧹 S ♿ ✽

Horncastle | Grange Farm Cottages

Enjoy England ★★★

Units: 3 Sleeps: 3-4
Open: closed in February

Low season p/w:
£210.00
High season p/w:
£400.00

Mrs Valerie Downes, Grange Farm, Salmonby, Horncastle, Lincolnshire LN9 6QS   t 01507 534101   e info@grangefarmholidaybreaks.co.uk
grangefarmholidaybreaks.co.uk

4D2

Beechwood cottage, well equipped, homely. A quiet retreat in the beautiful Wolds. Wildlife, birdwatching, fishing.

Access: 🐾🏚😊 General: 🅿️PⓈ Unit: ♿🚱♿WC✿

Lincoln | Cliff Farm Cottage

AS

Enjoy England ★★★★

Units: 1 Sleeps: 2-4
Open: All year

Low season p/w:
£250.00
High season p/w:
£395.00

Rae Marris, Cliff Farm, North Carlton, Lincoln LN1 2RP
t 01522 730475 Mobile 0797 0787 793   e info@cliff-farm-cottage.co.uk
cliff-farm-cottage.co.uk

4C2

Situated 3 miles north of historic Lincoln, charming cottage on working arable farm. Rural retreat.

Access: 😊 General: ⛵PⓈ Unit: ♿♿♿♿♿ⓈWC✿

North Somercotes | Nursery Cottage

AS

Enjoy England ★★★★

Units: 3 Sleeps: 2-4
Open: All year

Low season p/w:
£300.00
High season p/w:
£450.00

Mrs Linda Libell, Meals Farm, Marsh Lane, North Somercotes LN11 7NT
t 01507 358256   e nurserycottage@hotmail.co.uk
mealsfarm.com

4D2

Modern, luxurious cottages in peaceful rural setting close to beach/nature reserve and market towns.

Access: abc 🐾🏚 General: ⛵🅿️PⓈ Unit: ♿♿♿♿WCⓈ✿

Woodhall Spa | Petwood Hotel

Enjoy England ★★★

Open: All year
Rooms per night:
s: £95.00
d: £145.00
p/p half board:
d: £95.00
Meals: £22.95

Stixwould Road, Woodhall Spa LN10 6QG
t 01526 352411   e reception@petwood.co.uk
petwood.co.uk

4D2

A beautiful countryside retreat set in 30 acres. Only 20 miles from historic Lincoln.

Access: 🅿️🐾🏚♿♿ General: ⛵🍽✕🍷P♿✿⊡♿ Room: ♿♿♿WC☕

Oundle | **Oundle Cottage Breaks**

Enjoy England ★★★-★★★★

Units: 3   Sleeps: 1-4
Open: All year

Low season p/w:
£295.00
High season p/w:
£395.00

Richard Simmonds, Oundle Cottage Breaks, Mews Cottage, 30 Market Place, Oundle PE8 4BE
t 01832 275508   **e** richard@simmondsatoundle.co.uk
oundlecottagebreaks.co.uk

3A1

Three s/c cottages in a garden 'oasis' in the centre of this historic Market Town.

General: ⛋回⑤ Unit: ♨🍳🧺🖐️📶🦽🌸

Rugby | **Holiday Inn Rugby-Northampton**

Junc 18 M1, Crick, Northamptonshire NN6 7XR
t 0871 9429059   **e** rugbyhi@ihg.com
ichotelsgroup.com

Access: 🛗☺🦽 General: ⛋🍳✕🍷P♿⊞🖐️ Room: ☕

Wigsthorpe | **Nene Valley Cottages**

Enjoy England   ★★★★★

Units: 3   Sleeps: 2-4
Open: All year

Low season p/w:
£250.00
High season p/w:
£600.00

Heather Ball, The Cottage, Glapthorn PE8 5QB
t 01832 273601   **e** stay@nenevalleycottages.co.uk
nenevalleycottages.co.uk

4D3

Luxurious converted barns in secluded setting with Gold Award. One cottage is fully M3I compliant.

AS

General: ⛋回P⑤ Unit: ♨🍳🧺🖐️📶🚻🦽🌸

Newark | **Dairy Cottage**

Enjoy England   ★★★★

Units: 1   Sleeps: 1-4
Open: All year

Low season p/w:
£300.00
High season p/w:
£420.00

William Baird, Dairy Cottage, Hall Farm, Shelton, Newark NG23 5JG
t 01949 850309   **e** william-baird@btconnect.com
hallfarmaccommodation.co.uk

4C2

Quiet rural location with lovely views of open countryside to the rear of the property.

AS

Access: abc ✕✕🦽 General: ⛋10回P⑤ Unit: ♨🧺🖐️📶🚻⑤🦽🌸

Nottingham | Harts Hotel

AS

AA	★★★★
Open: All year	

Rooms per night:
s: £121.50-£206.50
d: £135.00-£220.00
Meals: £25.00-£50.00

Park Row, Nottingham, Nottinghamshire NG1 6GN
t 0115 988 1900 e reception@hartshotel.co.uk
hartsnottingham.co.uk

4C2

Hart's is Nottingham's highest rated Boutique hotel and award winning restaurant.

Access: 🔭😊♿ General: 🛏🍴✕🍷P&✿▣♿ Room: 🛋🚾📺♨

Sandiacre | Holiday Inn Derby/Nottingham

Bostocks Lane, Sandiacre, Nottingham, Nottinghamshire NG10 5NJ
t 0871 942 9062 e reservations-derby-nottingham@ihg.com
holidayinn.com

Access: abc 🐾🔭😊♿ General: 🛏🍴✕🍷P&✿& Room: 🛋📺♨

Worksop | Clumber Park Caravan Club Site — CARAVAN CLUB

AS

🚐 (183)	
	£15.70–£29.30
🚐 (183)	
	£15.70–£29.30

183 touring pitches
Open: All year

Shop: 5 miles
Pub: 5 miles

Lime Tree Avenue, Clumber Park, Worksop, Nottinghamshire S80 3AE
t 01909 484758
caravanclub.co.uk

4C2

There's a great feeling of spaciousness here, for the 20 acre site is set within 4,000 acres of parkland. Set in the heart of Sherwood Forest, also visit Nottingham Castle and the watersports centre at Holme Pierrepont.

Location: From junction of A1 and A57, take A614 signposted Nottingham for 0.5 miles. Turn right into Clumber Park site.

Access:
🅰🐾🔭😊♿
General:
🗄🖼🔌🚿🐾🕴🍳🚾
Pitch:
🚐🚐

Derbyshire

ASHBOURNE

Ancestral Barn
Mr & Mrs S Fowler, Church Farm, Stanshope, Ashbourne, Derbyshire DE6 2AD
t 01335 310243   **w** dovedalecottages.co.uk

BUXTON

Northfield Farm
Mrs Elizabeth Andrews, Flash, Nr Buxton, Derbyshire SK17 0SW
t 01298 22543   **e** info@northfieldfarm.co.uk
w northfieldfarm.co.uk

CALDWELL

Forest Lodges
Ms Marie Hall, Forest Lodges, Rosliston Forestry Centre, Burton Road, Swadlincote DE12 8JX
t 01283 519119   **f** 01283 565494
e marie@roslistonforestrycentre.co.uk
w roslistonforestrycentre.co.uk

EARL STERNDALE

Wheeldon Trees Farm
Deborah & Martin Hofman, Wheeldon Trees Farm, Earl Sterndale, Buxton SK17 0AA
t 01298 83219   **e** stay@wheeldontreesfarm.co.uk
w wheeldontreesfarm.co.uk

HARDSTOFT

Whitton Lodge
Chesterfield Road, Hardstoft S45 8AX
t 01773 875614   **e** pjohnthestud@aol.com
w whittonlodge.co.uk

HARTINGTON

Ash Tree Cottage
Mrs Clare Morson, Ash Tree Cottage, Nettletor Farm, Mill Lane, Buxton SK17 0AN
t 01298 84247   **e** nettletorfarm@btconnect.com
w nettletorfarm.co.uk

OLD BRAMPTON

Chestnut and Willow Cottages
Mr & Mrs Jeffrey & Patricia Green, Chestnut and Willow Cottages, Priestfield Grange, Old Brampton S42 7JH
t 0800 141 2926   **e** patricia_green@btconnect.com

Leicestershire

ASHBY-DE-LA-ZOUCH

Church View Barn
Mrs W Davis, Church View Barn, 20 Church Street, Swepstone LE67 2SA
t 01530 272481   **e** wendydavis39@hotmail.com

CROPSTON

Horseshoe Cottage Farm
Hallgates Roecliffe Road, Cropston, Leicester LE7 7HQ
t 0116 235 0038   **e** lindajee@ljee.freeserve.co.uk
w horseshoecottagefarm.com

DISEWORTH

Lady Gate Guest House
47 The Green, Diseworth, Castle Donington DE74 2QN
t 01332 811565   **e** ladygateguesthouse@tiscali.co.uk
w ladygateguesthouse.co.uk

GLOOSTON

Old Barn Inn & Restaurant
Main Street, Glooston, Market Harborough LE16 7ST
t 01858 545215   **e** mail@oldbarninn.co.uk
w oldbarninn.co.uk

HATHERN

Leys Guest House
Loughborough Road, Hathern, Loughborough LE12 5JB
t 01509 844373   **e** leysab2@msn.com

HEMINGTON

Spring Cottage
79 High Street, Castle Donington DE74 2PQ
t 01332 814289   **e** madge.stic@btinternet.com
w springcottagebb.co.uk

MARKET HARBOROUGH

Angel Hotel
37 High Street, Market Harborough LE16 7AF
t 01858 462702   **e** theangel@theangel-hotel.co.uk
w theangel-hotel.co.uk

MOIRA

YHA National Forest
48 Bath Lane, Moira, Ashby-de-la-Zouch DE12 6BD
t 0870 770 6141   **e** nationalforest@yha.org.uk
w yha.org.uk

THRUSSINGTON

Walton Thorns Farm Cottages
Mrs Liz Hollingshead, Walton Thorns Farm Cottages, Walton Thorns Farm, Paudy Lane, Nr Seagrave, Loughborough LE7 4TB
t 01509 880315   **e** liz@waltonthorns.co.uk
w waltonthorns.co.uk

Lincolnshire

ALFORD

Ash & Chestnut Holiday Cottages
Ann Graves, Farmhouse B&B Cottages and Caravans, Grange Farm, Maltby le Marsh, Alford LN13 0JP
t 01507 450267   **e** anngraves@btinternet.com
w grange-farmhouse.co.uk

The Granary and Yew Tree Holiday Cottage
Ann Graves, Farmhouse B&B Cottages and Caravans, Grange Farm, Maltby le Marsh, Alford LN13 0JP
t 01507 450267   **e** anngraves@btinternet.com
w grange-farmhouse.co.uk

Half Moon Hotel
25-28 West Street, Alford LN13 9DG
t 01507 463477   **e** halfmoonalford25@aol.com
w halfmoonhotelalford.com

ASHBY-CUM-FENBY

Hall Farm Hotel & Restaurant
Ashby Lane, Ashby Cum Fenby, Grimsby DN37 0RT
t 01472 220666   **e** info@hallfarmrestaurant.co.uk
w hallfarmhotelandrestaurant.co.uk

BELCHFORD

Poachers Hideaway
Jacki Harris, Flintwood Farm, Belchford LN9 5QN
t 01507 533555   **e** info@poachershideaway.com
w poachershideaway.com

BICKER

Supreme Inns
Bicker Bar, Bicker PE20 3AN
t 01205 822804   **e** sales@supremeinns.co.uk
w supremeinns.co.uk

BLYTON

Blyton (Sunnyside) Ponds
Sunnyside Farm, Station Road, Blyton, Gainsborough DN21 3LE
t 01427 628240   **e** blytonponds@msn.com
w blytonponds.co.uk

BOSTON

Crewyard Cottages
Colin Ash, Crewyard Cottages, Everards, Highgate, Leverton, Boston PE22 0AW
t 01205 871389   **e** gina@gina31.wanadoo.co.uk
w crewyardholidaycottages-boston.co.uk

CLEETHORPES

Tudor Terrace Guest House
11 Bradford Avenue, Cleethorpes DN35 0BB
t 01472 600800   **e** tudor.terrace@ntlworld.com
w tudorterrace.co.uk

CROWLAND, SPALDING

Fen-Acre Crowland
Julie Smith, Fen-Acre, 20 Barbers Drove North, Crowland, Spalding, Peterborough PE6 0BE
t 01733 211847   **e** julie@fen-acreholidaylet.com
w en-acreholidaylet.com

DONINGTON

Browntoft House
Browntoft Lane, Donington PE11 4TQ
t 01775 822091   **e** finchedward@hotmail.com
w browntofthouse.co.uk

EAST BARKWITH

Grange Farm Cottages
Mrs Sarah Stamp, Grange Farm Cottages, Torrington Lane, East Barkwith LN8 5RY
t 01673 858670   **e** sarahstamp@farmersweekly.net
w thegrange-lincolnshire.co.uk

EDLINGTON MOOR

Village Limits Motel & Restaurant
Stixwould Road, Woodhall Spa LN10 6UJ
t 01526 353312   **e** info@villagelimits.co.uk
w villagelimits.co.uk

GRAINTHORPE

Kents Farm Cottages
Mrs Sandra Carr, Kents Farm Cottages, Austen Fen, Grainthorpe, Louth LN11 0NX
t 01472 388264   **e** sandracarr500@msn.com
w kentsfarmcottages.net

HAGWORTHINGHAM

Kingfisher Lodge
Nick Bowser, E.W. Bowser & Son Ltd, The Estate Office, Leverton, Boston PE22 0AA
t 01205 870210   **e** office@ewbowser.com
w meridianretreats.com

HEMINGBY

Mon Abri
Mr Malcolm Hickson, Mon Abri, Hawthorne Lodge, Great Sturton, Horncastle LN9 5NX
t 01507 578630   **e** malc@aludrain.co.uk

HORNCASTLE

Best Western Admiral Rodney Hotel
North Street, Horncastle LN9 5DX
t 01507 523131   **e** reception@admiralrodney.com
w bestwestern.co.uk/admiralrodneyhotel

INGOLDMELLS

Ingoldale Park
Cathryn Whitehead, Ingoldale Park, Roman Bank, Ingoldmells PE25 1LL
t 01754 872335   **e** ingoldalepark@btopenworld.com
w ingoldmells.net

LOUTH

Bay Tree Cottage
Gordon Reid, Bay Tree Cottage, Goulceby Post, Ford Way, Goulceby, Louth LN11 9WD
t 01507 343230   **e** info@goulcebypost.co.uk
w goulcebypost.co.uk

The Thomas Centre
Mrs J Cream, Westfield Mews & Lodges, Westfield House, Covenham St Bartholomew, Louth LN11 0PB
t 01507 363217   **w** thethomascentre.co.uk

MABLETHORPE

Colours Guest House
Queens Park Close, Mablethorpe LN12 2AS
t 01507 473427   **e** info@coloursguesthouse.co.uk
w coloursguesthouse.co.uk

MARKET RASEN

Bainfield Lodge
Marian Walker, Bainfield Leisure, Bainfield House, Main Road, Market Rasen LN8 6JY
t 01507 313540   **e** dennis.walker1@btinternet.com
w bainfieldholidaylodge.co.uk

MARTIN

The Manor House Stables
Sherry Forbes, The Manor House Stables, The Manor House, Timberland Road, Martin LN4 3QS
t 01526 378717   **e** sherryforbes@hotmail.com
w manorhousestables.co.uk

MOULTON EUGATE

Stennetts Farm Holiday Cottages
Mrs Anne Ashton, Stennetts Farm Holiday Cottages, Stennetts Farm, Molton Eaugate, Spalding PE12 0SX
t 01406 380408   **f** 01406 380408
e info@stennettsfarmcottages.co.uk
w stennettsfarmcottages.co.uk

SKEGNESS

Chatsworth
16 North Parade, Skegness PE25 2UB
t 01754 764177   **e** info@chatsworthskegness.co.uk
w chatsworthskegness.co.uk

SPILSBY

Red Lion Inn - Accommodation
Skegness Road, Partney, Spilsby PE23 4PG
t 01790 752271   **e** chrishurrell@btconnect.com
w redlioninnpartney.co.uk

WOODHALL SPA

Kirkstead Old Mill Cottage
Tattershall Road, Woodhall Spa LN10 6UQ
t 01526 353637   **e** barbara@woodhallspa.co.uk
w woodhallspa.co.uk

Mill Lane Holiday Cottage
Ian Williamson, Mill Lane Holiday Cottages, 72 Mill Lane, Woodhall Spa LN10 6QZ
t 01526 353101   **e** janewill89@hotmail.com
w skegness.net/woodhallspa.htm

Wayside Cottage
Ian Williamson, Mill Lane Holiday Cottages, 72 Mill Lane, Woodhall Spa LN10 6QZ
t 01526 353101   **e** janewill89@hotmail.com
w skegness.net/woodhallspa.htm

Nottinghamshire

EDWINSTOWE

Sherwood Forest Youth Hostel
Forest Corner, Edwinstowe, Mansfield NG21 9RN
t 0870 770 6026   **e** sherwood@yha.org.uk
w yha.org.uk

SOUTH SCARLE

Greystones Guest Accommodation
Main Street, South Scarle, Newark NG23 7JH
t 01636 893969
e sheenafowkes@greystonesguests.co.uk
w greystonesguests.co.uk

WORKSOP

Browns
The Old Orchard Cottage, Holbeck, Worksop S80 3NF
t 01909 720659   **e** browns.holbeck@btconnect.com
w brownsholbeck.co.uk

Where to Go

Bolsover | **Bolsover Castle**

Open: For opening hours and prices, please call 0870 333 1181 or visit www.english-heritage.org.uk/properties

Castle Street, Bolsover, Derbyshire S44 6PR
t 0870 333 1181   **e** customers@english-heritage.org.uk
english-heritage.org.uk/bolsovercastle

Enjoy a family day out, there's lots to discover and places to rest and picnic.

Access: ♿🅦🖼️♿♿ General: 🅿️🗺️✿

Kenilworth | **Kenilworth Castle & Elizabethan Garden**

Open: For opening hours and prices, please call 0870 333 1181 or visit www.english-heritage.org.uk/properties

Kenilworth, Warwickshire CV8 1NE
t 0870 333 1181   **e** customers@english-heritage.org.uk
english-heritage.org.uk/kenilworth

With its new wheelchair accessible Elizabethan garden, restored gatehouse and exhibitions, there's lots to entertain.

Access: 🐾😊♿♿🗺️♿ General: 🅿️🗺️✿♿🖥️

Great Witley | **Witley Court**

Open: For opening hours and prices, please call 0870 333 1181 or visit www.english-heritage.org.uk/properties

Great Witley, Nr Worcester, Worcestershire WR6 6JT
t 0870 333 1181   **e** customers@english-heritage.org.uk
english-heritage.org.uk/witleycourt

Explore a stunning romantic ruin, beautiful woodland walks and Parterre Gardens and the spectacular fountains.

Access: 🐾♿♿🗺️♿♿ General: 🗺️✿♿🖥️

Where to Eat

Cleethorpes | Trawler Man

North Sea Lane, Cleethorpes DN35 0PP
t 01472 811893
tavernerscleethorpespub.co.uk

General: 🐕 🚶 ♿ WC ♿ 👥 abc **P**★★★

Grimsby | Pizza Hut

68-72 Victoria Street, Grimsby, North East Lincolnshire DN31 1BL
t 01472 242999
pizzahut.co.uk

General: 🐕 @FAX 🐾 🚶 ♿ WC abc

Northampton | Ask

10 St Giles Square, Northampton, Northamptonshire NN1 1DA
t 01604 230891
askrestaurants.com

General: 🐕 @FAX 🐾 🚶 WC WC 👥

Northampton | T.G.I. Friday's

Sixfields Leisure Park, Upton Way, Northampton, Northamptonshire
NN5 4EG   **t** 01604 589456 **e** 1658@crww.com
tgifridays.co.uk

General: 🐕 @FAX 🐾 🚶 WC WC 👥 .: abc ♪ ★★★

Newark | Farndon Boathouse Bar and Kitchen

Riverside, Farndon, Newark, Nottinghamshire NG24 3SX
t 01636 676578 **e** info@farndonboathouse.co.uk
farndonboathouse.co.uk

General: 🐕 @FAX 🚶 WC WC 👥 abc **P**★★★

Newark-on-Trent | Zizzi

The Ossington, Castle Gate, Market Hill, Newark-on-Trent, Nottinghamshire
NG24 1BH   **t** 01636 679599
zizzi.co.uk

General: 🐕 🚶 WC 👥

For more information on accommodation attractions activities **events** and holidays **contact the Tourist Information Centres** see regional listings for the nearest one.

200

Rufford Abbey Country Park

Ollerton, Nottinghamshire, NG22 9DF

- Open year round 10am - 5pm
- Romantic ruins of medieval Abbey
- Gardens, lake and woodland
- Exhibitions in the Craft Centre Gallery
- Home cooked lunches in the Savile Restaurant
- Coach House café for snacks and drinks
- Gift and Craft Shop
- Electric scooter hire and free wheelchair loan
- Free parking for blue badge holders
- Only three miles from historic Sherwood Forest.

Downloadable access map:

Nottinghamshire
County Council

www.nottinghamshire.gov.uk
/ruffordcp
Tel. 01623 821338

OPEN **DECIDED WHERE TO GO? SEE ATTRACTIONS FOR WHAT TO DO**
BRITAIN **Ideas and information at the end of each regional section**

The Heart of England – central, accessible, unmissable!

Welcome to The Heart of England – home to England's heritage and culture. From Stratford-upon-Avon, birthplace of Shakespeare, to our world heritage site of Ironbridge Gorge. From the imposing Warwick Castle to 'The Potteries', home to the famous Wedgwood brand. From the iconic Royal Shakespeare Company to the City of Birmingham Symphony Orchestra and Birmingham Royal Ballet.

Welcome to The Heart of England – home to world-class festivals and events. From annual events that celebrate our heritage such as the **Much Wenlock Olympian Games** – forerunner of the modern

Olympic Games. From food and drink festivals such as **Ludlow**, real ale festivals, asparagus, plum and apple festivals to internationally acclaimed events such as the **V Festival**, **Three Choirs Festival** and **Artsfest**.

Welcome to The Heart of England – home to quintessential English countryside. From Worcestershire's market town of Broadway – gateway to The Cotswolds, to Shropshire and Herefordshire with their **Black and White Village Trails** to the imposing **Trentham Estate** – England's largest garden restoration project and the dozens of Capability Brown designed landscape gardens.

Welcome to The Heart of England – home to great English food and drink. Devour home-made traditional food in country inns and pubs, experience Michelin starred restaurants in Ludlow and Birmingham, sample Black

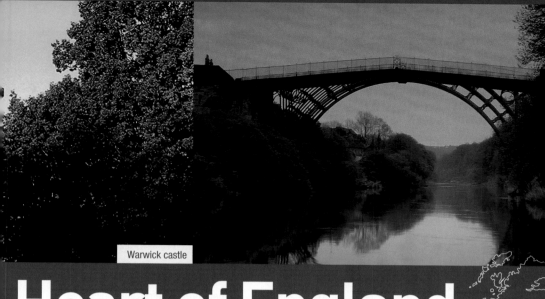

Warwick castle

Ironbridge

Heart of England

**Herefordshire, Shropshire, Staffordshire,
Warwickshire, West Midlands, Worcestershire**

Tourist Information Centres	204	Where to Go	212
Where to Stay	205	Where to Eat	213

Country 'faggots' and Staffordshire oatcakes, the Birmingham 'Balti' and a myriad of local cheeses. Be quenched by Bass beer, Bulmers cider, wine, perry, and discover the micro-breweries of the countryside.

Welcome to The Heart of England – home to a great accessible welcome from our accommodation providers – hotels, caravanning sites such as **Poston Mill**, bed and breakfast establishments like **Hidelow House**. From our attractions such as **Cadbury World**, the **Heritage Motor Centre** at Gaydon, **RAF Cosford** and **Drayton Manor Theme Park** to the many National Trust properties such as **Attingham Park** near Shrewsbury with its accessible walks, and **Croombe Park** near Worcester with its mobility buggies.

Not only will you find this a region that's easy to get to – at the heart of the UK road, rail and canal network, it's a region that's easy to get around. For a full list of accessible –friendly attractions and accommodations that are sure to deliver exactly what you're looking for visit our website.

Find out more
www.visittheheart.co.uk

Bullring, Birmingham

Tourist Information Centres

Tourist Information Centres are a mine of information about local and regional accommodation, attractions and events. Visit them when you arrive at your destination or contact them before you go:

Bewdley	Load Street	01299 404740	bewdleytic@wyreforestdc.gov.uk
Birmingham	The Rotunda	0844 888 3883	callcentre@marketingbirmingham.com
Bridgnorth	The Library	01746 763257	bridgnorth.tourism@shropshire.gov.uk
Church Stretton	Church Street	01694 723133	churchstretton.scf@shropshire.gov.uk
Coventry Cathedral	Coventry Cathedral	024 7622 5616	tic@cvone.co.uk
Hereford	1 King Street	01432 268430	tic-hereford@herefordshire.gov.uk
Ironbridge	Ironbridge Gorge Museum Trust	01952 884391	tic@ironbridge.org.uk
Leamington Spa	The Royal Pump Rooms	01926 742762	eamington@shakespeare-country.co.uk
Leek	Stockwell Street	01538 483741	tourism.services@staffsmoorlands.gov.uk
Lichfield	Lichfield Garrick	01543 412112	info@visitlichfield.com
Ludlow	Castle Street	01584 875053	ludlow.tourism@shropshire.gov.uk
Malvern	21 Church Street	01684 892289	malvern.tic@malvernhills.gov.uk
Oswestry	Mile End	01691 662488	tic@oswestry-bc.gov.uk
Ross-On-Wye	Swan House	01989 562768	tic-ross@herefordshire.gov.uk
Rugby	Little Elborow Street	01788 533217	visitor.centre@rugby.gov.uk
Shrewsbury	The Music Hall	01743 281200	visitorinfo@shrewsbury.gov.uk
Solihull	Central Library	0121 704 6130	artscomplex@solihull.gov.uk
Stafford	Gatehouse Theatre	01785 619619	tic@staffordbc.gov.uk
Stoke-On-Trent	Victoria Hall, Bagnall Street	01782 236000	stoke.tic@stoke.gov.uk
Stratford-Upon-Avon	Bridgefoot	0870 160 7930	stratfordtic@shakespeare-country.co.uk
Tamworth	29 Market Street	01827 709581	tic@tamworth.gov.uk
Warwick	The Court House	01926 492212	touristinfo@warwick-uk.co.uk
Worcester	The Guildhall	01905 728787	touristinfo@cityofworcester.gov.uk

Where to Stay

Hereford | **Grafton Villa Farm Cottages**

Enjoy England ★★★★

Units: 3 Sleeps: 2-6
Open: All year

Low season p/w:
£270.00
High season p/w:
£650.00

Mrs Jennie Layton, Grafton Villa Farm Cottages, Grafton Villa, Grafton, Hereford HR2 8ED **t** 01432 268689 **e** jennielayton@ereal.net
graftonvilla.co.uk

2A1

Award winning holiday cottages set within the farmhouse walled gardens overlooking beautiful countryside, just perfect.

Access: abc General: ➤P⑤ Unit: ⬛⬛⬛⬛⬛⬛⬛⬛✿

Ledbury | **Old Kennels Farm**

Enjoy England ★★★-★★★★

Units: 2 Sleeps: 2-6
Open: All year

Low season p/w:
£280.00
High season p/w:
£675.00

Mr Brian Wilce, Old Kennels Farm, Bromyard Road, Ledbury, Herefordshire HR8 1LG **t** 01531 635024 **e** wilceoldkennelsfarm@btinternet.com
oldkennelsfarm.com.uk

2B1

Very spacious wheelchair accessible cottage. please call to discuss your personal requirements.

General: ➤⬛P⑤ Unit: ⬛⬛⬛⬛⬛⬛⬛⬛✿

OPEN BRITAIN DECIDED WHERE TO GO? SEE ATTRACTIONS FOR WHAT TO DO
Ideas and information at the end of each regional section

Malvern | Hidelow House Cottages

AS

Enjoy England
★★★★-★★★★★
....
Units: 3 Sleeps: 2-12
Open: All year
....
Low season p/w:
£295.00
High season p/w:
£2800.00
Pub: 2.5 miles

Mrs Pauline Diplock, Acton Green, Acton Beauchamp, Worcester WR6 5AH
t 01886 884547 **e** openb@hidelow.co.uk
hidelow.co.uk

2B1

3 outstanding award-winning holiday cottages (sleeping 2, 5 and 12 people) in rural but accessible Elgar country. With wide selection of assistance aids available and carers if required, we aim to provide worry-free holidays for disabled guests and their carers.

Location: From M5 J7, take A44, A4440, then A4103 at top of hill towards Bromyard. After 2mls turn left at signboard.

Access:
🦽 abc 🐾 🏛 ☺ ♿
General:
🛏 📷 P Ⓢ
Unit:
🛁 🖥 ♨ ♿ 📺 📼 ♿ ☕ ❀

Ross-on-Wye | Merton House Hotel

AS

Open: All year
....
Rooms per night:
s: £40.00-£55.00
d: £70.00-£90.00
p/p half board:
d: £50.00-£70.00
Meals:
Shop: <0.5 miles
Pub: <0.5 miles

Edde Cross Street, Ross-on-Wye, Herefordshire HR9 7BZ
t 01989 563252 **e** merton.house@clara.co.uk
mertonhouse.org

2A1

A specialist hotel catering for people with disabilities and the elderly frail. A registered charity. Door to Door transport can be provided, we also have our own mini-bus with tail-lift for wheelchair access and daily trips out are arranged

Location: Off the A449/M50 to South Wales from the M5. M4/A449 Monmouth/Ross On Wye.

Access:
🦽 🐾 🏛 ☺ ♿
General:
🛏 🍽 ✕ ⚲ P ❀ ⬆ ♿
Room:
🛁 ♨ 📺 📼 Ⓢ

Ross-on-Wye | **Portland House**

AA	★★★★
Enjoy England	★★★★

Open: All year except Xmas and New Year

Rooms per night:
s: £70.00-£75.00
d: £75.00-£85.00

Whitchurch, Ross-on-Wye, Herefordshire HR9 6DB
t 01600 890757 **e** info@portlandguesthouse.co.uk
portlandguesthouse.co.uk

2A1

Uniquely placed in Wye Valley. Wide internal areas for wheelchairs. Luscious Lloyd Suite overlooking garden.

Access: abc 🦅 ☺ ♿ General: 🛏 🍴 ✗ P♿ ✿ ♿ Room: ♿ 🛏 📺 wc S 🍵

Ross-on-Wye | **Trevase Granary**

Enjoy England   ★★★★★

Units: 1 Sleeps: 1-16
Open: All year

Low season p/w:
£2400.00
High season p/w:
£4250.00

Mrs Liz Pursey, Trevase Granary, Trevase Farm, St Owens Cross HR2 8ND
t 01989 730210 **e** stay@trevasecottages.co.uk
trevasecottages.co.uk

2A1

Luxury 5* barn conversion beautifully furnished and equipped. Eight en suite bedrooms, sleeps sixteen. Stairlift.

Access: 🦅 General: 🛏 🖥 P S Unit: ♿ 🖨 🛏 ♿ 📺 wc S ♿ ✿

Ludlow | **Goosefoot Barn Cottages**

Enjoy England   ★★★★

Units: 4 Sleeps: 2-4
Open: All year

Low season p/w:
£235.00
High season p/w:
£485.00

Mrs Sally Loft, Goosefoot Barn Cottages, Pinstones, Diddlebury, Craven Arms SY7 9LB   **t** 01584 861326 **e** info@goosefootbarn.co.uk
goosefootbarn.co.uk

4A3

Four Star fully-equipped cottages in Corvedale, Nr Ludlow. Bedrooms en suite. Short breaks.

Access: abc 🦅 General: 🛏 🖥 S Unit: ♿ 🖨 🛏 ♿ 📺 🍵 ✿

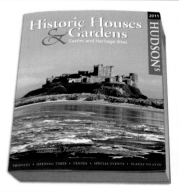

Shrewsbury | **Wroxeter Hotel**

Enjoy England ★★★

Open: All year

Rooms per night:
s: £50.00-£75.00
d: £55.00-£90.00
p/p half board:
d: £47.50-£70.00
Meals: £10.00-£35.00
Shop: 3 miles
Pub: 1 mile

Access:

General:

Room:

Wroxeter, Shrewsbury SY5 6PH
t 01743 761256 **e** info@thewroxeterhotel.co.uk
thewroxeterhotel.co.uk

4A3

Amidst beautiful countryside with 18 well appointed bedrooms, The Wroxeter is family run and excels in personal service. We have the specialist skills to cater for the needs of discerning visitors. If there's anything we can help with, we will!

Location: Situated on the B4380 halfway between Telford and Shrewsbury. Easy access from the M54 and A5.

Strefford, Nr Church Stretton | **Strefford Hall Self Catering - Robins & Swallows Nest**

Enjoy England ★★★★

Units: 2 Sleeps: 2
Open: All year

Low season p/w:
£180.00
High season p/w:
£300.00

Mrs Caroline Morgan, Strefford Hall, Strefford, Craven Arms SY7 8DE
t 01588 672383 **e** strefford@gmail.com
streffordhall.co.uk

4A3

In the South Shropshire countryside surrounded by fields and close to Wenlock Edge.

Access: General: Unit:

Tugford | **Tugford Farm B&B**

Enjoy England ★★★★

Open: All year

Rooms per night:
s: £55.00
d: £90.00
p/p half board:
d: £73.00
Meals: £18.00

Tugford Farm, Craven Arms SY7 9HS
t 01584 841259 **e** tugfordfarm@yahoo.co.uk
tugford.com

4A3

Top quality accommodation deep in the Corvedale valley. En suite, central heating. Hearty farmhouse breakfast.

Access: General: Room:

Burton-on-Trent | **Holiday Inn Express Burton-Upon-Trent**

2nd Avenue, Centrum 100, Burton-on-Trent, Staffordshire DE14 2WF
t 01283 504300 **e** reservations@exhiburton.co.uk
exhiburton.co.uk

Access: abc 🅿 🐕 🔭 ☺ ♿ 🦽 General: ⮂ ✕ 🍷 P 🔳 ♿ Room: 🛏 🗻 📺 📺 📱 ☕

Leek | **Blackshaw Moor Caravan Club Site**  AS

Enjoy England ★★★★★	Blackshaw Moor, Leek ST13 8TW
Open: Mar 2011 to Jan 2012	**t** 01538 300203
	caravanclub.co.uk

Access: 🚻 ☺ General: 📺 📶 📞 🚼 🍼 Pitch: 🚐 🚗

Peak District | **Quarry Walk Park** AS

AA ★★★★	Reception Park Managers, Quarry Walk, Coppice Lane, Freehay, Alton,
Enjoy England ★★★★	Staffordshire ST10 1RQ **t** 01538 723412
Units: 18 Sleeps: 2-6	**e** Quarry@quarrywalkpark.co.uk
Open: All year	quarrywalkpark.co.uk **4B2**
Low season p/w: £365.00	18 luxurious log cabins with private hot tubs, 46 acres of woodland, quiet and relaxing.
High season p/w: £1200.00	

Access: abc 🐕 🔭 ☺ 🦽 General: ⮂ 📺 P S Unit: 🛏 🗻 ♿ 📺 📱 🦽 ✿

Stoke-on-Trent | **Holiday Inn Stoke-on-Trent**

AA ★★★	Clayton Road, Newcastle-under-Lyme, Staffordshire ST5 4DL
	t 0871 942 9077 **e** wendy.salmon@ihg.com
	holiday-inn.co.uk

Access: ∴ abc 🅿 🐕 🔭 ☺ ♿ 🦽 General: ⮂ 🍽 ✕ 🍷 P ✿ 🦽 Room: 📺 ☕

Uttoxeter | **Uttoxeter Racecourse Caravan Club Site** CARAVAN CLUB AS

Enjoy England ★★	Uttoxeter Racecourse, Wood Lane, Uttoxeter ST14 8BD
Open: March to November	**t** 01889 564172
	caravanclub.co.uk

Access: 🐕 🔭 ☺ 🦽 General: 📺 🚐 📶 🚿 📞 🚼 🍼 WP Pitch: 🚐 🚗 ⛺

Stratford-upon-Avon | **Island Meadow Caravan Park**

Mill House, Aston Cantlow, Henley in Arden, Warwickshire B95 6JP
t 01789 488273 **e** holiday@islandmeadowcaravanpark.co.uk
islandmeadowcaravanpark.co.uk

Access: 🦽 General: 📺 ♿ 📶 🚿 📞 🚼 🍼 WP Pitch: 🚐 🏕 🚗 ⛺

Birmingham | Chapel Lane Caravan Club Site THE CARAVAN CLUB

AS

Enjoy England ★★★★★

🚐 (108)
£15.30–£27.20

🚎 (108)
£15.30–£27.20

108 touring pitches
Open: All year

Shop: 0.5 miles
Pub: 1 mile

Access:
🅰 🐾 🏢 ☺ ♿

General:
▯ ▱ 🐾 🚐 ⚡ 🕛 📦 🚰

Pitch:
🚐 🚎

Chapel Lane, Wythall, Birmingham, West Midlands B47 6JX
t 01564 826483
caravanclub.co.uk

4B3

A quiet, rural area yet convenient for Birmingham (9 miles) and the NEC (13 miles). Visit Cadbury's World, explore the surrounding countryside and local canals, or visit fascinating museums about our industrial heritage.

Location: M42 j3 onto A435 to Birmingham. At roundabout take 1st exit, Middle Lane. Turn right at church; site on right.

Birmingham | Holiday Inn Birmingham City Centre

AA ★★★

Smallbrook Queensway, Birmingham, West Midlands B5 4EW
t 0121 6346200 e reservations-birminghamcity@ihg.com
holidayinn.com/birminghamcity

Access: .: abc 🗐 🐾 🏢 ☺ ♿ General: 🛏 🍴 ✕ 🍷 🖽 ♿ Room: 🛏 📺 📺 ☕

Birmingham | Holiday Inn Birmingham M6 Junction 7

Chapel Lane, Great Barr, Birmingham, West Midlands B43 7BG
t 0871 9429009 e reservations-birminghamgreatbarr@ihg.com
holidayinn.com

Access: .: 🅰 abc 🗐 🐾 🏢 ☺ ♿ General: 🛏 🍴 ✕ 🍷 P ✿ ♿ Room: 📺 ☕

Birmingham Airport & NEC | Crowne Plaza Birmingham NEC

Pendigo Way, National Exhibition Centre, Birmingham, West Midlands B40 1PS t 0871 942 9160 e necsales@ihg.com
crowneplaza.com

Access: abc 🗐 🐾 🏢 ☺ ♿ General: 🛏 🍴 ✕ 🍷 P ✿ 🖽 ♿ Room: 📺 ☕

Coventry | Holiday Inn Coventry M6 J2

AS

AA ★★★

Hinckley Road, Walsgrave, Coventry, West Midlands CV2 2HP
t 0871 942 9021 e reservations-coventrym6@ihg.com
holiday-inn.com//coventrym6

Access: abc 🗐 🐾 🏢 ☺ ♿ General: 🛏 🍴 ✕ 🍷 P ✿ 🖽 ♿ Room: 📺 ☕

Worcester | **The Manor Coach House**

 AS

Enjoy England	★★★★

Open: All year except Xmas and New Year

Rooms per night:

s:	£49.00
d:	£70.00

Shop: 0.5 miles
Pub: 0.5 miles

Hindlip Lane, Hindlip, Worcester WR3 8SJ
t 01905 456457 **e** info@manorcoachhouse.co.uk
manorcoachhouse.co.uk

2B1

Beautiful B&B, semi-rural location close to Worcester/M5. Five rooms, one with disabled access, full wet-room. Wheelchair accessible bedroom leads into spacious, well lit ground floor room with en suite wet room, grab rails, disabled toilet and sink by the side.

Access:
abc 🏃‍♂️ ♿

General:
🛏 ⛵ P♿ ✿ ♿

Room:
♿ 🚿 📺 🅂 ☕

Worcester/ Upton-on-Severn | **Roseland Bungalow Annexe**

AS

Enjoy England ★★★★

Mr & Mrs Laurent, Roseland B&B & Holiday Bungalow, Roseland, Clifton, Severn Stoke WR8 9JF   **t** 01905 371463 **e** guy@roselandworcs.demon.co.uk
roselandworcs.demon.co.uk

Access: 🐾 🏃 General: 🛏 📷 P Unit: ♿ ♿ 🅂 ♿ ✿

Herefordshire

EWYAS HAROLD

Old King Street Farm
Robert Dewar, Old King Street Farm, Ewyas Harold, Golden Valley HR2 0HB
t 01981 240208 **e** info@oldkingstreetfarm.co.uk
w oldkingstreetfarm.co.uk

LEINTWARDINE

Mocktree Barns Holiday Cottages
Clive & Cynthia Prior, Mocktree Barns Holiday Cottages, Leintwardine, Ludlow SY7 0LY
t 01547 540441 **e** mocktreebarns@care4free.net
w mocktreeholidays.co.uk

LEOMINSTER

YHA Leominster
The Priory, Leominster HR6 8EQ
t 01568 620517 **e** leominster@yha.org.uk
w yha.org.uk

LITTLE TARRINGTON

Hereford Camping and Caravanning Club Site
Little Tarrington, Hereford HR1 4JA
t 01432 890243 **e** enquiries@millpond.co.uk
w campingandcaravanningclub.co.uk/hereford

LLANGARRON, ROSS-ON-WYE

Penblaith Barn
Mrs. Liz Pursey, Trevase Cottages, Trevase Farm, St. Owens Cross HR2 8ND
t 01989 730210 **f** 01989 730210
e stay@trevasecottages.co.uk
w trevase Cottages.co.uk

MICHAELCHURCH ESCLEY

Holt Farm
Nick Pash, Holt Farm, Michaelchurch Eskley, c/o Hideaways, Shaftesbury SP7 0HQ
t 01747 828170 **e** enq@hideaways.co.uk
w hideaways.co.uk/property.cfm/h189

WHITCHURCH

Tump Farm Holiday Cottage
Mrs Debbie Williams, Tump Farm Holiday Cottage, Tump Farm, Whitchurch, Ross-on-Wye HR9 6DQ
t 01600 891029 **e** clinwilcharmaine@hotmail.com

Shropshire

ALBRIGHTON

Boningale Manor Barns
Owner, Boningale Manor Barns, Holyhead Road, Albrighton WV7 3AT
w boningalemanor.com

BROSELEY

Coalport YHA
John Rose Building, High Street, Telford TF8 7HT
t 0870 770 5882 **e** ironbridge@yha.org.uk
w yha.org.uk

EATON-UNDER-HEYWOOD

Eaton Manor
Mrs Nichola Madeley, Eaton Manor, Eaton-Under-Heywood, Church Stretton SY6 7DH
t 01694 724814 **f** 01694 722048
e nichola@eatonmanor.co.uk
w eatonmanor.co.uk

FISHMORE

Fishmore Hall
Fishmore Road, Ludlow SY8 3DP
t 01584 875148 **e** reception@fishmorehall.co.uk
w fishmorehall.co.uk

LYTH BANK

Lyth Hill House
28 Old Coppice, Lyth Hill, Shrewsbury SY3 0BP
t 01743 874660 **e** bnb@lythhillhouse.com
w lythhillhouse.com

ROWTON

Church Farm Self Catering
Mrs Virginia Evans, Church Farm, Rowton, Wellington, Telford TF6 6QY
t 01952 770381 **e** churchfarm49@beeb.net
w churchfarmshropshire.com

STANTON LACY

Sutton Court Farm Cottages
Mrs Jane Cronin, Sutton Court Farm, Little Sutton, Ludlow SY8 2AJ
t 01584 861305 **e** enquiries@suttoncourtfarm.co.uk
w suttoncourtfarm.co.uk

WHEATHILL

The Malthouse
Mr & Mrs Brian & Janet Russell, The Malthouse, Bridgnorth WV16 6QT
t 01244 356666 **e** info@sykescottages.co.uk
w cottageselection.co.uk

Staffordshire

ASHBOURNE

Dale Bottom Cottage
Mrs Sue Fowler, Church Farm, Milldale, Nr Alstonefield, Ashbourne DE6 2GD
t 01335 310243 **e** sue@fowler89.fsnet.co.uk
w dovedalecottages.co.uk

DILHORNE

Little Summerhill Cottages
Beth Plant, Little Summerhill Cottages, Little Summerhill Farm, Tickhill Lane ST10 2PL
t 01782 550967 **f** 01782 550967
e info@holidaycottagesstaffordshire.com
w holidaycottagesstaffordshire.com

ILAM

Beechenhill Farm Cottages
Alexandra Gray, Beechenhill Farm, Beechenhill Farm, Ilam, Ashbourne DE6 2BD
t 01335 310274 **e** beechenhill@btinternet.com
w beechenhill.co.uk

YHA Ilam Hall
Ilam, Ashbourne DE6 2AZ
t 0870 770 5876 **e** ilam@yha.org.uk
w yha.org.uk

Warwickshire

KNIGHTCOTE

Arbor Holiday & Knightcote Farm Cottages
Mr & Mrs Craig Walker, The Bake House, Knightcote, Southam CV47 2EF
t 01295 770637 **e** fionawalker@farmcottages.com
w farmcottages.com

LIGHTHORNE

Church Hill Farm B&B
Lighthorne, Warwick CV35 0AR
t 01926 651251 **e** sue@churchillfarm.co.uk
w churchillfarm.co.uk

STRATFORD-UPON-AVON

The Stratford
Arden Street, Stratford-upon-Avon CV37 6QQ
t 0845 074 0060 **e** thestratford@qhotels.co.uk
w qhotels.co.uk

Worcestershire

CHADDESLEY CORBETT

Brockencote Hall
Chaddesley Corbett, Kidderminster DY10 4PY
t 01562 777876 **e** info@brockencotehall.com
w brockencotehall.com

Where to Go

Goodrich | **Goodrich Castle**

Open: For opening hours and prices, please call 0870 333 1181 or visit www.english-heritage.org.uk/properties

Goodrich, Ross-on-Wye, Herefordshire HR9 6HY
t 0870 333 1181 **e** customers@english-heritage.org.uk
english-heritage.org.uk/goodrich

Relive the history with our free audio tour. Explore the keep and maze of rooms.

Access: ✲ ⚹ ♿ ♿ 🗐 General: ♿ 🗐

Tamworth | **Drayton Manor**

near Tamworth, Staffordshire B78 3TW
t 0844 472 1950 **e** info@draytonmanor.co.uk
draytonmanor.co.uk

Birmingham | **Cadbury World**

Linden Road, Bournville, Birmingham, West Midlands B30 2LU
t 0845 450 3599
cadburyworld.co.uk

Edgbaston | **Birmingham Botanical Gardens & Glasshouses**

Westbourne Road, Edgbaston, Birmingham B15 3TR
t 01214 541860 **e** admin@birminghambotanicalgardens.org.uk
birminghambotanicalgardens.org.uk

Access: ∴ ✲ ♿ ♿ ✲ ♿ 🗐 📺 ♿ ♿ General: ♿ 🗐 ⚘ ♿ ▣

Where to Eat

Barton under Needwood | **Waterfront**

Barton Marina, Barton under Needwood, East Staffordshire DE13 8DZ
t 01283 711500
bartonmarina.co.uk

General: 🐕 @FAX ♨ 🧍 👤 WC ♿ 👥 abc P***

Burton upon Trent | **Old Vicarage**

2 Main Street, Branston, Burton upon Trent, East Staffordshire DE14 3EX
t 01283 533222 **e** pascalarnoux@hotmail.com
pascalattheoldvicarage.co.uk

General: 🐕 @FAX ♨ 🧍 👤 WC ♿ 👥 ***

Hanley | **Portofino**

38 Marsh Street, Hanley, Stoke-on-Trent ST1 1JD
t 01782 209444
portofino-italiana.co.uk

General: 🐕 @FAX 🧍 👤 👥

Trent Vale | **Bauhinia**

2 Lyme Drive, Trent Vale, Stoke-on-Trent ST4 6NW
t 01782 719709
bauhiniarestaurant.co.uk

General: 🐕 🧍 👤 WC ♿ 👥 P***

Dickens Heath | **Mortons Kitchen Bar & Deli**

7 Main Street, Dickens Heath, West Midlands B90 1UB
t 0121 744 2884 **e** foodtogo@mortonskitchen.co.uk
mortonskitchen.co.uk

General: 🐕 @FAX ♨ 🧍 👤 WC ♿ 👥 abc

Hampton in Arden | **Beeches Bar and Restaurant**

Marsh Lane, Hampton in Arden, West Midlands B92 0AH
t 01675 442277 **e** info@thebeecheshampton.co.uk
thebeecheshampton.co.uk

General: 🐕 @FAX ♨ 🧍 👤 WC ♿ 👥 abc P***

For more information on accommodation attractions activities **events** and holidays
contact the **Tourist Information Centres**
see regional listings for the nearest one.

access Rugby

Planning a visit to Rugby has never been so easy.

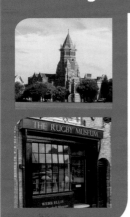

Visit our website for the latest availability and to book online.
enjoyrugby.co.uk can help with
- Where to stay
- Planning your visit
- What's On
- Visiting the birthplace of the game
- Ideas on things to see and do

Tel: **01788 533217**

Email: visitor.centre@rugby.gov.uk

www.enjoyrugby.co.uk

RUGBY
BOROUGH COUNCIL

RUGBY
THE BIRTHPLACE OF THE GAME

What's going on here then?

www.bclm.co.uk

- Meet the characters in the original shops and houses
- Underground Coal Mine Tours
- Working demonstrations
- New 1930's Street **and much more.**

THE BLACK COUNTRY LIVING MUSEUM
Dudley DY1 4SQ
tel: **0121 557 9643**

Mar to Dec: Every Day / Jan to Feb: Wed to Sun
Mar to Oct: 10am-5pm / Nov to Feb: 10am-4pm

NATIONAL FEDERATION OF Shopmobility 2011

The directory of Shopmobility Schemes in the UK, Channel Islands & ROI

Get trained - Get out - Get independent
The Shopmobility experience is not just about shopping!

www.shopmobilityuk.org

©Britain on View

OPEN BRITAIN **PLANNING A DAY OUT? WHY NOT MAKE IT A SHORT- BREAK?**
Fabulous 'Places to Stay' in every region

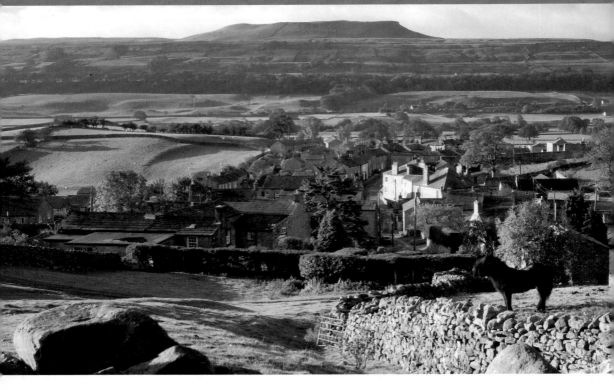

Welcome to Yorkshire

Yorkshire boasts an ever increasing choice of accessible accommodation, attractions and shops and we're confident you can enjoy Yorkshire to the full, whatever your needs may be. From the thrilling activity packed adventure, to the relaxing and peaceful, we asked European Champion sitskier Jo Willoughby how she enjoys Yorkshire...

Some might think it impossible to navigate the rough hills of **North Yorkshire** in a wheelchair, but on the path to **Malham Cove** and **Gordale scar**, that is not the case. Do you have a disability but want to kayak, abseil and aquaseil? Want to take part in archery or raft building? Then Yorkshire is the country for you. **Low Mill Outdoor Centre** in North Yorkshire offers these opportunities, as does **Hatfield Waterpark** in South Yorkshire.

Snozone in Xscape, Castleford offers accessible skiing and accessible scuba diving is offered by **Proscuba**, so leave your disability behind, and plunge into a frozen and watery world of fun. Why not try another medium and take to the air? This can be experienced with a microlight flight

from **Rufforth airfield**, East Yorkshire. Fancy a llama walking alongside your wheelchair during a ramble with **Nidderdale Llamas**. Fancy trekking through lema woods at **Yorkshire Wildlife Park** or flying a bird of prey at **Park Rose Bird of Prey Centre**; Yorkshire has all of these activities and more. Delve deep down into the earth's core at the **Yorkshire Mining Museum**, or journey into a dark canal tunnel built by navvy's hands at **Standedge Tunnell**. Each activity is disabled friendly whether the mode of travel is an accessible mine shaft cage or a boat with a wheelchair lift.

Visit the county's many colourful cities and enjoy **Huntfun's city treasure hunts**. Each hunt is designed with disabled people in mind and each city has a different flavour, so why not journey from city to city searching for Yorkshire treasure. Other such treasure includes The Forbidden Corner, in the **Tupgill Park Estate** in Coverham. This garden of secret treasures invites its visitors into a world of strange stone animals and sculptures; the stone path twists and turns through an elaborate maze of art work imaginatively situated within an earthen environment. The path here is only partially accessible for wheelchairs and

Askrigg

Woolley Edge

Yorkshire

Tourist Information Centres	218	Where to Go	229
Where to Stay	220	Where to Eat	231

partially sighted people need to take care, as often the path underfoot is the floor of a forest.

After such an experience, visitors might need a rest, so sit back, relax and settle into one of the **North of England Trike Tours**. The sight of the **Yorkshire Dales or Moors**, from the back of a trike, cannot fail to melt your heart, whatever your ability. Riding a trike can be as exhilarating as riding a motorbike, so for people who cannot ride, this activity is the perfect way to see Yorkshire. Finally, after all that, you might need to relax in a restful environment. Once such place is **York Yurts**; an import that transfers Mongolian accommodation into a Yorkshire field. Besides the issue of mud and wheelchair wheels, access is open to all, and inclusion in the hot tub is mandatory. Such an import suggests that the visitor is experiencing something foreign, but on the contrary: these yurts are one more example of how cosmopolitan and unique the county of Yorkshire is.

Sitting in the hot tub, bubbles frothing around your body and in your champagne glass, you can sit back and reflect: with all of these opportunities around you, why would you want to leave?

For more information on planning a trip to Yorkshire to suit your needs, click onto
www.yorkshire.com/disabled-go

Gordale Scar

Standedge T

Tourist Information Centres

Tourist Information Centres are a mine of information about local and regional accommodation, attractions and events. Visit them when you arrive at your destination or contact them before you go:

Aysgarth Falls	Aysgarth Falls NP Centre	01969 662910	aysgarth@yorkshiredales.org.uk
Beverley	34 Butcher Row	01482 391672	beverley.tic@eastriding .gov.uk
Bradford	City Hall	01274 433678	tourist.information@bradford.gov.uk
Bridlington	25 Prince Street	01262 673474	bridlington.tic@eastriding.gov.uk
Danby	The Moors Centre, Lodge Lane	01439 772737	moorscentre@northyorkmoors-npa.gov.uk
Doncaster	The Blue Building	01302 734309	tourist.information@doncaster.gov.uk
Filey	John Street	01723 383637	tourismbureau@scarborough.gov.uk
Grassington	National Park Centre	01756 751690	grassington@yorkshiredales.org.uk
Guisborough	Priory Grounds	01287 633801	guisborough_tic@redcar-cleveland.gov.uk
Halifax	Piece Hall	01422 368725	halifax@ytbtic.co.uk

Harrogate	Royal Baths	01423 537300	tic@harrogate.gov.uk
Hawes	Dales Countryside Museum	01969 666210	hawes@yorkshiredales.org.uk
Haworth	2/4 West Lane	01535 642329	haworth@ytbtic.co.uk
Hebden Bridge	Visitor and Canal Centre	01422 843831	hebdenbridge@ytbtic.co.uk
Helmsley	Helmsley Castle	01439 770173	helmsley.tic@englishheritage.org.uk
Holmfirth	49-51 Huddersfield Road	01484 222444	holmfirth.tic@kirklees.gov.uk
Huddersfield	3-5 Albion Street	01484 223200	huddersfield.tic@kirklees.gov.uk
Hull	1 Paragon Street	01482 223559	tourist.information@hullcc.gov.uk
Humber Bridge	North Bank Viewing Area	01482 640852	humberbridge.tic@eastriding.gov.uk
Ilkley	Station Road	01943 602319	ilkleytic@bradford.gov.uk
Knaresborough	9 Castle Courtyard	0845 389 0177	kntic@harrogate.gov.uk
Leeds	Gateway Yorkshire	0113 242 5242	tourinfo@leeds.gov.uk
Leeming Bar	The Yorkshire Maid	01677 424262	leeming@ytbtic.co.uk
Leyburn	4 Central Chambers	01748 828747	tic.leyburn@richmondshire.gov.uk
Malham	National Park Centre	01969 652380	malham@yorkshiredales.org.uk
Malton	Market Place	01653 600048	maltontic@btconnect.com
Otley	Otley Library	01943 462485	otleytic@leedslearning.net
Pateley Bridge	8 High Street	0845 389 0177	pbtic@harrogate.gov.uk
Pickering	Ropery House	01751 473791	pickeringtic@btconnect.com
Reeth	National Park Centre	01748 884059	reeth@yorkshiredales.org.uk
Richmond	Friary Gardens	01748 828742	tic.richmond@richmondshire.gov.uk
Ripon	Minster Road	01765 604625	ripontic@harrogate.gov.uk
Rotherham	40 Bridgegate	01709 835904	tic@rotherham.gov.uk
Scarborough	Brunswick Shopping Centre	01723 383636	tourismbureau@scarborough.gov.uk
Scarborough	Harbourside TIC	01723 383636	tourismbureau@scarborough.gov.uk
Settle	Town Hall	01729 825192	settle@ytbtic.co.uk
Sheffield	14 Norfolk Road	0114 2211900	visitor@yorkshiresouth.com
Skipton	35 Coach Street	01756 792809	skipton@ytbtic.co.uk
Sutton Bank	National Park Centre	01845 597426	suttonbank@northyorkmoors-npa.gov.uk
Thirsk	49 Market Place	01845 522755	thirsktic@hambleton.gov.uk
Todmorden	15 Burnley Road	01706 818181	todmorden@ytbtic.co.uk
Wakefield	9 The Bull Ring	0845 601 8353	tic@wakefield.gov.uk
Wetherby	Library & Tourist Info. Centre	01937 582151	wetherbytic@leedslearning.net
Whitby	Langborne Road	01723 383637	whitbytic@scarborough.gov.uk
Withernsea	131 Queen Street	01964 615683	withernsea.tic@eastriding.gov.uk
York	The De Grey Rooms	01904 550099	info@visityork.org
York Railway Station	Outer Concourse	01904 550099	info@visityork.org

Where to Stay

Bolton Abbey | Strid Wood Caravan Club Site ᴛʜᴇ CARAVAN CLUB

AS

Enjoy England ★★★★★

🚐 (57)
£15.30–£27.20

🚎 (57)
£15.30–£27.20

57 touring pitches
Open: 18 March - 2January 2012

Shop: 4 miles
Pub: 3 miles

Access:
🅰ᴴ ✳ 🚌 ☺ ♿ᵂᶜ
General:
🗓 🚐 🔥 🚗 💀 🗄 🛎 🔌ᵂᴾ ✕

Pitch:
🚐 🚎

Bolton Abbey, Skipton, North Yorkshire BD23 6AN
t 01756 710433
caravanclub.co.uk

4B1

One of the prettiest Club sites and part of the Bolton Abbey Estate in open glades surrounded by woodland and the glorious Yorkshire Dales. Within the boundaries of the estate are miles of footpaths through moors, woods and farmland.

Location: B6160 from A59 Bolton Bridge roundabout; after 3m turn right into car park. Do not approach on B6160 from north.

Brighouse | Holiday Inn Leeds/Brighouse

AA
★★★ Clifton Village, Brighouse, West Yorkshire HD6 4HW
t 0870 400 9013 e reservations-brighouse@ihg.com
holiday-inn.co.uk

Access: 📱 ✳ ☺ ♿ᵂᶜ ♿ᵂᶜ General: 🛎 🍽 ✕ ▼P♿ ✿ ♿ Room: ♿ 📺 ☕

©Britain on View/Tony Pleavin

Buckden | **Dalegarth and The Ghyll Cottages**

Enjoy England ★★★★

Units: 3   Sleeps: 2-6
Open: All year

Low season p/w:
£387.00
High season p/w:
£737.00
Shop: <0.5 miles
Pub: <0.5 miles

Access:
🅰 🏚 ☺
General:
🛏 🗄 P Ⓢ
Unit:
♨ 🏔 ♿ 🛗 📺 Ⓢ ♿ ✿

Mr & Mrs David Lusted, 11 Dalegarth, Buckden BD23 5JU
t 01756 760877 **e** info@dalegarth.co.uk
dalegarth.co.uk

5B3

Level access; downstairs double/twin bedroom with spa bath & level deck shower. Additional bedrooms/bathroom upstairs. Ground floor wheelchair friendly. Secluded sunny garden; stunning views; close to village centre.

Location: Buckden, Upper Wharfedale, between Skipton (30 min) and Aysgarth (20 min) on B6160. Convenient for visiting Wensleydale, Nidderdale, Swaledale, Malhamdale.

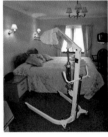

Ellerby | **Ellerby**

Enjoy England ★★★★

Open: All year

Rooms per night:
s: £55.00-£75.00
d: £85.00-£110.00
Meals: £9.00-£25.00

Ryeland Lane, Ellerby, Saltburn-by-the-Sea TS13 5LP
t 01947 840342 **e** relax@ellerbyhotel.co.uk
ellerbyhotel.co.uk

5D2

Run by the Alderson family since 1985 and located in a beautiful country, coastal setting.

Access: abc 🐾 🏚 ☺ ⁿᶜ 🦮 **General:** 🛏 🍳 ✕ 🍷 P ✿ ♿ **Room:** ♨ 🏔 🛗 ᵂᶜ Ⓢ ☕

Filey | **Muston Grange Farm**

Enjoy England ★★★

Units: 5   Sleeps: 5
Open: All year

Low season p/w:
£295.00
High season p/w:
£590.00

David & Gillian Teet, Muston Road, Filey, North Yorkshire YO14 0HU
t 01723 516620 **e** info@thecottagesfiley.co.uk
thecottagesfiley.co.uk

5D3

Group of five cottages, one being wheelchair friendly. Close to Filey on Yorkshire Coast.

Access: abc 🐾 **General:** 🛏 🗄 P Ⓢ **Unit:** ♨ 🏔 ♿ 🛗 ♿ ✿

Great Ayton | **Blackthorn Gate** AS

Enjoy England ★★★★

Units: 4 Sleeps: 4-5
Open: All year

Low season p/w:
£450.00
High season p/w:
£898.00
Shop: 2 miles
Pub: 1.5 miles

Mike & Rita Corrigan, Blackthorn Gate, Eastfields Farm, Nunthorpe, Nr Stokesley, North Yorkshire TS7 0PB **t** 01642 324496
e info@blackthorngate.co.uk
blackthorngate.co.uk

5C3

Wooden Swedish lodges four star gold rated, member of pet, family, cyclist, walker friendly schemes. Two bedrooms, ground floor one single one double bed, first floor king size bed, en suite shower room. Main bathroom and sauna on ground floor.

Location: From South A1, A168, A19, A172 three miles past Stokesley From North A19, A174, A172 300m past second roundabout.

Access:
General:
Unit:

Knaresborough | **Knaresborough Caravan Club Site** THE CARAVAN CLUB AS

Enjoy England ★★★★★

🚐 (74)
£15.30–£27.20
🚑 (74)
£15.30–£27.20
⛺ (5)

74 touring pitches
Open: 1 March 2011 to 14 February 2012

New Road, Scotton, Knaresborough HG5 9HH
t 01423 860196
caravanclub.co.uk

4B1

The Knaresborough Caravan Club Site is a perfect gateway to the Yorkshire Dales and the many attractions of the North of England. The caravan park is surrounded by mature trees and hedges.

Location: A1 j47 A59; right onto A59; left on A59 right onto B6165; right into New Rd. Site on right.

Access:
General:
Pitch:

Leeds | Crowne Plaza Leeds

AA ★★★★ Wellington Street, Leeds, West Yorkshire LS1 4DL
t 0871 942 9170 **e** sales.cpleeds@ihg.com
crowneplaza.co.uk

Access: abc 🔲 🏃 ☺ 🚽 ♿ 🛁 General: 🛏 🍽 ✕ ▼ P♿ ✿ ⊞ ♿ Room: 🔲 ☕

Leeds | Weetwood Hall Conference Centre & Hotel

AS

Enjoy England ★★★★	Otley Road, Leeds, West Yorkshire LS16 5PS
Open: All year	**t** 0113 230 6000 **e** reservations@weetwood.co.uk
Rooms per night:	weetwood.co.uk

4B1

Rooms per night:
s: £69.00-£159.00
d: £69.00-£159.00
p/p half board:
d: £59.00-£104.00
Meals: £24.50

Built around a 17th century Manor House, Weetwood Hall offers extensive hotel services and facilities.

Access: 🐕 ♿ 🛁 General: 🛏 🍽 ✕ ▼ P♿ ✿ ⊞ ♿ Room: 🛁 🏃 🛗 📺 🔲 ☕

Leyburn | Lower Wensleydale Caravan Club Site ~~THE CARAVAN CLUB~~

AS

Enjoy England ★★★

🚐 (92)
£11.40-£23.90

🚑 (92)
£11.40-£23.90

⚕ (5)

92 touring pitches
Open: 25 March to 7
November

Harmby, Leyburn DL8 5NU
t 01969 623366
caravanclub.co.uk

5C3

The Site is set within the hollow of a disused quarry that has a vast array of wild flowers and mosses, with ducks and rabbits roaming the site. A special area is set aside on site for tent campers.

Location: From East: A684 turn right Harmby just before Pheasant Inn; over bridge, left, follow signs to site.

Access:
🏃 ☺ ♿
General:
📖 🍴 🚐 💬 🚿 ☎ 🆆🅿
Pitch:
🚐 🚑 ⚕

Pickering | Keld Head Farm Cottages

 AS

Enjoy England ★★★★
Units: 9 Sleeps: 2-8
Open: All year

Low season p/w:
£215.00
High season p/w:
£1120.00

Penny & Julian Fearn, Keld Head, Pickering, North Yorkshire YO18 8LL
t 01751 473974 **e** julian@keldheadcottages.com
keldheadcottages.com

5D3

Picturesque stone cottages, emphasis on comfort and relaxation. Six cottages are easy access single storey.

General: 🛏️🗄️P🅂 Unit: ♿♿🚾🅂♿✿

Pickering | Keldlands Farm

AS

Enjoy England ★★★★
Units: 3 Sleeps: 4-7
Open: All year

Low season p/w:
£440.00
High season p/w:
£765.00
Shop: 3 miles
Pub: 0.5 miles

David Archer, Keldlands Farm Cottages, Yatts Road, Newton Upon Rawcliffe, Pickering, North Yorkshire YO18 8JP   **t** 01751 477656
e info@keldlandsfarmcottages.co.uk
keldlandsfarmcottages.co.uk

5D3

Three stone luxurious four star cottages, two, two bedroomed and one three with ground floor bedroom equiped for disabled. Cottages have two doubles or double and two singles. Ground floor WC, full central heating and pets welcome. BBQ, hot tub.

Location: Cottages are situated north past Pickering railway station, after 3.7 miles we are on your left just before the village.

Access:
✂️🏛️
General:
🛏️🗄️P🅂
Unit:
♿♿♿🅂♿✿

Pickering | Rawcliffe House Farm

Enjoy England ★★★★
Units: 1 Sleeps: 1-2
Open: All year

Low season p/w:
£400.00
High season p/w:
£544.00

Mr & Mrs Duncan & Jan Allsopp, Rawcliffe House Farm, Stape, Nr Pickering, North Yorkshire YO18 8JA   **t** 01751 473292
e stay@rawcliffehousefarm.co.uk
rawcliffehousefarm.co.uk

5D3

Cloth Fair Cottage, superior wheelchair accessible, one bedroom self catering holiday cottage, sleeping two persons.

Access: 🏛️☺ General: 🗄️P🅂 Unit: ♿♿♿♿🚾🅂♿✿

Richmond | Hargill House Caravan Club Site

THE CARAVAN CLUB

Enjoy England ★★★★

🚐 (66)
£12.10–£23.90

🚎 (66)
£12.10–£23.90

66 touring pitches
Open: 18 March – 7 November

Shop: 1 mile
Pub: 1 mile

Access:
⚠ 🐕 🔋 ☺ ♿

General:
🔲 🚐 📷 🚮 🛒 🛍 🏪 (WP)

Pitch:
🚐 🚎

Gilling West, Richmond, North Yorkshire DL10 5LJ
t 01748 822734
caravanclub.co.uk

5C3

A tranquil site in the old town of Richmond with breathtaking views over the Yorkshire Dales. It's Herriot country, and you'll find many of the locations used in the famous series. It's also where the artist Turner travelled and painted.

Location: Leave A1 at Scotch Corner onto A66. After 1.5m turn left at crossroads. Site entrance is 100yds on left.

Scarborough | Inglenook Guest House

Enjoy England ★★★★★

Open: All year except Xmas and New Year

Rooms per night:
s: £45.00–£50.00
d: £80.00–£90.00
p/p half board:
d: £56.00–£140.00
Meals: £8.00–£20.00

94a Scalby Road, Scarborough YO12 5QN
t 01723 369454 **e** inglenookguesthouse@live.co.uk
inglenookscarborough.co.uk

5D3

Small 5 star silver guest house. Award winning gardens. 1 family, 1 double, en suite.

Access: abc 🐕 🔋 General: 🛏 🍴 ✗ P♿ ❀ ♿ Room: 🛗 📻 (WC)

Wakefield | Campanile Hotel

Monckton Road, Wakefield, West Yorkshire WF2 7AL
t 01924 201054 **e** wakefield@campanile.com
campanile.com

Wakefield | Holiday Inn Leeds-Wakefield M1 J40

Queens Drive, Ossett, Wakefield, West Yorkshire WF5 9BE
t 0871 942 9082 **e** reservations-wakefield@ihg.com
holiday-inn.co.uk

Access: .: abc 🔲 🐕 🔋 ☺ (wc) ♿ ♿ General: 🛏 🍴 ✗ 🍷 P♿ ❀ 🔲 ♿ Room: 🔋 📻 🖥 🔲 S ☕

Whitby | **Whitby Holiday Park - Touring Park**

Enjoy England ★★★★

🚐 (18)
£16.00–£33.50

🚙 (93)
£16.00–£33.50

🛖 (111)
£140.00–£628.00

119 touring pitches
Open: 01/03 - 14/01

Whitby Holiday Park, Saltwick Bay, Whitby YO22 4JX
t 01947 602664 **e** info@whitbyholidaypark.co.uk
whitbypark.co.uk

5D3

Ideally situated on the cliff top overlooking Saltwick Bay, Whitby Holiday Park is perfectly located for exploring the nearby North Yorkshire National Park and stunning local beaches.

Location: Approch Whitby directing you to Whitby Abbey follow Green Lane T junction, turn right & look for tourist signs.

Access:
⚠ 🖉 🐕 🏢 ☺ ♿
General:
🔋 ♿ 🐾 🔌 🚻 🚿 WP
Pitch:
🚐 🛖 🚙

York | **Holiday Inn York**

Tadcaster Road, York, North Yorkshire YO24 1QF
t 0871 942 9085 **e** reservations-york@ihg.com
holidayinn.co.uk

Access: abc 🖉 🐕 🏢 ☺ ♿ General: 🛏 🍴 ✕ 🍷 P♿ ✿ 🖽 ♿ Room: 🖂 ☕

York | **Rowntree Park Caravan Club Site** THE CARAVAN CLUB

AS

Enjoy England ★★★★★

🚐 (102)
£16.40–£29.30

🚐 (102)
£16.40–£29.30

⛺ (6)

102 touring pitches
Open: All year

Shop: <0.5 miles
Pub: <0.5 miles

Terry Avenue, York, North Yorkshire YO23 1JQ
t 01904 658997
caravanclub.co.uk

4C1

On the banks of the river Ouse in the heart of York, this popular site is just a few minutes' walk from the city centre. York is a feast, there's so much to see and do.

Location: A64 onto A19 (York). After 2 miles join one-way system. Keep left. Left at caravan sign. Right onto Terry Avenue.

Access:
🅰 🐕 ♿ ☺ ♿wc
General:
📶 📻 🚐 ☠ 🚻 🚰 WP
Pitch:
🚐 🚐 ⛺

York | **South Newlands Farm Self Catering**

♿ AS

Enjoy England ★★★★

Units: 3   Sleeps: 2-6
Open: All year

Low season p/w:
£295.00
High season p/w:
£595.00
Shop: 1 mile
Pub: 1 mile

Mrs Peggy Swann, South Newlands Farm, Selby Road, Riccall, York
YO19 6QR   **t** 01757 248203 **e** info@southnewlandsfarm.co.uk
southnewlandsfarm.co.uk

4C1

Our aim is to provide excellent accommodation for people of all ages and abilities, generously proportioned rooms, ample wheelchair access, flat entry showers, double and twin bedrooms, lawn and paved patio all make for a comfortable and enjoyable stay.

Location: A19 York-Selby. From York pass 2 signs for Riccall take next left. From Selby pass turnoff A163 take next right.

Access:
🅰 🐕 ♿
General:
🐕 📶 P Ⓢ
Unit:
🛁 ♿ 🧹 ♿ 📺 wc Ⓢ ♿ ❀

York | **York Lakeside Lodges**

Enjoy England
★★★★-★★★★★

Units: 16   Sleeps: 2-7
Open: All year

Low season p/w:
£240.00
High season p/w:
£850.00

Mr Neil Manasir, York Lakeside Lodges, Moor Lane, York, North Yorkshire
YO24 2QU   **t** 01904 702346   **e** neil@yorklakesidelodges.co.uk
yorklakesidelodges.co.uk

4C1

Lodges in parkland overlooking a lake yet two miles from the centre of York.

Access: 🐾🚻♿ General: 🐴P Unit: 🍳🔥♿🛏🚽📺Ⓢ♿✿

Yorkshire

AMOTHERBY

Walnut Garth
Cas Radford, Walnut Garth, Havendale, Main Street, Swinton YO17 6SL
t 07530 383429   **f** 01653 691293
e cas@walnutgarth.co.uk
w walnutgarth.co.uk

BRIDLINGTON

The Bay View Hotel
52 South Marine Drive, Bridlington YO15 3JJ
t 01262 674225   **e** info@bay-view-hotel.com
w bay-view-hotel.com

Providence Place
11 North View Terrace, Bridlington YO15 2QP
t 01262 603840   **e** enquiries@providenceplace.info
w providenceplace.info

BRIGHOUSE

The Lodge @ Birkby Hall
Birkby Hall, Birkby Lane, Brighouse HD6 4JJ
t 01484 400321   **e** thelodge@birkbyhall.co.uk
w birkbyhall.co.uk

CLAPHAM

New Inn Hotel
Clapham LA2 8HH
t 01524 251203   **e** info@newinn-clapham.co.uk
w newinn-clapham.co.uk

CROW EDGE

Lazy Daisy's
Sally Howe, Lazy Daisy's, Daisy Hill Farm, Flouch S36 4HH
t 01226 763001   **e** daisyhillfarm@tiscali.co.uk
w lazydaisys.co.uk

DREWTON

Rudstone Walk Country Accommodation
Laura Greenwood, Rudstone Walk Country Accommodation, South Cave HU15 2AH
t 01430 422230   **e** office@rudstone-walk.co.uk
w rudstone-walk.co.uk

Rudstone Walk Country B&B
South Cave, Brough, Beverley HU15 2AH
t 01430 422230   **e** rooms@rudstone-walk.co.uk
w rudstone-walk.co.uk

DUNSLEY

The Old Granary
Mrs Jackie Richardson, Sandsend Bay Cottages, Raven Hill Farm, Dunsley YO21 3TJ
t 01947 893331   **f** 01947 893331
e jackie.richardson@btopenworld.com
w sandsendbaycottages.co.uk

EBBERSTON

Cow Pasture & Swallow-Tail Cottages
David & Brenda Green, Studley House Farm, 67 Main Street, Ebberston YO13 9NR
t 01723 859285   **e** brenda@yorkshireancestors.com
w studleyhousefarm.co.uk

FELLBECK

Brimham Rocks Cottages
Deborah Gray, Brimham Rocks Cottages, High North Farm, Fellbeck HG3 5EY
t 01765 620284   **e** brimhamrockscottages@yahoo.com
w brimham.co.uk

FILEY

5 Leys Holiday Accommodation
Mrs Kerry Welsby, 5 Leys Bar, Restaurant & Holiday Accommodation, 7-10 The Beach, Filey YO14 9LA
t 0845 094 5051   **e** kerry@icflimited.co.uk
w 5leys.co.uk

FLAMBOROUGH

Flamborough Rock Cottages
Mrs J Geraghty, 13 Dog & Duck Square, Bridlington YO15 1NB
t 01262 850996   **e** jannicegeraghty@hotmail.com
w flamboroughrockcottages.co.uk

GATEFORTH

Lund Farm Cottages
Mr Chris Middleton, Lund Farm Cottages, Lund Farm, Gateforth YO8 9LE
t 01757 228775   **e** lundfarm@talktalk.net
w lundfarm.co.uk

HARWOOD DALE

The Grainary
The Grainary, Harwood Dale, Scarborough YO13 0DT
t 01723 870026   **e** grainary@btopenworld.com
w grainary.co.uk

HELMSLEY

Helmsley YHA
Carlton Lane, Helmsley YO62 5HB
t 01439 770433   **e** helmsley@yha.org.uk
w yha.org.uk

HIGH CATTON

The Courtyard & Ruxpin Cottage
Sheila Foster, High Catton Grange, High Catton, York YO41 1EP
t 01759 371374   **e** foster-s@sky.com
w highcattongrange.co.uk

ILKLEY

Westwood Lodge, Ilkley Moor
Tim Edwards, Westwood Lodge Ilkley Moor, Westwood Drive, Ilkley LS29 9JF
t 01943 433430   **e** welcome@westwoodlodge.co.uk
w westwoodlodge.co.uk

INGLETON

Riverside Lodge
24 Main Street, Ingleton LA6 3HJ
t 01524 241359   **e** info@riversideingleton.co.uk
w riversideingleton.co.uk

KELFIELD

The Dovecote Barns York
Mrs Brigita Bramley, The Dovecote Barns York, Manor Farm, Kelfield YO19 6RG
t 01757 249332   **e** enquiries@dovecotebarnsyork.co.uk
w dovecotebarnsyork.co.uk

KIRKBYMOORSIDE

The Cornmill
Kirby Mills, Kirkbymoorside YO62 6NP
t 01751 432000   **e** cornmill@kirbymills.co.uk
w kirbymills.co.uk

Low Hagg Holidays
Mr J Lee, Low Hagg Holidays, Low Hagg, Starfitts Lane, York YO62 7JF
t 01751 430500   **e** info@lowhaggfarm.com

LEVEN

Agape
Heron House, Beverley Road, Beverley HU17 5PA
t 01964 541316   **e** enquiries@stayatagape.co.uk
w stayatagape.co.uk

LOCKTON

YHA Lockton
The Old School, Lockton YO18 7PY
t 01751 460376   **e** lockton@yha.org.uk
w yha.org.uk

MIDDLETON, NR PICKERING

The Hawthornes Lodges
Mrs Paula Appleby, The Hawthornes/ The Hawthornes Lodges, The Hawthornes, High Back Side, Middleton, near Pickering YO18 8PB
t 01751 474755   **e** info@thehawthornes.co.uk
w thehawthornes.co.uk

NEWTON-ON-RAWCLIFFE

Mel House Cottages
John Wicks, Let's Holiday, Mel House, Newton-on-Rawcliffe YO18 8QA
t 01751 475396   **e** holiday@letsholiday.com
w letsholiday.com

Sunset Cottage
Pat Anderson, Mrs Anderson's Country Cottages, Boonhill Cottage, Newton-on-Rawcliffe YO18 8QF
t 01751 472172   **e** bookings@boonhill.co.uk
w boonhill.co.uk/sunset.htm

NORTHALLERTON

Lovesome Hill Farm
Lovesome Hill Farm, Northallerton DL6 2PB
t 01609 772311   **e** lovesomehillfarm@btinternet.com
w lovesomehillfarm.co.uk

PICKERING

Eastgate Cottages
Kevin & Elaine Bedford, Eastgate Cottages Ltd, 117 Eastgate, Pickering YO18 7DW
t 01751 476653   **e** info@eastgatecottages.co.uk
w eastgatecottages.co.uk

PRESTON

Little Weghill Farm
Weghill Road, Preston, Hull HU12 8SX
t 01482 897650   **e** info@littleweghillfarm.co.uk
w littleweghillfarm.co.uk

SCARBOROUGH

The Scarborough Travel and Holiday Lodge
33 Valley Road, Scarborough YO11 2LX
t 01723 363537   **e** enquiries@scarborough-lodge.co.uk
w scarborough-lodge.co.uk

SEWERBY

Field House Farm Cottages
Mr & Mrs Foster, Field House Farm Cottages, Jewison Lane, Sewerby YO16 6YG
t 01262 674932   **e** john.foster@farmline.com
w fieldhousefarmcottages.co.uk

SHEFFIELD

The Cart Shed
Mr James Russell, Moorwood Farm, Riggs High Road, Sheffield S6 6GR
t 0114 230 2122   **e** moorwoodequine@googlemail.com
w cottage.moorwoodequine.co.uk

SLAITHWAITE

The Mistal Bed and Breakfast
The Mistal, Cop Hill Side, Huddersfield HD7 5XA
t 01484 845404   **e** carolineandphil1@tiscali.co.uk
w themistal.co.uk

SLEIGHTS

Groves Dyke Holiday Cottage
Niall Carson, Groves Dyke, Woodlands Drive, Sleights
YO21 1RY
t 01947 810220   **e** relax@grovesdyke.co.uk
w grovesdyke.co.uk

SUMMERBRIDGE

Helme Pasture Lodges & Cottages
Mrs Rosemary Helme, Helme Pasture Lodges & Cottages,
Hartwith Bank, Summerbridge, Harrogate HG3 4DR
t 01423 780279   **e** info@helmepasture.co.uk
w helmepasture.co.uk

THORGANBY

Thorganby Farm Cottages
Ms Judy Ruston, Thorganby Farm Cottages, Common Farm,
Southmoor Road YO19 6DL
t 01904 449653   **e** judyruston@btinternet.com
w thorganbyfarmcottages.org.uk

THORNTON DALE

Easthill Farm House and Gardens
Mrs Diane Stenton, Easthill Farm House and Gardens, Wilton
Road, Thornton Dale, Pickering YO18 7QP
t 01751 474561   **e** info@easthill-farm-holidays.co.uk
w easthill-farm-holidays.co.uk

THORPE BASSETT

The Old Post Office
Sandra Simpson, S Simpson Cottages, The Old Post Office,
Thorpe Bassett YO17 8LU
t 01944 758047   **e** ssimpsoncottages@aol.com
w ssimpsoncottages.co.uk

WHITBY

Captain Cook's Haven
Anne Barrowman, Captain Cook's Haven, Larpool Lane,
Whitby YO22 4NE
t 01947 893573   **e** mail@hoseasons.co.uk
w whitbyholidayhomes.co.uk

Dale House Farm Cottages
Mrs Welford, Dale House Farm Cottages, Dale House Farm,
Staithes, Whitby TS13 5DT
t 01947 840377   **e** em.welford@btinternet.com
w dalehousefarmcottages.co.uk

Whitby YHA
East Cliff, Whitby YO22 4JT
t 01947 602878

WRELTON

Beech Farm Cottages
Rooney Massara, Beech Farm Cottages, Wrelton YO18 8PG
t 01751 476612   **e** holiday@beechfarm.com
w beechfarm.com

YAPHAM

Wolds View Holiday Cottages
Margaret Woodliffe, Wolds View Holiday Cottages, Mill Farm,
Yapham YO42 1PH
t 01759 302172   **e** info@woldsview.co.uk

YORK

Best Western Monkbar Hotel
St. Maurice's Road, York YO31 7JA
t 01904 638086   **e** sales@monkbarhotel.co.uk
w bestwestern.co.uk/monkbarhotel

The Groves
St. Peters Grove, York YO30 6AQ
t 01904 559777   **e** info@thegroveshotelyork.co.uk
w thegroveshotelyork.co.uk

Stakesby Holiday Flats
Mr Anthony Bryce, Stakesby Holiday Flats, 4 St George's
Place, York YO24 1DR
t 01904 611634   **e** ant@stakesby.co.uk
w stakesby.co.uk

Where to Go

Brodsworth | Brodsworth Hall & Gardens

Open: For opening hours and prices, please call 0870 333 1181 or visit www.english-heritage.org.uk/properties

Brodsworth, Near Doncaster, South Yorkshire DN5 7XJ
t 0870 333 1181   **e** customers@english-heritage.org.uk
english-heritage.org.uk/brodsworth

Brodsworth Hall is a unique family day out. Explore the country house and beautiful gardens.

Access: General:

Harrogate | RHS Garden Harlow Carr

Crag Lane, Harrogate, North Yorkshire HG3 1QB
t 01423 565418   **e** harlowcarr@rhs.org.uk
rhs.org.uk

Leeds | Henry Moore Institute

74 The Headrow, Leeds, Yorkshire LS1 3AH
t 0113 246 7467
henry-moore-fdn.co.uk

Access: abc

Leyburn | Yorkshire Dales National Park Authority

Yoredale, Bainbridge, Leyburn, North Yorkshire DL8 3EL
t 0870 1666333 **e** rachel.briggs@yorkshiredales.org.uk

Rievaulx | Rievaulx Abbey

Open: For opening hours and prices, please call 0870 333 1181 or visit www.english-heritage.org.uk/properties

Rievaulx, Nr Helmsley, North Yorkshire YO62 5LB
t 0870 333 1181 **e** customers@english-heritage.org.uk
english-heritage.org.uk/rievaulx

Take a day out to find peace amongst the atmospheric ruins of Rievaulx Abbey.

Access: ♿ General: ⬚

Scarborough | Scarborough Castle

Open: For opening hours and prices, please call 0870 333 1181 or visit www.english-heritage.org.uk/properties

Castle Road, Scarborough, North Yorkshire YO11 1HY
t 0870 333 1181 **e** customers@english-heritage.org.uk
english-heritage.org.uk/scarboroughcastle

Enjoy a fun family day out visiting Scarborough Castle! Explore over 2,500 years of history!

Access: ⬚ General: ⬚ ✿ ♿ ⌨

Whitby | Whitby Abbey

Open: For opening hours and prices, please call 0870 333 1181 or visit www.english-heritage.org.uk/properties

Whitby, North Yorkshire YO22 4JT
t 0870 333 1181 **e** customers@english-heritage.org.uk
english-heritage.org.uk/whitby

The iconic ruins of Whitby Abbey offer a great family day out with great views.

Access: ♿ ☼ ⬚ ▦ General: ♿ ✿ ♿

York | Jorvik Viking Centre

Coppergate, York, North Yorkshire YO1 9WT
t 01904 543400 **e** jorvik@yorkat.co.uk
jorvik-viking-centre.co.uk

Where to Eat

Leeds | **De Fresh Restaurant**

Unit 5, Moor Allerton District Centre, King Lane, Leeds LS17 5NY
t 0113 2687799
defreshrestaurant.co.uk

General: 🐕 🐾 🧍 ♿ WC ♿ 🧑‍🦽 abc ★★★

Leeds | **Sous le Nez**

Quebec House, Quebec Street, Leeds LS1 2HA
t 0113 2440108
souslenez.com

General: 🐕 FAX ♿ abc

Leeds | **Spice Quarter**

Millennium Square, Electric Press Building, Great George Street, Leeds
LS2 3AD   **t** 0113 246 9241 **e** spicequarter@hotmail.co.uk
spicequarter.co.uk

General: 🐕 FAX 🐾 🧍 ♿ WC ♿ 🧑‍🦽

York | **Ask**

The Grand Assembly Rooms, Blake Street, York YO1 2QG
t 01904 637254
askrestaurants.com

General: 🐕 FAX 🐾 🧍 ♿ WC ♿ 🧑‍🦽 .: abc

York | **Fellini's Restaurant**

11-12 Fossgate, York YO1 9TA
t 01904 611154
fellinis.co.uk

General: 🐕 🧍 ♿ 🧑‍🦽

York | **Jaipur Spice**

103 Haxby Road, York YO31 8JS
t 01904 673550
jaipur-spice.com

General: FAX 🐾 🧍 ♿ ♿ P ★★★

York | **Lime House**

55 Goodramgate, York YO1 7LS
t 01904 632734 **e** fishers@limehouse.fsnet.co.uk
limehouserestaurant-york.co.uk

General: 🐕 FAX 🧍 ♿ 🧑‍🦽 abc

OPEN BRITAIN

2011 – Dates for your diary

2011

New Year's Day Bank Holiday	3rd Jan
Moving & Handling People	3rd – 4th Feb
Kidz in the Middle	10th Mar
The Care Show	29th – 30th Mar
Good Friday	22nd Apr
Easter Monday	25th Apr
Naidex National	5th – 7th Apr
May Day Bank Holiday	2nd May
Liberation Day (Channel Islands)	9th May
Spring Bank Holiday	30th May
Kidz South	9th June
The Mobility Roadshow	30th June – 2nd July
Summer Bank Holiday	29th Aug
Naidex Scotland	14th – 15th Sep
Naidex South	19th – 20th Oct
Beyond Boundries Live!	TBC
enABLE 2011	TBC
Kidz up North	TBC
Boxing Day Holiday	26th Dec
Christmas Bank Holiday	27th Dec

If there is an event going on in your area that you think we should know about, let us know!

info@openbritain.net

©Britainonview / Pawel Libera

©Britainonview / Grant Pritchard

©Britainonview / Liz Gander

Striking landscapes and vibrant cityscapes

An exciting and dynamic region, England's North West if full of striking landscapes and vibrant cityscapes. From the elegant and ancient city of Chester to the inspirational vistas of the Lake District; the award winning industrial heritage of Manchester and the outstanding cultural attractions of Liverpool, there's so much to see and do in England's North West. Add to these a spectacular coastline with Britain's favourite seaside resorts, and the delightfully undiscovered countryside of Lancashire, and you're spoilt for choice.

Individual and edgy, Manchester is a place like no other. From **Manchester Art Gallery's** Pre-Raphaelites to the cool and contemporary **Beetham Tower**, it's a dramatic mix of old and new. The city's industrial legacy lives on in its trail-blazing spirit, with cutting edge festivals and events all year round. Manchester is synonymous with sport, but equally famed for its vibrant cultural scene and fantastic nightlife; this is the original 24-hour city.

Elegant and ancient, the city of Chester is full of 21st century delights. This walled Roman city is the perfect place to treat yourself; indulge in some seriously sophisticated retail therapy or pamper yourself in luxurious spa hotels. **Chester's Rows** are unique to the city and these two-tiered shopping galleries are accessible to all. And when it comes to spectacular gardens, Cheshire can boast some of the finest examples in the world, including the glorious **Ness Botanic Gardens**.

Liverpool is truly awe-inspiring; with more museums and galleries than anywhere else outside London and the iconic architecture of its **World Heritage Site**, this really is a world-class city. With eight venues in the **National Museums** Liverpool family, not to mention the **Beatles story** and **Tate Liverpool**, it's easy to see why Liverpool remains a Capital of Culture.

Head North from Liverpool and discover a spectacular coastline sprinkled with Britain's favourite seaside resorts, including bold and bright **Blackpool** with its famous illuminations and white-knuckle rides; **Sandcastle Waterpark** is always a favourite. Lancashire is also home to the **Forest of Bowland**, **Ribble Valley** and **Pendle Hill**, all areas of renowned natural beauty where it's easy to get out and about, as well as offering top notch cuisine and plenty of farm fresh produce.

Wastwater

Liverpool

North West

Cheshire, Cumbria, Lancashire, Manchester, Merseyside

The spectacular vistas of the **Lake District**, the country's best outdoor playground, are inspirational at any time of year. Home to England's highest mountain and deepest lake, here you can follow the footsteps of the Romantic poets at **Dove Cottage** and the **Wordsworth Museum** or try your hand at something a little more vigorous with countless outdoor activity providers eager to show you the ropes whatever your ability.

England's North West is also home to England's **Golf Coast**, the highest concentration of championship links courses in the world. Add to this a sporting heritage that is second to none – the professional football game was born here and **Aintree Racecourse** is home to the most famous steeplechase on earth, the renowned **John Smiths Grand National** – and you're spoilt for choice.

With the myriad events, performances, exhibitions and gigs that keep the region buzzing all year long, we guarantee you'll be hooked.

Find out more
www.visitenglandsnorthwest.com

Bowland Forest

Blackpool

Tourist Information Centres

Tourist Information Centres are a mine of information about local and regional accommodation, attractions and events. Visit them when you arrive at your destination or contact them before you go:

Accrington	Town Hall	01254 380293	tourism@hyndburnbc.gov.uk
Altrincham	20 Stamford New Road	0161 912 5931	tourist.information@trafford.gov.uk
Ambleside	Central Buildings	015394 32582	amblesidetic@southlakeland.gov.uk
Ashton-Under-Lyne	Council Offices	0161 343 4343	tourist.information@tameside.gov.uk
Barnoldswick	The Council Shop	01282 666704	tourist.info@pendle.gov.uk
Barrow-In-Furness	Forum 28	01229 876505	touristinfo@barrowbc.gov.uk
Blackburn	50-54 Church Street	01254 53277	visit@blackburn.gov.uk
Blackpool	1 Clifton Street	01253 478222	tic@blackpool.gov.uk
Bolton	Central Library Foyer	01204 334321	tourist.info@bolton.gov.uk
Bowness	Glebe Road	015394 42895	bownesstic@lake-district.gov.uk
Burnley	Burnley Bus Station	01282 664421	tic@burnley.gov.uk
Bury	The Met Arts Centre	0161 253 5111	touristinformation@bury.gov.uk
Carlisle	Old Town Hall	01228 625600	tourism@carlisle-city.gov.uk

Chester	Town Hall	01244 402111	welcome@visitchesterandcheshire.co.uk
Cleveleys	Victoria Square	01253 853378	cleveleystic@wyrebc.gov.uk
Clitheroe	Ribble Valley Borough Council	01200 425566	tourism@ribblevalley.gov.uk
Congleton	Town Hall	01260 271095	tourism@congleton.gov.uk
Coniston	Ruskin Avenue	015394 41533	mail@conistontic.org
Ellesmere Port	McArthur Glen Outlet Village	0151 356 7879	cheshireoaks.cc@visitor-centre.net
Fleetwood	Old Ferry Office	01253 773953	fleetwoodtic@wyrebc.gov.uk
Garstang	Council Offices	01995 602125	garstangtic@wyrebc.gov.uk
Kendal	Town Hall	01539 797516	kendaltic@southlakeland.gov.uk
Keswick	Moot Hall	017687 72645	keswicktic@lake-district.gov.uk
Knutsford	Council Offices	01565 632611	knutsfordtic@cheshireeast.gov.uk
Lancaster	The Story Creative Industries Centre	01524 582394	lancastervic@lancaster.gov.uk
Liverpool City Centre	Whitechapel	0151 233 2008	info@08place.gov.uk
Liverpool Albert Dock	Anchor Courtyard	0151 233 2008	info@08place.gov.uk
Liverpool John Lennon Airport	Arrivals Hall, South Terminal	0151 907 1058	info@08place.gov.uk
Lytham St Annes	Town Hall, St Annes Rd West	01253 725610	touristinformation@fylde.gov.uk
Macclesfield	Macclesfield	01625 504114	informationcentre@macclesfield.gov.uk
Manchester	Lloyd Street	0871 222 8223	touristinformation@ marketingmanchester.co.uk
Morecambe	Old Station Buildings	01524 582808	morecambetic@lancaster.gov.uk
Nantwich	Civic Hall	01270 537359	touristi@crewe-nantwich.gov.uk
Northwich	The Arcade	01606 353534	tourism@valeroyal.gov.uk
Oldham	12 Albion Street	0161 627 1024	ecs.tourist@oldham.gov.uk
Pendle Heritage Centre	Park Hill	01282 661701	heritage.centre@pendle.gov.uk
Pendle, Discover	Boundary Mill Sores	01282 856186	discoverpendle@pendle.gov.uk
Penrith	Middlegate	01768 867466	pen.tic@eden.gov.uk
Preston	The Guildhall	01772 253731	tourism@preston.gov.uk
Rochdale	Touchstones	01706 924928	tic@link4life.org
Salford	The Lowry, Pier 8	0161 848 8601	tic@salford.gov.uk
Southport	112 Lord Street	01704 533333	info@visitsouthport.com
St Helens	The World of Glass	01744 755150	info@sthelenstic.com
Stockport	Staircase House	0161 474 4444	tourist.information@stockport.gov.uk
Warrington	The Market Hall	01925 428585	informationcentre@warrington.gov.uk
Whitehaven	Market Hall	01946 598914	tic@copelandbc.gov.uk
Wigan	62 Wallgate	01942 825677	tic@wlct.org
Wilmslow	Rectory Fields	01625 522275	i.hillaby@macclesfield.gov.uk
Windermere	Victoria Street	015394 46499	windermeretic@southlakeland.gov.uk

Where to Stay

Acton Bridge | Wall Hill Farm Guesthouse

 AS

Enjoy England ★★★★★

Open: All year

Rooms per night:
s: £45.00–£52.00
d: £68.00–£75.00

Acton Lane, Acton Bridge, Northwich CW8 3QE
t 01606 852654 **e** info@wallhillfarmguesthouse.co.uk
wallhillfarmguesthouse.co.uk

4A2

Five star luxury guest house with 7 double/twin bedrooms with en suite facilities.

Access: 🏛️♿♿ General: 🛁🍴🅿️❀♿ Room: 🛏️🧹📺📶Ⓢ☕

Chester | Chester Fairoaks Caravan Club Site ᴛʜᴇ CARAVAN CLUB

AS

Enjoy England ★★★★★

🚐 (100)
£16.40–£29.30

🚏 (100)
£16.40–£29.30

⛺ (5)

100 touring pitches
Open: All year

Shop: 0.5 miles
Pub: <0.5 miles

Rake Lane, Little Stanney, Chester, Cheshire CH2 4HS
t 0151 3551600
caravanclub.co.uk

4A2

A tranquil site edged with oak trees six miles from the walled city of Chester with its famous zoo, historic sites, and excellent entertainment and shopping. Take an open-top bus or walk around the walls to absorb the colourful atmosphere.

Location: Travel towards Queensferry on A5117 from M53. Turn left in Little Stanney at signpost Chorlton. Site 0.25 miles on left.

Access:
🅰️🐾🏛️☺♿🚾
General:
🚻🍴🏧🚐🛒🛗📶
Pitch:
🚐🚏⛺

Chester | Crowne Plaza Chester

AS

AA ★★★★

Trinity Street, Chester, Cheshire CH1 2BD
t 01244 899988 **e** cpchester@qmh-hotels.com
crowneplaza.com/chester

Access: 🅰️ abc 📱🐾🏛️☺♿♿ General: 🛁🍴✕🍷🅿️⬆️♿ Room: 📶📺📶📺📺Ⓢ☕

Chester | **Express by Holiday Inn Chester Racecourse**

New Crane Street, Chester, Cheshire CH1 2LY
t 0870 990 4065 **e** hotel@chester-races.com
hiexpress.com

Access: ♿ 🅿 ⚡ 🏨 ☺ ♿ ♿ General: 🐕 🛏 ✗ ♟ 🅿 ✿ 🈁 ♿ Room: 🛏 🔥 📺 ☕

Knutsford | **The Cottage**

Open: All year except Xmas and New Year
....

Rooms per night:
s: £50.00-£89.00
d: £50.00-£95.00
Meals: £9.00-£30.00

London Road, Allostock, Nr Knutsford, Cheshire WA16 9LU
t 01565 722470 **e** reception@thecottageknutsford.co.uk
thecottageknutsford.co.uk

4A2

The Cottage offers comfort and attentive service with friendliness and informality. Expect a warm welcome.

Access: 🏨 ☺ ♿ ♿ General: 🐕 🛏 ✗ ♟ ♿ Room: 🛏 ☕

Macclesfield | **Kerridge End Holiday Cottages**

 AS

Enjoy England   ★★★★★
Units: 3 Sleeps: 1-6
Open: All year

Low season p/w:
£300.00
High season p/w:
£900.00

Mr Ivor Williams, Kerridge End Holiday Cottages, Kerridge End House,
Rainow, Macclesfield, Cheshire SK10 5TF   **t** 01625 424220
e info@kerridgeendholidaycottages.co.uk
kerridgeendholidaycottages.co.uk

4B2

Northwest Tourism for All winner 2009. Cheshire's 'Self Catering Holiday of the Year' winner 2009.

Access: abc ⚡ 🏨 ☺ General: 🐕 🅟 P S Unit: 🛏 🍳 🔥 ♿ 📺 📠 S ♿ ✿

Middlewich | **The Boars Head Hotel**

Kinteron Street, Middlewich CW10 0JE
t 01606 833191 **e** boarsheadhotel@hotmail.com
theboars.com

North Rode Nr Congleton | **Ladderstile Retreat at Twin Oaks**

 AS

Enjoy England   ★★★★★
Open: All year except Xmas and New Year
....

Rooms per night:
s: £50.00-£55.00
d: £80.00-£90.00

Ladderstile Farm, North Rode, Nr Congleton, Cheshire CW12 2PH
t 01260 223338 **e** enquiries@ladderstileretreat.co.uk
ladderstileretreat.co.uk

4B2

Enjoy peace, tranquillity and stunning views as you relax in our luxurious ground floor suite.

Access: abc ⚡ ♿ General: 🐕 🛏 ✗ 🅿 ✿ ♿ Room: 🛏 🔥 📺 📠 ☕

Runcorn | Holiday Inn Runcorn

AA   ★★★   Wood Lane, Beechwood, Runcorn, Cheshire WA7 3HA
t 0871 942 9070   **e** reservations-runcorn@ihg.com
holiday-inn.co.uk

Access: .: abc 🗺 ⚐ 🏨 ☺ ♿ ♿   General: ⟆ 🍴 ✕ ♟ ₽ ❉ ⊞ ⚿   Room: ⚘ 🆂 ♨

Warrington | Holiday Inn Warrington

AA   ★★★   Woolston Grange Avenue, Woolston, Warrington, Cheshire WA1 4PX
Open: All year   **t** 01925 838779   **e** steve.hammersley@ihg.com
holidayinn.co.uk

Access: .: abc 🗺 ⚐ 🏨 ☺ ♿ ♿   General: ⟆ 🍴 ✕ ♟ ₽ ❉ ⊞ ⚿   Room: ⚘ 🏔 🆂 ♨

Ambleside | Nationwide Bungalow

Units: 1   Sleeps: 7

Low season p/w:
£240.00

High season p/w:
£550.00

Livability Self Catering Holidays, PO Box 36, Cowbridge, Vale of Glamorgan
CF71 7TN   **t** 08456 584478   **f** 01446 775060
e selfcatering@livability.org.uk
livability.org.uk

5A3

Fully accessible 4 bedroom bungalow set in the
heart of Cumbria close to Lake Windermere.

Access: 🅷 ☺ ♿   General: ⟆ P 🆂   Unit: ⚘ 🏔 ♿ 🏔 🖥 🆂 ⚿ ♨ ✿

Ambleside | Rothay Manor

 **AS**

AA   ★★★
Enjoy England   ★★★

Beds: 3 suites

Open: All year except 3rd
to 27th January 2011.

Rooms per night:
s: £95.00-£155.00
d: £150.00-£235.00
p/p half board:
d: £105.00-£195.00
Meals: £36.00-£48.00
Shop: <0.5 miles
Pub: <0.5 miles

Access:
⚐ ☺ ♿ ♿
General:
⟆ 🍴 ✕ ♟ ₽ ❉ ♿
Room:
⚘ 🏔 🏔 🖥 🆂 ♨

Rothay Bridge, Ambleside LA22 0EH
t 01539 433605   **e** hotel@rothaymanor.co.uk
rothaymanor.co.uk

5A3

This country house hotel close to
Ambleside and Windermere lake is
an ideal base for exploring the area.
Family-owned for more than 40
years it is renowned for the warm,
comfortable, relaxed and friendly
atmosphere and excellent food and
wine.

Location: M6, J36 follow A591
(Ambleside). Turn left at traffic lights
and left in $\frac{1}{4}$ mile. Entrance 200m
on right.

Cockermouth | **Irton House Farm**

AS

Enjoy England ★★★★

Units: 6 Sleeps: 2-6
Open: All year

Low season p/w:
£365.00
High season p/w:
£825.00

Isel, Cockermouth, Cumbria CA13 9ST
t 017687 76380 **e** joan@irtonhousefarm.co.uk
disabled-holiday.net

5A3

Self-catering cottages for up to 6 people, specially designed for wheelchair accessibility. Quiet, rural location.

General: ⚘🗎P Unit: ♿🖼🧹♿🛏📺🚾♿❀

Coniston | **Park Coppice Caravan Club Site** CARAVAN CLUB

AS

Enjoy England ★★★★★

🚐 (280)
      £14.70–£27.20
🚌 (280)
      £14.70–£27.20
⛺ (1)

280 touring pitches
Open: 18 March to 7 November

Coniston LA21 8LA
t 01539 441555
caravanclub.co.uk

5A3

Set in 63 acres of beautiful National Trust woodland. With pitches grouped in open glades and fast access to the fun attractions of Coniston Water, the caravan park offers a scenic holiday getaway that will keep the whole family happy.

Location: A590, Barrow; 5m turn right onto A5092; 2m fork right onto A5084; 6m turn right onto A593. Site on right.

Access:
🚿😊♿
General:
🗎📺🐾🚐🐷🍼♁🚰
Pitch:
🚐🚌⛺

Gatebeck | **Barkinbeck Cottage**

🖼

Enjoy England ★★★

Units: 1   Sleeps: 4
Open: All year except Xmas and New Year

Low season p/w:
£300.00
High season p/w:
£425.00

Mrs Ann Hamilton, Barkin House Barn, Gatebeck, Kendal LA8 0HX
t 01539 567122 **e** barkinhouse@yahoo.co.uk
barkinbeck.co.uk

5B3

Adapted accommodation for disabled guests between English Lakes and Yorkshire Dales on a family farm.

Access: ♿ General: ⚘12P Unit: ♿🖼🧹♿🛏♿❀

Grange-over-Sands | **Meathop Fell Caravan Club Site** THE CARAVAN CLUB

Enjoy England ★★★★★

🚐 (131)
   £14.90–£27.20

🚏 (131)
   £14.90–£27.20

131 touring pitches
Open: All year

Shop: 3 miles
Pub: 2 miles

Access:
🅰 ✳ 🎣 ☺ ♿ ᵂᶜ
General:
🔲 💷 📶 🚿 🎮 🕐 👕 🆖
Pitch:
🚐 🚏

Grange-over-Sands, Cumbria LA11 6RB
t 01539 532912
 caravanclub.co.uk

5A3

This gentle, peaceful site is an ideal base to explore the Lake District. You'll find literary associations everywhere, from Wordsworth to Beatrix Potter. Windermere and Coniston are great for water-based activities.

Location: M6 jct 36, A590 (Barrow). After 3 miles take slip road A590 (Barrow). At 1st roundabout follow International Camping signs.

Hawkshead | **Restharrow**

National Trust, Restharrow, nr Hawkshead, Cumbria LA22 0LH
t 0844 800 2070 **e** cottages@nationaltrust.org.uk
nationaltrustcottages.co.uk

Access: ☺ General: 🔲P🆂 Unit: 🛏 🧺 ♿ 📺 ♿

Ings Village Nr Windermere | **Meadowcroft Country Guest House**

Enjoy England ★★★★

Open: All year except Xmas

Rooms per night:
s: £55.00-£65.00
d: £74.00-£94.00
Shop: <0.5 miles
Pub: <0.5 miles

Ings Village, Nr Windermere, Cumbria LA8 9PY
t 01539 821171 **e** info@meadowcroft-guesthouse.com
meadowcroft-guesthouse.com

5A3

We have two ground floor rooms one wheelchair friendly including wet room. Plus one twin bedded for people with limited mobility with a large step in shower. We will try to make your stay as trouble free as possible.

Location: Leave M6 at J36 on to A590/591 and follow signs for Windermere. Watch for speed cameras as you approach Ings.

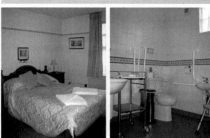

Access:

General:

Room:

Kendal | **Low Park Wood Caravan Club Site**

AS

Enjoy England ★★★★

(141)
£15.30-£27.20

(141)
£15.30-£27.20
141 touring pitches
Open: 18 March -7 November

Shop: 3 miles
Pub: 1 mile

Sedgwick, Kendal, Cumbria LA8 0JZ
t 01539 560186
caravanclub.co.uk

5B3

Set in extensive National Trust woodland, on the site of a 19thC gunpowder mill this peaceful country site is a haven for birdwatchers, fishermen and wild-flower enthusiasts. Kendal, a small market town famous for its mint cake, isn't far.

Location: M6 jct 36 onto A590 (South Lakes). After 3 miles take slip road (Milnthorpe, Barrow) at roundabout; follow caravan signs.

Access:

General:

Pitch:

Penrith | Crowdundle

National Trust, Acorn Bank, Temple Sowerby, Nr. Penrith, Cumbria CA10 1SP **t** 0844 800 2070 **e** cottages@nationaltrust.org.uk
nationaltrustcottages.co.uk

Access: General: Unit:

Saint Bees | Springbank Farm Lodges

AS

Enjoy England ★★★★
Units: 2 Sleeps: 2-5
Open: All year
Low season p/w: £300.00
High season p/w: £600.00

Mrs Carole Woodman, Springbank Farm, High Walton, Saint Bees, Cumbria CA22 2TY **t** 01946 822375 **e** stevewoodman@talk21.com
springbanklodges.co.uk **5A3**

New luxury log cabins in tranquil farm setting with spectacular open views. Wheelchair friendly.

Access: abc General: Unit:

Southwaite | Southwaite Green

AS

Enjoy England ★★★★★
Units: 4 Sleeps: 1-6
Open: All year
Low season p/w: £445.00
High season p/w: £930.00

Mrs Marna McMillin, Southwaite Green, Lorton, Cockermouth CA13 0RF **t** 01900 821055 **e** info@southwaitegreen.co.uk
southwaitegreen.co.uk **5B2**

Wheelchair friendly award winning 5 star eco cottage in Western Lakes.

Access: abc General: Unit:

Thurstonfield, Carlisle | Tranquil Otter

AS

Enjoy England ★★★★★
Units: 8 Sleeps: 2-6
Open: All year
Low season p/w: £600.00
High season p/w: £1160.00

Nick & Tazeem Kittoe, The Tranquil Otter, The Lough, Thurstonfield, Carlisle, Cumbria CA5 6HB **t** 01228 576661 **e** info@thetranquilotter.co.uk
thetranquilotter.co.uk **5A2**

Luxury lodges, wheelchair accessible, fully equipped, private lakeside deck. Fabulous views. Nr the Lake District.

Access: General: Unit:

OPEN BRITAIN
GETTING THERE IS NOT A PROBLEM!
See Getting there..... and back section (p314)
Everything you need for a hassle-free journey

Windermere | **Birch Cottage** AS

Enjoy England ★★★★

Units: 5 Sleeps: 2-6
Open: All year

Low season p/w:
£280.00
High season p/w:
£660.00

Mrs PM Fanstone, Deloraine Holiday Homes, Helm Road, Bowness-on-Windermere, Cumbria LA23 2HS **t** 015394 45557
e info@deloraine.demon.co.uk
deloraine.co.uk

5A3

Luxury fully wheelchair accessible cottage. Well equipped with private gardens. Located in central Lakes.

Access: abc 😊 ♿ General: 🛏️ 📷 P Ⓢ Unit: 🔧 🏔️ ♿ 📺 Ⓢ ♿ ✿

Windermere | **The Bowering** AS

Enjoy England ★★★★★

Units: 4 Sleeps: 6
Open: All year

Low season p/w:
£690.00
High season p/w:
£1150.00

Steven Turner & Helen Smith, The Bowering, Cavendish House, Aldon Road, Poulton Industrial Estate, Poulton-le-Flyde FY6 8JL
t 01253 881594 **e** Helen@thebowering.co.uk
thebowering.co.uk

5A3

The Bowering is a collection of four 5 star boutique style self catering apartments.

General: 🛏️ 📷 P Ⓢ Unit: 🔧 🏔️ ♿ Ⓢ ♿ ✿

Windermere | **Braithwaite Fold Caravan Club Site** CARAVAN CLUB AS

Enjoy England ★★★★

🚐 (66)
£15.30–£27.20

🚐 (66)
£15.30–£27.20

66 touring pitches
Open: 18 March - 7 November

Shop: 1 mile
Pub: <0.5 miles

Glebe Road, Bowness-on-Windermere, Windermere, Cumbria LA23 3HB
t 01539 442177
caravanclub.co.uk

5A3

An attractively laid out site, close to the shores of Windermere and within easy walking distance of the town. Windermere has an excellent sailing centre from which you can enjoy sailing, windsurfing and canoeing.

Location: From A592 follow signs for Bowness Bay, in 300yds turn right into Glebe Road. Site on right.

Access:
🅷 🐾 🛊 😊 ♿
General:
📷 🔌 📶 ♿ 💧 🚰 🚻 💧
Pitch:
🚐 🚐

Blackpool | **The Baron Hotel**

| Enjoy England | ★★★★ | 296 North Promenade, Blackpool, Lancashire FY1 2EY |
| AA | ★★★★ | **t** 01253 622729 **e** baronhotel@f2s.com |

baronhotel.co.uk

Access: ♿ General: 🛏✕🍷🔼♨ Room: 🔥📶🅂☕

Blackpool | **Chequers Plaza Hotel**

| Enjoy England | ★★★★ | 24 Queens Promenade, Blackpool, Lancashire FY2 9RN |

t 0800 0273107 **e** enquiries@chequersplaza.com

chequersplaza.com

Blackpool | **Promenade Apartments**

| Enjoy England | ★★★ |
| Units: 8 Sleeps: 2-4 |
| Low season p/w: £180.00 |
| High season p/w: £570.00 |

Mrs Christine Phillips, Promenade Apartments, 361 Promenade, Blackpool FY1 6BJ **t** 01253 343537 **e** promenade-apartments361@hotmail.co.uk
selfcateringflatinblackpool.com **4A1**

Eight self contained apartments sleeping 2-7. Three groundfloor suitable for guests with limited mobility.

Access: ∴ abc 🔲 ✳ General: ➰🅾Ｐ🅂 Unit: 🔥♨♨♿🚾🅂♿

Bolton | **Holiday Inn Bolton Centre**

| AA | ★★★★ | 1 Higher Bridge Street, Bolton, Lancashire BL1 2EW |

t 01204 879988 **e** reservations.hibolton@qmh-hotels.com

holiday-inn.co.uk

Access: abc 🔲 ✳ 🏢 ☺ ♿ General: ➰🛏✕🍷Ｐ🔼♨ Room: 🅂☕

Caton | **Croft, The - No. 4, Ground Floor Apartment**

| Enjoy England | ★★★★ |
| Units: 1 Sleeps: 6 |
| Open: All year |
| Low season p/w: £300.00 |
| High season p/w: £400.00 |

Mrs Sue Brierly-Hampton, 2 The Croft, Caton, Lancaster LA2 9QG **t** 01524 770725 **e** suebrierly@hotmail.com
holiday-rentals.co.uk (property number 10721) **5B3**

4 The Croft is a versatile ground floor apartment in the centre of Caton village.

General: ➰🅾Ｐ🅂 Unit: 🔥♨♨♿🚾🅂♿✿

Forest of Bowland | **Gibbon Bridge Hotel**

 AS

Enjoy England ★★★★

Open: All year

Rooms per night:

s: £100.00-£90.00
d: £140.00
p/p half board:
d: £85.00-£100.00
Meals: £30.00-£40.00
Shop: 0.8 miles
Pub: 0.8 miles

Chipping, Forest of Bowland, Preston, Lancashire PR3 2TQ
t 01995 61456 **e** reception@gibbon-bridge.co.uk
gibbon-bridge.co.uk

4A1

Situated in the beautiful Forest of Bowland, this four-star privately owned hotel, offers superior accommodation, elegant surroundings, delicious food and award-winning gardens.

Location: Exit M6 (from the North-32) (from south - 31A)

Access:
✶✶ ♿ ♿ ♿
General:
♿ ♿ ✕ ♿ P♿ ✿ ♿ ♿
Room:
♿ ♿ ♿ ♿

Lancaster | **Knotts Farm Holiday Cottages**

 AS

Enjoy England ★★★★

Units: 3 Sleeps: 2-4
Open: All year

Low season p/w:
£280.00
High season p/w:
£400.00

Mr Andrew Sheerin, Knotts Farm Holiday Cottages, Quernmore, Lancaster
LA2 9LU   **t** 07768 211842 **e** stay@knottsfarm.co.uk
knottsfarm.co.uk

5A3

Three 4 star new self catering cottages on a working farm at Quernmore near Lancaster.

Access: ✶✶ General: ♿ ♿ P ⑤ Unit: ♿ ♿ ♿ ♿ ♿ ♿ ⑤ ♿ ✿

Langho | **Best Western Mytton Fold Hotel and Golf Complex**

 AS

Enjoy England ★★★

Open: All year except Xmas and New Year

Rooms per night:
s: £57.00-£70.00
d: £72.00-£104.00
p/p half board:
d: £58.00-£81.50
Meals: £20.00-£28.00

Best Western Mytton Fold Hotel & Golf Complex, Langho, Nr Blackburn
BB6 8AB   **t** 01254 240662 **e** reception@myttonfold.co.uk
myttonfold.co.uk

4A1

Access for All Award Winner 2010, family owned & run. Located in Ribble Valley, Lancashire.

Access: abc ☺ ♿ ♿ General: ♿ ♿ ✕ ♿ P♿ ✿ ♿ ♿ Room: ♿ ♿ ♿ ♿

Ormskirk | Cross Farm Holiday Cottages

 AS

Enjoy England ★★★★

Units: 3 Sleeps: 2-4
Open: All year

Low season p/w:
£295.00
High season p/w:
£445.00

Mrs Linda Harrison, Cross Farm Holiday Cottages, Mairscough Lane, Downholland, Lancashire L39 7HT **t** 0151 526 1576
e ns.harrison@virgin.net
crossfarmholidaycottages.co.uk

4A1

Three newly converted cottages set in rural Lancashire yet near to Liverpool and Southport.

Access: 🏃 General: ⛄🗄P🅂 Unit: 🔥🛁🚿🍴💧🚾🧺✿

Bury | Burrs Country Park Caravan Club Site THE CARAVAN CLUB

AS

Enjoy England ★★★★★

🚐 (85)
£15.30–£27.20
🚛 (85)
£15.30–£27.20
85 touring pitches
Open: All year

Shop: 1.5 miles
Pub: <0.5 miles

Woodhill Road, Bury, Lancashire BL8 1DA
t 0161 761 0489
caravanclub.co.uk

4B1

On a historic mill site, Burrs offers easy access to relaxing river and countryside walks, the adjacent East Lancashire Steam Railway and Manchester. There are many opportunities for outdoor pursuits in the country park, such as climbing, abseiling and canoeing.

Location: From A676 (signposted Ramsbottom), follow signs for Burrs Country Park.

Access:
🅷✖🔔😊🚾♿
General:
🗄⛄📷🚗🚮🛒💧(WP)
Pitch:
🚐🚛

Manchester Airport | Crowne Plaza Manchester Airport

Terminal 3, Ringway Road, Manchester Airport M90 3NS
t 0871 942 9055 **e** reservations-manchesterairport@ihg.com
crowneplaza.co.uk

Access: 🅷 abc 🖊✖🔔😊🚾♿ General: ⛄🍴✖🍷P⬆♿ Room: 🔥♨

Ainsdale | **Willowbank Holiday Home and Touring Park**

  AS

AA ★★★
Enjoy England ★★★★★

🚐 (87)
£13.20–£17.85

🚐 (87)
£13.20–£17.85

🚐 (228)

Open: 1st Mar to 31st Jan

Coastal Road, Ainsdale, Southport PR8 3ST
t 01704 571566 **e** info@willowbankcp.co.uk
willowbankcp.co.uk

4A1

Within walking distance of the National Trust nature reserve and Sefton Coastline.

Access: abc 👥 ♿ General: 🔲 📷 🚐 👶 🍴 📶 Pitch: 🚐 🚐 🚐

Haydock | **Holiday Inn Haydock**

Lodge Lane, Newton-le-Willows, Merseyside WA12 0JG
t 0870 400 9039 **e** reservations-haydock@ihg.com
holiday-inn.co.uk

Access: ⋮ abc 🔲 🐾 👥 ☺ ♿ General: 🛏 🍽 ✕ 🍷 🅿 ❀ 🔲 ♿ Room: 🛏 📶 📺 abc 🔲 ☕ 🍵

Southport | **Vitalise Sandpipers**

AS

Fairway, Southport, Merseyside PR9 0AL
t 0845 345 1970 **e** bookings@vitalise.org.uk
vitalise.org.uk

Access: 🅷 👥 ☺ ♿ General: 🍽 ✕ 🍷 🅿 ❀ 🔲 ♿ Room: 🛏 📶 📺 wc 🔲 🍵

Thurstaston | **Wirral Country Park Caravan Club Site** THE CARAVAN CLUB

AS

Enjoy England ★★★★

Open: March to November

Station Road, Thurstaston, Wirral CH61 0HN
t 0151 648 5228
caravanclub.co.uk

Access: 🐾 👥 ☺ ♿ General: 🔲 🚐 📷 🚐 🚐 👶 🍴 📶 Pitch: 🚐 🚐

Cheshire

BOSLEY

The Old Byre
Mrs Dorothy Gilman, Woodcroft, Tunstall Road, Bosley, Macclesfield SK11 0BB
w farmstay.co.uk

CHESTER

Brookside Hotel
Brook Lane, Chester CH2 2AN
t 01244 381943 **e** info@brookside-hotel.co.uk
w brookside-hotel.co.uk

Grosvenor Pulford Hotel & Spa by Kasia
Wrexham Road, Pulford, Chester CH4 9DG
t 01244 570560
e reservations@grosvenorpulfordhotel.co.uk
w grosvenorpulfordhotel.co.uk

CONGLETON

Sandhole Farm Bed & Breakfast
Manchester Road (A34), Hulme Walfield, Congleton CW12 2JH
t 01260 224419 **e** veronica@sandholefarm.co.uk
w sandholefarm.co.uk

ELLESMERE PORT

Holiday Inn Ellesmere Port/Cheshire Oaks
Centre Island, Waterways, Ellesmere Port CH65 2AL
t 0151 356 8111 **e** reception@hiellesmereport.com
w hiellesmereport.com

MACCLESFIELD

Strawberry Duck Cottage
Mr B Carter, Strawberry Duck Cottage, Bryer Cottage, Bullgate Lane, Bosley, Macclesfield SK11 0PP
t 01260 223591 **e** 2007@strawberryduckholidays.co.uk
w strawberryduckholidays.co.uk/

Cumbria

ARNSIDE

YHA Arnside
Oakfield Lodge, Redhills Road, Arnside LA5 0AT
t 01524 761781 **e** arnside@yha.org.uk
w yha.org.uk

BASSENTHWAITE

Parkergate
Ian & Jane Phillips, Parkergate, Bassenthwaite, Keswick CA12 4QG
t 01768 776376 **e** info@parkergate.co.uk
w parkergate.co.uk

BOWNESS-ON-SOLWAY

The Old Chapel
Wigton, Cumbria, Bowness-on-Solway CA7 5BL
t 01697 351126 **e** oldchapelbowness@hotmail.com
w oldchapelbownessonsolway.com

CARLISLE

Bessiestown Farm Country Guesthouse
Catlowdy, Longtown, Carlisle CA6 5QP
t 01228 577219 **e** info@bessiestown.co.uk
w bessiestown.co.uk

Old Brewery Residences
Dee Carruthers, Impact Housing Association, Old Brewery Residences, Bridge Lane, Carlisle CA2 5SR
t 01228 597352 **e** deec@impacthousing.org.uk
w impacthousing.org.uk

GRANGE-OVER-SANDS

Netherwood Hotel
Lindale Road, Grange-over-Sands LA11 6ET
t 015395 32552 **e** enquiries@netherwood-hotel.co.uk
w netherwood-hotel.co.uk

GRASMERE

Rothay Lodge & Apartment
Lindsay Rogers, Rothay Lodge & Apartment, c/o 54A Trevor Road, West Bridgford NG2 6FT
t 0115 923 2618 **e** enquiries@rothay-lodge.co.uk
w rothay-lodge.co.uk

HEADS NOOK

Tottergill Farm
Stephen & Joyce Wightman, Tottergill Farm, Castle Carrock, Brampton CA8 9DP
t 01228 670615 **f** 01228 670727
e stephen@tottergill.co.uk
w tottergill.co.uk

ISEL

Linskeldfield
Pauline Young, Messrs GR & PM Young, Linskeldfield Farm, Isel, Cockermouth CA13 9SR
t 01900 822136 **f** 01900 821075
e info@linskeldfield.co.uk
w linskeldfield.co.uk

LONGTHWAITE

Borrowdale YHA
Longthwaite, Borrowdale, Keswick CA12 5XE
t 0870 770 5706 **e** borrowdale@yha.org.uk
w yha.org.uk

PENRITH

Howscales
Liz Webster, Kirkoswald, Penrith CA10 1JG
t 01768 898666 e liz@howscales.co.uk
w howscales.co.uk

STAVELEY

Avondale
Helen Hughes, Avondale, 2 Lynstead, Thornbarrow Road,
Windermere LA23 2DG
t 07811 670260 e enquiries@avondale.uk.net
w avondale.uk.net

THRELKELD

Scales Farm Country Guest House
Scales, Threlkeld, Penrith CA12 4SY
t 01768 779660 e scales@scalesfarm.com
w scalesfarm.com

WHINFELL

Cobblestone Cottage & Wallers Barn
Diane Barnes, Topthorn Holiday Cottages, Topthorn Farm,
Whinfell, Kendal LA8 9EG
t 01539 824252 e info.barnes@btconnect.com
w topthorn.com

WINDERMERE

Hawksmoor
Lake Road, Windermere LA23 2EQ
t 015394 42110

Lake District Disabled Holidays
Stuart & Jane Higham, Mitchelland Farm, off Crook Road,
Nr Bowness-on-Windermere, Kendal, Cumbria. LA8 8LL
t 01539 447421 w lakedistrictdisabledholidays.co.uk

Linthwaite House Hotel
Crook Road, Windermere, Cumbria LA23 3JA
t 01539 488600 e stay@linthwaite.com
w linthwaite.com

Lancashire

ALSTON

Proven House
Mrs Kathleen English, Laneside Farm, Alston Lane, Alston
PR3 3BN
t 01772 782653 e kenglish56@hotmail.co.uk
w theprovenhouse.co.uk/

ASHTON WITH STODDAY

Ashton Hall Cottages
Mrs Clark, Ashton Hall Cottages, The Long Barn, Ashton
With Stodday, Lancaster LA2 0AJ
t 01524 751325 e ashtonhallcottage@googlemail.com
w ashtonhallcottages.co.uk

BARNACRE

Barnacre Cottages
Mr Terence Sharples, Barnacre Cottages, The Old Shippon,
Arkwright Farm, Eidsforth Lane, Preston PR3 1GN
t 01995 600918 e sue@barnacre-cottages.co.uk
w barnacre-cottages.co.uk

BLACKPOOL

The Address
91-93 Reads Avenue, Blackpool FY1 4DG
t 01253 624238 e stay@theaddressblackpool.co.uk
w theaddressblackpool.co.uk

The Beach House
Mrs Estelle Livesey, The Beach House, 204 Queens
Promenade, Blackpool FY2 9JS
t 01253 826555 e info@thebeachhouseblackpool.co.uk
w thebeachhouseblackpool.co.uk

The Berkeley
Lord Lomax - Dwent, The Berkeley, 6 Queens Promenade,
Blackpool FY2 9SQ
t 01253 351244 e info@selfcatering.tv
w selfcatering.tv

Big Blue Hotel
Pleasure Beach Blackpool, Ocean Boulevard, Blackpool
FY4 1ND
t 0871 222 4000 e reservations@bigbluehotel.com
w bigbluehotel.com

Coast Apartments
Mr & Mrs Steven & Karen Livesey, Coast Apartments, 11
Empress Drive, Blackpool FY2 9SE
t 01253 351377 e enquiries@coastapartments.co.uk
w coastapartments.co.uk

Holmsdale
6-8 Pleasant Street, Blackpool FY1 2JA
t 01253 621008 e stay@holmsdalehotel-blackpool.com
w holmsdalehotel-blackpool.com

Langtrys
36 King Edward Avenue, Blackpool FY2 9TA
t 01253 352031 e info@langtrysblackpool.co.uk
w langtrysblackpool.co.uk

The Lawton
58-66 Charnley Road, Blackpool FY1 4PF
t 01253 753471 e thelawtonhotel@gmail.com
w thelawtonhotel.co.uk

Norbreck Castle Hotel
Queens Promenade, Blackpool FY2 9AA
t 0871 222 0031 e res722@britanniahotels.com
w britanniahotels.com

St Elmo
20-22 Station Road, Blackpool FY4 1BE
t 01253 341820 e hotelstelmo@hotmail.com
w hotelstelmo.co.uk

BLEASDALE

Bleasdale Cottages
Mr Gardner, Bleasdale Cottages, Lower Fairsnape Farm,
Bleasdale, Nr Preston PR3 1UY
t 01995 61343 e robert_gardner1@tiscali.co.uk
w bleasdalecottages.co.uk

BOLTON

Meadowcroft Barn B&B
Bury Road, Bolton BL7 0BS
t 01204 853270 e info@meadowcroftbarn.co.uk
w meadowcroftbarn.co.uk

CLITHEROE

Stonefold Holiday Cottage
Ms Helen Blanc, Stonefold Holiday Cottage, Slaidburn Road,
Newton-in-Bowland, Citheroe BB7 3DL
t 07966 582834 w stonefoldholidaycottage.co.uk

FORTON

Cleveley Mere Boutique Lakeside Lodges
Owner, Cleveley Mere Boutique Lodges, Cleveley Lodge,
Cleveley Bank Lane, Forton PR3 1BY
w cleveleymere.com

LYTHAM ST ANNES

Avondale
Mr Alvin Perkins, Avondale, 17 Chatsworth Road, Lytham St
Annes FY8 2PR
t 01253 789190 e alvinperkins20@totalise.co.uk

The Chadwick Hotel
113-115 South Promenade, Lytham St Annes FY8 1NP
t 01253 720061 e sales@thechadwickhotel.com
w thechadwickhotel.com

MORECAMBE

Eden Vale Luxury Holiday Flats
Mr Jason Coombs, 338 Marine Road, Morecambe LA4 5AB
t 07739 008301 e jicoombs@talktalk.net
w edenvalemorecambe.co.uk

POULTON-LE-FYLDE

Hardhorn Breaks
Mr Pawson, Hardhorn Breaks, High Bank Farm, Fairfield Rd,
Poulton Le Fylde FY6 8DN
t 01253 890422 e blackpoolnick@btinternet.com
w highbank-farm.com

RIBBLE VALLEY

Pinfold Farm
Mr Alan Davies, Preston Road, Ribchester PR3 3YD
t 01254 820740 e davies-pinfold@yahoo.co.uk
w pinfoldfarm.co.uk

RIBCHESTER

Riverside Barn
Riverside, Ribchester, Preston PR3 3XS
t 01254 878095 e relax@riversidebarn.co.uk
w riversidebarn.co.uk

SOUTHPORT

Sandy Brook Farm
Mrs Wendy Core, Sandy Brook Farm, Wyke Cop Road,
Southport PR8 5LR
t 01704 880337 e sandybrookfarm@gmail.com
w sandybrookfarm.co.uk

Sandy Brook Farm (B&B)
Wyke Cop Road, Scarisbrick, Southport PR8 5LR
t 01704 880337 e sandybrookfarm@gmail.com
w sandybrookfarm.co.uk

TURTON

Clough Head Farm
Mrs Ethel Houghton, Clough Head Farm - Self Catering,
Broadhead Road, Turton BL7 0JN
t 01254 704758 e ethelhoughton@hotmail.com
w cloughheadfarm.com

Greater Manchester

DENSHAW

Cherry Clough Farm House Accommodation
Cherry Clough Farm, Denshaw, Oldham OL3 5UE
t 01457 874369 e info@cherryclough.co.uk
w cherryclough.co.uk

MANCHESTER

Hilton Manchester Deansgate
303 Deansgate, Manchester M3 4LQ
t 0161 870 1600
e sales.manchesterdeansgate@hilton.com
w hilton.co.uk/manchesterdeansgate

Ibis Hotel Manchester
96 Portland Street, Manchester M1 4GX
t 0161 2340600 w ibishotel.com

Lancashire County Cricket Club & Old Trafford Lodge
Talbot Road, Old Trafford, Manchester M16 0PX
t 0161 874 3333 e lodge@lccc.co.uk
w oldtraffordlodgehotel.co.uk

Luther King House
Brighton Grove, Wilmslow Road, Manchester M14 5JP
t 0161 224 6404 e martincloves@lkh.co.uk
w lutherkinghouse.co.uk/

Macdonald Manchester Hotel
London Road, Manchester M1 7JG
t 0870 194 2137
e sales.manchester@macdonald-hotels.co.uk
w macdonaldhotels.co.uk

Manchester YHA
Potato Wharf, Castlefield, Manchester M3 4NB
t 0161 839 9960 e manchester@yha.org.uk
w yhamanchester.org.uk

Midland Hotel
Peter Street, Manchester M60 2DS
t 0161 236 3333 e midlandreservations@qhotels.co.uk
w qhotels.co.uk

Park Inn Manchester Victoria
4 Cheetham Hill Road, Manchester M4 4EW
t 0161 436 1931
e info.manchester-victoria@rezidorparkinn.com
w parkinn.co.uk

MANCHESTER AIRPORT

Bewleys Hotel Manchester Airport
Outwood Lane, Manchester Airport, Manchester M90 4HL
t 0044 161 498 1390
e manchester@bewleyshotels.com
w bewleyshotels.com

ROCHDALE

Fernhill B&B
Fernhill Lane, Rochdale OL12 6BW
t 01706 355671 e info@fernhillbreaks.co.uk
w fernhillbreaks.co.uk

SALFORD

Lowry Hotel
50 Dearmans Place, Chapel Wharf, Salford M3 5LH
t 0161 827 4000
e enquiries.lowry@roccofortecollection.com
w thelowryhotel.com

Merseyside

BIRKENHEAD

Mersey View - East Float Dock 2
Mill 1, Dock Road, Birkenhead CH41 1DN
t 07941 562879 e enquiries@merseyview.com
w merseyview.com

LIVERPOOL

Holiday Inn Liverpool City Centre
Lime Street, Liverpool L1 1NQ
t 0151 709 7090 e reservations@hiliverpool.com
w hiliverpool.com

Hotel Ibis
27 Wapping, Liverpool L1 8LY
t 0151 706 9800 e h3140@accor.com
w ibishotel.com

YHA Liverpool International
25 Tabley Street, off Wapping, Liverpool L1 8EE
t 0870 770 5924 e liverpool@yha.org.uk
w yha.org.uk

WEST KIRBY

Herons Well Cottage
Mrs Glynis Lavelle, Owner, Three Lanes End Farm, West
Kirby, Wirral CH48 1PT
t 0151 625 1401 e HeronsWell@btinternet.com
w HeronsWell.co.uk

Where to Go

Necton | **Ness Botanic Gardens**

Ness, Necton, Cheshire CH64 4AY
t 0151 353 0123 **e** nessgdns@liverpool.ac.uk
nessgardens.co.uk

Stockport | **Alexandra Park**

Edgeley Road, Edgeley, Stockport, Cheshire SK3 9NB
t 0161 474 4512 **e** parks@stockport.gov.uk
stockport.gov.uk

Stockport | **Bramall Hall**

Bramhall Park, Bramhall, Stockport SK7 3NX
t 0161 4853708 **e** bramall.hall@stockport.gov.uk
bramallhall.org.uk

Stockport | **Reddish Vale Country Park**

Mill Lane, Reddish Vale, Stockport SK5 7HE
t 0161 474 4512 **e** parks@stockport.gov.uk
stockport.gov.uk

Stockport | **Stockport Art Gallery & War Memorial**

Greek Street, Stockport, Cheshire SK3 8AB
t 0161 474 4453
stockport.gov.uk

Old Trafford | **Old Trafford**

Manchester United Football Club, Sir Matt Busby Way, Old Trafford,
Manchester M16 0RA **t** 0161 8688000
manutd.com

Ballaugh | **Curraghs Wildlife Park**

Off A3, Ballaugh, Isle Of Man IM7 5EA
t 01624 897323 **e** tina.hampton@curraghswlp.dtl.gov.im
gov.im

Where to Eat

Cheadle | Pizza Express

83-85 High Street, Cheadle, Stockport SK8 1AA
t 0161 491 1442
pizzaexpress.com

General: 🐕 FAX ♿ ♿ wc ♿ ♿ .: abc

Cheshire | American Bar & Grill

6-10 Victoria Road, Hale, Cheshire WA15 9AF
t 0161 929 9259 **e** info@theamericanbarandgrill.com
theamericanbarandgrill.com

General: 🐕 FAX ♿ ♿ wc ♿ ♿ P

Stockport | Beluga

26 Bramhall Lane South, Bramhall, Stockport, Cheshire SK7 1AF
t 0161 439 8080
belugaonline.co.uk

General: 🐕 ♿ ♿ ♿ ♿ P

Liverpool | HA! HA! Bar & Canteen

Atlantic Pavillion, Albert Dock, Liverpool, Merseyside L3 4AF
t 0151 707 7877 **e** haha.liverpool@bayrestaurantgroup.com
hahaonline.co.uk

General: 🐕 FAX ♿ ♿ ♿ wc ♿ ♿ P

Liverpool | Living Room

15 Victoria Street, Liverpool, Merseyside L2 5QS
t 0870 442 2535 **e** liverpool@thelivingroom.co.uk
thelivingroom.co.uk

General: 🐕 FAX ♿ ♿

Liverpool | Monro

Duke Street, Liverpool, Merseyside L1 5AG
t 0151 707 9933
themonro.com

General: 🐕 ♿ ♿ ♿

Liverpool | Pesto

Unit 9, Liverpool One, 14 Paradise Street, Liverpool, Merseyside L1 8JF
t 0151 708 6353 **e** liverpool@pestorestaurants.co.uk
pestorestaurants.co.uk

General: 🐕 FAX ♿ ♿ ♿ ♿ P

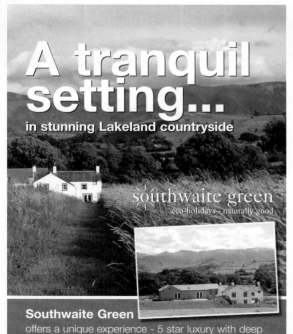

Coastline, castles, countryside and culture

Hadrian's Wall, Northumberland

World famous for our friendliness and hospitality, come and share our passion for this wonderful region of coastline and castles, countryside and culture!

Want to experience our sweeping countryside and idyllic coastline? Head for **Saltburn** where you can take the oldest water balanced cliff tramway in Britain down to the pier which extends 200 metres from the shoreline. Or spend the day in **Kielder**, where you can take a cruise on Europe's largest man-made lake, wander miles of forest paths and stay in a wheelchair accessible forest village.

If you love your history you won't want to miss the chance to marvel at **Hadrian's Wall** which still marks the

Saltburn

View of the city of Durham with the tops of the Norman Cathedral and Castle in the distance and the River Wear running through the centre of the city.

North East

County Durham, Northumberland
Tyne & Wear

Tourist Information Centres	258	Where to Go	268
Where to Stay	259	Where to Eat	270

northernmost limit of the Roman Empire after almost 2,000 years. There are amazing interactive exhibits and events at several of its forts, including **Segedunum** and **Arbeia** in North and South Tyneside respectively.

Walk along cobbled streets steeped in history amongst the **Castle** and **Cathedral** of Durhams city centre or travel back in time to 1825 and 1913 at the **Living Museum**, **Beamish**, via an easy access bus, to visit the town, farm, manor house and colliery village.

Feel our cities come alive with world-class culture and superb shopping.

Visit the **National Glass Centre** in Sunderland to see beautiful glass being hand-made and even have a go yourself! Be sure to check out the **Theatre Royal**, Newcastle, or **The Sage Gateshead**, for West-End shows or breathtaking concerts, or catch the latest vibrant art exhibitions at **mima**, **Middlesbrough's Institute of Modern Art**, or **BALTIC**, **Centre for Contemporary Art** on Newcastle Gateshead's Quayside. If it's shopping you're after then why not treat yourself to some retail therapy at **MetroCentre**, Europe's largest shopping and leisure complex.

Find out more:
www.visitnortheastengland.com

BALTIC, Centre for Contemporary Art

Tourist Information Centres

Tourist Information Centres are a mine of information about local and regional accommodation, attractions and events. Visit them when you arrive at your destination or contact them before you go:

Alnwick	2 The Shambles	01665 511333	alnwicktic@alnwick.gov.uk
Amble	Queen Street Car Park	01665 712313	amble.tic@alnwick.gov.uk
Barnard Castle	Woodleigh, Flatts Road	01833 690909	tourism@teesdale.gov.uk
Bellingham	The Heritage Centre, Hillside	01434 220616	bellinghamtic@btconnect.com
Berwick-Upon-Tweed	106 Marygate	01289 330733	tourism@berwick-upon-tweed.gov.uk
Bishop Auckland	Town Hall Ground Floor	01388 604922	bishopauckland.touristinfo@durham.gov.uk
Corbridge	Hill Street	01434 632815	corbridgetic@btconnect.com
Craster	Craster Car Park	01665 576007	crastertic@alnwick.gov.uk
Darlington	13 Horsemarket	01325 388666	tic@darlington.gov.uk
Durham	2 Millennium Place	0191 384 3720	touristinfo@durhamcity.gov.uk
Gateshead	Central Library	0191 433 8420	tic@gateshead.gov.uk
Gateshead	The Sage Gateshead	0191 478 4222	tourism@gateshead.gov.uk
Haltwhistle	Railway Station	01434 322002	haltwhistletic@btconnect.com
Hartlepool	Hartlepool Art Gallery	01429 869706	hpooltic@hartlepool.gov.uk
Hexham	Wentworth Car Park	01434 652220	hexham.tic@tynedale.gov.uk
Middlesbrough	99-101 Albert Road	01642 729700	middlesbrough_tic@middlesbrough.gov.uk
Morpeth	The Chantry	01670 500700	morpeth.tic@northumberland.gov.uk
Newcastle-Upon-Tyne	8-9 Central Arcade	0191 277 8000	tourist.info@newcastle.gov.uk
North Shields	Unit 18, Royal Quays	0191 2005895	ticns@northtyneside.gov.uk
Once Brewed	Northumberland NP Centre	01434 344396	tic.oncebrewed@nnpa.org.uk
Peterlee	4 Upper Yoden Way	0191 586 4450	touristinfo@peterlee.gov.uk
Redcar	West Terrace	01642 471921	redcar_tic@redcar-cleveland.gov.uk
Rothbury	Northumberland NP Centre	01669 620887	tic.rothbury@nnpa.org.uk
Saltburn By Sea	3 Station Buildings	01287 622422	saltburn_tic@redcar-cleveland.gov.uk
Seahouses	Seafield Car Park	01665 720884	seahousesTIC@berwick-upon-tweed.gov.uk
South Shields	South Shields Museum & Gallery	0191 454 6612	museum.tic@s-tyneside-mbc.gov.uk
South Shields	Sea Road	0191 455 7411	foreshore.tic@s-tyneside-mbc.gov.uk
Stanhope	Durham Dales Centre	01388 527650	durham.dales.centre@durham.gov.uk
Stockton-On-Tees	Stockton Central Library	01642 528130	touristinformation@stockton.gov.uk
Sunderland	50 Fawcett Street	0191 553 2000	tourist.info@sunderland.gov.uk
Whitley Bay	Park Road	0191 2008535	ticwb@northtyneside.gov.uk
Wooler	The Cheviot Centre	01668 282123	woolerTIC@berwick-upon-tweed.gov.uk

Where to Stay

Cockfield | Stonecroft and Swallows Nest

 AS

Enjoy England ★★★★	Mrs Alison Tallentire, Stonecroft and Swallows Nest, Lowlands Farm, Cockfield, Bishop Auckland DL13 5AW **t** 01388 718251
Units: 2	**e** info@farmholidaysuk.com
Open: All year	**farmholidaysuk.com**
Low season p/w: £160.00	
High season p/w: £360.00	

5C2

Beautifully renovated cottages, comfortable, cosy, own gardens/parking, friendly working farm, fantastic countryside, everyone welcome

Access: ✕ ♿ wc General: 🐴 📺 P Unit: 🛏 🖥 ♨ ♿ 📻 📼 📺 S ♿ ✿

Cornriggs | Alice & Nelly's Cottages

 AS

Enjoy England ★★★★★	Mrs Janet Elliot, Cornriggs Cottages, Low Cornriggs Farm, Cornriggs, Bishop Auckland DL13 1AQ **t** 01388 537600
Units: 2	**e** cornriggsfarm@btconnect.com
Open: All year	**cornriggsfarm.co.uk**
Low season p/w: £339.00	
High season p/w: £564.00	
Shop: 1.5 miles	
Pub: 1 mile	

5B2

Our cottages are large and to a very high standard, on one level, no steps, wide doors, bedrooms two en suite one bath. Roll in accessible showers, handrails and space by WC. Well-fitted Kitchen. Comfy lounge. Outside seating, flat parking.

Location: A689 midway between Stanhope and Alston. One mile On the right hand side of the road leaving Cowshill, towards Alston.

Access:
abc 🏠 wc ♿
General:
🐴 📺 P S
Unit:
🛏 🖥 ♨ ♿ 📻 📼 📺 S ♿ ✿

Darlington (8 miles) | East Greystone Farm Cottages

AS

Enjoy England

★★★★-★★★★★

Units: 2   Sleeps: 1-4
Open: All year

Low season p/w:
£275.00
High season p/w:
£460.00

Mrs Sue Hodgson, East Greystone, Gainford, Darlington, Co. Durham
DL2 3BL   t 01325 730236   e sue@holidayfarmcottages.co.uk
holidayfarmcottages.co.uk

5C3

Situated in glorious rolling Teesdale countryside. One
level accommodation. Ideal base to relax or explore.

Access: 🐾 General: ⟲P⑤ Unit: 🍳🔥♿🛏🚻Ⓢ🕯❀

Durham | The Grange Caravan Club Site CARAVAN CLUB

AS

Enjoy England   ★★★★★

🚐 (76)
          £15.30–£27.20
🚍 (76)
          £15.30–£27.20
⚊ (10)

76 touring pitches
Open: All year

Shop: 1 mile
Pub: 1.5 miles

Meadow Lane, Durham DH1 1TL
t 0191 384 4778
caravanclub.co.uk

5C2

An open, level site within easy
reach of the picturesque city of
Durham with walks from the site
into the city. Durham is steeped in
history, and a visit to Durham
Cathedral and Castle is a must.

Location: A1(M) jct 62, A690
towards Durham. Turn right after
50m. Signposted Maureen Terrace
and brown caravan sign.

Access:
🅷 🐾 🚮 ☺ ♿
General:
🔲🚐🐾🚰🔌🚿🚽☕🅌
Pitch:
🚐🚍⚊

Quebec | Hamsteels Hall Cottages

Enjoy England   ★★★★
Units: 4   Sleeps: 2-8
Open: All year

Low season p/w:
£280.00
High season p/w:
£530.00

Mrs June Whitfield, Hamsteels Hall Cottages, Hamsteels Hall, Hamsteels
Lane, Quebec DH7 9RS   t 01207 520388   e june@hamsteelshall.co.uk
hamsteelshall.co.uk

5C2

Spacious stone bungalows in open countryside with
all facilities. Parking. Wi-fi access. Close to Durham/
Beamish.

Access: 🅷 🐾🚮 General: ⟲🅿P⑤ Unit: 🍳♿🛏🚻Ⓢ🕯❀

Stockton on Tees | White Water Park Caravan Club Site

AS

Enjoy England ★★★★★

⊞ (115)
                    £12.10–£23.90
🚐 (115)
                    £12.10–£23.90
⚊ (5)

115 touring pitches
Open: All year

Shop: 1 mile
Pub: 0.5 miles

Access:
🅰 ✖ 🐾 😊 ♿

General:
▢ ⊞ 📶 ⛽ 😊 🔌 ☎ WP

Pitch:
⊞ 🚐 ⚊

Tees Barrage, Stockton-on-Tees, Co Durham TS18 2QW
t 01642 634880
caravanclub.co.uk   **5C3**

Pleasantly landscaped site, close to the largest white-water canoeing and rafting course in Britain. Nearby Teesside Park is great for shopping, restaurants, cinema and bowling. Birdwatchers, wildlife enthusiasts and walkers will enjoy 30 miles of coastline close by.

Location: Come off the A66 Teesside Park. Follow Teesdale sign, go over Tees Barrage Bridge, turn right. Site 200yds on left.

Alnwick | Doxford Hall Hotel & Spa

Enjoy England ★★★★

Open: All year

Rooms per night:
s: £96.00–£190.00
d: £132.00–£270.00
p/p half board:
d: £101.00–£165.00
Meals: £30.00–£41.00

Doxford Hall, Chathill, Alnwick, Northumberland NE67 5DN
t 01665 589700   **e** info@doxfordhall.com
doxfordhall.com   **5C1**

Located 8 miles north of Alnwick, Northumberland.

Access: ♿ 🅦🅒   General: 🍽️ 🍴 ✖ 🍷 P♿ ❀ 🖼️ ♿   Room: 🔌 🛏️ 📺 ☕

Bamburgh | **Alnwick Castle Cottages**

Enjoy England
★★★★-★★★★★

Units: 18 Sleeps: 2-12
Open: All year

Low season p/w:
£371.00
High season p/w:
£553.00
Shop: 2 miles
Pub: <0.5 miles

Access:
abc 🐾 🏠

General:
🐕 ⊡ P S

Unit:
🔥 🧹 ♿ 📺 📟 □ ☕ ✿

Mrs J Mallen, Alnwick Castle Cottages, Lucker Hall Steading, Belford, Northumberland NE70 7JQ   **t** 01668 219941
e info@alnwickcastlecottages.co.uk
alnwickcastlecottages.co.uk

5C1

With friendly efficient service we offer spacious cottages for 2 with twin or superking beds, in tiny village Nr Bamburgh Castle, beaches, Alnwick Castle & Gardens. We also have delightful groundfloor cottages for 4 and 6. ETB 4* and 5*

Location: In the centre of a tiny village, 5 mins from A1 and the beach at Bamburgh. Alnmouth Station 20 miles.

Berwick-Upon-Tweed | **Meadow Hill Guest House**

Enjoy England   ★★★★

Open: All year

Rooms per night:
s: £70.00
d: £70.00-£80.00
Meals: £12.95-£15.00

Duns Road, Berwick-upon-Tweed TD15 1UB
t 01289 306325 **e** christineabart@aol.com
meadow-hill.co.uk

6D2

Attractive 170-year-old house overlooking the River Tweed, Cheviot Hills, Berwick to Holy Island coastline.

Access: 🐕 General: 🐕 🍴 ✗ P ♿ ⛱ Room: 🔥 S ☕

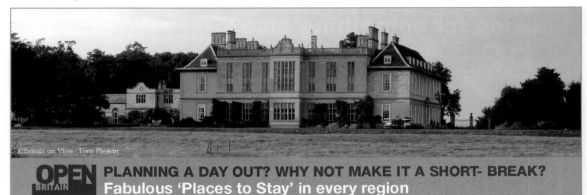
©Britain on View/Tony Pleavin

Berwick-Upon-Tweed | **Seaview Caravan Club Site** CARAVAN CLUB

AS

Enjoy England ★★★★

(98)
£13.10–£25.40

(98)
£13.10–£25.40

98 touring pitches
Open: 25 March to 2
January 2012

Billendean Road, Berwick-upon-Tweed TD15 1QU
t 01289 305198

caravanclub.co.uk

5B1

Site combines the spectacular scenery of Northumberland with visits across the border to Scotland. There are superb views to be seen from this caravan site, which overlooks the river estuary.

Location: A1 approaching Berwick at Morrisons roundabout continue on A1; left at roundabout onto A1167; right at roundabout. Site on right.

Access:

General:

Pitch:

Catton | **Station House Flat**

AS

Enjoy England ★★★★

Units: 1 Sleeps: 1-6

Low season p/w:
£275.00
High season p/w:
£440.00

Mr & Ms Michael & Verona Woodhouse, Station House Flat, Station House, Catton NE47 9QF   **t** 01434 683362 **e** info@allendale-holidays.co.uk

allendale-holidays.co.uk

5B2

Cosy Wood-burning stove. 1 mile from award-winning village Allendale. In beautiful North Pennines.

Access: abc General: ☆⬛P⬚ Unit: 🔥🧹🚾♿✿

Embleton | **Brunton House**

AS

Enjoy England ★★★★

Embleton, Alnwick, Northumberland NE66 3HQ
t 01665 589199

bruntonhouse.co.uk

Access: 🅷♿ General: ☆🍽✖P♿✿♿ Room: 🔥🧹🚾☕

Hexham | **The Hytte**

AS

Enjoy England ★★★★★
Units: 1 Sleeps: 1-8
Open: All year

Low season p/w:
£550.00
High season p/w:
£960.00

Mr & Mrs S R Gregory, The Hytte, Bingfield, Hexham, Northumberland
NE46 4HR **t** 01434 672321 **e** sgregory001@tiscali.co.uk
thehytte.com

5B2

Norwegian-style mountain lodge with grass roof, sleeps eight, four accessible bedrooms. Hot-tub. NAS Access exceptional

Access: ⓗ abc 🐾 🧴 ☺ General: 🎠🗔**P**Ⓢ Unit: ♿📺🗝🚿♿🛏🔳abc wc Ⓢ🚽 ❀

Hexham | **The Old Farmhouse**

AS

Enjoy England ★★★★
Units: 1 Sleeps: 1-5
Open: All year

Low season p/w:
£305.00
High season p/w:
£600.00

Mr CJ Armstrong, Grindon Farm, Haydon Bridge, Hexham, Northumberland
NE47 6NQ **t** 07904411054 **e** chris@grindonfarm.co.uk
grindonfarm.co.uk

5B2

Cosy barn conversion nestled in Hadrian's Wall country. Spectacular rural views. An ideal relaxing base.

Access: abc 🐾 🧴 General: 🎠🗔**P**Ⓢ Unit: ♿📺🛏♿🛏 wc Ⓢ🚽 ❀

Hexham | **Peel Bothy**

National Trust, Peel Bothy, Nr. Hexham, Northumberland NE47 7AW
t 0844 800 2070 **e** cottages@nationaltrust.org.uk
nationaltrustcottages.co.uk

Access: ☺ General: 🎠**P**Ⓢ Unit: ♿♿🚽

Newcastle upon Tyne | **Burradon Farm Houses and Cottages**

AS

Enjoy England
★★★★-★★★★★
Units: 2 Sleeps: 3-4
Open: All year

Low season p/w:
£375.00
High season p/w:
£650.00

Mrs Judith Younger, Burradon Farm, Cramlington, Northumberland
NE23 7ND **t** 0191 2683203 **e** judy@burradonfarm.co.uk
burradonfarm.co.uk

5C2

15 Luxury self-catering properties near city, coast & countryside ideally suited for holidays and business.

Access: abc 🐾 General: 🎠**P**Ⓢ Unit: ♿📺🛏♿🛏🚽 ❀

Powburn | **River Breamish Caravan Club Site**

AS

Enjoy England ★★★★★

🚐 (79)

£13.10–£25.40

🚎 (79)

£13.10–£25.40

⛺ (7)

79 touring pitches
Open: 25 March - 7 November

Shop: 0.8 miles
Pub: 0.8 miles

Access:
⚠ ⚥ 🏠 ☺ ♿

General:
🔲 🚐 📷 ♨ 🍴 ☕ 🚰

Pitch:
🚐 🚎 ⛺

Powburn, Alnwick, Northumberland NE66 4HY
t 01665 578320
caravanclub.co.uk

5B1

This site is set amid the Cheviot Hills, with excellent walking and cycling in the immediate area. A footbridge in Branton takes you over the river to the delightful Breamish Valley. There is a National Park Centre at Ingram.

Location: Take A697 from A1. In 20 miles (just past Powburn) turn left at service station on right. Site on right.

Rothbury | **Burnfoot Holiday Cottages**

Enjoy England ★★★-★★★★

Units: 14   Sleeps: 2-10
Open: All year

Low season p/w:
£235.00

High season p/w:
£1795.00

Mr & Mrs Gemma & Tim Stienlet, Burnfoot Holiday Cottages, Burnfoot, Netherton, Northumberland NE65 7EY   **t** 01912 811900
e stay@burnfootholidaycottages.co.uk
burnfootholidaycottages.co.uk

6D3

Luxury converted barns with opulent interiors and a fascinating history, in a breathtaking setting.

Access: ⚥ 🏠♿ General: 🌾 📱P Ⓢ Unit: 🔌 ♿ 🛁 🚾 Ⓢ ⛱ ✿

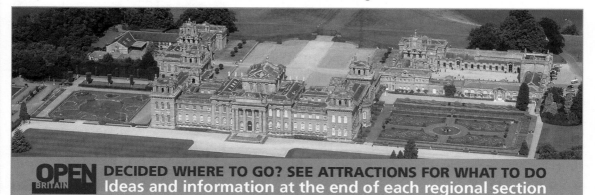

OPEN BRITAIN **DECIDED WHERE TO GO? SEE ATTRACTIONS FOR WHAT TO DO**
Ideas and information at the end of each regional section

Wooler | **Crookhouse Cottages**

Enjoy England ★★★★

Units: 2   Sleeps: 2-12
Open: All year

Low season p/w:
£470.00
High season p/w:
£950.00
Shop: 4 miles
Pub: 4 miles

Lynney Holden, Crookhouse Cottages, Crookhouse, Kirknewton, Wooler,
Northumberland NE71 6TN
t 01668 216113 **e** stay@crookhousecottages.co.uk
crookhousecottages.co.uk

5B1

A small traditional Northumbrian Steading, superior accommodation in a secluded, tranquil location with outstanding views of the College Valley and Cheviots. Two 4 star luxury cottages, each sleeping 4-6, can easily transform into one to sleep 12+. Dogs welcome.

Location: A697, 3 miles north of Wooler, turn left to Lanton, single track for 3 miles over cattle grids & uphill.

Access:

General:

Unit:

Marley Hill | **Hedley Hall Cottages**

Enjoy England ★★★★

Units: 2   Sleeps: 4
Open: All year

Low season p/w:
£350.00
High season p/w:
£580.00
Shop: 2 miles
Pub: 1.5 miles

Mrs Brenda Fraser, Hedley Hall Cottages, Hedley Lane, Nr Sunniside,
Gateshead, Tyne & Wear NE16 5EH   **t** 01207 231835
e hedleyhall@aol.com
hedleyhallcottages.com

5C2

Set in tranquil countryside, close to major attractions, each cottage has been designed with comfort in mind and all cottages are wheelchair accessible. Zip & link beds, en suite level entry shower, family bathroom with overhead shower.

Location: From the A1 heading north take the junction after the Angel of the North statue, signposted Team Valley Retail World.

Access:

General:

Unit:

Washington | **Holiday Inn Washington**

AS

Open: All year

Rooms per night:
s: £65.00-£150.00
d: £65.00-£150.00
p/p half board:
d: £47.50-£95.00
Meals: £15.00-£35.00

Emerson, Washington, Tyne & Wear NE37 1LB
t 0871 942 9084 **e** reservations-washington@ihg.com
holidayinn.co.uk

5C2

Holiday Inn Washington is a short drive from the Cities of Newcastle, Durham and Sunderland.

Access: **General:** **Room:**

Co. Durham

BOWES

Mellwaters Barn
East Mellwaters Farm, Stainmore Road, Barnard Castle DL12 9RH
w mellwatersbarn.co.uk

DARLINGTON

Mill Granary Cottages
Mr & Mrs Richard & Kate Hodgson, Mill Granary Cottages, Middleton House, Ingleton, Darlington DL2 3HG
t 01325 730339 **e** info@millgranary.co.uk
w millgranary.co.uk

EGGLESTON

Stable Court
Owner, Stable Court, High Shipley, Eggleston, Barnard Castle DL12 0DP
w stablecourt.co.uk

FROSTERLEY

Cromer House Camping Barn
48 Front Street, Frosterley, Bishop Auckland DL13 2QS
t 01388 526632
e inquiries@cromerhousecampingbarn.co.uk
w cromerhousecampingbarn.co.uk

HIGH HESLEDEN

The Ship Inn
Main Street, High Hesleden TS27 4QD
t 01429 836453 **e** sheila@theshipinn.net
w theshipinn.net

LYNESACK

Little Owl Lodge
Mrs Yvonne Wilkinson, Little Owl Lodge, East Howle Farm, Lynesack, Bishop Auckland DL13 5QG
t 01388 710749 **e** yvonne@alpacas-easthowle.co.uk
w alpacas-easthowle.co.uk

RUFFSIDE

Hadrian & Derwent Country Escapes
Ms Loraine Maddison, Cowie Holiday Cottage Developments LLP, Estate Office, Lanchester DH7 0TD
t 01207 529663 **e** sara@sirtomcowie.com
w hadrianandderwent.com

WINSTON

Alwent Mill Cottage
Mrs Libby Hampson, Alwent Mill Cottage, Alwent Mill, Alwent Mill Lane, Darlington DL2 3QH
t 01325 730479 **e** libby@alwentmill.co.uk

Northumberland

ALNWICK

Bog Mill Farm Holiday Cottages
Mrs Ann Mason, Bog Mill Farm Holiday Cottages, Bog Mill Farm, Alnwick NE66 3PA
t 01665 604529 **e** stay@bogmill.co.uk
w bogmill.co.uk

Doxford Cottages
Ms Sue Pringle, Manager, Doxford Cottages, Doxford Estate, Chathill NE67 5DW
t 01665 589393 **e** stay@doxfordcottages.co.uk
w doxfordcottages.co.uk

Village Farm
Mrs Crissy Stoker, Village Farm, Town Foot Farm, Alnwick NE66 2HG
t 01665 575591 **e** crissy@villagefarmcottages.co.uk
w villagefarmcottages.co.uk

AMBLE

Eden Bungalow
Mrs Jeanette Young, Eden Bungalow, 1 Stafford Villas, Springwell Village, Gateshead NE9 7SL
t 01914 167607 **e** edenjenyoung@googlemail.com
w edenbungalow.co.uk

BAMBURGH

Outchester & Ross Farm Cottages
Mrs Shirley McKie, Outchester & Ross Farm Cottages, 1 Cragview Road, Belford NE70 7NT
t 01668 213336 **e** stay@rosscottages.co.uk
w rosscottages.co.uk

BARDON MILL

Coach House Bed & Breakfast
Southview, Tavern House, Bardon Mill NE47 7HZ
t 01434 344779 **e** mail@bardonmillcoachhouse.co.uk
w bardonmillcoachhouse.co.uk

High Shield
Michael High Shield, Bardon Mill, Hexham, Northumberland NE47 7AJ
t 01434 340188 **f** 01434 344791
e highshield@btinternet.com
w highshield.co.uk

BELFORD

Elwick Farm Cottages
Mrs Roslyn Reay, Elwick Farm Cottages, Elwick, Belford NE70 7EL
t 01668 213242 **e** w.r.reay@talk21.com
w elwickcottages.co.uk

BELLINGHAM

Brownrigg Lodges
Mrs Morag MacLeod, Brownrigg, Bellingham NE48 2HR
t 01434 220272 **e** mac.kent@virgin.net
w brownrigglodges.com

BERWICK-UPON-TWEED

Fenham Farm Bed & Breakfast
Beal, Berwick-upon-Tweed TD15 2PL
t 01289 381245 **e** gillcurry@hotmail.com
w fenhamfarm.co.uk

West Ord Holiday Cottages
Mrs Carol Lang, West Ord Holiday Cottages, West Ord Farm, Berwick-upon-Tweed TD15 2XQ
t 01289 386631 **e** stay@westord.co.uk
w westord.co.uk

CORNHILL-ON-TWEED

Collingwood Arms Hotel
Main Street, Cornhill-on-Tweed TD12 4UH
t 01890 882424 **e** enquiries@collingwoodarms.com
w collingwoodarms.com

CRASTER

Craster Pine Lodges
Mr & Mrs Michael & Fyona Robson, Craster Pine Lodges, 19 Heugh Road, Alnwick NE66 3TJ
t 01665 576286 **e** pinelodges@barkpots.co.uk
w crasterpinelodges.co.uk

FALSTONE

Falstone Barns
Mrs Nicolette Forster, Falstone Barns, Falstone Farm, Hexham NE48 1AA
t 01434 240251 **e** redstone@btinternet.com
w falstonebarns.com

HAYDON BRIDGE

Grindon Cartshed
Haydon Bridge, Hexham, Northumberland NE47 6NQ
t 01434 684273 **e** cartshed@grindon.force9.co.uk
w grindon-cartshed.co.uk

Shaftoe's
4 Shaftoe Street, Haydon Bridge NE47 6BJ
t 01434 684664 **e** bookings@shaftoes.co.uk
w shaftoes.co.uk

KIELDER

Calvert Trust Kielder
Kielder Water, Kielder NE48 1BS
t 01434 250232 **e** enquiries@calvert-kielder.com
w calvert-trust.org.uk/kielder

LONGHIRST

Longhirst Hall
Longhirst NE61 3LL
t 01670 795000 **e** enquiries@longhirst.co.uk
w longhirst.co.uk

LONGHORSLEY

Macdonald Linden Hall Golf & Country Club
Longhorsley NE65 8XF
t 0870 194 2123 **e** lindenhall@macdonald-hotels.co.uk
w lindenhall-hotel.co.uk

MORPETH

Beacon Hill Farm
Alun Moore, Beacon Hill Farm, Longhorsley, Morpeth, Northumberland NE65 8QW
t 01670 780900 **e** alun@beaconhill.co.uk
w beaconhill.co.uk

The Game Keepers Lodge
Cavil Head Farm, Morpeth NE65 9DF
t 01670 761110 **e** gd.charlton@hotmail.co.uk
w thegamekeeperslodge.co.uk

NEWBROUGH

Carr Edge Farm
Newbrough NE47 5EA
t 01434 674788 **e** stay@carredge.co.uk
w carredge.co.uk

NORTH CHARLTON

The Reading Rooms
Mrs Jane Robson, The Reading Rooms, Northumberland Cottages, The Old Stable Yard, Chathill NE67 5DE
t 01665 589434
e enquiries@northumberlandcottages.com
w northumberlandcottages.com

OTTERBURN

Redesdale Arms
Rochester, Otterburn NE19 1TA
t 01830 520668 **e** info@redesdale-hotel.co.uk
w redesdale-hotel.co.uk/

SLALEY

Rye Hill Farm (Old Byre)
Mrs Elizabeth Courage, Rye Hill Farm (Old Byre), The Old Byre, Slaley NE47 0AH
t 01434 673259 **e** info@ryehillfarm.co.uk
w ryehillfarm.co.uk

WARK

Battlesteads Hotel
Wark, Hexham, Northumberland NE48 3LS
t 01434 230209 **e** info@battlesteads.com
w battlesteads.com

WOOLER

Fenton Hill Farm Cottages
Mrs Margaret Logan, Fenton Hill Farm Cottages, Fenton Hill Farm, Wooler NE71 6JJ
t 01668 216228 **e** stay@fentonhillfarm.co.uk
w fentonhillfarm.co.uk

Tyne and Wear

GATESHEAD

Hilton Newcastle Gateshead
Bottle Bank, Gateshead NE8 2AR
t 01914 909700 **e** reservations.newcastle@hilton.com
w hilton.co.uk/newcastlegateshead

Where to Go

Durham | **Barnard Castle**

Open: For opening hours and prices, please call 0870 333 1181 or visit www.english-heritage.org.uk/properties

Barnard Castle, Durham DL12 8PR
t 0870 333 1181 **e** customers@english-heritage.org.uk
english-heritage.org.uk/barnardcastle

Above the banks of the River Tees is one of northern England's largest medieval castles.

Access: 🚻♿🚹 General: ✏️🌼

Alnwick | **The Alnwick Garden**

Denwick Lane, Alnwick, Northumberland NE66 1YU
t 01665 511350 **e** info@thealnwickgarden.com
alnwickgarden.com

Belsay | **Belsay Hall, Castle & Gardens**

Open: For opening hours and prices, please call 0870 333 1181 or visit www.english-heritage.org.uk/properties

Belsay, Northumberland NE20 0DX
t 0870 333 1181 **e** customers@english-heritage.org.uk
english-heritage.org.uk/belsayhallcastleandgardens

With something to delight and inspire everyone, Belsay Hall is a wonderful family day out.

Access: ♿🚻♿🔥♿♿ General: 🅿️♿✏️🌼♿

Hexham | **Northumberland Park Authority**

Eastburn, South Park, Hexham, Northumberland NE46 1BS
t 01434 605555
northumberland-national-park.org.uk

Prudhoe | **Prudhoe Castle**

Open: For opening hours and prices, please call 0870 333 1181 or visit www.english-heritage.org.uk/properties

Prudhoe, Northumberland NE42 6NA
t 0870 333 1181 **e** customers@english-heritage.org.uk
english-heritage.org.uk/prudhoecastle

Explore the fortress remains, visit the exhibition and enjoy play and picnics in the grounds.

Access: ∴ ⚲ ♿ ♿ General: ▨ ♿

Warkworth | **Warkworth Castle & Hermitage**

Open: For opening hours and prices, please call 0870 333 1181 or visit www.english-heritage.org.uk/properties

Warkworth, Northumberland NE65 0UJ
t 0870 333 1181 **e** customers@english-heritage.org.uk
english-heritage.org.uk/warkworthcastleandhermitage

One of the most impressive fortresses in northern England offers a fun family day out.

Access: ♿ ♿ ▨ ♿ ♿ General: ♿ ▨ ✿ ♿

Where to Eat

Newcastle Upon Tyne | Adriano's

90 High Street, Gosforth, Newcastle Upon Tyne NE3 1HB
t 0191 284 6464
adrianos.co.uk

General: 🐕 🚶 ♿ wc ♿

Newcastle upon Tyne | Fisherman's Lodge

Jesmond Dene, Newcastle upon Tyne NE7 7BQ
t 0191 281 3281
fishermanslodge.co.uk

General: 🐕 🚶 ♿ ♿ ♿

Newcastle upon Tyne | Jesmond Dene House

Jesmond Dene Road, Newcastle upon Tyne NE2 2EY
t 0191 212 3000 **e** frontdesk@jesmonddenehouse.co.uk
jesmonddenehouse.co.uk

General: 🐕 FAX 🏊 🚶 ♿ wc ♿ ♿ abc ? P★★★

Newcastle upon Tyne | La Tasca

106 The Quayside, Newcastle upon Tyne NE1 3DX
t 0191 230 4006 **e** newcastle@latasca.co.uk
latasca.co.uk

General: 🐕 FAX 🏊 🚶 ♿ ♿ ♿

Newcastle upon Tyne | Zizzi

42-50 Grey Street, Newcastle upon Tyne NE1 6AE
t 0191 261 8360
zizzi.co.uk

General: 🐕 🚶 ♿ wc ♿

Newgate Street | Nando's

Unit F8, The Gate, Newgate Street, Newcastle NE1 5XE
t 0191 261 0131
nandos.co.uk

General: 🐕 FAX 🏊 🚶 ♿ wc ♿ .: abc P★★★

For more **information** on **accommodation**
attractions activities **events** and holidays
contact the **Tourist Information Centres**
see regional listings for the nearest one.

Small Country, Big Heart

Scotland's heritage is what makes the country unique. The first-time visitor may expect only tartan, bagpipes and haggis, but Scotland's heritage is much more than that – it encompasses castles and historic houses, tweeds and fine textiles, malt whisky, gardens galore, and wild countryside.

Scotland is a small country and easy to get around, thanks to the network of roads and rail; you can stay in just one or two places, explore on day trips, enjoy the variety of scenery – and feel that you've got to know the country. **Edinburgh** and **Glasgow**, the two main cities, may be only forty miles and a short train ride apart, but they are very different in character. Edinburgh's Old and New Towns, together, are deservedly a **World Heritage Site**, whilst her festivals (arts, film, theatre, book, science) ensure plenty to do all year round. Glasgow is much bigger, with the best shopping in Britain outside London, and **Kelvingrove Art Gallery and Museum** is rated as one of the best. The easiest way to get around the cities is with the hop-on hop-off tour buses; in the capital city all the **Edinburgh Tour Buses** are wheelchair-accessible.

Scotland's countryside is a mix of mountains and glens, farms and woods, rocky coastlines and sandy beaches. **The National Parks** (the **Cairngorms** in the Highlands and **Loch Lomond and the Trossachs** north of Glasgow) have mountains, glens and lochs (**Loch Ness** and **Loch Lomond**) as well as wildlife – eagles, red deer and roe deer, ospreys and otters, wildcats and pine martens. If you are touring by car, look for the brown signposts with the thistle logo, because they denote national tourist routes, chosen for the scenery and the quiet roads.

Food and drink are important when you are on holiday and Scotland's restaurants make a feature of local produce such as Aberdeen Angus steak, lamb from the hills, salmon from the rivers, venison and pheasant from the moors, and strawberries and raspberries freshly picked. A visit to Scotland is incomplete, of course, without a dram of whisky – take your choice of malts from the **Highlands**, the **Lowlands** or the **islands**; each is subtly different, so if you have a favourite, try something new.

Getting around Scotland by car does give you the most flexibility, but if you want to leave the car at home (a good idea in the cities), then **ScotRail** operates the trains and

Edinburgh Castle

The West Highland Line

Scotland

Visitor Information Centres	274	Where to Go	293
Where to Stay	280	Where to Eat	294

there is a dedicated helpline to provide information if you need some, whilst **Traveline Scotland** can advise on buses, ferries and trains.

For tartan and bagpipes, visit one of the **Highland Games** which take place during the summer and ask for haggis as a starter to your meal in a Scottish restaurant.

Where to stay

Finding the right place to stay is important for all visitors and especially so if you have limited mobility. Scotland has bed and breakfasts, guest houses, hotels, hostels and self-catering. **VisitScotland**, the national tourist board, operates a grading scheme for accommodation (one to five stars) and also checks accessibility, where relevant, every three years, using criteria based on advice from organisations which are aware of the need for accuracy. In serviced accommodation the assessment covers bedrooms, bathrooms and public areas. In self-catering, everything is checked. Attractions are assessed for the core attraction, the toilets and, where relevant, the restaurant and the shop.

The **VisitScotland** website will inspire you and help you plan your holiday. On it you can also find information on accommodation and visitor attractions both by level of accessibility or by location. Or you can contact the call centre who will help you find the place that's right for you.

Live it. Visit *Scotland.*
visitscotland.com

Get in touch

For general information and advice on accommodation:

VisitScotland
t: +44 (0)131 625 8625 (from overseas) or 0845 22 55 121 (UK)
e: info@visitscotland.com
web: www.visitscotland.com

Accessible accommodation:
www.visitscotland.com/
accommodation/
accessiblescotland

Cairngorms National Pa

Visitor Information Centres

Visitor Information Centres are a mine of information about local and regional accommodation, attractions and events. Visit them when you arrive at your destination or contact them before you go.

All the Visitor Information Centres listed below can give you detailed information on Scotland and book your accommodation wherever you want to go. You can email **info@visitscotland.com** for information and to book your holiday. The Visitor Information Centres listed below are open all year. See **www.visitscotland.com** for a full listing including centres that open seasonally.

Aberdeen	23 Union St, Aberdeen AB11 5BP	01224 252212
Aberfeldy	The Square, Aberfeldy PH15 2DD	01887 820276
Aberfoyle	Trossachs Discovery Centre, Main St, Aberfoyle FK8 3UQ	01877 382352
Abington	Welcome Break Services, Junction 13, off M74, Biggar ML12 6RG	01864 502571
Arbroath	Harbour Visitor Centre, Fishmarket Quay, Arbroath, DD11 1PS	01241 872609
Aviemore	7 The Parade, Grampian Rd, Aviemore PH22 1PP	01479 810930
Ayr	22 Sandgate, Ayr KA7 1BW	01292 290300
Ballater	Old Royal Station, Station Square, Ballater AB35 5RB	013397 55306
Balloch	Old Station Building, Balloch Rd, Balloch G83 8LQ	01389 753533
Blairgowrie	26 Wellmeadow, Blairgowrie PH10 6AS	01250 872960
Bowmore	The Square, Main St, Bowmore, Islay PA43 7JP	01496 810254
Braemar	The Mews, Mar Rd, Braemar AB35 5YP	01339 741600
Brechin	Pictavia Centre, Brechin Castle Centre, Haighmuir, Brechin DD9 6RL	01356 623050
Brodick	The Pier, Brodick, Arran KA27 8AU	01770 303774
Callander	Ancaster Sq, Callander FK17 8ED	01877 330342
Campbeltown	MacKinnon House, The Pier, Campbeltown PA28 6EF	01586 552056
Craignure	The Pierhead, Craignure, Mull PA65 6AY	01680 812377
Crathie	The Car Park, Crathie, By Ballater AB35 5UL	013397 42414
Crieff	High St, Crieff PH7 3HU	01764 652578
Drumnadrochit	The Car Park. Drumnadrochit IV63 6TX	01456 459086
Dumfries	64 Whitesands, Dumfries DG1 2RS	01387 253862
Dundee	Discovery Point, Discovery Quay, Dundee DD1 4XA	01382 527527
Dunfermline	1 High St, Dunfermline KY12 7DL	01383 720999

Dunkeld	The Cross, Dunkeld PH8 0AN	01350 727688
Dunoon	7 Alexandra Parade, Dunoon PA23 8AB	01369 703785
Dunvegan	2 Lochside, Dunvegan, Skye IV55 8WB	01470 521878
Durness	Sango, Durness IV27 4PZ	01971 511368
Edinburgh	3 Princes St, Edinburgh EH2 2QP	0131 473 3844
Edinburgh Airport	Edinburgh International Airport, Edinburgh EH12 9DN	0131 473 3120
Elgin	Elgin Library, Cooper Park, Elgin, Moray IV30 1HS	01343 562608
Falkirk	Falkirk Wheel, Lime Road, Tamfourhill, Falkirk FK1 4RS	01324 620244
Fort William	15 High Street, Fort William PH33 6DH	01397 701801
Glasgow	11 George Square, Glasgow G2 1DY	0141 204 4400
Glasgow Airport	International Arrivals Hall, Glasgow Airport, Paisley PA3 2ST	0141 848 4440
Gretna	Unit 10, Gateway Outlet Village, Glasgow Rd, Gretna DG16 5GG	01461 337834
Hawick	Heart of Hawick Tower Mill, Kirkstile, Hawick TD9 0AE	01450 373993
Inveraray	Front St, Inveraray PA32 8UY	01499 302063
Inverness	Castle Wynd, Inverness IV2 3BJ	01463 252401
Jedburgh	Murray's Green, Jedburgh TD8 6BE	01835 863171
Kelso	Town House, The Square, Kelso TD5 7HF	01573 228055
Kirkcaldy	The Merchant's House, 339 High St, Kirkcaldy KY1 1JL	01592 267775
Kirkwall	The Travel Centre, West Castle Street, Kirkwall, Orkney KW15 1GU	01856 872856
Lanark	Horsemarket, Ladyacre Rd, Lanark ML11 7LQ	01555 661661
Lerwick	Market Cross, Lerwick, Shetland ZE1 0LU	01595 693434
Melrose	Abbey House, Abbey St, Melrose TD6 9LG	01896 822283
North Berwick	1 Quality St, North Berwick EH39 4HJ	01620 892197
Oban	Albany St, Oban PA34 4AN	01631 563122
Paisley	9A Gilmour St, Paisley PA1 1DD	0141 889 0711
Peebles	23 High St, Peebles EH45 8AG	01721 723159
Perth	Lower City Mills, West Mill St, Perth PH1 5QP	01738 450600
Pirnhall	M9/M80 Junction 9 Service Area, Pirnhall FK7 8EU	01786 814111
Pitlochry	22 Atholl Rd, Pitlochry PH16 5BX	01796 472215
Portree	Bayfield House, Bayfield Rd, Portree, Skye IV51 9EL	01478 614906
Rothesay	Isle of Bute Discovery Centre, Victoria St, Rothesay PA20 0AH	01700 502151
Southwaite	M6 Service Area, Southwaite, Carlisle CA4 0NS	01697 473445
St Andrews	70 Market St, St Andrews KY16 9NU	01334 472021
Stirling	41 Dumbarton Rd, Stirling FK8 2QQ	01786 475019
Stornoway	26 Cromwell St, Stornoway, Lewis HS1 2DD	01851 703088
Stranraer	28 Harbour St, Stranraer DG9 7RA	01776 702595
Sumburgh	Sumburgh Airport, Wilsness Terminal, Sumburgh ZE3 9JP	01950 460905
Tobermory	The Pier, Main St, Tobermory, Mull PA75 6NU	01688 30218
Tyndrum	6 Main Street, Tyndrum FK20 8RY	01838 400324

Abbotsford

Scotland's Heritage

What comes to mind when you think about Scotland? Bagpipes and kilts, whisky and Loch Ness? These are part of our heritage, but Scotland is much more; the history of religion, textiles, architecture, literature, ship-building and golf are all to be found at the visitor attractions featured here.

Hopetoun House

Sir Walter Scott, the 19th century novelist, wrote romantic tales of courage and derring-do and his poem "The Lady of The Lake" inspired people to visit the Trossachs. He spent many years at Abbotsford, his home near Melrose, where he built up a collection of historical items, including a quaich (a drinking cup) made from a tree cut down on the battlefield of Waterloo. Robert Burns is Scotland's national poet; whose poems and songs are known far beyond the country. He refined the words to the haunting melody of "Auld Lang Syne", a song sung wherever friends gather at Hogmanay. A new visitor centre celebrating his life and works opens in early 2011 in Alloway in Ayrshire, where he was born in 1759.

Hopetoun House, in extensive parkland near Edinburgh, is an outstanding example of Georgian architecture, which was built in the early 1700, designed by two of Scotland's most famous architects, William Bruce and William Adam.

The Royal Yacht Britannia

It houses magnificent collections of paintings, tapestries and ceramics. The same Georgian magnificence can be seen in Edinburgh's New Town, in pleasing contrast to the medieval skyscrapers of the Old Town.

Scotland has been the scene of many battles. In 1746 a desolate moor near Inverness was the scene of the last battle to be fought on British soil; this was Culloden, where the forces of Bonnie Prince Charlie, the Catholic pretender to the British throne, were beaten by the Government army. In the visitor centre you can follow the story through pictures, voices, maps and a thrilling depiction of the battle, as well as trace the pathways across the moor to the memorials to the fallen clans.

Religion is an integral part of Scotland's heritage; once a Catholic country, Scotland became largely Protestant in the decades following the 16th century Reformation. St. Giles' Cathedral in Edinburgh, founded in the Catholic

Mary Queen of Scots jewellery
National Museum of Scotland

11th century reflects this change. John Knox, the leading preacher in the Reformation, first preached at St. Giles in June 1559 and only a week later he was elected minister and stayed in office for 13 years. Still a place of worship, the magnificent Glasgow Cathedral is the only Scottish mainland medieval cathedral to have survived intact the ravages of the Reformation. Tucked away in the South West is the village of Whithorn, the "Cradle of Christianity", once a place of pilgrimage for Scottish monarchs, including Robert the Bruce and Mary, Queen of Scots; you can find out more in the Whithorn Trust Discovery Centre.

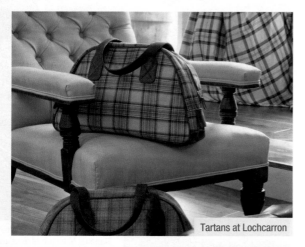

Tartans at Lochcarron

For many years ship-building was an important part of Scottish industry and the RRS *Discovery* and the Royal Yacht *Britannia* are two of the best examples. In 1901 Captain Scott set sail on his first voyage to the Antarctic on board the *Discovery*, a former whaling ship built in Dundee, now berthed on the shores of the River Tay in her home town. The on-shore visitor centre gives a comprehensive idea of life on board and in the Antarctic, and visitors who can't access the below-decks can watch the simulated tour.

Britannia, built on Glasgow's Clydeside, for decades world-famous for ship-building, was the floating home of the British royal family on their overseas tours from 1953 to 1997. Visitors can see the state dining room, the royal bedrooms, the captain's cabin and much more, with the audio guide providing insights into life on board for the royals and the crew. A lift means that all the decks are accessible.

Scotland is known as the Home of Golf and at the heart of it is St. Andrews, where, whether or not you are a golfer, you will find the British Golf Museum a fascinating place. You can learn about the history of golf and how the equipment has evolved (with golf balls and clubs from the earliest times) and find out more about golfing greats such as Greg Norman, Tony Jacklin, Jack Nicklaus and Colin Montgomerie.

Scotland is also the home of fine tweeds, tartans and woollens and before you buy that special gift which will last

Courtesy of Edinburgh Bus Tours

Johnston's of Elgin

a lifetime, you can see how it is made in two mills — in Lochcarron in the Borders there are tours of the mill and then you can browse and buy in the shop, perhaps choosing something from the 700 tartans in stock. In the North East, at Johnston's of Elgin, as well as the mill tour there is a small exhibition where visitors can see and touch the range of textiles, then enjoy tea and scones whilst deciding what to buy!

Finally, before you set out on your tour, take time to browse through Scotland's heritage and culture. There are two museums which are not to be missed — the National Museum of Scotland in Edinburgh and Kelvingrove Museum and Art Gallery in Glasgow.

Find out more about Scotland's heritage this year!

Access

All the attractions mentioned above are accessible for wheelchair-users. In some places not all areas can be accessed, but there may be a video for virtual exploration. If you have particular requirements, we recommend that you call in advance.

Contact details

Abbotsford
01896 752043
scottsabbotsford.co.uk

British Golf Museum
01334 460046
britishgolfmuseum.co.uk

Burns Cottage
0844 493 2601
nts.org.uk

Culloden
0844 493 2159
nts.org.uk

Edinburgh Bus Tour
0131 220 0770
edinburghtour.com

Glasgow Cathedral
0141 552 8298
glasgow-cathedral.com

Hopetoun House
0131 331 2451
hopetoun.co.uk

Johnston's of Elgin
01343 554094
johnstonscashmere.com

Kelvingrove Museum
0141 276 9599
glasgowlife.org.uk/museums

Lochcarron of Scotland
01750 726000
lochcarron.com

National Museum of Scotland
0131 225 7534
nms.ac.uk

RRS Discovery
01382 201245
rrsdiscovery.com

Royal Yacht Britannia
0131 555 5566
royalyachtbritannia.co.uk

St. Giles
0131 225 4363
st.gilescathedral.org.uk

Whithorn Trust
01988 500508
whithorn.com

For general information, call VisitScotland on 0845 22 55 121 or visitscotland.com

Where to Stay

Aberdeen | Holiday Inn Express Aberdeen City Centre

Visit Scotland ★★★

Chapel Street, Aberdeen AB10 1SQ
t 01224 623500 **e** reservations@hieaberdeen.co.uk
hiexpress.com/exaberdeencc

Access: General: Room:

Ballater | Crathie Opportunity Holidays

Visit Scotland ★★★★

Units: 4 Sleeps: 4-6

Low season p/w:
£315.00

High season p/w:
£695.00

Ms Maggie MacAlpine, Crathie Opportunity Holidays, The Manse Courtyard, Crathie, Ballater, Aberdeenshire AB35 5UL **t** 01339 742100
e info@crathieholidays.org.uk
crathieholidays.org.uk **7D3**

Four beautifully restored cottages, designed and equipped to the highest standard for disabled people.

Access: H abc General: Unit:

Ardmaddy | Caddleton Farmhouse

Visit Scotland ★★★★

Units: 5 Sleeps: 4-12

Open: All year

Low season p/w:
£351.00

High season p/w:
£2112.00

Mrs Minette Struthers, Ardmaddy Castle Holiday Cottages, By Oban, Argyll PA34 4QY **t** 01852 300353 **e** ardmaddycastle@btinternet.com

One of five 4* cottages, stunning rural seaside location nr Oban. Hillwalking, wildlife, fishing, boats.

Access: General: Unit:

Campbeltown | **Dunvalanree**

Visit Scotland ★★★★

Rooms per night:
s: £75.00
d: £100.00-£135.00
Meals: £22.00-£28.00

Port Righ, Carradale, Campbeltown, Argyll PA28 6SE
t 01583 431226 **e** book@dunvalanree.com
dunvalanree.com

6A2

Dunvalanree, a small hotel in Carradale on the Mull of Kintyre, ideal to explore the history and natural beauty of Kintyre. Only five rooms. The food is recognised by the Good Food Guide. Licensed.

Location: A83 towards Campbeltown, turn onto the B8001 which becomes the B842. Continue south into Carradale. At the crossroads turn right.

Access:

General:

Room:

Oban | **North Ledaig Caravan Club Site**

Visit Scotland ★★★★★

(230)
£15.30-£22.50
(50)
£15.30-£22.50
280 touring pitches
Open: 25/3/2011 to 31/10/2011

Pub: 2 miles

Connel, Oban, Argyll PA37 1RU
t 01631 710291
caravanclub.co.uk

6B1

We are situated right on shore with fabulous views over the sea to the Isle of Mull. Enjoy a peaceful escape or an activity holiday touring the local area, visiting gardens or cruising to the off-shore islands.

Location: From south, turn at Connel onto A828 (sign posted Fort William), site is on left about 1 mile.

Access:

General:

Pitch:

Salen | Ard Mhor House

Visit Scotland ★★★	
Open: All year except Xmas and New Year	

Rooms per night:	
s:	£35.00-£50.00
d:	£50.00-£90.00
Meals:	£20.00

Pier Road, Salen, Isle of Mull, Argyll & Bute PA72 6JL
t 01680 300 255 **e** davidclowes@ardmhorguesthouse.fsnet.co.uk
ardmhor-guesthouse.co.uk **6A1**

Friendly guesthouse overlooking Salen Bay. Ideal jumping off point for the whole Island of Mull.

Access: ♿ General: ✕ P Room:

Castle Douglas | Rusko Holidays

Visit Scotland ★★★-★★★★★

Lady Vaux, Rusko Holidays, Rusko, Gatehouse of Fleet, Castle Douglas
DG7 2BS **t** 01557 814215 **e** enquiries@ruskoholidays.co.uk
ruskoholidays.co.uk

Access: abc General: P S Unit:

Port Logan | New England Bay Caravan Club Site

Visit Scotland ★★★★★

Open: March to November

Port Logan, Stranraer DG9 9NX
t 01776 860275
caravanclub.co.uk

AS

Access: General: Pitch:

Sanquhar | Nith Riverside Cottages

Visit Scotland ★★★

Mr. McAndrew, Nith Riverside Cottages, BlackaddieHouse Hotel, Blackaddie
Rd, Sanquhar DG4 6JJ **t** 01659 50270 **e** enquiries@blackaddiehotel.co.uk
nithriversidecottages.co.uk

Access: General: P S Unit:

Dundee | Holiday Inn Express Dundee

41 Dock Street, Dundee DD1 3DR
t 01382 314330 **e** info@hiexpressdundee.com
hiexpress.com/exhidundee

Access: General: Room:

©Britain on View/Tony Pleavin

Dirleton | **Yellowcraig Caravan Club Site** ~~THE~~ CARAVAN CLUB

AS

Visit Scotland ★★★★★

🚐 (116)
£14.70–£27.20

🚚 (116)
£14.70–£27.20

116 touring pitches
Open: 25 March to 07 November

Access:
🐾 🏠 😊 ♿ ᵂᶜ

General:
🔋 🚐 📶 🔥 🚐 ᵍ 📞 🚐ᵂᴾ

Pitch:
🚐 🚚

Dirleton EH39 5DS
t 01620 850217
caravanclub.co.uk

6D2

Yellowcraig Caravan Club Site is an attractive location with several pitching areas separated by grass banking, shrubs and roses - a splendid choice for family holidays with acres of flat golden sands and rock pools nearby. Great for nature lovers.

Location: From South turn off A1 at signpost Haddington onto A199 (signposted Drem); at roundabout turn right onto A6137 (signposted Aberlady).

Edinburgh | **Atholl Brae - The Harland**

♿ **AS**

Visit Scotland ★★★★

Units: 1   Sleeps: 1
Open: All year

Low season p/w:
£398.00
High season p/w:
£948.00
Shop: <0.5 miles
Pub: <0.5 miles

General:
🐎 Ⓢ

Unit:
♿ 🌼

Mrs Elizabeth (Liz) Bentley, Partner, Atholl Brae, 20 Bellfield Crescent, Eddleston, Peebles, Peebleshire EH45 8RQ   **t** 01721 730679 home and fax mobile - 07769 224224 **e** stay@athollbrae.co.uk

athollbrae.co.uk

6C2

4 * luxury for 4 - comfort for 6 Friendly, personal service. Lift. Bedroom 1 - king-sized bed, en suite. Bedroom 2 - 2 singles Bed-settee and folding beds to accomodate up to 6 Bathroom. Cot. High-chair. Parking. Wi-fi

Location: The apartment address is - Flat 10, 6 Pilrig Heights, Edinburgh, EH6 5BF. - Google map on our web-site www.athollbrae.co.uk

Edinburgh | Edinburgh Caravan Club Site

AS

Visit Scotland ★★★★★

Open: All year

Marine Drive, Edinburgh EH4 5EN
t 01313 126874
caravanclub.co.uk

Access: General: Pitch:

Edinburgh | Gillis Centre

Visit Scotland ★★★

100 Strathearn Road, Edinburgh EH9 1BB
t 0131 623 8933 e gilliscentre@staned.org.uk
gilliscentre.org.uk

Access: General: Room:

Edinburgh | Holiday Inn Edinburgh

AS

AA ★★★★

132 Corstophine Road, Edinburgh EH12 6UA
t 0871 942 9026 e edinburghhi@ihg.com
holiday-inn.co.uk

Access: abc General: Room:

Edinburgh | Holiday Inn Express - Edinburgh, Royal Mile

AS

300 Cowgate, Edinburgh EH1 1NA
t 0131 524 8400 e info@hiexpressedinburgh.co.uk
hiexpressedinburgh.co.uk

Access: General: Room:

Glenrothes | Balbirnie Park Caravan Club Site

AS

Visit Scotland ★★★★

(76) £13.10–£25.40

(76) £13.10–£25.40

(2)

76 touring pitches

Open: March to November

Access:

General:

Pitch:

Balbirnie Road, Markinch, Glenrothes KY7 6NR
t 01592 759130
caravanclub.co.uk

6C2

The tranquil rural surroundings let you unwind from the bustle of everyday life. For those who fancy some activity, the sporting and leisure facilities in nearby Glenrothes and Kirkcaldy make for a fun day out.

Location: M90 junction 2A (j3 from North) onto A92; 15m at roundabout right onto B9130. Left into Balbirnie Park.

Glenrothes | Express by Holiday Inn - Fife

AA ★★★

Leslie Roundabout, Leslie Road, Glenrothes, Fife KY6 3EP
t 01592 745509 **e** reservations@hiexpressglenrothes.co.uk
hiexpress.co.uk

Access: General: Room:

Kelty | Benarty Holiday Accommodation

Units: 4 Sleeps: 6-7
Open: All year

Low season p/w: £245.00
High season p/w: £440.00

Mrs Barbara Constable, Benarty Holiday Accommodation, Benarty House, Kelty, Fife KY4 0HT **t** 01383 830235
e barbara@benartyholidaycottages.co.uk
benartyholidaycottages.co.uk **6C2**

Rural setting, working estate. Horsemill renovated with basic wheelchair access and wet floor shower.

General: P Unit:

Glasgow | Crowne Plaza Hotel Glasgow

Congress Road, Glasgow, Lanarkshire G3 8QT
t 0871 942 9091 **e** cpglasgow@qmh-hotels.com
cpglasgowhotel.co.uk

Access: abc General: Room:

Aviemore | The Highland Council @ Badaguish

Visit Scotland ★★★

Units: 4 Sleeps: 12-17
Open: All year

Low season p/w: £835.00
High season p/w: £1895.00

Mr. Phil Swainson, The Highland Council, Outdoor education @ Badaguish, Badaguish, Aviemore PH22 1QU **t** 01463 870797
e badaguish@highland.gov.uk
highland.gov.uk/learninghere/communitylearning/outdoorlearning/badaguish.htm **7C3**

Visitscotland 3 star lodges in forest location nr Aviemore.

Access: General: P Unit:

Brora | Dalchalm Caravan Club Site

THE CARAVAN CLUB

AS

Visit Scotland ★★★★★

Open: April to October

Brora KW9 6LP
t 01408 621479
caravanclub.co.uk

Access: General: Pitch:

Gairloch | **Willow Croft** **AS**

Visit Scotland ★★★	Mrs Beryl Leslie, 40 Big Sand, Gairloch, Ross-Shire IV21 2DD
Units: 1 Sleeps: 6	**t** 01445 712448 **e** bigsand@waitrose.com
Open: All year	sites.ecosse.net/iml **7B2**

Low season p/w:
£200.00
High season p/w:
£490.00

Magnificent sea/mountain views from patio or rooms. Peaceful situation. Wildlife watching. Relax in comfort.

Access: 🐾✕🚻 General: 🚐🗑P Unit: ♨🔥♿🎛📺🔥❀

Inchcree | **Bunree Caravan Club Site** THE CARAVAN CLUB **AS**

Visit Scotland ★★★★★

🚐 (99)
      £14.90–£27.20

🚐 (99)
      £14.90–£27.20

99 touring pitches
Open: 25 March 2011 to 2 January 2012

Onich, Fort William PH33 6SE
t 01855 821283
caravanclub.co.uk   **6B1**

Visit magnificent Ben Nevis, take a cable car to the upper terminal (2,300ft) of the Aonach Mor Mountain, for fabulous views of the whole mountain range, the Great Glen and the islands of Skye and Rhum.

Location: Left off A82 (Glencoe - Fort William) 1m past Onich. At Club Site sign into narrow track. Site in $\frac{1}{4}$m.

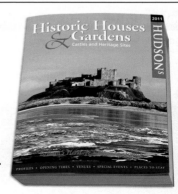

Access:
🐾🔥☺🚻♿
General:
🗑🚐📶🎣😊👶🚿🚰
Pitch:
🚐🚐

Kinlochewe | **Kinlochewe Caravan Club Site** THE CARAVAN CLUB

Kinlochewe, Achnasheen IV22 2PA
t 01445 760239
caravanclub.co.uk

7B3

Visit Scotland ★★★★★

🚐 (56)
£11.40–£23.90

🚍 (56)
£11.40–£23.90

56 touring pitches
Open: 25 March to 3 October

Peaceful and intimate , Kinlochewe Caravan Club Site is set at the foot of the rugged slopes of Ben Eighe, at the end of a beautiful drive along the valley from Achnasheen, with glittering lochs, lush woodland and mountains.

Location: A9 Tore left at roundabout onto A835; at rndabt in Maryburgh A835; Achnasheen roundabout follow A832. Site on left 10m.

Access:
🐾🏛️☺️♿🚻
General:
🗄️📠📻🚿💀👜🚰♻️
Pitch:
🚐🚍

Thurso | **Dunnet Bay Caravan Club Site** THE CARAVAN CLUB

Dunnet, Thurso KW14 8XD
t 01847 821319
caravanclub.co.uk

Enjoy England ★★★★★

Open: April to October

Access: 🏛️☺️♿ General: 🗄️📠📻🚿💀👜♻️ Pitch: 🚐🚍⚐

Glenshee | New Steading Cottage/Old Steading Cottage

Visit Scotland ★★★★

Units: 2 Sleeps: 2-4
Open: All year

Low season p/w:
£330.00
High season p/w:
£580.00
Shop: 5 miles
Pub: 5 miles

Sue Smith, Dalnoid Holiday Cottages, Dalnoid Farmhouse, Glenshee, Blairgowrie, Perthshire PH10 7LR **t** 01250 882200 **e** info@dalnoid.co.uk
dalnoid.co.uk   **6C1**

2 single-storey cottages both sleep 4, stunning mountain views. King-size with en suite, twin bedroom, family bathroom with grab rails, large open-plan kitchen/lounge/dining area, patio, no internal steps. Heating, power, logs included. Ideal for wildlife watching, Royal Deeside and Perthshire.

Location: On the A93, Deeside National Tourist Route. Nearest Station - Pitlochry 19 milesNearest Airports - Edinburgh 1 1/2 hrs

Access:

General:

Unit:

Glasgow Airport | Holiday Inn Glasgow Airport

AA ★★★

Abbotsinch, Paisley, Renfrewshire PA3 2TE
t 0870 400 9031 **e** reservations-glasgow@ihg.com
holidayinn.co.uk

Access: General: Room:

Coldstream | Little Swinton Cottages

Visit Scotland ★★★

Units: 3 Sleeps: 3-7
Open: All year

Low season p/w:
£180.00
High season p/w:
£420.00

Mrs Sue Brewis, Leet Villa, Leet Street, Coldstream, Berwickshire TD12 4BJ **t** 01890 882173 **e** suebrewis@tiscali.co.uk
littleswinton.co.uk   **6D2**

A row of comfortable, clean, well-equipped single storey farm cottages in beautiful border countryside.

Access: General: Unit:

Duns | **Green Hope**

Visit Scotland ★★★	Mrs. Alison Landale, Ellemford, Duns, Berwickshire TD11 3SG
Units: 2 Sleeps: 1-10	**t** 01361 890242 **e** alison@greenhope.co.uk
Open: All year	**greenhope.co.uk** 6D2

Low season p/w: £250.00	Secluded, peace-filled, river-side accommodation. Bird & wild-life interesting & varied. Border attractions & Edinburgh, accessible.
High season p/w: £1000.00	

Access: ⚇ General: ⚇ Unit: ⚇

Hawick | **Whitchester Christian Guest House**
 AS

Visit Scotland ★★★	Borthaugh, Hawick, Scottish Borders TD9 7LN
	t 01450 377477 **e** enquiries@whitchester.org.uk
	whitchester.org.uk

Access: abc ⚇ General: ⚇ Room: ⚇

Melrose | **Eildon Holiday Cottages**
♿ **AS**

Visit Scotland ★★★-★★★★★	Mrs Jill Hart, Eildon Holiday Cottages, Dingleton Mains, Melrose, Scottish
Units: 6 Sleeps: 2-6	Borders TD6 9HS **t** 01896 823 258 **e** info@eildon.co.uk
Open: All year	**eildon.co.uk** 6C2

Low season p/w: £294.00	Winner of Holiday Care Service award for the best self-catering accommodation for disabled people in Britain. On slopes of Eildon Hills in the beautiful Scottish Borders. 40 mins. from Edinburgh. Category1 accessibility. Two cottages with overhead ceiling hoists.
High season p/w: £777.00	
Shop: 0.5 miles	
Pub: 0.5 miles	

Location: From Melrose centre, take B6359 Dingleton Road for $\frac{1}{2}$ mile. Turn left into Melrose Golf Club and past clubhouse.

Access:
🅷 ⚇
General:
⚇
Unit:
⚇

Scottish Borders | **Bunnahabhain, Strathisla and Tomatin Lodges**

Visit Scotland ★★★★★	Mr. John Pilling, Strathmore, West Fishwick, Berwick Upon Tweed
	TD15 1XQ **t** 01289 386 279 **e** info@lazydaycottages.co.uk
	lazydaycottages.co.uk

General: ⚇ Unit: ⚇

Ayr | Craigie Gardens Caravan Club Site THE CARAVAN CLUB   AS

Visit Scotland ★★★★★	Craigie Road, Ayr KA8 0SS
Open: All year	**t** 01292 264909
	caravanclub.co.uk

Access: 🏕️ ☺ General: ▢ ▣ 🐾 🚐 ⚡ ☗ 🔒 ⓦⓟ Pitch: 🚐 🚙

Ayr | Holiday Inn Express Ayr   ♿

Visit Scotland ★★★★★	Wheatpark Place, Ayr, South Ayrshire KA8 9RT
	t 01292 272300 **e** info@hiexpressayr.com
	hiexpressayr.com/exhiayr

Access: ▣ 🐾 🏕️ ☺ ♿ ♿ General: 🪑 ✗ ⚟ 🅿️ ⬆️ ♿ Room: 🛏️ ♨️ 📺 📼 📺 ☕

Dunblane | Cambushinnie Croft   ♿

Visit Scotland ★★★★	Mrs Fiona Lyle, Mid Cambushinnie Farm, Cromlix, Dunblane, Perthshire
Units: 1 Sleeps: 1-6	FK15 9JU **t** 01786 880631/07977135071
Open: All year	**e** info@cambushinniecroft.co.uk
Low season p/w: £586.00	cambushinniecroft.co.uk **6C1**
High season p/w: £1092.00	

Spacious family house on working farm. Stunning countryside and ideal central location for exploring Scotland.

Access: 🐾 General: 🪑 ▢ **P** Ⓢ Unit: 🛏️ ♨️ ♿ 📺 📼 📺 ♿ 🌸

North Uist | Temple View Hotel   🚶

Visit Scotland ★★★★	Carinish, North Uist, Western Isles HS6 5EJ
	t 01876 580676 **e** templeviewhotel@aol.com
	templeviewhotel.co.uk

Access: 🏕️ ♿ ♿ General: 🪑 🍽️ ✗ ⚟ 🅿️ 🌸 ♿ Room: 🛏️ 📼 📺 📺 ☕

Killin | Maragowan Caravan Club Site THE CARAVAN CLUB   AS

	Aberfeldy Road, Killin FK21 8TN
	t 01567 820245
	caravanclub.co.uk

Access: 🏕️ ☺ ♿ General: ▢ ▣ 🐾 🚐 ⚡ ☗ 🔒 ⓦⓟ Pitch: 🚐 🚙

Aberdeenshire

ABERDEEN

Copthorne Hotel ♿
122 Huntly Street, Aberdeen, Aberdeenshire AB10 1SU
e reservations.aberdeenemill-cop.com
w milleniumhotels.com

Hilton Double Tree Hotel ♿
Beach Boulevard, Aberdeen, Aberdeenshire AB24 5EF
t 01224 633339
e sales.doubletreeaberdeen@hilton.com
w patiohotels.com

King's Hall ♿
University of Aberdeen, Aberdeen AB24 3FX
t 01224 273444 **e** conf.events@abdn.ac.uk
w abdn.ac.uk/confevents

Thistle Aberdeen Airport Hotel ♿
Aberdeen Airport, Argyll Road, Dyce, Aberdeen,
Aberdeenshire AB21 0AF
t 01224 725252 **w** thistlehotels.com

University of Aberdeen, King's Hall ♿
Kings College, Regent Walk, Aberdeen AB24 3FX
e conf.events@abdn.ac.uk
w abdn.ac.uk/confevents

ALTENS ABERDEEN

Thistle Aberdeen Altens ♿
Souterhead Road, Altens, Aberdeen, Aberdeenshire
AB12 3LF
t 01224 877000 **w** thistlehotels.com

BALLATER

Glenernan Guest House ♿
37 Braemar Road, Ballater, Aberdeenshire AB35 5RQ
t 01339 753111 **e** enquiries@glenernanguesthouse.com
w glenernanguesthouse.com

CRAIBSTONE ESTATE BUCKSBURN

Craibstone Estate ♿
Facilities Office, Hunter Annexe, Craibstone Estate,
Bucksburn, Aberdeen, Aberdeenshire AB21 9TR
t 01224 711012 **e** g.bruce@ab.sac.ac.uk
w sac.ac.uk/holidayletsaberdeen

PITFODELS, NEAR ABERDEEN

The Marcliffe Hotel and Spa ♿
North Deeside Road, Cults, Aberdeen, Aberdeenshire
AB15 9YA
t 01224 861000 **w** marcliffe.com

TURRIFF

Ashwood ♿
Mrs. Joan Johnson, Delgatie Castle Trust Self Catering,
Delgatie Castle, Turriff, Aberdeenshire AB53 5TD
t 01888 563479
e jjohnson@delgatie-castle.freeserve.co.uk
w delgatiecastle.com

Deveron Lodge B&B Guesthouse ♿
Bridgend Terrace, Turriff, Aberdeenshire AB53 4ES
t 01888 563613 **e** deveron.lodge@gmx.com
w deveronlodge.com

WESTHILL ABERDEEN

Holiday Inn Aberdeen West ♿
Westhill Drive, Westhill, Aberdeenshire AB32 6TT
t 01224 270300 **w** holiday-inn.com/aberdeenwest

Angus
BRECHIN

Northern Hotel
2 Clerk Street, Brechin, Angus DD9 6AE
t 01356 625400 **e** info@northern-hotel.co.uk
w northern-hotel.co.uk

BROUGHTY FERRY

Forbes of Kingennie - Glen Esk
Ms. Gail Forbes, Forbes of Kingennie (SC), Omachie Farm, Kingennie, By Dundee, Angus DD5 3RE
t 01382 350777 **e** info@forbesofkingennie.com
w forbesofkingennie.com

BY MONTROSE

Anniston Farm Cottages
Mrs. Seonaid Turnbull, Firm of R & S Turnbull, Anniston Farm, Inverbervie, Montrose, Angus DD10 0PP
t 01561 361402

Argyll & Bute
BY HELENSBURGH

Rosslea Hall Hotel
Ferry Road, Rhu, By Helensburgh, Argyll & Bute G84 8NF
e rossleahall@mckeverhotels.co.uk
w mckeverhotels.co.uk

CONNEL BY OBAN

Wide Mouthed Frog
Dunbeg, Oban, Argyll & Bute PA37 1PX
t 01631 567005 **e** enquiries@widemouthedfrog.co.uk
w widemouthedfrog.co.uk

KILKENZIE

Dalnaspidal Guest House
Dalnaspidal, Tangy, Kilkenzie, Campbeltown, Argyll & Bute PA28 6QD
t 01586 820466 **e** relax@dalnaspidal-guesthouse.com
w dalnaspidal-guesthouse.com

KINLOCHLEVEN

Tigh-Na-Cheo
Garbhein Road, Kinlochleven, Argyll & Bute PH50 4SE
t 01855 831434 **e** reception@tigh-na-cheo.co.uk
w tigh-na-cheo.co.uk

STRONTIAN

Honeysuckle
Susanna Barber, Acharacle, Argyll PH36 4JA
t 01967 402226 **w** bluebellcroft.co.uk

Dumfries & Galloway
AUCHENCAIRN BY CASTLE DOUGLAS

Balcary Bay Hotel
Shore Road, Auchencairn, Castle Douglas, Dumfries & Galloway DG7 1QZ
t 01556 640217 **e** graeme@balcary-bay-hotel.co.uk
w balcary-bay-hotel.co.uk

AULDGIRTH

The Byre
Ms & Mr Zan & J Kirk, Low Kirkbride, Auldgirth, Dumfries & Galloway DG2 0SP
t 01387 820258 **e** lowkirkbride@btinternet.com
w lowkirkbridebyre.com

DALBEATTIE

Kerr Cottage
Port Road, Dalbeattie, Dumfries & Galloway DG5 4AZ
t 01556 612 245 **e** l.wilbur@site-electrical.co.uk
w kerrcottage.co.uk

DUMFRIES

Ae Farm Cottages
Mr. David Stewart, Gubhill Farm, Ae Forest, Dumfries DG1 1RL
t 01387 860 648 **e** david@creaturefeature.co.uk
w aefarmcottages.co.uk

Gubhill Farm - Shepherd's Flat
Mr D Stewart, Ae Forest Cottages, Dumfries DG1 1RL
e david@creaturefeature.co.uk
w aefarmcottages.co.uk

GRETNA

Bojangles Guest House
103 Annan Road, Gretna, Dumfries & Galloway DG16 5DN
t 01461 338291 **e** info@bojangles-guesthouse.co.uk
w bojangles-guesthouse.co.uk

The Garden House Hotel
Sarkfoot Road, Gretna, Dumfriesshire DG16 5EP
e june@gardenhouse.co.uk
w gardenhouse.co.uk

Hunters Lodge Hotel
Annan Road, Gretna, Dumfriesshire DG16 5DL
t 01461 338214 **e** reception@hunterslodgehotel.co.uk
w hunterslodgehotel.co.uk

GRETNA GREEN

Smiths @ Gretna Green
Gretna Green, Dumfries, Dumfries & Galloway DG16 5EA
t 0845 3676768 **e** info@smithsgretnagreen.com
w smithsgretnagreen.com

KIRKCUDBRIGHT

Fludha Guest House
Fludha, Tongland Road, Kirkcudbright, Dumfries & Galloway DG6 4UU
t 01557 331443 **e** stay@fludha.com
w fludha.com

LOCHMABEN

The Crown Hotel
Bruce Street, Lochmaben, Dumfriesshire DG11 1PD
e lorraine@crownlochmaben.freeserve.co.uk
w crownlochmaben.co.uk

MOFFAT

Lochhouse Farm Retreat Centre
Lochhouse Farm Retreat Centre, Beattock, Moffat, Dumfries & Galloway DG10 9SG
t 01683 300451 **e** accom@lochhousefarm.com
w lochhousefarm.com

STRANRAER

Culmore Bridge Cottages
Mr. J.W. Sime, Oak Cottage, Sandhead, Stranraer DG9 9DX
t 01776 830539 **e** jandmsime@aol.com
w culmorebridge.co.uk

Dundee
BROUGHTY FERRY DUNDEE

The Fisherman's Tavern Hotel
10-16 Fort Street, Broughty Ferry, Dundee DD5 2AD
t 01382 775941 **w** fishermanstavern.co.uk

DUNDEE

The Landmark Hotel
Kingsway West, Invergowrie, Dundee DD2 5JT
t 01382 641122 **w** thelandmarkdundee.com

West Park Centre
319 Perth Road, Dundee DD2 1NN
t 01382 647171 **e** caroline.rankin@westpark.co.uk
w westpark.co.uk

East Ayrshire
KILMARNOCK

Park Hotel
Rugby Road, Kilmarnock, Ayrshire KA1 2DP
t 01563 545999 **e** nh@theparkhotelayrshire.co.uk
w theparkhotelayrshire.co.uk

East Lothian
DIRLETON

Denis Duncan House
Mrs. Miriam Toosey, Eastgate House, Upper East Street, Sudbury, Suffolk CO10 1UB
t 01787 372343 **e** info@thelinberwicktrust.org.uk
w thelinberwicktrust.org.uk

HADDINGTON

Maitlandfield House Hotel
24 Sidegate, Haddington, East Lothian EH41 4BZ
t 01620 826513 **e** info@maitlandfieldhouse.co.uk
w maitlandfieldhouse.co.uk

MUSSELBURGH

QMU Capital Campus
Queen Margaret University Drive, Musselburgh, East Lothian EH21 6UD
t 0131 474 0000 **e** spattersonl@qmu.ac.uk
w qmu.ac.uk/services/holiday-accommodation.htm

Edinburgh
EDINBURGH

Ardgarth Guest House
1 St. Mary's Place, Portobello, Edinburgh EH15 2QF
t 0131 669 3021 **e** stay@ardgarth.com
w ardgarth.com

Edinburgh City Centre(Morrison St) Premier Inn
1 Morrison Street Link, Edinburgh EH3 8DN
t 0870 238 3319 **w** premiertravelinn.com

Express By Holiday Inn
Express by Holiday Inn, Britannia Way, Ocean Drive, Edinburgh EH6 6LA
t 0131 555 4422 **w** hiex-edinburgh.com

Jurys Inn Edinburgh
43 Jeffrey Street, Edinburgh EH1 1DH
t 0131 200 3300 **w** jurysinn.com

Novotel Edinburgh Centre
80 Lauriston Place, Edinburgh EH3 9DE
e iuge.vanooteghem@accor.com
w novotel.com

Ramada Mount Royal Hotel
53 Princes Street, Edinburgh EH2 2DG
t 0131 225 7161 **w** ramadajarvis.co.uk

Thistle Edinburgh
107 Leith Street, Edinburgh EH1 3SW
t 0131 556 0111 **w** thistlehotels.com/edinburgh

Toby Carvery & Innkeepers Lodge Edin/Wes
Payments & Control Dept, 27 Fleet Street, Birmingham, West Midlands B3 1JP
t 0870 2430500 **w** innkeeperslodge.com

Fife
BURNTISLAND

Kingswood Hotel
Kinghorn Road, Burntisland, Fife KY3 9LL
t 01592 872329 **e** rankin@kingswoodhotel.co.uk
w kingswoodhotel.co.uk

DUNFERMLINE

Express By Holiday Inn Dunfermline
Halbeath, Dunfermline, Fife KY11 8DY
t 01383 748220 **w** hiexpress.com/dunfermline

ELIE

Lobster Pot Cottage
Mrs Kim Kirkaldy, Incharvie Farmhouse, Kilconquhar, Elie, Fife KY9 1JU
t 01333 340640 **e** info@lobster-pot.co.uk
w lobster-pot.co.uk

KINGHORN

Bay Hotel
Burntisland Road, Kinghorn, Fife KY3 9YE
t 01592 892222 **e** catherine.cameron@pettycur.co.uk
w thebayhotel.net

ST ANDREWS

The Old Station Country Guest House
Stravithie Bridge, St. Andrew's, Fife KY16 8LR
t 01334 880505 **e** info@theoldstation.co.uk
w theoldstation.co.uk

Glasgow
GLASGOW

Carlton George Hotel
44 West George Street, Glasgow G2 1DH
t 0141 353 6373 **e** resgeorge@carltonhotels.com
w carltonhotels.com

Glasgow Hilton
1 William Street, Glasgow G3 8HT
t 0141 204 5555 **w** hilton.co.uk/glasgow

Glasgow Marriott
500 Argyle Street, Anderston, Glasgow G3 8RR
t 0141 226 5577
e mhrs.gladt.frontdesk@marriotthotels.com
w marriott.co.uk/gladt

Holiday Inn
161 West Nile Street, Glasgow G1 2RL
t 0141 352 8300 **e** carolynn.morrison@higlasgow.com
w higlasgow.com

Jurys Inn Glasgow
80 Jamaica Street, Glasgow G1 4QG
t 0141 314 4800 **w** jurysdoyle.com

Premier Inn Glasgow City Centre South
80 Ballater Street, Glasgow G5 0TW
t 0870 423 6452 **e** Glasgowccsouth.PI@premierinn.com
w tulipinnglasgow.co.uk

Highland
ACHNASHEEN

The Torridon
Annat, Achnasheen, Highland IV22 2EY
t 01445 791242 **e** roger@lochtorridon.co.uk
w lochtorridonhotel.com

AULDEARN

Covenanters' Inn
Auldearn, Nairn, Highland IV12 5TG
t 01667 452456   e covenanters@aol.com
w covenanters-inn.co.uk

AVIEMORE

Braeriach High Range Holiday Lodges
Mr. F Vastano, High Range Holiday Lodges, Grampian Road,
Aviemore, Inverness-Shire PH22 1PT
t 01479 810636   e info@highrange.co.uk
w highrange.co.uk

DAVIOT

The Lodge at Daviot Mains
Daviot, Inverness, Highland IV2 5ER
t 01463 772215
e margaret.hutcheson@btopenworld.com
w daviotlodge.co.uk

FARR

Rowan, Woodpecker
Mr F Forbes, Inverarnie House, Inverarnie, Inverness IV2 6XA
t 01808 521467 / 521747
e farquharforbes@onetel.com

FORT WILLIAM

Bluebell Croft, Honeysuckle House and Rose Cottage
Mrs Sukie Barber, Strontian, Ardnamurchan, Highlands
PH36 4JA
t 01967 402226   e billandsukie@bluebellcroft.co.uk
w bluebellcroft.co.uk

INVERNESS

Kingsmills Hotel Inverness Ltd
Culcabock Road, Inverness, Highland IV2 3LP
t 01463 237166   e arlene.petrie@kingsmillshotel.com
w kingsmillshotel.com

Lochletter Lodges
Miss Mary Brook, Lochletter Lodges, Balnain,
Drumnadrochit, Inverness IV63 6TJ
t 01456 476 313   e info@lochletter.com
w lochletter.com

ISLE OF SKYE

La Bergerie
Mrs Chantal MacLeod, 33 Lochbay, Waternish, Isle Of Skye
IV55 8GD
t 01470 592282   f 01470 592 282
e enquiries@la-bergerie.co.uk
w la-bergerie-skye.co.uk

KINCRAIG

Loch Insh Chalets - Drumguish
Mr. Andrew Freshwater, Loch Insh Log Chalets, Loch Insh
Chalets Ltd, Insh Hall, Kincraig, Inverness-shire PH21 1NU
t 01540 651 272   e office@lochinsh.com
w lochinsh.com

NAIRN

Windsor Hotel
16 Albert Street, Nairn, Highland IV12 4HP
t 01667 453108   e jag@ehd.co.uk

NEWTONMORE

Crubenbeg House
Falls of Truim, Newtonmore PH20 1BE
t 01540 673300   e enquiries@crubenbeghouse.com
w crubenbeghouse.com

NR FORT WILLIAM

Isles of Glencoe Hotel & Leisure Centre
Ballachulish, Nr Fort William PH49 4HL
e gm.glencoe@foliohotels.com
w foliohotels.com

PORTREE

Cuillin Hills Hotel
Portree, Isle of Skye, Highland IV51 9QU
t 01478 612003   e info@cuillinhills-hotel-skye.co.uk
w cuillinhills-hotel-skye.co.uk

Number 6
Mrs. Margaret MacDonald, Maligan, Achachork, Portree, Isle
Of Skye IV51 9HT
t 01478 613 167   e No6chalet@aol.com

SPEAN BRIDGE

Old Pines Hotel and Restaurant
Gairlochy Road, Spean Bridge, Highland PH34 4EG
t 01397 712324   e info@oldpines.co.uk
w oldpines.co.uk

STRONTIAN

Ariundle Bunkhouse
Strontian, Argyll, Argyll & Bute PH36 4JA
t 01967 402279   e ariundle@aol.com
w ariundle.co.uk

THURSO

Park Hotel
Oldfield, Thurso, Highland KW14 8RE
t 01847 893251   e karen@parkhotelthurso.co.uk
w parkhotelthurso.co.uk

Pentland Lodge House
Pentland Lodge House, Granville Street, Thurso, Caithness
KW14 7JN
t 01847 895103   e info@pentlandlodgehouse.co.uk
w pentlandlodgehouse.co.uk

WATERNISH

Ardmore Holiday Cottage
Mrs. Margaret MacDonald, Mrs M J MacDonald, 3 Ardmore,
Waternish, Isle of Skye, Highland IV55 8GW
e info@ardmorecottage.co.uk
w self-catering-skye.co.uk

Inverclyde
GREENOCK

Express by Holiday Inn
Cartsburn, Greenock, Inverclyde PA15 4RT
t 01475 786666
e gm.greenock@expressbyholidayinn.net
w hiexpressgreenock.co.uk

James Watt College
Halls of Residence, Waterfront Campus, Custom House Way,
Greenock, Renfrewshire PA15 1EN
e kfullerton@jameswatt.ac.uk

Moray
LOSSIEMOUTH

Ceilidh B&B
34 Clifton Road, Lossiemouth, Moray IV31 6DJ
t 01343 815848   e ceilidh.b-b@whsmithnet.co.uk
w ceilidhbandb.co.uk

North Ayrshire
BRODICK

Auchrannie Spa Resort
Auchrannie Spa Resort, Brodick, North Ayrshire KA27 8BZ
t 01770 302234   e rsmall@auchrannie.co.uk
w auchrannie.co.uk

GAILES

Gailes Hotel and Restaurant
Marine Drive, Gailes, Irvine, North Ayrshire KA11 5AE
t 01294 204040   e enquiries@gaileshotel.com
w simpsinns.com

IRVINE

Menzies Irvine
46 Annick Road, Irvine KA11 4LD
e irvine.hotel@menzieshotels.co.uk
w menzieshotels.co.uk

KILDONAN

Kildonan Hotel
Kildonan, Isle of Arran, North Ayrshire KA27 8SE
t 01770 820207   e info@kildonanhotel.com
w kildonanhotel.com

North Lanarkshire
MOTHERWELL

Express By Holiday Inn
Strathclyde Country Park, 1 Hamilton Road, Motherwell,
Lanarkshire ML1 3RB
e james.rush@ichotelgroup.com
w hiexpress.com

Motherwell College
Dalzeil Drive, Motherwell, North Lanarkshire ML1 2DD
t 01698 261890   w motherwell.ac.uk

Orkney
KIRKWALL

Auldkirk Apartments
Mr. Robert Clouston, Clouston Properties, 5 Clumly Avenue,
Kirkwall, Orkney KW15 1YU
t 01856 875488   e enquiries@r-clouston.co.uk

Lav'rockha Guest House
Inganess Road, St. Ola, Kirkwall, Orkney KW15 1SP
e rooms@lavrockha.co.uk
w lavrockha.co.uk

Perth and Kinross
AUCHTERARDER

The Gleneagles Hotel
Auchterarder, Perthshire, Perth and Kinross PH3 1NF
t 01764 662231   e bernard.j.murphy@gleneagles.com
w gleneagles.com

CRIEFF

Phase 1 & Phase 2 Lodges
Ms. Lynne Anderson, Crieff Hydro Hotel (Self Catering),
Crieff Hydro Hotel, Crieff, Perthshire PH7 3LQ
t 01764 655555   e enquiries@crieffhydro.com
w crieffhydro.com

FORGANDENNY

Battledown Bed & Breakfast
Battledown, Forgandenny, Perth and Kinross PH2 9EL
t 01738 812471   e i.dunsire@btconnect.com
w battledown.net

Renfrewshire
PAISLEY

Express by Holiday Inn Glasgow Airport
St Andrew's Drive, Glasgow Airport, Paisley, Renfrewshire
PA3 2TJ
t 0141 842 1100
e gm.glasgowairport@expressholidayinn.co.uk
w hiex-glasgow.com

Scottish Borders
COLDSTREAM

Cotoneaster
Mrs S Brewis, Leet Villa, Leet St, Coldstream, Berwickshire
TD12 4BJ
t 01890 882173   e suebrewis@tiscali.co.uk
w littleswinton.co.uk

NR HAWICK

Mosspaul
Teviothead, Nr Hawick, Scottish Borders TD9 0LP
e mosspaulinn@aol.com
w mosspaulinn.co.uk

PEEBLES

Cringletie House Hotel
Edinburgh Road, Peebles EH45 8PL
t 01721 725750   e enquiries@cringletie.com
w cringletie.com

SWINTON

The Wheatsheaf at Swinton
Main Street, Berwickshire, Scottish Borders TD11 3JJ
t 01890 860257   e chris@wheatsheaf-swinton.co.uk
w wheatsheaf-swinton.co.uk

Shetland
BRESSAY

Northern Lights Holistic Spa
Sound View Uphouse, Bressay, Shetland ZE2 9ES
e northernlightsholisticspa@fsmail.net

WALLS

Burrastow House
Walls, Shetland ZE2 9PD
t 01595 809307   w burrastowhouse.co.uk

South Ayrshire
AYR

Ramada Jarvis
Dalblair Road, Ayr, South Ayrshire KA7 1UG
t 01292 269331   e gm.ayr@ramadajarvis.co.uk
w ramadajarvis.co.uk

TURNBERRY

The Westin Turnberry Resort
Turnberry, Ayrshire, South Ayrshire KA26 9LT
t 01655 331000   w westin.com/turnberry

South Lanarkshire
BIGGAR

The Glenholm Centre
Broughton, Biggar, Lanarkshire ML12 6JF
t 01899 830 408   e info@glenholm.co.uk
w glenholm.co.uk

NEW LANARK

New Lanark Mill Hotel
Mill Number One, New Lanark Mills, Lanark, South
Lanarkshire ML11 9DB
t 01555 667200   e hotel@newlanark.org
w newlanark.org

Stirling

STIRLING

Express by Holiday Inn - Stirling
Springkerse Business Park, Stirling FK7 7XH
t 01786 449922 **e** gm.stirling@expressholidayinn.co.uk
w expressstirling.co.uk

Stirling Management Centre
University of Stirling Campus, Stirling FK9 4LA
t 01786 451666 **e** smc.sales@stir.ac.uk
w smc.stir.ac.uk

West Dunbartonshire

ALEXANDRIA

De Vere Cameron House
Cameron House, Loch Lomond, West Dunbartonshire
G83 8QZ
t 01389 755565 **w** devere.co.uk

CLYDEBANK

The Beardmore Hotel & Conference Centre
Beardmore Street, Clydebank, West Dunbartonshire G81 4SA
t 0141 9516000 **w** thebeardmore.com

Western Isles

ISLE OF LEWIS

The Cross Inn
Cross, Ness, Isle Of Lewis HS2 0SN
e info@crossinn.com
w crossinn.com

SOUTH UIST

Crossroads
Crossroads, Stoneybridge, South Uist, Western Isles
HS8 5SD
e macrury.321@tascali.co.uk

STORNOWAY

Broad Bay House
Back, Nr Stornoway, Isle of Lewis HS2 0LQ
t 01851 820990 **e** enquiries@broadbayhouse.co.uk
w broadbayhouse.co.uk

UIG

Tigh-nan-Eilean
Mr. Murdo MacLeod, 17 Uigen, Uig, Stornoway, Isle of
Lewis HS2 9H5
t 01851 672377 **e** murdomac@btinternet.com
w mountainviewholidays.co.uk

Angus

BY BRECHIN

Brechin Castle
Dalhousie Estates Office, Brechin, Angus DD9 6SG
w brechincastlecentre.co.uk

Dumfries & Galloway

DUMFRIES

Dumfries Museum and Camera Obscura
The Observatory, Dumfries, Dumfries & Galloway DG2 7SW
e siobhanr@dumgal.gov.uk
w dumgal.gov.uk/museums

Edinburgh

EDINBURGH

National Museum of Scotland
Chambers Street, Edinburgh EH1 1JF
t 0131 225 7534 **e** info@nms.ac.uk
w nms.ac.uk

LASSWADE

Edinburgh Butterfly & Insect World
c/o Spiritmedia Scotland, 24 Broughton Street, Edinburgh
EH1 3RH
e info@edinburgh-butterfly-world.co.uk
w edinburgh-butterfly-world.co.uk

Glasgow

GLASGOW

People's Palace & Winter Gardens
Glasgow Green, Glasgow, Strathclyde Region G40 1AT
t 0141 276 0789 **e** museums@cls.glasgow.gov.uk
w glasgowmuseums.com

Where to Go

Brechin | **Brechin Cathedral**

Church Street, Brechin, Angus DD9 6EU
t 01356 629360 **e** brechincathedral@tiscali.com
brechincathedral.org.uk

Edinburgh | **Edinburgh Castle**

Castle Hill, Edinburgh EH1 2ND
t 0131 225 9846
historic-scotland.gov.uk

North Queensferry | **Deep Sea World**

Battery Quarry, North Queensferry, Fife, Scotland KY11 1JR
t 01383 411880
deepseaworld.com

Orkney | **The Orkney Museum**

Tankerness House, Broad Street, Kirkwall, Orkney KW15 1DH
t 01856 873535
orkney.gov.uk

Where to Eat

Aberdeen | Pier Bistro

Esplanade Sea Beach, Aberdeen AB24 5NS
t 01224 583357 **e** martin@pierbistro.com
pierbistro.com

General: 🐕 FAX 🚶 ♿ ♿ ♿ P★★

Aberdeen | Rustico

62-66 Union Row, Aberdeen AB10 1SA
t 01224 632111
rustico-restaurant.co.uk

General: 🐕 🦽 🚶 ♿ ♿

Edinburgh | Browns Restaurant & Bar

George Street, Edinburgh EH2 4JS
t 0131 225 9353 **e** browns.edinburgh@robplc.com

General: 🐕 FAX 🚶 ♿ wc ♿ ♿

Edinburgh | Lauriston Farm Restaurant

69 Lauriston Farm Road, Edinburgh EH4 5EX
t 0131 312 7071 **e** edinburgh.lauristonfarm@whitbread.com

General: 🐕 🦽 🚶 wc ♿ ♿ .:🔊

Edinburgh | Pizza Express

23 North Bridge, Edinburgh EH1 1SB
t 0131 557 6411
pizzaexpress.com

General: 🐕 FAX 🦽 🚶 wc ♿ .:

St Andrews | Maisha

5 College Street, St Andrews, Fife KY16 9AA
t 01334 476666 **e** info@maisharestaurant.co.uk
maisharestaurant.co.uk

General: 🐕 FAX ♿

Glasgow | AntiPasti

305 Sauchiehall Street, Glasgow G2 3HQ
t 0141 332 9002
antipasti.co.uk

General: 🐕 FAX 🚶 ♿ wc ♿

295

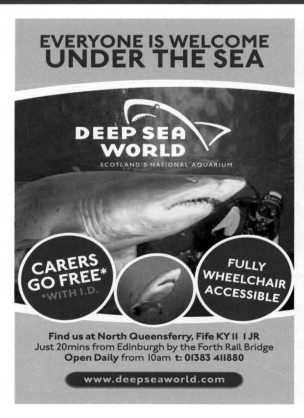

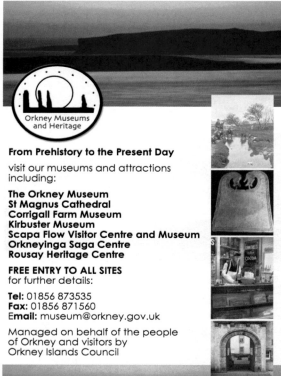

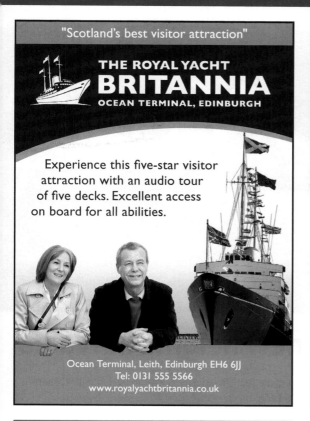

Accessibility reaches new heights in Wales

The tourism industry in Wales provides opportunities for staying in traditional resorts, large cities, country towns or more rural locations. Well established resorts for families that are set within mostly level terrain, are to be found around most of the coast.

In the North these include Rhyl, Colwyn Bay and Llandudno. Aberdovey, Barmouth and Towyn are on the West coast and Tenby and Porthcawl in the south. Hillier sections of the coast have many historic towns, some with castles such as Harlech, Caernarfon and Conwy or with attractive harbours like New Quay.

But the landscape in Wales is changing through a greater awareness, bringing with it a variety of accessible solutions to satisfy our individual lifestyles. A common factor linking attractions; restaurants; museums and accommodation is the provision of an Access Statement that, in giving accurate and up-to-date information, allows you, the visitor, the choice of where to visit.

There is a saying here in Wales that "you don't have to flatten Snowdon for us all to walk over", illustrating the fact that access is not just about physical features. Take for instance, cordless kettles; personal loop systems; suction support rails; large print menus; easy grip cutlery; bath seats. These little things make a BIG difference to many

and the tourism industry is alive to this, and have them to hand.

Let's take a brief tour across this accessible tapestry, starting with yes, that Mountain, the roof of Wales -**Snowdon**. Several heritage railways horizontally criss-cross the face of Wales – Vale of Rheidol, Bala, Ffestiniog, Talyllyn, Llanberis, Welshpool, Fairbourne, Welsh Highland (Portmadog) but the **Snowdon Mountain Railway** climbs vertically from Llanberis to the summit at 3650ft.

At the summit, **Hafod Eryri**, has a welcome for all. A lift complements steps from the station platform to the level floor of the new Visitor Centre. Views are audio described from window vantage points. Baby change and toilet facilities are designed inclusively.

Perhaps mountains are not for you, rather the coast, visible from the summit of **Yr Wyddfa**. There are several award winning beaches; bays, headlands and harbours dotted along the 750 miles of coastline, which is the subject of more access initiatives to create **The All Wales Coastal Path**. If you are lucky you could spot dolphins along the coast of **Cardigan Bay**. A Pembrokeshire initiative using a wheelchair attachment allows you to dip your toes in the sea without getting beached!

There are three National Parks, **Brecon Beacons**, **Snowdonia** and a coastal one in **Pembrokeshire**,

National Botanic Garden of Wales

Tal-y-Llyn, Snowdonia

Wales

Tourist Information Centres	301	Where to Go	310
Where to Stay	303		

all of which have easy access routes for families with pushchairs and wheelchair users.

Gardens, large and small, will delight the senses through all seasons, with perhaps the most fascinating ones being the **National Botanic Garden of Wales** in Carmarthenshire, and the walled gardens at **Aberglasney** that may evoke poetry from your inner self…as it has in poets since 1477.

The past is always around you wherever you travel, with Roman legends fact and fiction at for instance **Llangollen** and **Caernarfon**. Castles are our forte – hanging over a cliff face at **Harlech**; on a hilltop at **Llandielo**, and on river estuaries at **Conwy** and **Caernarfon**. Once built to keep the enemy at bay, new initiatives such as those at Caernarfon and Cardiff allow more and more people through their fortified ramparts.

As opposed to Castles, motorways are a rarity in Wales, being confined mostly to the South. This creates more opportunities to drink in the countryside along quieter roads, passing cottages, hostels, caravan parks, farms and Country Houses in idyllic settings just waiting to greet you.

At some of these you can fish a lake for your dinner from a safe platform or an adapted wheely boat, as on **Tal-y-Llyn**, under the shadow of the **Cader Idris** mountain ridge.

Visit Wales
Croeso Cymru

Aberaeron Coast

Observation area Hafod Eryri Visitors Centre Snowdon, Snowdonia

St David's Shopping Centre, Cardiff

Bryn Bach Country Park

Aberystwyth

You could have a film show after dinner, in a purpose built cinema in the once cellar of one country house near **Aberaeron**, without hardly leaving your seat. On clear nights, starry skies put on another show in the unspoilt darkness and complete quietness of the countryside.

Witness the agricultural activity at many of the **Farm Stay** Cottage properties with, if you time if right, the smell of shoeing the family pony as the horn receives the hot shoe, or the bleating of new born spring lambs.

Or just sink into the luxurious splendour of days gone by, amidst the smell of beeswax on the antique furniture, as the chiming of the grandfather clock announces dinner.

And food is high on the menu, not only on the dinner plate, but at the many local farmers markets and Food Festivals held throughout the year.

Accessibility is not an extra on your bill, but a natural consequence of accommodating you, the visitor and ensuring a quality holiday experience.

Let Wales touch all your senses and speak to you through its sights, sounds, smells and tastes...giving a real Sense of Place...and that Place is Wales.

Tourist Information Centres

Tourist Information Centres are a mine of information about local and regional accommodation, attractions and events. Visit them when you arrive at your destination or contact them before you go:

Aberaeron	The Quay	01545 570602	aberaerontic@ceredigion.gov.uk
Aberdulais Falls	The National Trust	01639 636674	aberdulaistic@nationaltrust.org.uk
Aberdyfi*	The Wharf Gardens	01654 767321	tic.aberdyfi@eryri-npa.gov.uk
Abergavenny	Swan Meadow	01873 853254	abergavenny.ic@breconbeacons.org
Aberystwyth	Terrace Road	01970 612125	aberystwythtic@ceredigion.gov.uk
Bala *	Pensarn Road	01678 521021	bala.tic@gwynedd.gov.uk
Barmouth	The Station	01341 280787	barmouth.tic@gwynedd.gov.uk
Barry Island *	The Promenade	01446 747171	barrytic@valeofglamorgan.gov.uk
Beddgelert *	Canolfan Hebog	01766 890615	tic.beddgelert@eryri-npa.gov.uk
Betws y Coed	Royal Oak Stables	01690 710426	tic.byc@eryri-npa.gov.uk
Blaenavon *	World Heritage Centre	01495 742333	Blaenavon.tic@torfaen.gov.uk
Borth *	Cambrian Terrace	01970 871174	borthtic@ceredigion.gov.uk
Brecon	Cattle Market Car park	01874 622485	brectic@powys.gov.uk
Bridgend	Bridgend Designer Outlet	01656 654906	bridgendtic@bridgend.gov.uk
Caerleon	5 High Street	01633 422656	caerleon.tic@newport.gov.uk
Caernarfon	Oriel Pendeitsh	01286 672232	caernarfon.tic@gwynedd.gov.uk
Caerphilly	The Twyn	029 2088 0011	tourism@caerphilly.gov.uk
Cardiff	The Old Library	08701 211 258	visitor@cardiff.gov.uk
Cardigan	Theatr Mwldan	01239 613230	cardigantic@ceredigion.gov.uk
Carmarthen	113 Lammas Street	01267 231557	carmarthentic@carmarthenshire.gov.uk
Chepstow	Castle Car Park	01291 623772	chepstow.tic@monmouthshire.gov.uk
Conwy	Castle Buildings	01492 592248	conwytic@conwy.gov.uk
Dolgellau	Ty Meirion	01341 422888	tic.dolgellau@eryri-npa.gov.uk
Fishguard Harbour	Ocean Lab	01348 872037	fishguardharbour.tic@pembrokeshire.gov.uk
Fishguard Town	Town Hall	01437 776636	fishguard.tic@pembrokeshire.gov.uk
Harlech *	Llys y Graig	01766 780658	tic.harlech@eryri-npa.gov.uk
Haverfordwest	Old Bridge	01437 763110	haverfordwest.tic@pembrokeshire.gov.uk

Holyhead	Stena Line	01407 762622	holyhead@nwtic.com
Knighton	Offa's Dyke Centre	01547 528753	oda@offasdyke.demon.co.uk
Llanberis *	41b High Street	01286 870765	llanberis.tic@gwynedd.gov.uk
Llandovery	Heritage Centre	01550 720693	llandovery.tic@breconbeacons.org
Llandudno	Library Building	01492 577577	llandudnotic@conwy.gov.uk
Llanelli	Millennium Coastal Park Visitor Centre	01554 777744	DiscoveryCentre@carmarthenshire.gov.uk
Llanfairpwllgwyngyll	Station Site	01248 713177	llanfairpwll@nwtic.com
Llangollen	Y Chapel	01978 860828	llangollen@nwtic.com
Merthyr Tydfil	14a Glebeland Street	01685 727474	tic@merthyr.gov.uk
Milford Haven *	Suite 19,Cedar Court	01646 690866	milford.tic@pembrokeshire.gov.uk
Mold	Library Museum & Art Gallery	01352 759331	mold@nwtic.com
Monmouth	Market Hall	01600 713899	monmouth.tic@monmouthshire.gov.uk
Mumbles	The Methodist Church	01792 361302	info@mumblestic.co.uk
New Quay *	Church Street	01545 560865	newquaytic@ceredigion.gov.uk
Newport	Museum & Art Gallery	01633 842962	newport.tic@newport.gov.uk
Newport (Pembs) *	2 Bank Cottages	01239 820912	NewportTIC@Pembrokeshirecoast.org.uk
Oswestry Mile End	Mile End Services	01691 662488	oswestrytourism@shropshire.gov.uk
Oswestry Town	The Heritage Centre	01691 662753	ot@oswestry-welshborders.org.uk
Pembroke	Visitor Centre	01437 776499	pembroke.tic@pembrokeshire.gov.uk
Porthcawl *	Old Police Station	01656 786639	porthcawltic@bridgend.gov.uk
Porthmadog	High Street	01766 512981	porthmadog.tic@gwynedd.gov.uk
Presteigne *	The Judge's Lodging	01544 260650	presteignetic@powys.gov.uk
Pwllheli	Min y Don	01758 613000	pwllheli.tic@gwynedd.gov.uk
Rhyl	Rhyl Childrens Village	01745 355068	rhyl.tic@denbighshire.gov.uk
Saundersfoot *	The Barbecue	01834 813672	saundersfoot.tic@pembrokeshire.gov.uk
St Davids	The Grove	01437 720392	enquiries@stdavids. pembrokeshirecoast.org.uk
Swansea	Plymouth Street	01792 468321	tourism@swansea.gov.uk
Tenby	Upper Park Road	01834 842402	tenby.tic@pembrokeshire.gov.uk
Welshpool	The Vicarage Gardens Car Park	01938 552043	ticwelshpool@btconnect.com
Wrexham	Lambpit Street	01978 292015	tic@wrexham.gov.uk

*seasonal opening

Where to Stay

Cardiff | Holiday Inn Cardiff City
AS

Castle Street, Cardiff CF10 1XD
t 0871 942 9240 **e** reservations-cardiffcity@ihg.com
holidayinn.com/cardiff

Access: ⓐ abc 🔲 �╳ 🏢☺️🚻♿ General: 🛋️🍳╳🍷Ⓟ♿✻⊞♿ Room: 🛏️Ⓢ☕

Cardiff | Holiday Inn Express Cardiff Bay

Off Schooner Way, Atlantic Wharf, Cardiff, Wales CF10 4EE
t 02920 449000 **e** reservations@exhicardiff.co.uk
exhicardiff.co.uk

Access: abc 🔲 🌳 🏢☺️♿🚻 General: 🛋️🍷Ⓟ⊞♿ Room: ♨️⚱️🛏️🚻Ⓢ☕

Cardiff | Parc Coed Machen Country Cottages
AS

Visit Wales ★★★★ Mr P Trivett, Parc Coed Machen Country Cottages, St Brides Super Ely, Cardiff, Wales CF5 6EZ **t** 01446 760684 **e** prtrivett@hotmail.com
Parccoedmachen.co.uk

Access: 🌳🏢 General: 🛋️🗃️ⓅⓈ Unit: ♨️♿🛏️🚻✻

Felingwm Uchaf | Allt-y-Golau Farmhouse
AS

AA ★★★★ Allt-y-Golau Uchaf, Felingwm Uchaf, Carmarthenshire SA32 7BB
Visit Wales ★★★★ **t** 01267 290455 **e** alltygolau@btinternet.com
Open: All year alltygolau.com

Access: abc 🌳🏢 General: 🛋️🍳✻ Room: ♨️🛏️🚻Ⓢ☕

Llanelli | Pembrey Country Park Caravan Club Site
THE CARAVAN CLUB **AS**

Visit Wales ★★★★★ Pembrey, Llanelli, Carmarthenshire, Wales SA16 0EJ
Open: March 2011 to **t** 01554 834369
January 2012 caravanclub.co.uk

Access: 🏢☺️🚻 General: 🗃️🏪🚐💧🚿🚾 Pitch: 🚐🚍

©Britain on View / Tony Pleavin

OPEN BRITAIN PLANNING A DAY OUT? WHY NOT MAKE IT A SHORT- BREAK?
Fabulous 'Places to Stay' in every region

Pendine | **Homeleigh Country Cottages**

AS

Visit Wales ★★★★

Units: 6 Sleeps: 2-7
Open: All year except Xmas and New Year

Low season p/w:
£320.00
High season p/w:
£1030.00
Shop: 5 miles
Pub: <0.5 miles

Mrs Morfydd Turner, Red Roses, Whitland, Dyfed SA34 0PN
t 01834 831765 **e** enquiries@homeleigh.org
homeleigh.org

8A3

6 spacious cottages to offer a warm welcome to guests who need a little extra help to make their holiday perfect. Disabled aids included in price, eg. electric bed, wheel in shower chair, commode, walking frame. Hoist available to hire.

Location: M4 to Wales. A40 Carmarthen, A477 St. Clears/Tenby, Red Roses B4314 Pendine. Homeleigh Country Cottages 300m on left.

Access:
⚠ 🐾 🏠 ☺ ♿

General:
🛏 🖥 P Ⓢ

Unit:
🛁 🔥 ♿ 🔔 🧺 S 💡 ♿ ✿

Aberaeron | **Ty Mawr Mansion Country House**

AS

Visit Wales ★★★★★

Open: Not Xmas & New Yr

Rooms per night:
s: £110.00-£180.00
d: £120.00-£280.00
p/p half board:
d: £85.00-£200.00
Meals: £24.95-£45.95

Cilcennin, Ceredigion SA48 8DB
t 01570 470033 **e** info@tymawrmansion.co.uk
tymawrmansion.co.uk

8A2

Beautiful family run 5 star restaurant with rooms including our 2 AA Rosette restaurant.

Access: abc 🐾 🏠 ♿ ♿ ♿ General: 🍴 ✕ 🍷 P ✿ ♿ Room: 🛏 ♿ 💡 ♨

Llandudno | **The West Shore**

Open: All year

Rooms per night:
s: £25.00-£50.00
d: £50.00-£100.00
p/p half board:
d: £40.00-£70.00
Meals: £14.95
Shop: <0.5 miles
Pub: <0.5 miles

West Parade, Llandudno, Conwy LL30 2BB
t 01492 876833 **e** westshore@livability.org.uk
livability.org.uk

8B1

The West Shore is a fully adapted wheelchair accessible hotel with 18 en suite bedrooms all with level access shower. Located on the west shore of Llandudno with stunning views across the Conwy Estuary towards the Snowdonia National Park.

Location: Conveniently located just off the A55 North Wales coast road, close to the historic castle town of Conwy.

Access:
Ⓗ 🗒 ☺ ♿ ♿ ♿
General:
🐂 🍲 ✕ 🍷 P 🌸 ⊞ ♿
Room:
♿ 🛁 📻 📺 Ⓢ ♨

Llangollen | **Dee Valley Cottages**   AS

Visit Wales ★★★★★

Units: 1   Sleeps: 4
Open: All year

Low season p/w:
£295.00
High season p/w:
£495.00

Mrs Jenny Scowcroft, Dee Valley Cottages, Ty Isar Plwyf, Glyndyfrdwy,
Corwen, Denbighshire, Wales LL21 9HW   **t** 01490 430342
e stay@deevalleycottages.com
deevalleycottages.com

8B1

Beautiful cottage situated in the Dee Valley 2.5 miles from Llangollen. Quiet, rural location.

Access: 🐎 🏛 General: 🐂 P Ⓢ Unit: ♿ 🛁 ♿ 📻 Ⓢ ♿ 🌸

Aberdaron | **Manaros**   AS

Visit Wales ★★★★★

Mr P Hewlett, Manaros, Capel Deunant Rd, Aberdaron, Pwllheli, Gwynedd,
Wales LL53 8BP   **t** 01758 760652 **e** enquiries@aberdaroncottage.co.uk
aberdaroncottage.co.uk

Access: abc 🏛 ♿ General: 🐂 📱 P Ⓢ Unit: ♿ 🛁 ♿ 📻 Ⓢ ♿ 🌸

Caernarfon | **Coed Helen Caravan Club Site** THE CARAVAN CLUB   AS

Visit Wales ★★★★
Open: March to November

Coed Helen Road, Caernarfon, Gwynedd, Wales LL54 5RS
t 01286 676770
caravanclub.co.uk

Access: 🏛 ☺ ♿ General: 🎫 📷 🚗 🐕 🕐 🍷 📱 Pitch: 🚐 🚏

Porthmadog | **Garreg Goch Caravan Park**

`AS`

Visit Wales ★★★★

 (54)
£15.00–£19.00

🚐 (25)
£15.00–£19.00

🏠 (8)
£160.00–£534.00

25 touring pitches
Open: 01/03 to 10/01

Black Rock Sands, Morfa Bychan, Porthmadog, Gwynedd, Wales LL49 9YD
t 01766 512210 **e** enquiries@garreggochcaravanpark.co.uk
garreggochpark.co.uk

8A1

Ideally located within a ten minute stroll from Black Rock Sands, Garreg Goch Caravan Park is perfectly situated for exploring the spectacular scenery of Snowdonia and the Llyn Peninsula.

Access:
🅷 📷 🐎 🎣 ☺ ♿ ♿

General:
📼 🛒 📠 💷 🛗 🚰 (WP)

Pitch:
🔌 🛗 🚐

Benllech | **Penrhos Caravan Club Site** THE CARAVAN CLUB

`AS`

Visit Wales ★★★★
Open: March to October

Brynteg, Benllech, Isle of Anglesey, Wales LL78 7JH
t 01248 852617
caravanclub.co.uk

Access: 🏛☺♿ General: 📼🔲📠🚐💷🛗🚰(WP) Pitch: 🔌🚐

Abergavenny | **Pandy Caravan Club Site** THE CARAVAN CLUB

AS

Visit Wales ★★★★

🚐 (53)
£13.90–£25.40

🚛 (53)
£13.90–£25.40

53 touring pitches
Open: 25 March to 31 October

Pandy, Abergavenny, Monmouthshire, Wales NP7 8DR
t 01873 890370
caravanclub.co.uk

8B3

The natural landscape of this location means you'll be surrounded by nature at its finest. Located at the western boundary of the River Honddu, visitors to the park are treated to the majestic Skirrid.

Location: Left off A465; turn into minor road by The Old Pandy Inn. Site on left after passing under railway bridge.

Access:
🏭 ☺ ♿

General:
📷 🐾 🚮 🔌 ♨ 🛒 (WP)

Pitch:
🚐 🚛

Boncath | **Clynfyw Countryside Centre**

AS

Visit Wales ★★★★

Jim Bowen, Abercych, Boncath, Pembrokeshire SA37 0HF
t 01239 841236 **e** jim.clynfyw@virgin.net
clynfyw.co.uk

Access: 🅷 abc 🐎 🏭 ☺ ♿ General: 🐎 📷 P S Unit: 🍳 🍽 🚿 ♿ 🛏 📺 📻 🎣 ❀

Pembroke | **Freshwater East Caravan Club Site** THE CARAVAN CLUB

AS

Visit Wales ★★★★
Open: March to October

Trewent Hill, Freshwater East, Pembroke SA71 5LJ
t 01646 672341
caravanclub.co.uk

Access: 🏭 ☺ ♿ General: 📷 🐾 🚮 🔌 ♨ 🛒 (WP) Pitch: 🚐 🚛 ⛺

Pembrokeshire | **Cuffern Manor Country House Guest Acconnodation**

Visit Wales ★★★

Roch, Haverfordwest, Pembrokeshire, Wales SA62 6HB
t 01437 710071 **e** enquiries@cuffernmanor.co.uk
cuffernmanor.co.uk

Access: 🅷 abc 🐎 🏭 ☺ ♿ ♿ General: 🐎 🍽 ✕ 🍷 P ⊡ ♿ Room: 🛏 📺 📻 ☕

St Davids | Lleithyr Meadow Caravan Club Site

AS

Visit Wales ★★★★

🚐 (120)
£13.10–£25.40

🚍 (120)
£13.10–£25.40

120 touring pitches
Open: 25 March - 10 October

Whitesands, St Davids, Haverfordwest, Pembrokeshire, Wales SA62 6PR
t 01437 720401
caravanclub.co.uk

8A3

Nestled between three headlands of the dramatic Pembrokeshire Coast, Lleithyr Meadow Caravan Club Site offers swimming, surfing, windsurfing and sailing from Whitesands Bay, just over a mile from the site.

Location: A40 onto B4331; left onto A487; in abt 9m B4583; turn left; 2nd X-rds turn sharp right; Site on left.

Access:
🚿 ☺ ♿ wc

General:
▢ ▦ 📷 ⛽ 🔌 🚻 🚰 WP

Pitch:
🚐 🚍

Brecon | Brynich Caravan Club Site

AS

Visit Wales ★★★★★

🚐 (144)
£14.90–£27.20

🚍 (144)
£14.90–£27.20

⛺ (1)

144 touring pitches
Open: 25 March to 31 October

Brecon, Powys, Wales LD3 7SH
t 01874 623325
cavavanclub.co.uk

8B3

Brynich Caravan Club Site features facilities that include two toilet blocks, a well stocked shop, play areas and a play barn adjacent. The caravan site can lay claim to some of the best views of the central Beacons.

Location: On A470 (Brecon - Builth Wells) 200yds past roundabout junc A40 (eastern end Brecon By-pass).

Access:
🚿 ☺ ♿ wc

General:
▢ ▦ 📷 ⛽ 🔌 🚻 🚰 WP

Pitch:
🚐 🚍 ⛺

Llanfair Caereinion | **Madog's Wells**

 **AS**

Visit Wales ★★★★★	

Units: 3 Sleeps: 1-6
Open: All year

Low season p/w:
£100.00
High season p/w:
£530.00

Ann & Michael Reed, Madogs Wells, Llanfair Caereinion, Welshpool, Powys SY21 0DE **t** 01938 810446 **e** info@madogswells.co.uk
madogswells.co.uk **8B2**

3 cottages, 5,4,3* 2 spacious sleeps 6, 1 cosy sleeps 3, in quiet countryside.

Access: 🅗 General: ⛵📶P⑤ Unit: ♿🔥🔥♿📻🚾⑤♿✿

Welshpool | **Lake Vyrnwy Hotel & Spa**

AS

AA ★★★★
Visit Wales ★★★★
Open: All year

Rooms per night:
s: £106.00-£211.50
d: £131.00-£236.50
p/p half board:
d: £94.00-£138.68
Meals: £39.95

Lake Vyrnwy, Llanwddyn, Powys, Mid Wales SY10 0LY
t 01691 870692 **e** info@lakevyrnwyhotel.co.uk
lakevyrnwyhotel.co.uk **8B2**

Lake Vyrnwy Hotel & Spa enjoys one of the finest locations in Wales.

Access: 🐾🏨🚾♿♿ General: ⛵🍴✕🍷P✿⊞♿ Room: 🔥📻⑤☕

Gowerton | **Gowerton Caravan Club Site**

AS

Visit Wales ★★★★
Open: March to November

Pont-Y-Cob Road, Gowerton, Swansea, Wales SA4 3QP
t 01792 873050
cavavanclub.co.uk

Access: 🚿😊🚾 General: ◻️📶📡🚙🐶☂️WP Pitch: 🚐🚛

Horton | **Bank Farm**

Visit Wales ★★★

Mr B H Richards, Bank Farm Leisure Park, Horton, Swansea SA3 1LL
t 01792 390228 **e** bankfarmleisure@aol.com
bankfarmleisure.co.uk

Access: 🚾 General: ◻️P⑤ Unit: ♿🔥🔥♿📻⑤♿

GETTING THERE IS NOT A PROBLEM!
OPEN See Getting there..... and back section (p314)
BRITAIN Everything you need for a hassle-free journey

Where to Go

Burry Port | Pembrey Country Park

Pembrey, Burry Port, Carmarthenshire, Wales SA16 0EJ
t 01554 833913 **e** naperry@sirgar.gov.uk
carmarthenshire.gov.uk

Pontrhydfendigaid | Strata Florida Abbey

Ystrad Meurig, Pontrhydfendigaid, Ceredigion, Wales SY25 6ES
t 01974 831261
cadw.wales.gov.uk

Beaumaris | Beaumaris Castle

Beaumaris, Isle of Anglesey, Wales LL58 8AP
t 01248 810361
cadw.wales.gov.uk

Holyhead | Holyhead Maritime Museum

Beach Road, Newry Baech, Holyhead, Isle of Anglesey, Wales LL65 1ES
t 01407 741859 **e** ray.rowlands@tiscali.co.uk
holyheadmaritimemuseum.co.uk

Abergavenny | White Castle

Llantilio Crosenny, Abergavenny, Monmouthshire, Wales NP7 8UD
t 01600 780380
cadw.wales.gov.uk

Lamphey | Lamphey Bishops Palace

Lamphey, Pembrokeshire, Wales SA71 5NT
t 01646 672224
cadw.wales.gov.uk

Welshpool | Powis Castle and Garden

Powis Castle and Gardens, Welshpool, Powys SY21 8RF
t 01938 551944 **e** powiscastle@nationaltrust.org.uk
nationaltrust.org.uk

OPENBRITAIN.NET

The one-stop-shop for all your travel needs.

OPEN BRITAIN

Go online and see how we can help you get in, out ...and about.

- Fully searchable database of accommodation, days out and where to eat and drink
- MyOpenBritain trip planner
- User reviews, blogs and forums

Join today!

Bank Farm Leisure Park is situated on the beautiful Gower Peninsula in the village of Horton. We have facilities for camping, touring and motor caravans and self catering accommodation. There is a licensed bar and restaurant on site and a shop, swimming pool and childrens play area.

Our bungalows are situated at the Bank Farm holiday complex about five minutes walk from the main facilities. They are double glazed and are of sound brick-built construction with a tiled pitched roof. They have two bedrooms, a lounge/dining area, kitchen and bathroom and are fully equipped with a colour television, fridge, cooker, microwave, cutlery and crockery. Bedding is available on request.All heating and electricity is included in the price. There is a dedicated parking space for each bungalow.

Telephone: 01792 390228 / 01792 390452 Fax: 01792 391282
Email: bankfarmleisure@aol.com Website: www.bankfarmleisure.co.uk

Cyngor Sir Ceredigion - yn ymrwymedig i wella eich teithiau ar fws.

Mae pob llwybr craidd y bysiau sy'n teithio trwy Geredigion nawr yn cael eu gwasanaethu gan fysiau modern a chyffordcus sy'n cydymffurfio â DDA, sy'n cynnwys:

● Mynediad lefel isel

● Mynediad hygyrch i rai sy'n defnyddio cadair olwyn

● Cyhoeddiadau gweledol a chlywedol am arosfannau bws

Dewch i deithio'n gyfforddus ac mewn steil trwy sir hyfryd Ceredigion yng ngorllewin Cymru - i gael gwybodaeth am amserlenni a siwrneiau, cysylltwch â Traveline ar **0871 200 22 23**

Ceredigion County Council - committed to improving your travel by bus.

All core bus routes travelling through Ceredigion are now serviced by modern and comfortable DDA compatible buses which include:

● Low level access

● Easily accessible for wheelchair users

● Visual and audio announcement of bus stops

Come and travel in style and comfort through the beautiful west Wales county of Ceredigion - for timetable and journey information contact Traveline on **0871 200 22 23**

OPEN LONDON

OpenLondon is the definitive guide for visitors to London with access needs. The guide contains everything required to enjoy London to the full.

  VISIT LONDON   tourismforall

www.openbritain.net | openlondon@hhgroup.co.uk | 01603 813740

Wheelchair Hire Scheme

P. I. P. P. A.

The Basement
Haverfordwest Registry Office
Tower Hill
Haverfordwest
Pembrokeshire
SA65 9LX
01437 760999

Getting there...

© ATO

Visit our website at:

Three Graces, Liverpool © Britain on View

and back

Central pier, Blackpool © Britain on View

Travel planning

Deciding between different means of transport for any particular journey depends on a range of individual factors and practical considerations that can include price, time, convenience and personal requirements and preferences. Security concerns require longer check-in times, which may make the overall time spent on flying between some cities longer than on a rail journey.

The journey may be anticipated as an enjoyable or relaxing experience: an overnight ferry crossing or railway journey may be used as such before or after a visit to a major city. If a person's regular means of transport is a private car, the convenience or lack of alternative transport will be a major consideration. If a car has been substantially altered to meet the disabled owner's needs, then the difficulty/ impossibility of hiring an alternative mode of transport away from home may require enduring long ferry routes and/or long driving times.

To make choices effectively one needs to know the available options – and these are always changing. Eurostar's links to St Pancras and King's Cross stations have increased these options for many people. Buses that can carry passengers in wheelchairs and wheelchair-accessible taxis have been of great benefit – although many local railway stations require the use of steps, as do the majority of long-distance coaches.

Top tip

- In general, if assistance may be required at any point in the journey advance notification will usually be required.

Information sources

County and unitary councils have some responsibilities for public transport for most of England and Wales, through a public transport information officer. Most publish specific information for disabled passengers. In major conurbations passenger transport executives oversee this facility. In Greater London, public transport planning and regulation of all forms of public transport and other functions are carried out by Transport for London. In Scotland, Regional Transport Partnerships deal with transport planning and some have more direct functions. The main public transport operations in Northern Ireland include Ulster Bus, Metro bus services in Belfast, NI Rail and Goldline coach services.

Detailed listings for these organisations are on page 318

The internet

Some sources of information are only available through the web. Information can be updated more quickly than in print and from the point of view of the transport companies or other providers, it costs less to provide and update information through the internet than in print.

Using the internet to make bookings is widespread and recommended. If assistance is required a telephone call is also advisable. People who do not have the use of a computer may, understandably, be irritated by an assumption that the internet is not only the major way of obtaining information but also that other methods are inferior. This is not helped when web addresses are publicised without other contact information being given. In general, assistance is available for people who want to start using the internet – a good starting point would be a local library/ideas store.

National Key Scheme for toilets

The NKS is used widely throughout the UK. The principle of the NKS is that if local authorities and other organisations decide to lock toilets for disabled people to prevent misuse they should use a standard lock. Local authorities taking part should have arrangements for disabled people in their area to obtain a NKS key that can be used throughout the country. If you have difficulty obtaining a key (price £3.50) contact RADAR on **020 7250 3222** or through **www.radar.org.uk.** RADAR also maintains a list of the toilets fitted with the NKS list, which is published annually in the National Key Scheme Guide and is updated on **www.directenquiries.co.uk t 01344 360101 e customerservices@directenquiries.com.**

Concessionary fares

Separate national concessionary fares schemes exist in England, Northern Ireland, Scotland and Wales. In England and Wales, free travel is available for people aged 60+ and qualifying disabled people. Individual local bodies may offer more extensive concessions – such as extending the concession to all buses or other forms of public transport, or widening the range of disabled people covered. Applications should be made to local authorities, PTEs or their agents.

Information sources

Door-to-door

e dptac@dft.gsi.gov.uk
web www.dptac.gov.uk/door-to-door

This is an internet source of regularly updated information for disabled people on all forms of transport.

GMPTE

9 Portland Street, Piccadilly Gardens,
Manchester M60 1HX
t 0871 200 2233 textphone 0871 200 2233
web www.gmpte.com

Highlands & Islands RTP

Building 25, Inverness Airport, Inverness IV2 7JB
t 01667 460464 web www.hitrans.org.uk

MerseyTravel

24 Hatton Garden, Liverpool L3 2AN
t/textphone 0151 227 5181
web www.merseytravel.gov.uk

Metro

Wellington House, 40-50 Wellington Street
Leeds LS1 2DE
t 0113 251 7272 web www.wymetro.com

Network West Midlands

Centro House, 16 Summer Lane,
Birmingham B19 3SD
t 0121 200 2700 textphone 0871 200 2233
web www.centro.org.uk

Nexus

Nexus House, St James Boulevard
Newcastle upon Tyne NE1 4AX
t 0191 203 3333 e contactus@nexus.org.uk
web www.nexus.org.uk

North East RTP

27-29 King Street, Aberdeen AB24 5AN
t 01224 625524 web www.nestrans.org.uk

Shetland TP

11 Hill Lane, Lerwick ZE1 0HA
t 01595 744868 e info@shetland.gov uk
web www.shetland.gov.uk/transport
Also see Shetland Islands Council t 01595 693535

South East RTP

1st Floor, Hopetoun Gate, 8B MacDonald Road
Edinburgh EH7 4LZ
t 0131 524 5150 web www.sestran.gov.uk

South West PT

c/o Dumfries & Galloway Council, Kirkbank House
English Street, Dumfries, DG1 2HS
t 01387 260102 web www.dumgal.gov.uk

South Yorkshire PT

11 Broad Street West, Sheffield S1 2BQ
t 0114 276 7575 web www.travelsouthyorkshire.com

Strathclyde PT

Consort House, 12 West George Street,
Glasgow G2 1HN
t 0141 332 6811 e enquiry@spt.co.uk
web www.spt.co.uk

Visit our website at:

Tayside & Central RTP

Bordeaux House, 31 Kinnoull Street, Perth PH1 5EN
t 01738 475775 web www.tactran.gov.uk

Translink

Central Station, Belfast BT1 3PB
t 028 9066 6630 textphone 028 9035 4007
web www.translink.co.uk

Timetables and a guide are available in alternative formats.
Website can be used with Browsealoud.

Transport for London

Travel Information, 55 Broadway, London SW1H 0BD
t 020 7222 1234 textphone 020 7222 1234
e travinfo@tfl.gov.uk web www.tfl.gov.uk

Traveline

t 0871 200 2233 web www.traveline.org.uk

Traveline is a partnership of transport operators and
local authorities formed to provide impartial advice and
comprehensive information about public transport within
England, Scotland and Wales.

© Transport for London

Useful websites

Mobilise
web **www.mobilise.info**

Mobilise was formed in 2005 from a merger
of two charities, the Disabled Drivers`
Association and the Disabled Drivers` Motor
Club. Mobilise is not just an organisation for
drivers, they also campaign for and support
passengers, scooter and wheelchair users,
families and carers. The organisation is run by
and for disabled people and their core belief is
that personal mobility impacts on every aspect
of disabled people's lives.

By leading the fight to improve mobility
and access, Mobilise seek to promote a
better way of life for all disabled people
irrespective of age, gender or race; and to
end discrimination and segregation.

When it comes to finding solutions to the
mobility problems that their members face,
they believe that choice and affordability are
paramount. They work closely with Motability
in a role that ensures the benefits of co-
operation and the ability to be constructively
critical when necessary. They also participate
in mobility events at dealerships throughout
country as a way of engaging with the public
and publicising the services they provide.

Transport for All
web **www.transportforall.org.uk**

Transport for All provides specialised advice,
information, advocacy and training to both
service users and providers of accessible
transport in London. The organisation can
help with all your general enquiries regarding
accessible transport in the capital and
can be contacted every day about service
information, complaints, appeals and
application assistance.

They have also published a comprehensive
48 page booklet '*Get Moving*' containing
information, contact numbers and helpful tips
about all of London's Transport services and
travel schemes visit **www.transportforall.
org.uk/services/guide**

Air travel

Since July 2007 it has been illegal for an airline, travel agent or tour operator in Europe to refuse a booking on the grounds of disability or to refuse to embark a disabled person who has a valid ticket and reservation under EC Regulation 1107/206. In Britain, the rules mean that anyone who has been refused boarding on the grounds of disability or reduced mobility may complain to the Commission on Equalities and Human Rights (CEHR). The Commission will advise them and could refer the matter to the Civil Aviation Authority (CAA), which has the power to prosecute. An airline could face an unlimited fine if found guilty.

Airports are required to organise the provision of services required by disabled passengers to board, disembark and transit between flights, with the airlines providing those services on board the aircraft. Airports may provide the services or contract them out. Passengers should not be charged for such services. Procedures must be in place to ensure information is gathered and exchanged to ensure the smooth operation of the service to passengers. All staff dealing directly with travellers should receive disability awareness and equality training.

Top tip

- Book assistance in advance: With air travel, more organisations may be involved than with other forms of transport, particularly if the flight is by charter aircraft as part of a holiday package. There can be failures in the communication chain; it is advisable to check that appropriate messages have been passed on and to emphasise the importance of the requests.

Visit our website at:

Safety and security

Airlines have to ensure that passengers understand the emergency instructions given at take-off. Accompanied passengers with sensory impairments or learning disabilities are asked to make themselves known, although they may consider that they do not need any particular assistance. Airlines may choose not to provide any particular safety instruction services, such as large print information or sub-titled videos.

Security enhancements - Anyone leaving a vehicle unattended outside a terminal should expect it to be removed. At some airports disabled people are helped into the building by a short free-parking period at the nearest car park. Wheelchair users/other disabled people obviously can not go through the regular metal detectors and can ask to be searched in private. Security staff are instructed to take particular care in re-packaging any luggage belonging to visually impaired people whom they search. A form of certification, such as a passport or driving licence is required for domestic flights.

Medicine and injections - Any medicines should be carried in hand luggage and contained in their original packaging. It is advisable to have a note saying what these medicines are, both to satisfy security personnel and to obtain further supplies if anything goes wrong. Despite the general ban on sharp objects, people who require injections must have a letter explaining the medical need for it, usually from their doctor.

Heightened security - At times of heightened security, additional restrictions may be imposed, relating to the use of private cars and even taxis in the area around airport terminals and on what may be taken onto aircraft.

Minimum requirements

The minimum requirements for assistance are laid down in the EC regulation; see Access to Air Travel for Disabled Persons and Persons with Reduced Mobility – Code of Practice 2008. This takes account of matters such as the wider definition of disability in the Disability Discrimination Act than in the regulation, although the regulation does include people with a temporary impairment.

Depending on the airline and the size of the aircraft, there may be an on-board wheelchair for transport to the seat, and it may be possible to request a seat in a particular area. The seats behind emergency exits, which have more space, will be allocated to people who are perceived as having the dexterity and strength to open the doors if necessary.

Most pieces of equipment are carried free of charge. Larger items, including wheelchairs, are carried in the hold. Smaller items, such as sticks and crutches, can be taken into the cabin, although will have to be stowed away. Check with the airline on any equipment, particularly if it may be required during the flight. Some airlines impose a weight limit on equipment that can be loaded into their hold.

DPTAC

The Disabled Persons Transport Advisory Committee (DPTAC) is an independent organisation; meetings are usually held in London. **www.dptac.gov.uk** explains the activities of its working groups, and focuses on air travel, buses, ferries, motoring, rail, taxis and walking. DPTAC has a travel guide for disabled people –'Door to Door'.

Contact DPTAC, Great Minster House, 76 Marsham Street, London SW1P 4DR t 020 7944 8011 e dptac@dft.gsi.gov.uk

General air enquiries

Holiday Taxis

1st Floor Martlet Heights' 49 The Martlets,
Burgess Hill, West Sussex RH15 9NN
t 0870 444 1880 textphone info@holidaytaxis.com
web www.holidaytaxis.com

Holiday Taxis arrange for its clients to be transferred between the airport and their hotel. This avoids the need to use transfer buses, find car hire offices, etc while also dealing with luggage. The service is available at airports serving a large number of cities and resorts in Europe, USA, the Caribbean, North Africa and the Middle East.

A wide range of vehicles are offered, from a standard saloon car taxi for up to 4 passengers, to people-carriers and minibuses and coaches for larger groups. At about 25 destinations, mainly in Europe, there are vehicles that have been adapted for wheelchair users. Individuals or travel agents and tour operators can make bookings.

Aetas Services

141 boulevard MacDonald 75019 Paris
t +33 (0)1 30 53 69 97
web www.aetas.fr

Aetas have vehicles that can carry wheelchair users and other disabled people on transfers to and from Paris airports and rail stations within the Paris region and the rest of France.

Air Transport Users Council

CAA House, 45-59 Kingsway, London WC2B 6TE
t 020 7379 7311
web www.caa.co.uk

The AUC is the consumer council for passengers of the British aviation industry. It is funded through the Civil Aviation Authority with an independent council and secretariat. It can take up complaints against airlines and airports when customers' previous written complaints have not been satisfactorily dealt with and offers advice in other cases. There is advice on many matters relating to air travel on the website.

Aviatours Ltd

Eglinton Road, Rushmoor, Farnham GU10 2DH
t 01252 793250 e fearofflying@aviatours.co.uk
web www.aviatours.co.uk

Aviatours Ltd offer private and group courses to help control or overcome the fear of flying.

ResortHoppa.com

Oakfield House, Small Heath Business Park,
Talbot Way, Birmingham B10 0HJ
t 0871 855 0350 web www.resorthoppa.com

ResortHoppa provides pre-booked transfers between airports and popular holiday destinations in Europe and beyond. These may be through shuttle services, often using coaches and minibuses, or private transfers by car or larger vehicles depending on the size of the booking. Folded, manual wheelchairs are carried without extra charge for passengers who transfer to a standard seat.

Airports

In the past at most British airports, airlines have been responsible for any assistance required by disabled passengers from the check-in desk on departure to baggage reclaim on arrival. This has now changed as a result of European Union regulation (EC) 1107/2006 so that the airline is only responsible for services on the aircraft with the airport being required to ensure that assistance as far as boarding and from disembarkation. Airports can contract out the provision of assistance, perhaps to airlines, and should establish procedures to ensure that advance requests and information are passed on smoothly to those involved. At the time of writing few Airports have published their revised arrangements.

Aberdeen Airport

Dyce, Aberdeen AB21 7DU
t 0844 481 6666 textphone 0141 585 6161
web www.aberdeenairport.com

By Road - Aberdeen Airport is 7 miles north of the city centre off the A96. It has scheduled services to around 35 domestic and European destinations.

Parking - There are parking spaces for Blue Badge holders in the short-stay car park close to a telephone help point for people who need assistance in getting to the terminal. There are also bays for disabled motorists in the long-stay park close to the Customer Service office. The buses between there and the terminal are accessible to wheelchair users. For assistance, information or if you need to take your Blue Badge with you for use elsewhere call **0844 335 1000**.

By Public Transport - The nearest rail station to the airport is Dyce, a short taxi ride away, which is used by trains between Aberdeen and Inverness. There are regular bus services into central Aberdeen, some using low-floor vehicles. Information can be obtained from Stagecoach Bluebird on **01224 212266** or First Bus on **01224 650065**. Wheelchair accessible cars can be ordered from Comcab by calling **01224 353535**, or Aberdeen Airport Taxis Ltd on **01224 775555**.

Accessiblity - The terminal is accessible with toilets for disabled people in both landside and airside areas. There are help points for requesting assistance on the terminal forecourt, in baggage reclaim and at a number of places around the terminal. There are reserved seating areas for passengers with special needs and induction loops have been installed and are signposted.

Assistance for disabled passengers through the airport and on and off the aircraft is provided by G4S. It is requested that any assistance is requested at least 48 hours before flying, and preferably as far in advance as possible. Therefore in addition to contacting the airline of your requirements, it is suggested that you separately contact **G4S** on **01224 725767**.

Belfast City George Best Airport

Airport Road, Belfast BT3 9JH
t 028 9093 9093
web www.belfastcityairport.com

By Road - Belfast City Airport has scheduled services mainly to other airports in Britain and Ireland.

Parking - There are spaces designated for disabled motorists in the short-stay car park near the Terminal entrance. These are available at the long-term rate by paying at the Information Desk. A telephone for requesting assistance is located in the car park.

By Public Transport - It is about 5km east of Belfast city centre off the A2. A shuttle bus service runs between the Airport Terminal and Sydenham Rail Halt for rail services to destinations elsewhere in Ireland. There is an express Airlink bus service between the airport and the Belfast Europa Bus Station at 20 minute intervals during the day and also regular services between Sydenham and the city centre. There are also regular Airporter coach services between the airport and Londonderry. Wheelchair accessible taxis are available on the rank.

Accessiblity - All areas of the Terminal are accessible with a lift between the floors, toilets for disabled people at each level and lowered counters at the Information Desk and other public enquiry points. Induction loops are installed at check-in areas and the Information Desk, where there is also a textphone. A public BT Textphone that can send emails is also available. An alerter, linked to the fire alarm, can be obtained from the Information Desk by deaf and hard-of-hearing travellers. A number of staff members are trained to basic sign language level. An exercise area for assistance dogs is available outside the terminal.

An Ambulift is available for boarding the aircraft.

Belfast International Airport

Belfast, BT29 4AB
t 028 9448 4848
e info.desk@bfs.aero
web www.belfastairport.com

By Road - Belfast International Airport is near Antrim 18 miles north-west of Belfast city centre. It has scheduled flights to destinations in Britain, Europe and North America and also a number of chartered services.

Parking - There is an area for passengers to be set down outside the terminal. When picking up people, drivers should use the 10-minute free period in the short-stay car park and collect passengers from the Meeting Point. There are also medium and long-term car parks on site with an accessible bus between the long-stay car park and the terminal entrance. To pre-book or get information in long-stay parking call **Q-park 0870 013 4781**.

By Public Transport - The frequent Airport Express coach service, using a low floor vehicle, between the airport and central Belfast is operated by Ulsterbus. For information on onward connections by bus or rail and also local bus services contact **Translink 028 9066 6630** or **www.translink.co.uk**. Coach services from the Airport to Derry, whether direct, through Omagh or via Coleraine are operated by **AirPorter 028 7126 9996**. For information in taxis contact **Belfast International Airport Taxi Company** on **028 9448 4353**.

Accessiblity - The Terminal is on 2 floors with lifts between and with toilets in all areas. Assistance, including a porter service, can be requested from helpline telephones at the entrance and elsewhere in the building. The Information Desk has a low counter and low level; text telephones are available. An Ambulift is available to airlines boarding or disembarking passengers with impaired mobility, which needs to be pre-booked.

Birmingham International Airport

Birmingham B26 3QJ
t 0844 576 6000
textphone 0121 767 8084
web www.bhx.co.uk

By Road - Birmingham International Airport has scheduled and chartered services to around 100 destinations in Europe, North America and the Middle East. It is located 8 miles east of central Birmingham and near M42 J6.

Parking - The Rapid Drop-Off parking area near the terminal can be used by Blue Badge holders for up to 30 minutes without charge, by taking their badge to the NCP Desk in Terminal One. There are spaces for disabled motorists in both long and short-stay car parks, which have call-for-assistance buttons at their entrances.

By Public Transport - The airport is next to Birmingham International Station, from where there are direct services to many destinations around the country as well as frequent services to Birmingham New Street from where other connections can be made. The Air-Rail link between the airport and the station is accessible to disabled people and makes the transfer every 2 minutes. The airport has its own bus/coach station serving both long-distance National Express coaches and local bus services. Information on which of the latter use accessible buses can be obtained from **Network West Midlands 0871 200 2233**. Metered taxis that can carry a passenger in a wheelchair are available on the taxi rank. Information on these can be obtained on **0121 782 3744**.

Accessiblity - The terminal building is accessible with lifts between floors and toilets for disabled people in all areas. There is a Textphone at the Terminal 1 Information Desk and staff who can use sign language both there and at the Special Assistance Reception Desk on the ground floor of Terminal 1. Deaf Alerters, linked to the fire alarm, are also available. Wheelchairs are available and anyone needing assistance to get to check-in should call **0121 767 7878** or Textphone **0121 767 8084**. Wheelchairs and a special lift to help with boarding are available.

Blackpool International Airport

Squires Gate Lane, Blackpool FY4 2QY
t 0844 482 7171
e info@blackpoolairport.com
web www.blackpoolinternational.com

By Road - The airport is close to the end of the M55 north of Blackpool town centre. It has flights to over 25 destinations in Britain, Ireland and Southern Europe.

Parking - There is a set-down and pick-up point in front of the terminal and both short and long-stay car parks are nearby.

By Public Transport - Taxis and nearby local buses provide a service into town and the nearby Squires Gate Station has an hourly rail service to Preston.

Accessiblity - The terminal building, which was extended and modernised in 2006, is accessible and has lowered check-in desks and pay phones and toilets for disabled people in all areas. A mobile lift is available for boarding.

Bournemouth International Airport

Christchurch BH23 6SE
t 01202 364000
web www.bournemouthairport.com

By Road - Bournemouth Airport is 6 miles north east of Bournemouth and signposted from the A338 and the A31. It handles both scheduled and holiday flights to an increasing number of destinations.

Parking - There are parking spaces for disabled motorists in Car Park 1 opposite the terminal and also a set-down/pick-up area. Assistance can be provided to and from the long-stay car park.

By Public Transport - The Bournemouth Airport Shuttle operates at hourly intervals using buses with a space for a passenger in a wheelchair and a low-level floor. Contact **Discover Dorset 01202 557007**.
www.bournemouth-airport-shuttle.co.uk
Buses stop at Bournemouth Travel Interchange for passengers using South West Trains, Southern and CrossCountry rail services. Taxis to and from the airport can be booked from **United Taxis 01202 556677**.

Accessiblity - The terminal is single storey with automatic doors. The Information Desk is just inside the entrance and from there staff can provide assistance or a wheelchair if required. Toilets for disabled people are located in the main terminal and the Arrivals Hall; there are wide aisles in shops and restaurants. A lift and ambulance chairs are available for boarding and exiting. In bad weather wheelchair capes are available for crossing to the aircraft.

Bristol International Airport

Bristol BS48 3DY
t 0871 334 4450
textphone 01275 473670
e specialassistance@bristolairport.co.uk
web www.bristolairport.co.uk

By Road - The airport is 8 miles south of central Bristol off the A38 and is among the most rapidly growing in the country.

Parking - Although cars cannot be left unattended beside the terminal, there is a pick-up area 100m from the Terminal. There are help buttons at car park barriers, which have designated bays for blue badge holders. Buses equipped with ramps are available for transfers from the long-stay car park.

By Public Transport - There is an express coach service between the Airport and Central Bristol including the bus station and Bristol Temple Meads railway station. Through tickets are available. This runs at 20-minute intervals but cannot carry passengers in wheelchairs. The taxi company serving the airport has minibuses adapted for disabled passengers. Contact **Checker Cars 01275 475000** or **bristol@checkercars.com**

Accessiblity - The terminal has lifts between floors, Braille signs, special assistance points and toilets for disabled people. There is an induction loop and wheelchairs are available without charge. To arrange assistance call the **OCS** Special Assistance Desk **0871 334 4444**.

Cardiff International Airport

Vale of Glamorgan CF62 3BD
t 01446 711111 web www.cwlfly.com

By Road - The airport is on the outskirts of Rhoose, 12 miles west of Cardiff and 10 miles from M4 junction 33. It has scheduled flights to over 40 domestic and international destinations.

Parking - There are designated parking bays for disabled motorists in both the short and long-stay car parks close to call-for assistance points. There is a ramp from the short-stay/business car park to the terminal. For long-stay parking enquiries contact **NCP 01446 710 313**.

Places can be booked at discounted rates by pre-booking online. Passengers can be dropped off near the Terminal entrance and picked-up from the short-stay car park.

By Public Transport - Rhoose Cardiff International rail station has regular services to Cardiff Central and Bridgend. There is an accessible shuttle bus between the station and the airport that is free to people with a rail ticket. Express bus services that can carry passengers in wheelchairs run between the airport and central Cardiff, both non-stop and via Barry. Taxis are available and can be booked by calling **Checker Cars** on **01446 711474** or **cardiff@checkercars.com**

Accessiblity - There are dropped kerbs at the entrances to the terminal, which has lifts to all floors. There are toilets for disabled people in all areas. The Information Desk has a Minicom and is equipped with an induction loop, which are also fitted at most check-in desks and other areas. Information is given visually on monitor screens and also by public address announcements. Wheelchairs are available and passengers can stay in their own wheelchairs up to boarding.

There is an assistance service to board aircraft and an Ambulift for those who cannot manage aircraft steps.

City of Derry Airport

**Airport Road, Eglinton,
Co. Londonderry BT47 3GY
t 028 7181 0784
web www.cityofderryairport.com**

By Road - The airport is 7 miles north east of the city, off the A2 Londonderry-Coleraine main road. It has scheduled domestic services and also a number of chartered flights.

Parking - There are spaces for Blue Badge Holders in the car parks adjacent to the terminal and concessionary rates are available.

By Public Transport - Ulsterbus operates various services between the airport and the main Foyle Street Bus Station in the city centre for onward services by bus and rail. For information contact **Translink 028 9066 6630** or **www.translink.co.uk**. There is a taxi rank outside the terminal.

Accessiblity - There is a ramp into the terminal and all the passenger facilities are on the ground floor with toilets for disabled people off the main concourse and the departure lounge. An induction loop is installed.

Wheelchairs are available, and the airport has stairclimbers for use both by airlines to assist in loading and disembarking passengers and also for wheelchair users who may need to go to the first floor conference room or administrative offices. Advance booking for these is requested.

Coventry Airport

**Siskin Parkway West, Coventry CV3 4PB
t 024 7630 8600 e info@coventryairport.co.uk
web www.coventryairport.co.uk**

By Road - Coventry Airport is to the south-east of Coventry. In addition to holiday flights it has scheduled budget services to 14 overseas destinations.

Parking - Parking spaces for Blue Badge holders are available. These cannot be booked in advance.

By Public Transport - There is an hourly bus service between the airport and the city centre and Coventry railway station. This uses vehicles that can carry wheelchair users. For information see **www.traveldecourcey.com**. To book a taxi contact **Central Taxis 024 7633 3333**.

Accessiblity - The present small terminal has all public areas on the ground floor with an accessible entrance. An induction loop is available. For assistance or wheelchair loan book in advance or contact **Thompsonfly** Customer Services **024 7633 3333**.

Durham Tees Valley Airport

**Darlington DL2 1LU
t 01325 332811 e enquiries@dtva.co.uk
web www.durhamteesvalleyairport.com**

By Road - Durham Tees Valley Airport is 10 miles east of Darlington on the A26.

Parking - There is a set down/pick-up area at the side of the terminal. Designated spaces for disabled motorists are located at the front of the main car park.

By Public Transport - A range of bus services operated by Arriva Link Durham Tees Valley Airport to the towns and villages surrounding the airport. Service 12 - Darlington to Airport and Service 20 - Middlesborough to airport via Stockton, Hartburn, Yarm, Taglescliffe and Long Newton.

See **www.arriva.co.uk** There is a taxi rank at the airport, for more information call **07855 642947**.

Accessiblity - The terminal building was designed to be accessible to disabled passengers. There is an induction loop at the Information Desk.

Wheelchairs and an Ambulift are available and should be booked in advance.

East Midlands Airport

Castle Donington, Derby DE74 2SA
t 0871 919 9000 textphone 0845 108 8545
web www.eastmidlandsairport.com

By Road - East Midlands Airport is between Derby, Leicester and Nottingham and close to the M1 Junctions 23a and 24. It has scheduled flights to many domestic, European and Mediterranean destinations and also handles chartered flights.

Parking - There are designated spaces for Blue Badge holders in the Short Stay Car Park where there are also help points connected to customer services staff. The long and medium stay car parks have accessible shuttle buses to the terminal. The Pick-up zone is situated at the terminal side of the short stay car park.

By Public Transport - At present the nearest rail stations are Loughborough (8 miles) and Long Eaton (5 miles), both served by East Midlands Trains. The new East Midlands Parkway Station is a couple of miles away with regular shuttle buses to the airport. A regular express Skylink service, using wheelchair accessible buses, runs between the airport and central Nottingham with connections with Nottingham Station and the NET tram system. There is also a half-hourly accessible Skylink service to Leicester. Local buses serve Derby, Long Eaton and Loughborough Stations and National Express coaches to towns in the Midlands and Yorkshire.

Accessiblity - The Terminal building is accessible, being mainly on the ground floor with a lift to the 1st floor part of the Departure Lounge. First aid rooms can be used for medication if required. There are two lounges equipped for passengers needing assistance in the Departure area. Wheelchairs are available free of charge. A booklet 'Access: a guide for passengers with a disability' is available or can be downloaded from the website.

Edinburgh Airport

Edinburgh, EH12 9DN
t 0844 481 8989 textphone 0141 585 6161
web www.edinburghairport.com

By Road - Edinburgh Airport is west of the city, off the A8. It is used by over 40 airlines flying to around 90 destinations. The airport has direct flights to 25 different foreign countries. £240m is being invested in developing the airport over the next several years.

Parking - Blue Badge holders can use the designated bays in the multi-storey short-stay car park, free for 15 minutes, for set-down/pick-up purposes. This is linked to the terminal by a covered walkway. Both short and long-stay car parks have designated spaces and help buttons. People wishing to take their Blue Badge for use elsewhere should contact the car park operator via the help button or by visiting the customer services points. For further information on parking **t** 0844 335 1000.

By Public Transport - The 100 express Airlink bus service, which uses wheelchair accessible buses, connects the airport with central Edinburgh including Edinburgh Waverley Station for onward journeys by First Scotrail and National Express East Coast. There are plans for both direct rail and tram links to the airport. Airlink also stops at Haymarket Station for some local services. For further information contact Lothian Buses **t** 0131 555 6363, **e** mail@lothianbuses.com or got to **www. flybybus.com** There is also an Airdirect service, again using easy access buses, between the airport and Inverkeithing Station in Fife, providing a more direct transport link to the East of Scotland. Accessible taxis are usually available on the airport taxi rank. Information on taxis can be obtained from Executive Onward Travel **t** 0131 333 2255.

Accessiblity - The terminal building is accessible with reserved seating areas for disabled passengers and others with special requirements and toilets for disabled people in all areas. All payphones can be used by hearing aid users and there is a Textphone in the international arrivals area. In addition to the car parks there are help points in the coach station taxi ranks and several places within the terminal. Assistance for disabled passengers through the airport and on and off the aircraft is provided by THS. It is requested that any assistance is requested at least 48 hours before flying, and preferably as far in advance as possible. In addition to contacting the airline concerning your requirements, it is suggested that you separately contact THS on **t** 0131 344 3449.

Exeter International Airport

Exeter EX5 2BD
t 01392 367433
web www.exeter-airport.co.uk

By Road - The airport is east of Exeter off the A30 near M5 junction 29. Vehicles using the drop-off area must be attended at all times.

Parking - Designated bays for Blue Badge holders are located near the pay station in the short-stay car park 1, from where assistance can be called for transfer into the terminal. Car park 2 is for car rental/return, disability and Blue Badge spaces, charged at standard rate. There are also designated spaces by the Shuttle Bus Shelter in car parks 3 and 4. Pre-booking discount of up to 30% if booking online.

By Public Transport - There are bus services that normally use low-floor buses, during the day between the airport and Exeter St Davids Station for First Great Western and South West Trains services. Call the taxi operator at the airport, Exeter Airport Taxis **01395 234 100** or Corporate cars **01395 233 728** for information or booking.

Accessiblity - The entrances to the terminal buildings are ramped and have automatic doors. The information desks are equipped with induction loops and information sheets in Braille are available at check-in and security areas. Deaf or hard of hearing passengers should make themselves known so that they can be alerted to announcements. Assistance, including wheelchair loan if required, can be provided to the boarding gate and between the aircraft and final point of departure from the airport.

Low-floor coaches with ramps are used between the terminal and the aircraft and an Ambulift, which must be booked in advance through the airline, is available for people who would have difficulty with the aircraft steps.

Glasgow Airport

Paisley, PA3 2ST
t 0844 481 5555 textphone 01224 725082
web www.glasgowairport.com

By Road - Glasgow Airport is to the west of Glasgow, near Paisley, off the M8, junction 28. It is the busiest airport in Scotland, handling services to 80 destinations by 40 airlines.

Parking - There is a drop-off/pick-up zone for Blue Badge holders on the ground floor of short-stay car park 2 giving 30 minutes free parking. Users should take their ticket and Blue Badge to the customer service desk in the car park for validation. There are spaces for Blue Badge holders in car parks 1, 2 and 3 close to the terminal. The multi-storey car park 2 has a height limit of 2 metres. People who wish to take their Blue Badge with them should contact the customer services office in car park 2. There are also reserved spaces for disabled motorists in the long-stay car parks and to ensure accessible transport to the terminal disabled people are advised to contact BAA information line on **0844 335 1000.**

By Public Transport - Arriva operate a regular Glasgow Flyer bus service into central Glasgow, including both main railway stations and Buchanan Street bus station. The Airport Link service serves other points in the city including Charing Cross bus station. These, and a number of other local bus services, use vehicles that can carry a passenger in a wheelchair. Wheelchair-accessible taxis are available at the airport. Contact the warden controlling the taxi rank at the arrivals end of the terminal.

Accessiblity - The terminal building has reserved seating areas for disabled passengers on the ground floor and the International Departure Lounge, unisex toilets in most toilet areas and induction loops in marked areas. Help points are located in car parks, outside the terminal, in the T2 check-in area and the baggage reclaim hall. A public text phone is located in the 1st floor shopping area. Assistance for disabled passengers through the airport, including to and from car parks, and on and off the aircraft is provided by THS (Scotland). It is requested that any assistance is requested at least 48 hours before flying, and preferably as far in advance as possible. Therefore, in addition to contacting the airline of your requirements, it is suggested that you separately contact THS on **0141 842 7700** or **info@thsscotland.co.uk**

Glasgow Prestwick Airport

Aviation House, Prestwick KA9 2PL
t 0871 223 0700
web www.gpia.co.uk

By Road - Prestwick Airport, north of Ayr, is just over 30 miles south west of Glasgow. It handles scheduled services to 25 domestic and European destinations and chartered flights to 11 holiday destinations.

Parking - It can be reached from the A77. Two short-term car parks are close to the Terminal entrance, both with designated bays for Blue Badge holders. Car park 1 is free of charge for the first 30 minutes on producing a valid Blue Badge at the car park information desk and should be used to set down and pick up passengers. Spaces in the medium and long-stay car parks can be booked 24 hours in advance (**0871 2222 883**) and are linked to the terminal by accessible shuttle bus.

By Public Transport - Prestwick Airport Station has regular half-hourly train services (hourly on Sundays) from Glasgow Central Station. The station has a lift to each platform, a unisex toilet and is linked to the Terminal by a covered walkway. Discounted fares are available from any First ScotRail Station. There are also express bus services to Glasgow Buchanan Street Bus Station. Taxis, of various sizes, serving the airport can carry wheelchair users. Contact **Ayr Black Cabs 01292 284545/471600** or **ayrblackcabs@aol.com**

Accessiblity - The Terminal is accessible with a lift, between the ground and upper floors and toilets, for disabled people on the ground floor and in departure lounges. A stairlift provides access to the Aviator Suite.

Wheelchairs are available. Staff assist disabled passengers who are pre-boarded, without charge.

Guernsey Airport

La Viliaze, Forest, Guernsey GY8 0DS
t 01481 237766 e airport@gov.gg
web www.guernsey-airport.gov.gg

By Road - Guernsey Airport is in the south of the island, 4 miles from St Peter Port. There are scheduled inter-island flights and also services to destinations in England, France, Germany and the Netherlands.

Parking - There are designated spaces for disabled motorists in the car park and a set down/pick up point for blue badge holders by the Terminal entrance.

By Public Transport - The regular Island Coastway bus service between the Airport and St Peter Port can carry passengers in wheelchairs and accessible vehicles are used on some other services around Guernsey. Taxis that can carry folded wheelchairs can be pre-booked, **01481 244444**.

Accessiblity - All areas of the Terminal, are accessible to wheelchair users. There are toilets for disabled people in both the main concourse and the arrivals hall.

A hoist for boarding is provided by Flybe. Other passengers unable to manage aircraft steps may have to be carried.

Highlands & Islands Airports Ltd (HIAL)

Inverness Airport, Inverness IV2 7JB
t 01667 462455 web www.hial.co.uk

By Road - HIAL, owned by Ministers in the Scottish Government, operates 11 airports providing commercial, tourist and emergency air services in northern Scotland. HIAL Airports are Inverness (see below), Sumburgh in Shetland, Kirkwall, Wick, Stornoway, Benbecula, Barra (the world's only beach airport with scheduled services), Tiree, Islay, Campbelltown and Dundee.

Accessiblity - Facilities at the smaller airports are not extensive but all have basically accessible terminals and most have Ambulifts for passengers who cannot use the steps to the aircraft. Information on each of these is available on the above website.

Humberside International Airport

Kirmington, North Lincolnshire DN39 6YH
t 01652 688456 web www.humbersideairport.com

By Road - Humberside Airport is between Scunthorpe and Grimsby off the A18, near the end of M180. It has scheduled flights to Amsterdam for connections to many other destinations. There are also direct charter flights to holiday destinations.

Parking - There are spaces designated for Blue Badge holders in the nearby short-stay car park with charges at standard rather than short-stay rates. There is a help point to call for assistance into the terminal. It is possible to book spaces in the long-stay car parks by calling **0871 310 4111**.

By Public Transport - An express coach service between Hull and Grimsby calls at the Airport from Monday to Saturday. The nearest rail station is Barnetby, 3 miles away, which has regular services to Doncaster for connections to other destinations. Taxis can be booked **01652 688132**.

Accessiblity - The public parts of the Terminal are on the ground floor and incorporate unisex toilets for disabled passengers in all area. A First Aid room is available.

An Ambulift is available for boarding and disembarking.

Inverness Airport

Dalcross, Inverness IV2 7JB
t 01667 464000 f 01667 462041
web www.hial.co.uk/inverness-airport

By Road - Inverness Airport has over 300 scheduled flights a week to airports throughout Britain. There are also a number of holiday charter flights.

Parking - The airport is 9 miles east of the city, situated just off the A96. The car park has designated parking bays for disabled motorists and there is also a designated set down/pick up point for disabled passengers at the entrance to the Terminal.

By Public Transport - There are regular bus services to the railway and bus stations in central Inverness using a low floor bus. The taxi company serving the airport (**Highland Taxis 01463 222222**) has vehicles that can carry passengers in wheelchairs.

Accessiblity - The terminal is single storey. There are unisex toilets for disabled people. Assistance dogs can be exercised in the dog walk area. Anyone who may need assistance should contact the Airport Information Desk on **01667 464000**.

An Ambulift and stairclimbers are available for the boarding and disembarkation of disabled passengers.

Isle of Man Airport

Ballasalla, Isle of Man IM9 2AS
t 01624 821600 web www.iom-airport.com

By Road - Isle of Man (Ronaldsway) Airport is at the south of the Island near Castletown but less than an hour's drive from all points on the Island. There are currently 5 airlines flying between the Isle of Man and airports in Britain and Ireland.

Parking - There are designated spaces for Blue Badge holders in both the main and the long-stay car parks. There are also reserved spaces outside the terminal to set down or pick up disabled passengers.

By Public Transport - Bus services run between the airport and Douglas and other major towns. For information on low floor buses and on arrangements for disabled passengers on their railways, contact **Isle of Man Transport**, Banks Circus, Douglas IM1 5PT. **01624 662525**. **info@busandrail.dtl.gov.im** **www.iombusandrail.info**

Accessiblity - Within the terminal there is a lift to the first floor, toilets for disabled people, lowered pay phones and an induction loop for announcements. Vehicles to lift wheelchair users to the aircraft are available, the use of which is arranged through the airline.

Jersey Airport

St Peter, Jersey JE1 1BY
t 01534 446000 e information@jerseyairport.com
web www. jerseyairport.com

By Road - The airport is located near the coast, west of St Helier and has flights to and from over 30 airports in Britain and Ireland.

Parking - There is a taxi rank and set down/pick up point outside the terminal.

By Public Transport - There is a regular bus service between the Airport and St Helier. Most of the public bus services on Jersey use vehicles that can carry a passenger in a wheelchair. Contact **Connex Transport Jersey 01534 877772**. **www.mybus.je**

Accessiblity - The terminal building is largely on the ground floor with a lift to the viewing gallery and restaurant. There are toilets for disabled people in the departure lounge and the arrivals area. Wheelchairs are available free of charge. Boarding and disembarking assistance can be provided, with advance notice, through the airline.

Leeds Bradford International Airport

Leeds LS19 7TU
t 0871 288 2288 e customerservices@lbia.co.uk
web www.lbia.co.uk

By Road - The airport is 11 miles from central Leeds and 7 miles from Bradford, signposted from the M1, M62 and A1. It is the largest airport in the region with flights to 74 domestic and international destinations.

Parking - There are reserved spaces for Blue Badge holders in the short stay car park. Stays of over 24 hours in these can be charged at the pre-booked long stay rate to people who call **0113 391 1607** or contact the Information Desk as soon as possible. There is also an intercom to call for assistance if required.

By Public Transport - There are regular bus services, usually using low floor buses that can carry a passenger in a wheelchair, between the airport and mainline rail stations in Leeds and Bradford. For further information call **0113 245 7676** or see **www.wymetro.com**

Leeds Airport Service provides a service between the airport terminal building and the long-stay car park.

Accessiblity - For wheelchairs and assistance contact Interserve **0113 391 1607.** An Ambulift is available for boarding and getting off the plane.

Liverpool John Lennon Airport

South Terminal, Liverpool L24 1YD
t 0870 129 8484
web www.liverpoolairport.com

By Road - The airport is 7 miles south of central Liverpool at Speke and signposted from the M56, M57 and M62. It has scheduled services to over 50 destinations in Britain and Europe and also chartered holiday flights.

Parking - There is a set down/pick up area opposite the Terminal and designated parking spaces for disabled motorists at the front of the short-stay and long-stay 1 car parks. Pre-book for discounts. There are no disabled parking bays within long-stay car park 2.

By Public Transport - There are regular bus services, using vehicles that can carry wheelchair users between the Airport and Liverpool South Parkway from where there are Merseyrail and Northern Rail services to central Liverpool and other destinations in the North West and the Midlands. From Lime Street Station there are main line connections. There are also other local bus services from the airport, including a night bus service into the City Centre. Mersey Travel has an information point for information about public transport in the area located in the Airport Tourist Information Centre. A taxi rank is located in front of the terminal by the arrivals area. For information about taxis at the airport contact **Mersey Cabs** on **0151 298 2060**.

Accessiblity - The terminal building is accessible and has toilets for disabled people and low level payphones.

Wheelchairs are available and there is an Ambulift for passengers unable to use the aircraft steps. These services should be requested when booking a flight.

London City Airport

Royal Docks, London E16 2PX
t 020 7646 0088   e CSC1@londoncityairport.com
web www.londoncityairport.com

By Road - London City Airport is 5 miles east of the City of London and 10 miles from the West End. It handles flights in comparatively small aircraft to 30 domestic and European destinations predominately for business travellers.

Parking - There are designated spaces for disabled motorists in the car park close to the terminal. However, the long-term car park is not far away. A valet parking service is available which could be useful to some disabled people. There is no additional charge for this beyond the parking fee.

By Public Transport - A station on the accessible Docklands Light Railway is integrated into the terminal. This is served by trains from Bank and Canning Town where it connects with the Jubilee Line for accessible transfers to London Bridge, Waterloo and Stratford rail stations. The DLR line continues south of the Thames to Woolwich. Local buses that can carry wheelchair users stop near the airport and there is a taxi rank where accessible cabs can be obtained.

Accessiblity - The terminal has toilets for disabled people, a first-aid room and a lift from the concourse to the departure lounge and to the apron for boarding.

For assistance when passing through the airport or boarding and disembarking, contact Customer Services **020 7646 0000** or **cssupervisor@londoncityairport.com**

London Gatwick Airport

Gatwick, West Sussex RH6 0NP
t 0844 335 1802
textphone 01293 513179
web www.gatwickairport.com

By Road - Gatwick, the second busiest airport in UK, is 28 miles south of London off the M23 junction 9.
Parking - For the South Terminal there is a set down area on the Lower Forecourt including an area specifically for disabled people. The Orange Short-stay car park 3 is now the dedicated area for passengers being picked up. There are spaces for Blue Badge holders in the short-stay multi-storey car parks beside each of the terminals. These are near help points and signposted accessible routes into the terminal. They are subject to a height limit of 2 metres but there is a parking area for higher vehicles nearby. For information on both short and long-term parking call **0844 335 1000**.

Travel-Care Gatwick is an independent agency, with charitable status, offering assistance to anyone at the airport who has a problem. It is located in The Village, South Terminal and is open during office hours 7 days a week. **01293 504283**.

Help-me-Park offers a meet and greet parking service at both Gatwick Terminals avoiding the need for disabled members of a family to be dropped off or having to hang around while another member of the party parks the car or the use of transfer coaches. They can be contacted via **0870 300 6009** or **www.help-me-park.com**

By Public Transport - Gatwick Station is immediately beside the South Terminal. In addition to the frequent non-stop services to London Victoria by Gatwick Express, there are also direct rail services to other London terminals and elsewhere in southern England. There are also CrossCountry services on a number of longer routes. The airport is well served by long-distance coach services although these cannot carry passengers in wheelchairs. Local bus services into Crawley do use accessible vehicles.
Checker Cars operate taxis from Gatwick and can supply cars with swivel seats, contact **01293 567 700** or **gatwick@checkercars.com**

Accessiblity - As with all multi terminal airports, it is important to make sure that you know which you will be using before setting out or making arrangements to be met. The South and North Terminals are linked by a frequent transit system that has level entrances and space

for wheelchair users. The terminals have lifts or ramps for changes in level, toilets for disabled people near or in toilets blocks, reserved seating areas and induction loops. In addition to the short stay car parks and the railway and coach stations, help points are located on terminal forecourts, baggage reclaim halls and on some of the long pedestrian routes around the buildings.

Assistance for disabled passengers through the airport, including to and from car parks, and on and off the aircraft is provided by G4S. It is requested that any assistance is requested at least 48 hours before flying, and preferably as far in advance as possible. Therefore in addition to contacting the airline of your requirements, it is suggested that you separately contact **G4S** on **01293 507502**.

London Heathrow Airport

234 Bath Road, Hayes, UB3 5AP
t 0844 335 1801 textphone 020 8745 7950
web www.heathrowairport.com

By Road - Heathrow, situated on the western edge of Greater London near the M4 and M25, has more international flights than any other airport in the world with 90 airlines serving 180 destinations in over 90 countries. It has 5 terminals with Terminals 1, 2 and 3 being grouped together in the centre of the airport, Terminal 4 on the southern edge and Terminal 5 at the west.

Parking - Short-stay car parks by each terminal have spaces for blue badge holders near routes into the terminal and help points where assistance can be called. People who wish to take their blue badge with them to notify the car park operator can also use the help points. The general height limit in multi-storey car parks is 2 meters. Higher cars than this can park on the ground floor of car park 3 for Terminals 1, 2 & 3 or the roof of car park 4. There are also designated spaces in the business and long stay car parks for which the operators can provide information on the accessibility of their transfer arrangements. For other information on parking at Heathrow or for pre-booking call **0844 335 1000**.

By Public Transport - Heathrow is linked by train to Paddington in central London using the accessible, non-stop Heathrow Express service and also the Heathrow Connect service that also serves some stations in west London. Both go to Terminals 1, 2 and 3 with Heathrow Connect continuing to Terminal 4 while Heathrow Express goes to Terminal 5. There are also London Underground

(Piccadilly Line) services to and from all terminals at the airport. Although the underground stations at Heathrow can be reached without using stairs or escalators the same is true of few other underground stations particularly in central London. For information call **020 7222 1234** or see **www.tfl.gov.uk**

The central bus station at the airport is close to Terminals 1, 2 & 3 and is equipped with a help point for people needing assistance to get into the terminal. Local bus services, long distance coach services and also the coaches linking with the rail network at Reading, Woking, Feltham and elsewhere use this. Many coach services also serve Terminals 4 and 5. Although most of the local bus services can carry passengers in wheelchairs, this is not yet a regular feature of coach services. Accessible taxis are available on taxi ranks.

The rail services can be used without charge to get between Terminal 4, Terminal 5 and Terminals 1, 2 & 3. An alternative is the Heathrow Help Bus, a free, accessible service for disabled passengers and those with heavy luggage. The bus serves all terminals and the central bus station and can be called from help points, the information desk or by phoning **020 8745 6261**.

Accessiblity - There are help points at the entrances to the terminals, in the baggage reclaim halls and along routes with long walking distances as well as in car parks and

stations. Lifts and ramps are provided for changes of level. Most toilet blocks contain a unisex WC for disabled passengers. Induction loops have been installed at various points in the terminals and their locations are indicated. Text pay phones are sited in the arrivals area of each terminal. Airbridges between the terminal and the aircraft are used for most flights at Heathrow.

Assistance is provided for disabled passengers through the airport, including to and from car parks, and on and off the aircraft. It is requested that any assistance is requested at least 48 hours before flying, and preferably as far in advance as possible.

Therefore in addition to contacting the airline of your requirements, it is suggested that you separately contact:

- Terminal 1 – Mitie on **020 8745 2165**

- Terminal 2 – Mitie on **020 8745 2195**

- Terminal 3 – OCS on **020 8745 2227**

- Terminal 4 – Mitie on **020 8745 2357**

- Terminal 5 – OCS on **020 3165 0285**

Terminal 5 opened in March 2008 and will handle British Airways flights. As this changeover is completed there will be changes to the Terminals used by other airlines and major developments in the existing area over forthcoming years.

Travel-Care Heathrow is an independent social work agency offering assistance to anyone at the airport who has a problem. It can be contacted on weekday office hours through help points or on **020 8745 7495**

London Luton Airport

Navigation House, Airport Way, Luton LU2 9LY
t 01582 405100 e disabledfacilities@ltn.aero
web www.london-luton.co.uk

By Road - The airport is to the south of Luton town centre, two miles from M1 junction 10. It has scheduled flights to a large number of domestic, European and Mediterranean airports and also chartered flights to holiday destinations.

Parking - A set down and pick-up area is located near the terminal with a strictly enforced 10 minute time limit during which vehicles must be attended at all times. Cars with a Blue Badge can use spaces in the nearby short-term car park without charge for the first hour. There are designated parking bays for disabled people in all car parks with Special Assistance points in those for mid and long-stay car parks, which also have accessible transfer buses to the terminal.

Parking places can be booked online in advance at a discounted rate. Users of powered wheelchairs should contact APCOA parking, which manages a variety of airport car parks, on **0845 210 2100 www.apcoa.co.uk**

By Public Transport - The Hire Car Centre is accessible, has a Special Assistance Help Point and is served by an accessible shuttle bus from the terminal.

There is also a shuttle bus between the airport and Luton Parkway Station, which is served by Capital Connect and East Midlands trains to London and parts of South East England and the Midlands. Local buses and a range of longer distance coach services also serve the airport. Among these, the Green Line 757 Express route to and from Central London has some coaches that are equipped with lifts. At present passengers wishing to use this service are asked to give a day's notice so that the correct vehicles can be put into the schedule – **www.greenline.co.uk**.

Luton Taxis with a fleet of wheelchair accessible vehicles operates from the airport **01582 735555.**

Accessiblity - The terminal has been rebuilt over recent years during which accessible features were incorporated. The large automatic revolving entrance doors can be slowed and two can be set open.

A Special Assistance Waiting Area is available for disabled people while cars are being parked or collected. Assistance telephones are located around the terminal and porters can give help or act as escorts to the check-in desks. Wheelchairs can be borrowed without charge from beside the entrance and near the check-out desks. Information points have lowered desks for wheelchair users and check-in desks and airport service counters are fitted with induction loops. There are toilets for disabled people in all main areas. There are covered walkways to the aircraft.

Boarding and disembarking are normally via steps to the aircraft. Aviance Care Assistants will pre-board disabled passengers using an Ambulift if appropriate. On return Aviance staff will escort disabled passengers as far as the baggage reclaim hall, after which free assistance, if required, will be available from porters. A booklet, "Access and Facilities Guide for Customers with Disabilities", is available in normal or large print, on the website or on a CD – contact **01582 405100** or **disabledfacilities@ltn.aero** All general information leaflets can be obtained in large print.

London Stansted Airport

**Enterprise House, Bassingbourn Road, Stansted, Essex CM24 1QW
t 0844 335 1803 textphone 01279 663725
web www.stanstedairport.com**

By Road - Stansted is Britain's 3rd busiest airport with flights to 160 destinations in 36 countries. It is located north of London and south of Cambridge off the M11, junctions 8 and 8A.

Parking - There are designated spaces for Blue Badge holders in all car parks, including the short-stay car parks close to the terminal. There are help buttons in the short-stay areas and at the bus shelters in the mid and long-stay car parks. Transfer buses can carry passengers in wheelchairs. Blue Badge holders wanting to take their badge with them should contact the car park operator on arrival. For further information or pre-booking contact **0844 355 1000**.

By Public Transport - Stansted Airport Station is directly under the terminal with lifts and escalators to the platforms. There are frequent Stansted Express trains to London Liverpool Street and also stopping trains to London. There is also a regular service between Stansted and Birmingham with connections to other parts of the rail network at Cambridge, Peterborough and Leicester. At the time of writing few of the long-distance coach services to and from the airport can carry passengers in wheelchairs. Wheelchair accessible taxis can be booked from **Checker Cars 01279 661111**.

Accessiblity - There are help points outside the terminal entrance doors for people needing assistance to check-in. The main areas of the terminal are on one level with lifts to the upper level catering outlets. There are toilets, some fitted with the National Key Scheme Lock, for disabled people in the main concourse and the departure lounge. Reserved seating areas have induction loops and low level flight information screens. Induction loops are also fitted in other areas and there are public text phones in the Satellite Two departure lounge and the international arrivals area. Most boarding gates are off satellites, which are reached by an accessible rail transit system. However, even using this, the distances to travel can be quite long for many disabled people who do not usually use a wheelchair.

Assistance for disabled passengers through the airport, including to and from car parks, and on and off the aircraft, is provided by Mitie. It is requested that any assistance is requested at least 48 hours before flying, and preferably as far in advance as possible. In addition individuals and groups who are unfamiliar with airport procedures can request an escort service either through security and the departure lounge to the aircraft or from the aircraft to the Arrivals area in the main terminal. This should be booked in advance by calling **Aviation Location Services** on **07715 171316**.

Manchester Airport

Manchester, M90 1QX
t 0871 271 0711 (general enquiries)
t 090 10 10 1000 (flight information)
t 0871 310 2200 (car park bookings)
web www.manchesterairport.co.uk

By Road - Manchester Airport is the UK's third largest airport and the busiest outside the London area with flights to over 200 destinations worldwide. It is located 10 miles south of central Manchester off the M56.

Parking - Cars cannot wait or be left unattended outside the terminals although there are areas where passengers can be set down and picked up. The short-stay car parks near each terminal have bays reserved for Blue Badge holders near the lifts. There are also reserved spaces near the entrance or reception office of each of the long-stay car parks. However, disabled people can also make arrangements to keep their car in the short-stay parks, at long-term rates, by calling **0871 310 2200.** The same number should be used by people wishing to take their Blue Badge for use elsewhere.

By Public Transport - There is a transport interchange with lifts or ramps between levels for Manchester Airport's rail, bus and coach stations and covered walkways to each of the terminals. There are frequent rail services to Manchester Piccadilly Station and also direct services to destinations in northern and central England. Many Transpennine Express train routes terminate at Manchester Airport. Future plans include extending the Metronet tram service to the airport. National Express has wheelchair accessible coaches on the 538 route serving Manchester Airport from Scotland and the Midlands.

Information on local bus services, including those using accessible vehicles, can be obtained from GMPTE **0161 228 7811.** There are taxi ranks outside each terminal and some of the taxis serving the airport can carry passengers in wheelchairs. For information call **0161 489 2313.**

Accessiblity - The terminals are accessible with ramps or lifts for changes of level and toilets for disabled people in all areas. Assistance can be obtained by using the courtesy telephones by entrances and elsewhere. Customer Service Agents are available to assist passengers with hearing difficulties and additional voice announcements are made in areas where there are induction loops. However, this is a large and quite complex airport. All 3 terminals have their own car parks. It is not necessary to pre-book parking.

Special vehicles are available to transfer passengers who are unable to walk between the terminal and the aircraft; contact the terminal manager.

Newcastle International Airport

Woolsington, Newcastle upon Tyne, NE13 8BZ
t 0871 882 1121 textphone 0191 214 3333
e enquiries@newcastleinternational.co.uk
web www.newcastleinternational.co.uk

By Road - Newcastle International is off the A1 north of Newcastle city centre. It acts as a regional airport with flights to almost 100 destinations by scheduled and chartered operators. An area to set down and pick up passengers is located at the front of the short-stay car park. There are designated parking bays for disabled people in both short and long-stay car parks with assistance points nearby. The shuttle bus to and from the long-stay car park can carry passengers in wheelchairs.

By Public Transport - The Tyne & Wear Metro system, which provides accessible connections to rail services at Newcastle Central Station, has a station at the airport terminal. There are also a number of local bus services. Airport Taxis is the only company that can use the taxi rank at the airport entrance. They have wheelchair accessible vehicles and operate both locally and for longer distances. Contact Airport Taxis **0191 214 6969** or see **www.airport-taxis.co.uk**

Accessiblity - The entrance to the terminals has large revolving doors that can be slowed down for disabled people. The Information Desk has a lowered counter. There are lifts between the ground floor to the 1st floor departure lounge, security area and departure gates. Toilets for disabled people are on both levels.

For passengers who use or require a wheelchair, assistance will be provided by the airport's airside operations or community service teams and will be taken through security and on to the aircraft and on their return to Newcastle. There is no charge for use of wheelchairs or cabin lifts for boarding, but it should be noted that the latter have no space for more than one person accompanying a disabled person. For information about services for disabled passengers at the airport call **0191 214 3305.**

Norwich International Airport

Amsterdam Way, Norwich NR6 6JA
t 01603 420672 web www.norwichairport.co.uk

By Road - The airport is to the north of Norwich off the A140 and handles domestic and international flights, both scheduled and chartered.

Parking - Both long and short-stay car parks are close to the terminal and there are designated bays for disabled people opposite the entrance. For information contact **NCP** on **0845 050 7080**.

By Public Transport - Rail passengers should use local buses or taxis from Norwich Station. There is a taxi rank at the airport and information can be obtained from **Norwich Airport Taxis** on **01603 424 044**.

Accessiblity - The terminal building is single storey and has toilets for disabled people in the main concourse and the departure lounge. Assistance can be provided and advance notice is requested.

Robin Hood Airport Doncaster Sheffield

Heyford House, First Avenue, Doncaster DN9 3RH
t 0844 481 7777 web www.robinhoodairport.com

By Road - Robin Hood Airport Doncaster Sheffield is the UK's newest airport having opened in 2005. The airport currently offers both scheduled and holiday flights to over 35 worldwide destinations.

Parking - Robin Hood Airport is located just 7 miles from Doncaster and 25 miles from Sheffield and offers excellent access by road, rail and bus. The airport is located within 20 minutes of 5 major motorway networks including the A1(M), M1, M18, M62 and M180. Disabled passengers can park just yards from the terminal building in designated spaces for Blue Badge holders at the front of the main passenger car park.

By Public Transport - There is a dedicated bus service, the Airlink Service 91, between the Doncaster Transport Interchange and the airport that uses accessible buses; for further information call **01709 56600**. Through ticketing is available from any National Express East Coast rail station. For information and booking taxis call **01302 625555**.

Accessiblity - The terminal is mainly on the ground floor with a lift to the 1st floor catering and retail areas. The reception desk has an induction loop and there are toilets for disabled people in all areas. Wheelchairs are available. For assistance call **01302 625099.**

Southampton Airport

Southampton, SO18 2NL
t 0844 481 7777 textphone 023 8062 7032
web www.southamptonairport.com

By Road - Southampton Airport offers flights by 14 airlines to 40 destinations. The Airport is north of Southampton near Eastleigh and the M3/M27 interchange.

Parking - There are designated spaces for Blue Badge holders in the main short-stay car park and disabled people wishing to take their badge with then should notify the car parks customer services office on the ground floor. Help Points are available for assistance with transferring luggage to the terminal or, if the ticket payment slot is out of reach, in the short-stay car park and also by the bus stop in the long-stay car park.

By Public Transport - Southampton Airport Parkway Station is immediately outside the airport and is also equipped with a Help Point for passengers needing assistance. There are frequent services to Southampton Central and London Waterloo stations and other on services operated by South West Trains. However, there is a footbridge to the northbound platform, for services towards London. Assistance with an alternative route may be provided. The U1C bus service, which can carry passengers in wheelchairs, runs 4 times an hour from the airport, via the University, to central Southampton, including the main railway station and the Red Funnel ferry terminals for the Isle of Wight. This service is operated by Uni-Link **023 8059 5974**.

Accessiblity - The terminal is mainly single storey, with a lift to the upper floor departure lounge. Assistance can be requested at the information desk.

There are toilets for disabled people in the main concourse and the departure lounge. Reserved seating areas for disabled passengers have been provided. Induction loops are fitted in these areas and elsewhere in the terminal. Text payphones are available in the main concourse and the departure lounge.

Assistance for disabled passengers through the airport, including to and from car parks, and on and off the aircraft is provided by Aviance. It is requested that any assistance is requested at least 48 hours before flying, and preferably as far in advance as possible. Therefore in addition to contacting the airline of your requirements, it is suggested that you separately contact Aviance on **023 8062 7391**.

Southend Airport

Southend-on-Sea SS2 6YF
t 01702 608100
e enquiries@southendairport.com
web www.southendairport.com

By Road - London Southend Airport is located just north of Southend. At present it is used for scheduled services to Jersey and also some chartered flights.

Accessiblity - It has a single-storey terminal and assistance is provided for disabled passengers by **Southend Handling 01702 608 150**.

A major development for a new terminal and more extensive services is planned. There are plans for a new railway station on the line between Southend and London Liverpool Street check website for details. At present the nearest rail station is Rochford, a short taxi ride away. Flybe runs a weekly service to Jersey.

Fear of flying

A number of organisations run courses for people who are scared of flying. These include:

Aviatours Ltd

Eglinton Road, Rushmoor, Farnham GU10 2DH
t 01252 793250 e fearofflying@aviatours.co.uk
web www.aviatours.co.uk

Virgin Atlantic Flying without Fear

PO Box 289, Betchworth RH3 7WX
t 01423 714900 e info@flyingwithoutfear.info
web www.flyingwithoutfear.info

Virtual Aviation

Sheraton House, Castle Park, Cambridge CB3 0AX
t 01223 890214 e info@virtualaviation.co.uk
web www.virtualaviation.co.uk

Road travel

Motoring

For many disabled people, motoring is the major means of independent mobility. General motoring organisations provide particular services for their disabled members and provide advice/assistance with route planning and insurance.

The Highways Agency is responsible for the motorways and major trunk roads in England and has duties in relation to construction and maintenance as well as safety and traffic management. Regional leaflets outlining planned road works, regional events likely to cause congestion and other news/advice are published quarterly.
Contact the Information Line t **08700 660 115 or** textphone **0102 335 8300** web **www.highways.gov.uk**

Information on main roads elsewhere in the UK is available from:
Trafficwatch N. Ireland t **0845 712 3321** web **www.trafficwatchni.com**
Traffic Scotland t **0800 028 1414** web **www.trafficscotland.org**
Traffic Wales t **0845 602 6020** web **www.traffic-wales.com**

Taxis

Information on companies and independent drivers with accessible vehicles should be available from local authorities. Two national websites with information on taxi companies with accessible vehicles are web **www.transportdirect.info** and web **www.traintaxi.co.uk**

Top tip

- The 100% London Congestion Charge discount applies to the person who is the Blue Badge holder and not the vehicle that is being used.

Visit our website at:

Road travel in London

Two particular factors affect disabled people using cars in central London:

On street parking - the Blue Badge Scheme does not apply in the City of London, Kensington & Chelsea, Westminster and the southern part of Camden. There are a limited number of marked parking spaces for Blue Badge holders and the badge may also be recognised for reserved bays in car parks. The location of Blue Badge spaces, car parks and other useful information is shown in "Blue Badge Parking Guide" price £4.99 from bookshops or the publishers. **t 0844 847 0875 web www.thepieguide.com**

An interactive map showing parking bays for Blue Badge holders in over 100 towns and cities and spaces on Red Routes in London as well as parking rules for all councils in the UK is at **www.direct.gov.uk/bluebadgemap**

Congestion Charge – disabled people's cars that are exempt from Vehicle Excise Duty are also exempt from the Central London Congestion Charge. Blue Badge holders can register for 100% discount from the charge. Registration takes 10 days to be administered and costs £10. The initial registration lasts for a year but can be renewed for free. It is possible to register both for long-term vehicles or those used on a short-term basis such as hire cars. **t 0845 900 1234 web www.cclondon.com**

London taxis

In London, which has a different system to the rest of the country, all licensed taxis must be able to carry a passenger in a standard wheelchair. All of the 'London black cabs' manufactured since 1989 must have space to carry a passenger in a manual wheelchair and carry or be equipped with a ramp. Computer Cab plc operates a booking service for taxis in the London area using wheelchair accessible black cabs. Their drivers have the necessary licence and experience with disabled people through their provision of services to disabled London Taxicard Users. Contact Computer Cab **t 020 7908 0207** (cash bookings – there is a £2 booking fee); customer services **t 020 7908 0271 e customerservices@comcab.co.uk; web www.comcab.co.uk**; for information about international airport transport services go to **www.cabchargeinternational.com**

Car hire

For some journeys it may be appropriate to hire a car or other vehicle that has been adapted for a disable driver or that can carry a passenger in a wheelchair. There are organisations that include both major car hire companies with outlets throughout the country and elsewhere including ports, airports, major railway stations and also more specialist organisations.

See page 342 for listings.

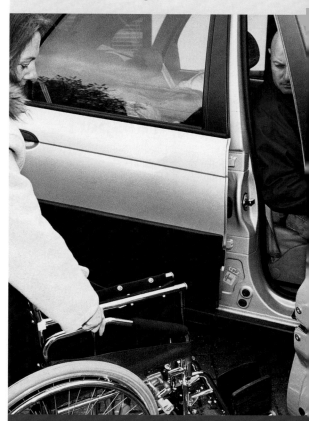

Driving abroad

Advice is available from motoring organisations and at **www.fco.gov.uk**

The Blue Badge is recognised throughout most of Europe, giving British Blue Badge holders the same parking arrangements as local disabled people. However, the concessions vary from country to country. For more information contact the **Institute of Advanced Motorists, IAM House, 510 Chiswick High Road, London W4 5RG, www.iam.org.uk 020 8996 9600.**

Door-to-door and community transport

Special transport schemes exist in some localities for disabled people who are not able to use public transport. The principle is that a disabled person can phone to book an adapted vehicle to carry them on a specific door-to-door journey. More general Community Transport schemes exist where no other public transport is available, often but not exclusively in rural areas. Generally, community transport schemes use vehicles adapted to carry disabled people. The demand for such a service is always likely to exceed the resources available, so a variety of restrictions are likely to be in place – people may be limited to a number of journeys in any given period of time, journeys may be limited to a particular administrative area, for example. Essentially, all special transport schemes are locally run with their own priorities.

Park and ride

These schemes usually provide secure parking areas on the approaches to towns with transport into the town centres, thereby avoiding some parking problems and reducing congestion. In many instances the transport provided is by accessible buses or other vehicles, for example trams. Information on Park and Ride schemes can be obtained from the appropriate local authorities; **web www.parkandride.net** and **www.transportdirect.info**

Coaches

Costs are generally lower than alternative means of transport. Coach stops in towns are often close to local transport services and are usually adjacent to passenger terminals at ports and airports. Drivers can provide some assistance and information when getting on and off, however finding information can be difficult.

Coaches are in general inaccessible for disabled people, particularly for wheelchair users and others with impaired mobility, due to the shallow steps and steep narrow entrances. A few operators have pioneered more accessible services, and from 2006 all new vehicles used for scheduled services have to be capable of carrying disabled passengers.

The situation will improve, but it will be some time before all the existing vehicles have been replaced and staff trained. Coaches, available for private hire or used on holidays, are not covered even by the accessibility regulations for those on scheduled services. However, some coach companies do have adapted vehicles. **See page 345 for listings.**

Bus services

Regulations have come into effect ensuring that all new buses are equipped with lifts or ramps with a level floor space to carry a passenger in a wheelchair, and incorporate features such as colour contrasted handrails, easy to operate bell-pushes etc. In London all general bus routes have been served with accessible buses since 2006, but elsewhere older vehicles may continue to be in use for years.

In some areas travel training is available to disabled people who may need assistance and encouragement to use accessible buses and other forms of public transport, for example the GMPTE in Greater Manchester **web www.gmpte.com** has a travel Training Guide that can be downloaded. 'Coolmove' is a network of people involved with independent travel training **e info@coolmove.org.uk web www.coolmove.org.uk**

Motoring organisations

AA

Norfolk House, Priestly Road, Basingstoke RG24 9NY
t 0870 5500 600 textphone 0870 243 2456
web www.theaa.com

Disabled Motorists' Federation

c/o 145 Knoulberry Road, Blackfell,
Washington NE37 1JN
t 0191 416 3172 e jkillick2214@yahoo.co.uk
web www.disabledmotoristsfederation.org.uk

A grouping of local organisations of disabled motorists.

Green Flag Assistance

3 Eldridge Road, Croydon, Surrey CR9 TAG
t 0845 246 1557 web www.greenflag.com

Motability

City Gate House, 22 Southwark Bridge Rd,
London SE1 9HB
t 0845 456 4566 textphone 01279 632213
web www.motability.co.uk

RAC Motoring Services

Great Park Road, Bradley Stoke, Bristol BS32 4QN
t 0870 572 2722 e info@citylink.co.uk
web www.rac.co.uk

The Mobilise Organisation

Ashwellthorpe, Norfolk NR16 1EX
t 01508 489449 e enquiries@mobilise.info
web www.mobilise.info

Mobilise, formed from a merger of the Disabled Drivers'
Association and the Disabled Drivers Motor Club, can
advise their members on a wide range of matters including
concessions on ferries and tolls.

Car hire

Adapted Vehicle Hire Ltd

Poplar House, Cowley Business Park, Cowley Road,
Uxbridge UB8 2AD
t 0845 257 1670 e admin@avhldt.com
web www.avhltd.com

This company has a variety of vehicles for hire including
those with adaptations and fittings for disabled drivers and
that are accessible to wheelchair users.

Atlas Vehicle Conversions Ltd

3 Aysgarth Road, Waterlooville, Hampshire PO7 7UG
t 023 9226 5600 web www.avcltd.co.uk

In addition to selling adapted cars, Atlas has a number of
accessible vehicles for hire including the Renault Kangoo,
which can carry one passenger in a wheelchair and a minibus
with removable seats that can carry up to two wheelchair
users. Daily, weekly and monthly terms are available with
special rates for weekends. Drivers must be over 25.

Autobility

Unit 2, Newburgh Ind. Estate, Cupar Rd, Newburgh,
Fife KY14 6HA
t 0800 298 9290 web www.autobility.co.uk

Autobility has cars and vans that can carry people in
wheelchairs for hire on weekend, weekly and monthly
rates. From its base in Scotland, this family-run company
can arrange delivery throughout Britain and deliver vehicles
to airports and rail stations. Used wheelchair accessible
vehicles are available for sale.

Avis

Avis House, Park Rd, Bracknell, Berkshire RG12 2EN
t 0844 581 0147 web www.avis.co.uk

Avis can fit Lynx hand controls to any automatic cars in
its fleet. These controls are designed for people with good
upper body function and hand dexterity. This service is
available at all its UK rental locations with 48 hours notice.

Brotherwood Automobility

Lambert House, Pillar Box Lane, Beer Hackett,
Sherborne, Dorset DT9 6QP
t 01935 872603 **e** sales@brotherwood.com
web www.brotherwood.com

Brotherwood has long experience of converting cars for
wheelchair users and have a range of cars available for long
or short term hire from it's premises in North Dorset.

Budget Rent-a-Car

Park Road, Bracknell RG12 2BW
t 0844 544 3407 **e** info@quotezone.co.uk
web www.budget.co.uk

Budget has Lynx hand controls that can be fitted to most
automatic cars in its hire fleet. These are available with 48
hours notice from all their rental locations with advice and
test drives available if required.

Hertz Rent-a-Car

700 Bath Rd, Cranford, Middlesex TW5 9SW
t 0870 844 8844 (Reservations)
web www.hertz.co.uk

Hertz can fit hand controls to cars from all its locations in
the UK, most of those in North America and the main entry
points in Western Europe for any length of hire and also for
periods of 5 days or more in a number of other European
countries. Advanced reservation of 48 hours for this service
is required in Britain and 72 hours elsewhere.

Healthcare Travel Ltd

44 Weir Road, London SW19 8UG
t 0845 3720 999

Offers a variety of vehicles for hire including wheelchair
accessible vans and minibuses and drivers with wide
experience of disability. These are available for outings
and transfers to and from stations and airports in the
London area.

Pyehire

Ovangle Road, Morcambe LA3 3PF
t 01524 598598 **web** www.pyemotors.co.uk

Pyehire has a range of self-drive accessible vehicles that can
carry between 1 and 4 passengers in wheelchairs and 2-8
other people. These are available on daily or weekly hire.

Thorntrees Garage

Wigan Road, Leyland, Lancashire PR25 5SB
t 01772 622688 **e** vicki@thorntreesgarage.co.uk
web www.thorntreesgarage.co.uk

Cars and vans that can carry passengers in wheelchairs
are available for hire for between 1 day and 6 months.
Thorntrees Garage is near M6 J28 and the M61 and M65
or customers can be picked up from Preston mainline rail
station from where there are direct services from many
parts of the country including Manchester Airport.

Morton Park Automobility

Unit H4, Morton Park, Darlington DL1 4PH
t 01325 389900
e info@wheelchairaccessibles.co.uk
web www.wheelchairaccessibles.co.uk

This company has for hire a range of self-drive adapted
vans that can carry wheelchair users. Delivery or collection
from Darlington Station can be arranged at additional cost.

Wheelchair Travel

1 Johnston Green, Guildford GU2 9XS
t 01483 233640 **e** info@wheelchair-travel.co.uk
web www.wheelchairtravel.co.uk

Wheelchair Travel is a well-established self-drive rental
company with wheelchair accessible cars and minibuses
available for any period of domestic and continental use by
both UK and non-UK licence holders. Minibuses have lifts,
wheelchair securing points and seatbelts. Fiat Doblo cars
can carry a wheelchair user, driver and 2 passengers. Cars
with fixed hand controls are also available. Vehicles can be
delivered to home, hotel or airport. A wheelchair taxi service
using luxury adapted minibuses is also offered.

Coach travel

National Express

Customer relations, National Express, PO BOX 9854, Birmingham B16 8XN
t 0871 781 8178 (bookings) or t 0871 781 8179 (disabled persons travel helpline)
textphone 0121 455 0086
web www.nationalexpress.com

National Express operates Britain's largest network of long distance coach services serving around 1000 destinations including city centres, small towns, airports and major ferry terminals. Folding wheelchairs can be carried and drivers can give some assistance on all services. Information on facilities for disabled people at National Express Coach Stations is available from the Helpline, on the website and in a booklet, "Serving our disabled customers". They are also the UK partner of Eurolines with services through Ireland and Continental Europe. National Express is introducing coaches equipped with a lift at the main entrance door and space for a passenger in a wheelchair. These also have less steep steps than previous models, no internal steps and a larger, though not wheelchair accessible toilet. These new vehicles

are being rolled out across their network with the intention that they will become the norm by 2012.

At present accessible coaches are used for all or most services on the following routes:

240	Leeds-Sheffield-Coventry-Heathrow-Gatwick
314	Liverpool-Stoke-Birmingham-Coventry-Northampton-Bedford-Cambridge
333	Blackpool-Bolton-Manchester-Stoke-Bristol-Yeovil-Weymouth-Poole-Bournemouth
341	Burnley-Blackburn-Bolton-Manchester-Birmingham-Weston-Exeter-Torquay
403	Bath-Swindon-Chippenham-Heathrow-London
538	The Midlands-Manchester Airport-Manchester-Preston-Carlisle-Scotland
560	Barnsley-Sheffield-London
562	Hull-Doncaster-London
591	Edinburgh-Newcastle-London
737	Oxford-High Wycombe-Luton Airport-Stansted

© National Express

Goldline Translink

t 028 9066 6630 e feedback@translink.co.uk
textphone 028 9038 7505 web www.translink.co.uk

Megabus

Customer Services, Megabus.com, Buchanan Bus
Station, Killermont St, Glasgow G2 3NW
t 0900 160 0900
web www.megabus.com

Megabus has a growing network of inter-city services using
double deck buses, most of which radiate from London to
around 40 cities. If you are a wheelchair/scooter user and
are able to climb a few steps into the bus, your wheelchair
or scooter can be stored in the luggage bay and assistance
is offered to ensure you are seated safely. However, if you
need to remain in your wheelchair for the duration of the
journey contact Megabus directly, at least 48 hours before,
on 0141 322 9841 to discuss your requirements as buses
with wheelchair lifts or ramps may be available.

Oxford Tube

Customer Services, Freepost SCE 15567,
Oxford OX4 2RY
t 01865 772250
web www.oxfordtube.com

Oxford Tube has services at frequent intervals through
the day, and at least hourly overnight, between Victoria
in London and Gloucester Green in Oxford with additional
stops in each city, one of which is at Thornhill Park & Ride
on the outskirts of Oxford. All of their 25 vehicles can carry
one passenger in a wheelchair and have easy access to
the lower deck. Guide dogs are carried free of charge.
Drivers can usually assist with luggage.

Scottish Citylink Coaches Ltd

Buchanan Bus Station, Killermont Street,
Glasgow G2 3NW
t 0871 266 33 33 e info@citylink.co.uk
web www.citylink.co.uk

Citylink is the largest network of inter-city coaches in
Scotland serving some 200 destinations. Wheelchair
accessible vehicles are in use on its regular service

between Edinburgh and Glasgow. Scottish holders of the
Entitlement Card for disabled and elderly people can travel
free on Citylink services within Scotland.

Victoria Coach Station

164 Buckingham Palace Road, London SW1W 9TP
web www.tfl.gov.uk

Passengers with impaired mobility can pre-book assistance
from the Mobility Lounge. t 020 7027 2520 for assistance on
and off the coaches. This service is free, although if you require
a porter for luggage, a payment may be expected. Customers
can arrange to be set down or picked up by taxi, minicab or
private car at the Mobility Lounge. There are toilets for disabled
people in the Mobility Lounge and in Arrivals and Departures.

Coach hire

Belle Vue (Manchester) Ltd

The Travel Centre, Discovery Park, Crossley Road
Stockport SK4 5DZ
t 0161 947 9477 t 07747 602 852 (emergency)
web www.bellevue-mcr.com

Britannia Coaches

Britannia House, Hollow Wood Road, Dover CT17 0UB
t 01304 228111 t 07968 570727 (emergency)
web www.britannia-coaches.co.uk

Bugler Coaches

29 Victoria Buildings, Lower Bristol Road,
Bath BA2 3EH
t 01225 444 422 e info@buglercoaches.co.uk
web www.buglercoaches.co.uk

Caldew Coaches

6 Caldew Drive, Dalston, Carlisle CA5 7NS
t 01228 711690/710963
e caldewcoachesltd@aol.com
web www.caldewcoaches.co.uk

Chalfont Line

Chalfont House, 4 Providence Road, West Drayton
Middlesex UB7 8HJ
t 01895 459540 web www.chalfont-line.co.uk

Community Transport Association UK

Highbank, Halton Street, Hyde, Cheshire SK14 2NY
t 0161 351 1475 e info@ctauk.org
web www.ctauk.org

CTA UK gives advice and support on establishing and
improving community transport schemes and provides
training. Transport schemes for elderly and disabled
people, including escorting people on public transport and
providing volunteer drivers, are provided by a number of
community organisations including British Red Cross and
WRVS.

Coopers Tours

114 Bridge Street, Killamarsh, Sheffield S21 1AH
t 0114 248 2859 e specialtravel@cooperstours.co.uk
web www.cooperstours.co.uk

Copelands Tours

1005 Uttoxeter Road, Meir, Stoke on Trent ST3 6HE
t 01782 334466 e enquiry@copelandstours.co.uk
web www.copelandstours.co.uk

Cruisers Ltd

Unit M, Kingsfield Business Centre, Redhill,
Surrey RH1 4DP
t 01737 770036 web www.cruisersltd.co.uk

Golden Stand Coaches (Southern)

13 Waxlow Road, London NW10 7NY
t 020 8961 9974 e info@goldenstand.co.uk
web www.goldenstand.co.uk

H C Chambers & Son

Chambers Bus Garage, High Street, Bures,
Suffolk CO8 5AB
t 01787 227233
web www.chamberscoaches.co.uk

Hatts Travel

Foxham, Chippenham, Wiltshire SN15 4NB
t 01249 740444
e info@hattstravel.co.uk
web www.hattstravel.co.uk

Holmeswood Coaches

Sandy Way, Holmeswood, Nr Ormskirk L40 IUB
t 01704 821245
web www.holmeswood.uk.com

© National Express

© Stagecoach Group

London Hire

14 Dock Offices, Surrey Quays, Lower Road,
London SE16 2XU
t 0845 257 4257
e lauras@londonhireltd.com
web www.londonhireltd.com

MCT Group Travel

Nethan Street Depot, Nethan Street,
Motherwell ML1 3TF
t 01698 253091
e enquiries@mctgrouptravel.com
web www.mctgrouptravel.com

Meridien Line Travel

Unit 2, Wireless Station Park, Chestnut Lane
Bassingbourne, Royston, Herts SG8 5JH
t 01763 241999
e meridianline@dial.pipex.com
web www.mltravel.co.uk

Reliance Travel

Unit 8, Norfolk Road, Gravesend, Kent DA12 2PS
t 01474 322002 e info@reliance-travel.co.uk
web www.reliance-travel.co.uk

Star Coaches of Batley

t 01924 477111 web www.star-coaches.com

Star Coaches of Batley, private coach hire service in West
Yorkshire, covers a wide area through all the major towns
and cities in Yorkshire and beyond.

Tellings Golden Miller

Building 16300 MTZ, Electra Avenue
London Heathrow Airport, Hounslow TW6 2DN
t 020 8757 4700
e info@tellings.co.uk
web www.tellingsgoldenmiller.co.uk

Translinc

Jarvis House, 157 Sadler Road, Lincoln LN6 3RS
t 01522 503400
e enquiries@translinc.co.uk
web www.translinc.co.uk

Travel De Courcey

Rowley Drive, Coventry CV3 4FG
t 024 7630 2656
web www.traveldecourcey.com

Rail travel

The Trains

All newly-built trains that have come into service since 1998 must incorporate access features, including spaces for passengers travelling in manual wheelchairs, visible and audible information and appropriate toilet facilities. Many trains introduced before 1998 have some of these features, either inherently or following refurbishment. Some pre-1998 carriages will be used for the next 10 years or so.

The Stations

These often date from the Victorian era and represent the range of disability access levels. The process of adapting premises is lengthy and has concentrated on larger stations and those that were being modernised in any event. Many smaller stations rely on the approach to platforms by steps; however, an Access for All programme funded by the Department of Transport is underway and is due to provide step-free routes and other access improvements for more than 200 stations.

Mind the Gap!

A remaining potential problem is the gap or step that exists between the train and the platform. There are portable ramps at stations and on trains, although staff need to be available to place and remove the ramp as well as providing assistance when required. In spite of continuing improvements, the railway system still has problem areas and many disabled passengers will need help at some points of their journey.

Top tips

- Book assistance: recommended 24 hours in advance. This allows the stations involved time to allocate appropriately trained staff and for them to check their equipment.

- Taxi assistance: TrainTaxi is a database providing information on the availability of taxis at rail, underground and tramsystems - **www.traintaxi.co.uk**

Disabled person's railcard

Some disabled people can get the Disabled Person's Railcard, which gives a third-off most rail fares for the cardholder and an adult companion. The qualifying criteria are:

- registered as visually impaired
- registered deaf
- have epilepsy, and are disabled by repeated attacks
- receipt of Attendance Allowance
- receipt of Disability Living Allowance (at either rate of the mobility component or the higher or middle level of the care component)
- receipt of Severe Disablement Allowance
- receipt of war or Service Disablement Pension for 80% or more disability
- buying or leasing a vehicle through Motability.

For further information on the railcard go to web www.disabledpersons-railcard.co.uk or t 0845 605 0525, textphone 0845 601 0132.

Underground railways

There are two long-established underground systems – London and Glasgow.

London – an increasing number of stations have step-free access to platforms and 25% of stations now have step-free access. Contact **web www.tfl.gov.uk** or for detailed information on each station go to **web www.directenquiries.com**

Glasgow – staff can assist disabled passengers who can manage the steps to the platforms. For information on each station for blind and partially sighted people go to **web www.describe-online.com** or **t 0845 128 4025** or **web www.spt.co.uk**, **t 0141 332 6811**; **e enquiry@spt.co.uk**

Wheelchairs and powered scooters

Most trains can accommodate wheelchairs that are up to 700mm wide and 1200mm long and that have a combined weight for the wheelchair and passenger of up to the safe working load of the portable ramp (between 230kg and 300kg).

However, scooters are of a far wider variety of sizes and weights. There can be problems caused by exceeding the safe load or tipping backwards on the ramp and being unable to manoeuvre safely inside the train. While many train companies accept scooters that are within the dimensions given above, there are some that only carry folded scooters or require the users to obtain a special pass. There have been some examples of rigidly restrictive rules being relaxed over the last year or so. However, at present anyone thinking of making a rail journey with a scooter should check on the policy of the train operator(s) involved.

Accessibility rail maps

National Rail has produced maps showing accessibility around Britain's rail network. For links and other information go to **www.openbritain.net/openbritain/travel/**

General rail enquiries

National Rail Enquiries

t 0845 748 49 50
textphone 0845 605 0600
web www.nationalrail.co.uk

National Rail Enquiries provides up-to-date information on train timetables, disruptions to services and also has information on the accessibility of individual stations.

Network Rail

Kings Place, 90 York Way, London N1 9AG
t 020 7557 8000
textphone 18001 0845 711 4141
web www.networkrail.co.uk

Network Rail owns and operates the track, signals and other infrastructure of Britain's rail network. Although this includes the stations, most of these are managed by individual train operating companies. However, Network Rail does directly run 17 major stations including 10 London terminals, Birmingham New Street, Edinburgh Waverley, Gatwick, Glasgow Central, Leeds, Liverpool Lime Street and Manchester Piccadilly.

Passenger Focus

Freepost (RRRE-ETTC-LEET) PO BOX 4257, Manchester M60 3AR
t 0300 123 2350
e info@passengerfocus.org.uk
web www.passengerfocus.org.uk

Passenger Focus is the independent body established by Government to represent the interests of rail passengers. They can take up complaints when no satisfactory response has been obtained from the relevant train operating company or other service provider, perhaps if assistance that had been booked was not provided.

They can also advise on making complaints and welcome hearing of people's experiences even when they are not formally representing them.

Train operators

Arriva Trains Wales

St Mary's House, 47 Penarth Road,
Cardiff CF10 5DJ
t 0845 300 3005 textphone 0845 605 0600
web www.arrivatrainswales.co.uk

Arriva Trains Wales operates rail services in Wales and the border counties, including services to Cardiff Airport and ferry ports at Holyhead, Fishguard and Pembroke Dock. A regularly up-dated booklet, 'Guide for Customers with Disabilities', gives information on services and accessibility of the stations. It is available from staffed stations in Wales, the above address or can be downloaded from the website.

C2C

Freepost ADM3968, Southend SS1 1ZS
t 01702 357640 textphone 0845 606 7245
web www.c2c-online.co.uk

C2C operates services between London and Southend through East London and South Essex.

Chiltern Railways

Banbury ICC, Merton Street, Banbury, Oxon OX16 4RN
t 0845 6005 165 textphone 0845 7078 051
web www.chilternrailways.co.uk

Chiltern runs trains from London to Aylesbury and through Banbury to Birmingham, Kidderminster and Stratford-upon-Avon.

CrossCountry

t 0844 811 0125 textphone 0844 811 0126
web www.crosscountrytrains.co.uk

CrossCountry has a network of long distance routes, from Aberdeen to Penzance, all of which use Birmingham New Street Station as a terminus or for connections. Airports that are directly served by CrossCountry trains include Birmingham, Gatwick, Southampton and Stansted.

East Midland trains

t 0845 712 5678 textphone 18001 08457 125 678
e getintouch@eastmidlandtrains.co.uk
web www.eastmidlandstrains.co.uk

East Midlands has mainline services between
St Pancras International in London and Sheffield,
Nottingham, Derby and Leicester and also local services
around the eastern Midlands with extensions into
East Anglia and the North West. At St Pancras there
are connections with Eurostar services. Luton and
East Midlands Airports can be reached from East Midlands
services, with transfers to the latter improved with the
opening of East Midlands Parkway Station.

Eurostar

Eurostar House, Waterloo Station, London SE1 8SE
t 08432 186 186 web www.eurostar.com

Eurostar train services currently run through the Channel
Tunnel from London St Pancras International to Brussels
and Paris. This provides straightforward connections for
passengers from services to St Pancras and also into the
adjacent King's Cross Station. It is also close to Euston Station
for passengers from the North West and West Midlands.

Some services stop at Ebbsfleet International, off M25
J2, at Ashford International in Kent, where there are
connections to many stations in southeast England, and
Lille where connections can be made to high speed
rail services for many cities across France. There are
also simple connections at Brussels to destinations in
the rest of Belgium, Germany and the Netherlands. The
Paris terminal of Eurostar is quite close to Gare d'Est for
accessible high-speed rail services to Eastern France
and parts of Germany and Switzerland. Eurostar operates
some direct services to Disneyland Paris all year, to ski
resorts in the French Alps in the winter and to Avignon in
the south of France in the summer.

There are spaces for passengers in a wheelchair on
each Eurostar train. These are available at the lowest
available standard class fare for the wheelchair user and a
companion. These spaces should be booked in advance on
08432 186 186.

All Eurostar stations are accessible. Assistance can be
provided on request at check-in although anyone who
may need help is asked to arrive as early as possible.
Assistance dogs covered by the "Passports for Pets"
scheme can be carried.

First Capital Connect

Customer Relations, Freepost ADM 3973,
London SW1Y 1YP
t 0845 026 4700 textphone 0800 515 152
web www.firstcapitalconnect.co.uk

Operates rail services through central London from
Brighton and south-west London to Bedford, serving
both Gatwick and Luton Airports and the Eurostar
Terminal at St Pancras International and also from
London King's Cross and Moorgate to Cambridge
through Hertfordshire.

First Great Western

Customer relations, Freepost (RRBR-REEJ-KTKY)
PO BOX 443, Plymouth PL4 6WP
t 0800 197 1329 e fgw@custhelp.com
textphone 18001 0800 197 1329
web www.firstgreatwestern.com

Operates InterCity services between London Paddington and
the West of England and South Wales and also regional and
local services through the west country, the Thames Valley
and the Cotswolds. It also has a service to Gatwick Airport
from Reading. Heathrow airport can be reached on the
Heathrow Connect service from stations in west London
and by a coach link service from Reading. The Night Riviera
service operates overnight between Paddington and
Penzance. Significant improvements to the disabled facilities
are in progress for First Great Western high speed trains.

© ATOC

Scotrail

PO Box 7030, Fort William PH33 6WX
t 0800 912 2901 textphone 0800 912 2899
web www.scotrail.co.uk

Operates both long distance and local rail services in Scotland. Tickets to include bus transfers are available for Aberdeen, Edinburgh and Glasgow Airports, while Prestwick International Airport has its own rail station. Inclusive rail and ferry fares are available to and from Scottish stations for Stena services between Stranraer and Belfast and for many of the Caledonian MacBrayne services to the islands off the west coast. First Scotrail also operates the Caledonian Sleepers between London Euston and Aberdeen, Edinburgh, Fort William, Glasgow and Inverness and a number of intermediate stations. These incorporate a berth that can be used by a wheelchair user.

First Transpennine Express

Customer Relations, Admail 3876, Freepost Manchester M1 9YB
t 0800 107 2149 (Assisted Travel)
textphone 0800 107 2061 web www.tpexpress.co.uk

Transpennine Express has regional services from Manchester and Liverpool to Yorkshire, Humberside, the North East and southern Cumbria. Many of their routes are direct to and from Manchester Airport. Through tickets are also available to a number of other airports on their network including Leeds/Bradford from Leeds, Liverpool John Lennon from Liverpool Lime Street, Robin Hood from Doncaster and Durham Tees Valley from Darlington. Barnetby, on the hourly service to Cleethorpes is the nearest station to Humberside.

Gatwick Express

52 Grosvenor Gardens, London SW1W 0AV
t 0845 850 1530 web www.gatwickexpress.com

Services run non-stop between Gatwick Airport and London Victoria Station every 15 minutes during the day. As there are staff on both the trains and the platforms, assistance can usually be provided even without advanced notice. All trains have spaces for passengers in wheelchairs.

Grand Central Railway

River House, 17 Museum Street, York YO1 7DJ
t 0845 603 4852 (Customer Services)
e info@grandcentralrail.com
web www.grandcentralrail.com

Grand Central operates direct services between London King's Cross and Sunderland, Hartlepool and North Yorkshire. A service also runs between London and West Yorkshire.

Heathrow Express

Customer Services, Freepost RLXYETJG-XKZS, London W2 6LG
t 0845 600 1515 web www.heathrowexpress.com

The Heathrow Express runs non-stop at frequent intervals between London Paddington and Heathrow. Each of their trains has two spaces for wheelchair users in Express (or standard) Class, by an accessible toilet, and one on First Class. Railcard holders can obtain discounted fares at Heathrow Express ticket offices, or for holders of the Disabled Persons Railcard on the train. The trolley barriers at the Heathrow platforms can be raised by Customer Service Assistants to give access to wheelchair users. A free service for disabled people needing assistance or help with luggage between the Heathrow platforms and airport check-in is available and can be pre-booked by calling Skycaps **020 8745 6011/5727**.

© www.freeimages.co.uk

Hull Trains

4th Floor, Europa House, Ferensway, Hull HU1 3UF
t 0845 071 0222 textphone 0845 678 6967
e customer.services@hulltrains.co.uk
web www.hulltrains.co.uk

Hull Trains operates inter-city services between Hull and London King's Cross. There is a bus link between Hull Station and Ferry Terminal. The company won the Enhanced Accessibility Rail Award at RADAR's 2006 People of the Year Awards following a poll among disabled railcard holders

Island Line

Ryde St Johns Road Station, Ryde,
Isle of Wight PO33 2BA
t 0845 6000 650 (opt 4) textphone 0800 692 0792
web www.island-line.com

Island Line operates rail services between Ryde and Shanklin on the Isle of Wight. Passengers from Wightlink Catamaran services can connect with services at Ryde Pier Head and those from Hovertravel at Ryde Esplanade where there is a new transport interchange. Disabled people needing assistance for journeys entirely on Island Rail call **01983 562492**; for those on journeys from the mainland call **0800 528 2100**. **Textphone: 0800 692 0792.**

London Midland

t 0800 092 4260 textphone 0844 811 0134
web www.londonmidland.com

London Midland operates services between London Euston and Birmingham, via Northampton and also local services around the western Midlands and to the North West. Among the airports served are Birmingham and Liverpool.

London Overground

t 0843 222 1234 textphone 020 7918 3015
web www.tfl.gov.uk

London Overground, part of Transport for London, runs train services between London Euston and Watford Junction, Richmond and Stratford, Gospel Oak and Barking and Willesden Junction and Clapham Junction. Although primarily used for local journeys, it can be a useful means of avoiding changing stations in Central London. The East London Line extension provides additional links with eastern and southern parts of Greater London.

Merseyrail

Rail House, Lord Nelson Street Liverpool L1 1JF
t 0151 702 2071 (Mobility Helpline)
textphone 0151 702 2071 web www.merseyrail.org

Merseyrail provides local rail services over most of Merseyside and the Wirral. The primary connection is at Liverpool Lime Street. There is an ongoing programme to improve interchange links to accessible bus services with MerseyTravel (see **www.merseytravel.gov.uk**).

National Express East Anglia

Customer Relations, Norwich Railway Station, Station Approach, Norwich NR1 1EF
t 0845 600 7245 textphone 0845 606 7245
web www.nationalexpresseastanglia.com

National Express East Anglia operates Intercity and local services from London Liverpool Street and local services throughout East Anglia. These include Stansted Express trains between London and Stansted Airport and also services to Harwich International for ferry services to Denmark, Germany and Holland.

OPENBRITAIN.NET
The one-stop-shop for all your travel needs. Go online and see how we can help you get in, out ...and about.

East Coast

t **08457 225 111**
textphone **0845 1202 067**
web **www.eastcoast.co.uk**

East Coast runs long-distance services between London and Scotland through Yorkshire and North East England. The London terminal is King's Cross which is next to the Eurostar Terminal at St Pancras International. Established connections for other means of transport can be made at Newcastle for both the airport and ferries to Darlington for Humberside Airport, Leeds for Leeds/Bradford Airport and Doncaster for Robin Hood Airport.

© ATOC

Northern Rail

Customer Relations, Freepost (RLSL-ABEC-BGUU)
Northern Rail Ltd, Leeds LS1 4DY
t **0845 600 0125**
textphone **0845 604 5608**
e **assistance@northernrail.org**
web **www.northernrail.org**

Northern Rail operates local and regional rail services across northern England. A booklet, "A Guide for Customers with Disabilities" is available from their staffed stations and can be downloaded from the website. There are connections to Inter-City services at many locations and services to Manchester Airport and Liverpool South Parkway for Liverpool John Lennon Airport

South West Trains

Customer Service Centre, Overline House,
Blechynden Terrace, Southampton SO15 1GW
t **0845 6000 650 (opt 4)** textphone **0800 692 0792.**
web **www.southwesttrains.co.uk**

South West Trains run from London Waterloo through south-west London, Surrey, Berkshire, Hampshire, Dorset and parts of Wiltshire and Devon. There are also services to Bristol, Brighton and Reading allowing connections to many other parts of the national rail network. Interchanges include Southampton Airport Parkway that adjoins Southampton Airport, Feltham, Woking and Reading that all have coach links to Heathrow, Portsmouth Harbour and Lymington Pier for Wightlink services to the Isle of Wight and Weymouth for services to the Channel Islands.

Southeastern Trains

PO Box 63428, London SE1P 5FD
t **0800 783 4524 (assisted travel)**
textphone **0800 783 4548**
web **www.southeasternrailway.co.uk**

South Eastern operates services in southeast London, Kent and parts of East Sussex. Stations served include Ashford International for connections to Eurostar and Dover Priory for transfer to Dover Ferry Port. It also has services from Kent to Gatwick. A booklet 'Helping you access our railway network' and a station map guide 'Planning an accessible journey with southeastern' are available.

Southern

PO Box 277, Tonbridge TN9 2ZP
t 08451 272 920 textphone 08451 272 940
e comments@southernrailway.com
web www.southernrailway.com

Southern trains serve much of south London, Surrey and Sussex and parts of Kent and Hampshire. Among the stations served regularly is Gatwick Airport and there are also direct services between Brighton to Ashford International, for Eurostar, and from East Croydon to Watford Junction, which can avoid the need to change stations in London for people travelling between the south coast and the Midlands and north west of England. From June 2008 the Gatwick Express and Southern franchise merged.

Virgin Trains

Customer relations, Freepost BM6613, PO BOX 713, Birmingham B5 4HH
t 0845 744 3366 (JourneyCare)
textphone 0845 744 3367
web www.virgintrains.co.uk

Virgin Trains operates InterCity services between London Euston, the west Midlands, north west England and Scotland. Many Virgin services stop at Birmingham International for Birmingham International Airport. Other destinations include Holyhead Ferry Terminal, Gatwick Airport and Reading for transfers to Heathrow Airport.

Wrexham & Shropshire

The Pump House, Coton Hill,
Shrewsbury SY1 2DP
t 0845 260 5200 (Customer Services)
e info@wrexhamandshropshire.co.uk
web www.wrexhamandshropshire.co.uk

Operates direct services between London Marylebone and Wrexham, Shrewsbury and Telford, with connections for other rail services at Wolverhampton, Tame Bridge Parkway and Banbury. Trains are being renovated to include spaces for wheelchair users and adapted toilets.

Light Railways and Trams

Blackpool Transport Services

Rigby Road, Blackpool FY1 5DD
t 01253 473001
e jean.cox@blackpooltransport.com
web www.blackpooltransport.com

Blackpool's old tram system survived the tram services closures of the 1960s. It was not designed for use by disabled people but upgrades are underway and due for completion Easter 2012.

Croydon Tramlink

5 Suffolk House, George Street, Croydon CRO 1PE
t 020 8681 8300 web www.tfl.gov.uk/trams

Croydon Tramlink crosses southern greater London between Wimbledon and Beckenham through central Croydon with lines to New Addington and Elmers End. It has accessible connections with the national rail network at Wimbledon, East Croydon, (where there are trains to Gatwick Airport) and Beckenham Junction. At Wimbledon there are passenger lifts providing connections to other rail services as well as from street level. There are tactile strips along the length of each stop to assist blind and partially sighted people. Wheelchair users can easily board and alight; next to the wheelchair space is an intercom to speak to the driver in an emergency and a stop request button, both at low level.

© ATOC

Greater Manchester

Metrolink House, Queens Road, Manchester M8 0RY
t 0161 205 2000 e customerservices@metrolink.co.uk
web www.metrolink.co.uk

Metrolink has services to Manchester Piccadilly Station from Altrincham, Bury and Eccles, via Salford Quays and also through services between Altrincham and Bury. Where required, mainly sections that had been railway lines, lifts have been provided to the platforms. Most platforms have tactile edges for visually impaired passengers and all platforms have designated wheelchair/pushchair access points for step-free access. Each tram has designated disabled/pushchair areas with its own emergency and information call points. Bus interchanges and Park & Rides have been established at several points and the service provides an accessible link between Victoria and Piccadilly stations. A £1bn investment project is ongoing to replace all Metrolink tram track, with 4 new tram lines now under construction. There are lower fares and free travel for some disabled people.

London Docklands

t 020 7363 9700 textphone 020 7093 0999
e cservice@dlr.co.uk web www.tfl.co.uk

The Docklands Light Railway operates an expanding network of routes from the City of London through east and south-east London. It was designed from the outset to be accessible by disabled people, with carriage entrances level with the platforms. There is an extension by covered walkway with London City Airport. The line extension to Woolwich Arsenal Station is completed. Other useful accessible interchanges with the national rail network are at Greenwich, Lewisham and Stratford. Persons over 18 who live in Greater London should check the Travel Mentoring Scheme - **t 020 3054 4361**

Nottingham

t 0115 942 7777 e info@thetram.net
web www.thetram.net

Nottingham Express Transit (NET) runs from Hucknall, north of Nottingham, through the city centre to Nottingham railway station. It also has a branch to Phoenix Park Park & Ride near M1 Junction 26. NET incorporates 5 free Park & Ride sites. There are accessible buses to Nottingham East Midlands Airport.

Sheffield

t 0114 272 8282
e enquiries@supertram.com
web www.supertram.com

Stagecoach Supertram has 3 light rail routes, which go through the city centre, and 5 Park & Ride sites that give easy access to the rail station, shopping areas, the 2 universities, the cathedral, sports arenas and entertainment venues. All platforms are accessible and the trams accommodate wheelchair users, have priority seating and low-level driver alert buttons. The Supertram Link bus service extends the network. Staff are trained in disability awareness.

Tyne & Wear

Nexus House, St James Boulevard, Newcastle upon Tyne NE1 4AX
t 0191 203 3199 textphone 0191 303 3216
e contactus@twmetro.co.uk
web www.nexus.org.uk

There are ramps or lifts to all platforms. There is a gap/step between platforms and train that may be difficult for some wheelchair users. Work on the second and final phase of a £7m modernisation project at Sunderland Station is now underway. Newcastle Central, Sunderland, Heworth and Metro Centre have level, ramped or lift access to all stations. You can book assistance when travelling on mainline services for your complete journey with the operator that you start your journey from. A Metro Access Guide is available on request from Nexus.

West Midlands

National Express Ltd, Customer Relations, PO BOX 9854, Birmingham, B16 8XN
t 0121 254 7272 web www.travelmetro.co.uk

The Metro Tram runs from Birmingham Snow Hill to Wolverhampton through West Bromwich. All stations have step-free access. There are Park & Ride sites along the route and bus interchanges. Concessionary travel passes are available for blind and disabled persons.

Sea travel

There are many journeys within the British Isles and beyond using sea and air travel, or for which a ferry is appropriate. Many people will make their choice based on personal taste, convenience and cost. A particular advantage of ferries for some disabled people, especially drivers, is that they can take their cars with them and so do not have to hire one, possibly with adaptations, at their destination. Also, motorists are not as restricted in the amount of luggage that they take with them, up to the capacity of the car. Equipment remains under the control of the ferry passenger whether directly of left in the car – unlike with air travel, where it may have to be carried in the hold.

When deciding between sea and air travel, factors that need to be taken into account include the ability to move around, availability of toilets designed for disabled people and the chance to relax during a long journey. This can be relevant to some channel crossings where there may be a choice between longer driving distances and length of crossing times.

Port assistance

Port accessibility will vary from location to location but the only real difficulty you should encounter is if the port is too small or too shallow for the ship to dock. In such cases you will have to transfer from the ship to the dockside by tender. Many of these smaller boats are now able to convey wheelchairs, but you are advised to confirm this beforehand. Try and get confirmation regarding the suitability for disabled travellers of the onshore tours.

Top tip

- If a passenger needs assistance or information, get in touch with the ferry operator in advance, preferably at the time of booking, and get to the port in good time.

- Depending on the ferry operator, your pet may have to remain in the car for the duration of the crossing. Other than registered guide dogs accompanying a visually impaired passenger, your pet will not be allowed access to any area other than the designated pet areas on any ferry.

Ferry/cruise operators

Ferry companies and cruise operators will often insist that a disabled passenger be accompanied by an able-bodied companion for the journey, depending on the nature and extent of the disability. One reason for this is that in the event of rough seas, a disabled passenger may encounter difficulties. If you are planning to take the journey alone you should discuss this possibility with the company first.

Ferries can vary from large modern ships used on international journeys, which in most cases are accessible with lifts between decks, toilet facilities and adapted cabins, through to much simpler vessels on estuary crossings with open car decks that may be accessible by virtue of their lack of facilities, and the short space of time that they are used.

When travelling by sea, note that getting around the ship can be difficult in rough weather; in catering areas furniture will be more likely to be fixed or difficult to move. Doors, particularly to deck areas, will usually be heavy and many staircases will be steep.

Cabins for the disabled, especially on more modern ships, are usually placed with better access to all public areas and lifts. They are designed with wider doorways, hand bars, low level controls, low door peep holes and specially designed spacious bathrooms. It is worth checking that balcony suites have ramps onto the verandah, that outside decks can be reached without assistance and that lifts are wide enough for your wheelchair.

Some cruise companies may ask that you are medically fit to travel, and provide proof of this, before travelling. It is essential that you confirm any requirements that the ferry or cruise company may have before booking your trip.

Try and give the cruise company you are travelling with as much notice as possible of your disability. They may ask that you book through their reservation centre in order that any requirements you may have can be noted on your booking, which will avoid any confusion later on. For this reason it is important that you are frank about your disability and any special needs you may have. Also some of the company's fleet of ships may be more disabled friendly than others.

Boarding

Boarding procedures will vary depending on whether you travel with a vehicle or as a foot passenger. If any member of a party travelling by car has impaired mobility this must be brought to the attention of the boarding staff, so that the car may be parked near the lift. This will require early check-in but does not necessarily mean early boarding.

Boarding is usually via a ramped walkway (which may be long) for foot passengers, although there may be a step or a steep lip when entering or leaving the ship. In some instances foot passengers use the car deck and its associated lifts. Some people who do not usually use a wheelchair may be advised to use one for boarding and disembarking

Assistance dogs

If you are considering taking an assistance dog on a cruise you must inform the cruise company and ensure your dog complies with the Pet Travel Scheme. You will also be responsible for clearing up after your dog. However, you may not be allowed to take your dog ashore in many foreign countries, so you should check this before travelling, along with any vaccinations that may be required for your dog. On board cruise ships Braille facilities are fairly standard, with lift buttons, deck numbers and cabin numbers in Braille. You should also be able to request a menu in Braille.

For deaf and hearing-impaired passengers, many cruises have special equipment such as telephone amplifiers, and lights that indicate someone has knocked on the cabin door, or that the smoke alarm has been activated.

Ferry companies

Brittany Ferries

Millbay, Plymouth, PL1 3EW
t 0871 244 0744   textphone 0871 244 0425
web www.brittanyferries.co.uk

Plymouth	► Roscoff / Santander
Poole	► Cherbourg
Portsmouth	► Caen / Cherbourg / St Malo / Santander
Cork	► Roscoff

Brittany Ferries is the major operator on the Western Channel with the above routes from England and Ireland, Normandy, Brittany and Spain:

The ships include both fast and traditional ferries with lifts between decks and toilets for disabled people, details available from the above telephone number. Those used on overnight crossings have some cabins designed for wheelchair users, which should be booked by telephone. If assistance is likely to be required it should be requested as far in advance as possible and disabled passengers are asked to check in at least 1 hour before departure.

© Britain on View

Caledonian MacBrayne Ltd

The Ferry Terminal, Gourock, PA19 1QP
t 0800 066 5000 (Enquiries)
e reservations@calmac.co.uk
web www.calmac.co.uk

Sails to 24 destinations on the west coast of Scotland.

A variety of vessels are in use. The timetable indicates whether there are facilities for disabled passengers. Anyone who may need assistance should notify the company when booking and checking in. Fare concessions for disabled drivers are available on production of appropriate documents.

Celtic Link Ferries

t 00353 53 91626 88 (Reservations)
web www.celticlinkferries.com

| Rosslare | ► Cherbourg |

Celtic Link operates an overnight service for vehicles and their passengers three times a week between Rosslare and Cherbourg. The crossing takes 18-20 hours. There is a lift between the car and passenger decks but no specific facilities for disabled passengers.

Condor Ferries

Ferry Terminal Building, Weymouth DT4 8DX
t 0845 609 1024
e reservations@condorferries.co.uk
web www.condorferries.co.uk

Weymouth	► Guernsey / Jersey / St Malo
Poole	► Guernsey / Jersey / St Malo
Portsmouth	► Guernsey / Jersey / Cherbourg

Condor Ferries operates a fast ferry service from the south coast ports of Weymouth and Poole to the Channel Islands of Jersey and Guernsey, and the French port of St Malo. A conventional ferry service also operates daily all year round excluding Sundays from Portsmouth to the Channel Islands and a Sunday service operates from Portsmouth to Cherbourg from May until September, recommended for taking caravans and motor homes.

On the fast ferries there is a lift from the car deck to the main cabin level where most of the passenger facilities are located including access to the outside viewing decks and a toilet for disabled passengers. The conventional ferry has two cabins with toilet facilities adapted for disabled passengers. Passengers with a hearing impairment can obtain information and make bookings at **sign-it5@hotmail.com**. Any passengers who require assistance must request it at the time of booking.

DFDS Seaways

Scandinavia House, Parkeston,
Harwich CO12 4QG

International Ferry Terminal, Royal Quays,
North Shields NE29 6EE
t **0871 522 9955**
e **travel.sales@dfds.co.uk**
web **www.dfds.co.uk**

| Harwich | ▶ Esbjerg (west coast of Denmark) |
| Newcastle | ▶ Ijmuiden (near Amsterdam) |

DFDS operate the above services which carry both foot and vehicle passengers.

The ferry terminal at Harwich is next to Harwich International railway station, there are coaches that connect with sailings to and from the main stations at Newcastle and Amsterdam and regular bus services from the terminal at Esbjerg.

Eurotunnel

UK Terminal, Ashford Road, Folkestone CT18 8XX
t **0844 335 3535** web **www.eurotunnel.com**

Eurotunnel carries cars and other vehicles, with their passengers, on frequent shuttle trains through the Channel Tunnel between the outskirts of Folkestone and Calais. For disabled people an advantage of this service is that they can stay in their car throughout the 35-minute journey if they wish. Drivers of cars carrying disabled people should arrive at least 45 minutes ahead of their booked departure time make themselves known at check-in. Vehicles carrying anyone who may need assistance in the event of an emergency will be loaded at the front of the shuttle. The single-storey Terminal Buildings, with shops and catering outlets, have low level telephones and toilets for disabled people. Eurotunnel is approved under PETS and can therefore carry assistance dogs with appropriate documentation.

Hovertravel Ltd

Quay Road, Ryde, Isle of Wight PO33 2HB
t **01983 811000**
e **info@hovertravel.com**
web **www.hovertravel.co.uk**

| Southsea | ▶ Ryde (Isle of Wight) |

Hovertravel operates a fast crossing for foot passengers between Southsea and Ryde by hovercraft – the only hovercraft service in British waters. There is a lift for boarding and spaces for two passengers in wheelchairs on each craft. Their most modern craft has an additional wheelchair space and an induction loop. The terminals have adjacent parking, toilets for disabled people and wheelchairs for transfer to and from the craft. There is a shuttle bus service between the Southsea Terminal t **023 9281 1000** and rail stations in Portsmouth. There are easy connections to bus and rail at the Ryde Terminal.

Irish Ferries

Contact Centre, PO Box 19,
Alexandra Road Ferryport, Dublin 1
t **+ 35 31 0818 300 400**
e **info@irishferries.com**
web **www.irishferries.com**

UK office: Corn Exchange,
Brunswick Street, Liverpool L2 7TP
t **08717 300 400**
web **www.irishferries.co.uk**

| Holyhead | ▶ Dublin |
| Pembroke | ▶ Rosslare |

Irish Ferries is Ireland's leading ferry company carrying passengers and their cars between Ireland, Great Britain and France. All vessels have toilets and lifts for disabled passengers, designated seating areas and adapted cabins as well as port terminals which have been built to be accessible. Advance notification at the time of booking is requested if passengers feel they have more specific requirements. All information for disabled passengers can be found on their website under 'More Information' and anyone with more specific requests should contact the Disability Officers directly through the Contact Centre or
e **disabilityofficer@irishferries.com**

Isle of Man Steam Packet Co.

Imperial Buildings, Douglas, Isle of Man IM1 2BY
t **08722 992 992**
web **www.steam-packet.com**

Liverpool	▶ Douglas (Isle of Man)
Heysham	▶ Douglas (Isle of Man)
Belfast	▶ Douglas (Isle of Man)
Dublin	▶ Douglas (Isle of Man)

Operates services to Douglas from Heysham and Liverpool all year and from Belfast and Dublin from late March to September. The 'Ben-my-Chree' ferry on the Heysham route has a lift to all decks and two cabins adapted for disabled passengers. The Liverpool service uses Super SeaCats that have lifts for disabled people. However the SeaCats on the Belfast and Dublin services cannot be used by wheelchair users. A new large fast ferry came into service in 2009 and a new terminal in Liverpool is now in use. When making a reservation please notify the company of any assistance that may be required.

Isles of Scilly Steamship Co

Isles of Scilly Travel Centre, Quay Street, Penzance TR18 4BZ
t **0845 710 5555**
e **sales@islesofscilly-travel.co.uk**
web **www.islesofscilly-travel.co.uk**

Penzance	▶ St Mary's

The 'Scillonian III' makes a return journey between Penzance and St Mary's 6 days a week from spring to autumn with additional Sunday services in August and a reduced service in winter. The Penzance terminal is a 15-minute walk or a short taxi journey from Penzance Station. Passengers can board and disembark using wheelchairs. Powered scooters have to be carried as cargo but a manual wheelchair is available for scooter users; this should be requested in advance. There is a stair lift on the main staircase on board to which wheelchair users have to transfer independently. Information on services between St Mary's and the other islands can also be obtained from the Tourist Information Centre t **01720 424031**.
For information on Shop Mobility Scheme see web **www.gopenzance.com**
or t **01736 351792.**

John O'Groats Ferries

Ferry Office, John O'Groats, Caithness KW1 4YR
t **01955 611353**
e **office@jogferry.co.uk**
web **www.jogferry.co.uk**

John O'Groats	▶ Burwick (South Ronaldsay)

A ferry service for foot passengers operates from May to September. The ferry can carry passengers in wheelchairs for the 40-minute crossing although there is no lift between decks and at tidal extremes it is necessary to use a different deck when getting off from that used on boarding. Staff can provide help but it is advisable to check in advance. The large car park at John O'Groats has a toilet fitted with the NKS lock for disabled people.

Coach transfers are available from Burwick to Kirkwall and between John O'Groats and Thurso and Wick rail stations. There is also an express coach service to and from Inverness. There are no specific facilities for disabled passengers on the coach connections although folded wheelchairs can be carried.

LD Lines

Continental Ferry Port, Wharf Road, Portsmouth PO2 8QW
t **0844 576 8836** e **mailto:booking@ldlines.co.uk**
special assistance t **+33 2 35 19 78 78**
web **www.ldlines.com**

Portsmouth	▶ Le Havre
Dover	▶ Boulogne
Newhaven	▶ Dieppe
Rosslare	▶ Cherbourg / Le Havre

LD Lines operates ferry services between Portsmouth and Le Havre with day and night sailings in each direction. Disabled passengers and those with animals are asked to check in 90 minutes before departure. The main vessel on the route, 'Norman Spirit', has lifts between decks and toilets for disabled passengers. However, there are no adapted cabins and the reclining seats have fixed armrests, although in rows of no more than two. LD Lines also operates services between Newhaven and Dieppe (in association with Transmanche Ferries), a new fast ferry service (since June 2009) between Dover and Boulogne and a new service (from September 2009) between Cherbourg and Rosslare.

North Link Ferries

Kiln Corner, Ayre Road, Kirkwall, Orkney KW15 1QX
t **0845 6000 449 (Reservations),**
t **01856 885500 (Administration)**
e info@northlinkferries.co.uk
e reservations@northlinkferries.co.uk
web www.northlinkferries.co.uk

Aberdeen	► Kirkwall / Lerwick
Scrabster	► Stromness
Kirkwall	► Lerwick

Operates ferry services to Orkney and Shetland from Aberdeen and between Scrabster in Caithness and Stromness on Orkney, using three modern vessels. Each has toilets for disabled passengers and lifts between decks. Those used for overnight sailings have 4 cabins designed for disabled people of which two have enhanced facilities including hoists.

Concessionary rates and special boarding arrangements are available for disabled people. There are toilets for disabled people at each of NorthLink's terminals, and people using powered wheelchairs can board at all ports except Scrabster. Advance notice of passengers requiring assistance is appreciated.

Norfolk Line

Norfolk House, Eastern Docks, Dover CT16 1JA
t **0870 870 1020**
web www.norfolkline.com

12 Quays Terminal, Tower Road, Birkenhead CH41 1FE
t **0844 499 0007 (UK)**
or t **01 819 2999 (Ireland)**
web www.norfolkline.com

Dover	► Kirkwall / Lerwick
Dover	► Dunkirk
Liverpool	► Belfast / Dublin
Rosyth	► Zeebrugge

Norfolk Line operates a round-the-clock car ferry service using modern vessels. Ferries to France, Ireland, Scotland, Belgium and Dover. Foot passengers and coaches are not carried. Advance notice is requested for passengers who may need assistance.

Orkney Ferries

Shore Street, Kirkwall, Orkney KW15 1LG
t **01856 872044** e info@orkneyferries.co.uk
web www.orkneyferries.co.uk

Orkney Mainland to 13 of the smaller islands.

Facilities for disabled passengers vary according to the vessels used.

P&O Ferries

Channel House, Channel View Road,
Dover CT17 9TJ
t **0871 664 2121** e help@poferries.com
web www.poferries.com

Dover	► Calais
Hull	► Rotterdam / Zebrugge
Portsmouth	► Bilbao

Advice on the facilities on the ship is available when booking and at least 48 hours notice is requested for any assistance that may be required.

P&O Irish Sea

Larne Harbour, Larne BT40 1AW
t **0871 664 4999** textphone **01304 223090**
web www.poirishsea.com

Liverpool	► Dublin
Troon	► Larne
Cairnryan	► Larne

Operates both fast craft and conventional ferries between Larne and Cairnryan and fast craft on a summer seasonal service between Larne and Troon. On board there are lifts between car and passenger decks and toilets for disabled passengers. A minibus is available at both terminals for foot passengers. There is also a car ferry service between Dublin and Liverpool. However, the vessels used for this do not have lifts between the car deck and the main passenger areas. Advice on the suitability of vessels is available when booking and at least 48 hours notice is requested for any assistance that may be required.

Pentland Ferries

Pier Road, St Margaret's Hope, South Ronaldsay
Orkney KW17 2SW
t **01856 831226** t **Gill's Bay 01955 611773**
web **www.pentlandferries.co.uk**

Gill's Bay   ► St Margaret's Hope (South Ronaldsay)

Operates car ferries on the 1-hour crossing between
Gill's Bay in Caithness and St Margaret's Hope on the
southern Orkney island of South Ronaldsay. No specific
facilities are available for disabled passengers.

Red Funnel Ferries

12 Bugle Street, Southampton SO14 2JY
t **0844 844 9988** e **post@redfunnel.co.uk**
web **www.redfunnel.co.uk**

Southampton   ► Cowes

Operates both car ferries and hi-speed passenger services
between Southampton and Cowes on the Isle of Wight. Ferries
have lifts and there are toilets for disabled passengers on
board and at terminals. At Southampton a free bus service,
which can carry wheelchair users, links the ferry terminals
with the main railway station and the city centre.

SeaFrance

Whitfield Court, Honeywood Close,
Whitfield, Kent CT16 3PX
t **0871 423 7119** web **www.seafrance.com**

Dover   ► Calais

SeaFrance operates vehicle and foot passenger ferries
between Dover and Calais. The vessels used are modern
with facilities for disabled passengers. Advance notice of
any assistance that may be required is requested. Any car
driver carrying a disabled passenger should advise the call
centre or click the box on the website when booking and
should also make themselves known at check-in.

Shetland Islands Council Ferry

Port Administration Building, Sella Ness,
Shetland ZE2 9QR
t **01806 244200**
e **ferries@sic.shetland.gov.uk**
web **www.shetland.gov.uk/ferries**
t **Shetlands Island Council 01595 693 535**

Shetland Islands Council operates 13 ferries serving
9 islands from 16 terminals.

Facilities for disabled passengers at terminals, which are
often unmanned and built around 30 years' ago, and on
board, vary. Crew members can give assistance if required
especially if passengers indicate their needs when booking
or on arrival at the terminal.
To discuss requirements in advance call the above
number. Information on facilities for disabled passengers
at terminals and on board ferries is available on a website
hosted by Disability Shetland.
**www.shetlandcommunities.org/disabilityshetland/
shetland-access-guide**

SpeedFerries Ltd

Hoverport, Western Docks, Dover CT17 9TG
t **0800 917 1201**
e **customerservice@speedferries.com**
web **www.speedferries.co.uk**

Dover   ► Boulogne

SpeedFerries operate a fast, 55-minute crossing between
their sole-use terminals at Dover and Boulogne for vehicles
and their passengers. There is a ramped approach from
the car deck to the main passenger lounge and cafeteria,
where there are toilets for disabled people, although there
are steps to an upper deck level. Early check-in may be
required for appropriate loading. Disabled people who
may need assistance can make bookings through the call
centre, rather than the website, without the £10 charge
that is otherwise incurred.
Foot passengers cannot be carried.

OPENBRITAIN.NET
**The one-stop-shop
for all your
travel needs.**

Stena Line

Stena House, Station Approach,
Holyhead LL65 1DQ
t 0844 770 7070 (Reservations)
e info.uk@stenaline.com
web www.stenaline.com

Harwich	▶ Hook of Holland
Fleetwood	▶ Larne
Stranraer	▶ Belfast
Holyhead	▶ Dublin / Dun Laoghaire
Fishguard	▶ Rosslare

Stena Line operates 18 ferry routes across Europe and offers a ferry travel service to Ireland, Britain and Holland. There is a range of hotel breaks, self-catering and landbreak holidays, with the option to travel by car, rail, coach or on foot.

Two new superferries will be introduced to the Harwich and the Hook route, which will offer 30% more capacity and improved onboard facilities. Check website for details.

At present there are 2 crossings daily – day and overnight sailing. Assistance can be provided at both ports and on board, although as much notice as possible is requested. Pets can travel free of charge to Ireland; dogs must stay in the vehicle.

Transeuropa Ferries

t 0184 359 5522
e infouk@transeuropaferries.com
web www.transeuropaferries.com

Ramsgate	▶ Ostend

TransEuropa Ferries runs ferries for vehicles and their passengers from Ramsgate to Ostend on a crossing time of approximately 4 hours; 8 sailings per day cater to passengers with cars. The crossings do not carry foot passengers.

Facilities for disabled passengers on board the ships vary. Although some can carry passengers in wheelchairs, two have no lifts from the car deck and two others have small lifts with entrance steps. Therefore it is essential that anyone who cannot manage stairs notify the company at the time of booking. Guide and assistance dogs cannot be carried.

Transmanche Ferries

t 0844 576 8836 (Reservations)
web www.transmancheferries.com

Newhaven	▶ Dieppe

Transmanche has ferries for vehicles and foot passengers between Newhaven in Sussex and Dieppe in Normandy. Wheelchairs are available in both terminals to assist in transfer to the vessels and there are lifts between the car and passenger decks. One of the vessels has a 4-person cabin that has been adapted for disabled passengers. The terminal at Newhaven is within walking distance of Newhaven Town railway station and there is an adapted minibus between the ship and terminal at Dieppe.

Wightlink Isle of Wight Ferries

PO Box 59, Portsmouth PO1 2XB
t 0871 376 1000   e bookings@wightlink.co.uk
web www.wightlink.co.uk

Portsmouth	▶ Fishbourne / Ryde
Lymington	▶ Yarmouth

Wightlink operates car ferries on the Portsmouth-Fishbourne and Lymington-Yarmouth routes and FastCat catamaran services for foot passengers only between Portsmouth and Ryde. The vessels on the Portsmouth-Fishbourne service are equipped with lifts and toilets for disabled passengers and new vessels have been introduced onto the Lymington-Yarmouth route. Wheelchairs are available at all terminals and Wightlink can give contact details of companies with accessible taxicabs on the island. A Wightlink Disabled Persons Card is available giving discounted fares. For assistance **t 0871 376 1000**

Map 1

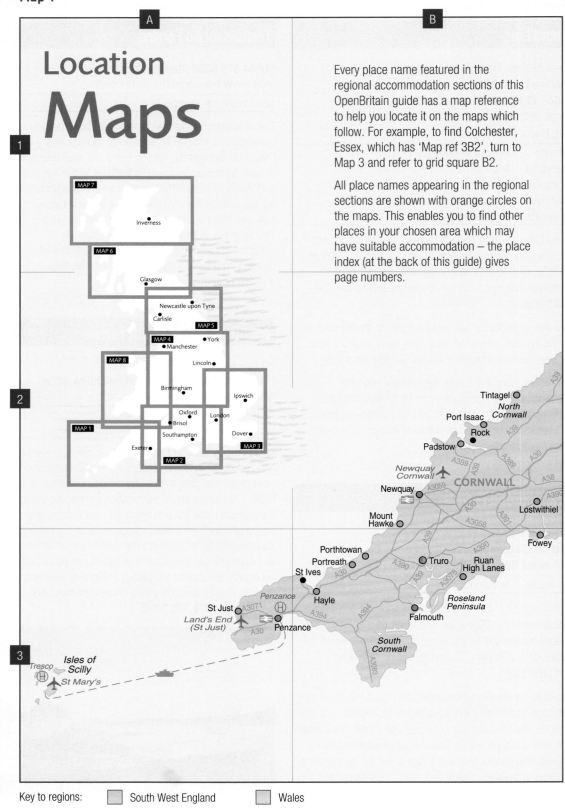

Location
Maps

Every place name featured in the regional accommodation sections of this OpenBritain guide has a map reference to help you locate it on the maps which follow. For example, to find Colchester, Essex, which has 'Map ref 3B2', turn to Map 3 and refer to grid square B2.

All place names appearing in the regional sections are shown with orange circles on the maps. This enables you to find other places in your chosen area which may have suitable accommodation – the place index (at the back of this guide) gives page numbers.

Key to regions: ■ South West England ■ Wales

Map 1

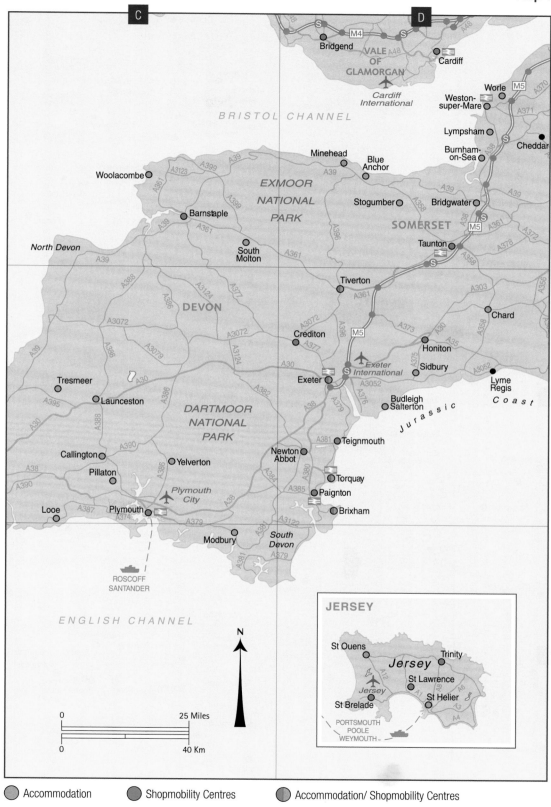

C

D

Bridgend

M4

VALE OF GLAMORGAN

A48

Cardiff

Worle

M5

A370

Weston-super-Mare

A371

Cardiff International

Lympsham

Cheddar

BRISTOL CHANNEL

Burnham-on-Sea

Minehead

Blue Anchor

A39

EXMOOR NATIONAL PARK

Stogumber

A358

Bridgwater

Woolacombe

A3123

A399

A39

A361

SOMERSET

M5

A361

A372

Barnstaple

A361

A399

A39

A396

Taunton

A358

A378

North Devon

A39

South Molton

A361

A303

A356

DEVON

A386

A3124

A377

Tiverton

A361

Chard

A35

A3072

A373

A30

A358

Crediton

A396

M5

Honiton

A375

A3052

Tresmeer

A3072

A3124

A30

A382

Exeter International

Sidbury

Lyme Regis

A395

Launceston

A388

A386

Exeter

A3052

A376

Budleigh Salterton

Coast

DARTMOOR NATIONAL PARK

A38

A379

Jurassic

Callington

A390

A386

Yelverton

A381

Teignmouth

Pillaton

A38

A390

Plymouth City

A38

Newton Abbot

A380

Torquay

A384

A385

Paignton

Looe

A387

Plymouth

A374

A379

Brixham

Modbury

A3122

South Devon

A381

A379

ROSCOFF SANTANDER

ENGLISH CHANNEL

N

0   25 Miles

0   40 Km

JERSEY

St Ouens

Trinity

Jersey

A12

St Lawrence

Jersey

St Helier

St Brelade

A3

PORTSMOUTH POOLE WEYMOUTH

⬤ Accommodation   ⬤ Shopmobility Centres   ◐ Accommodation/ Shopmobility Centres

Map 2

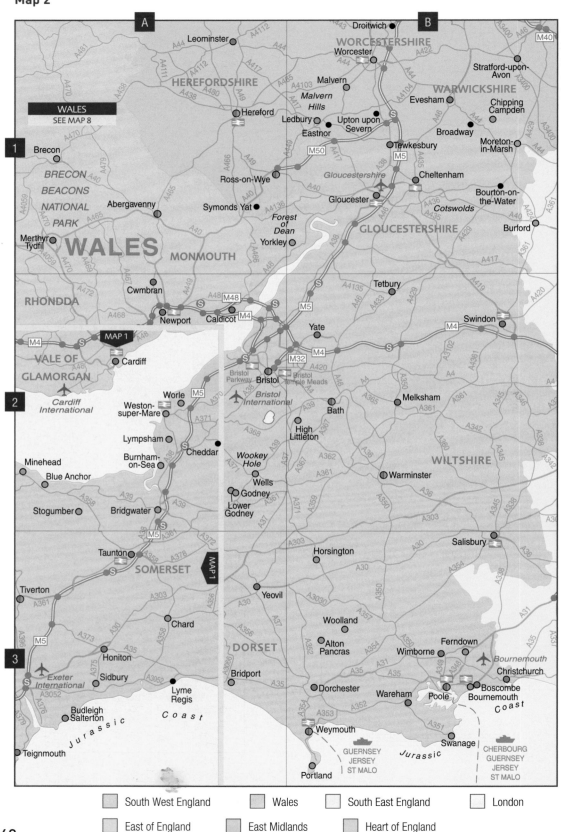

South West England | Wales | South East England | London
East of England | East Midlands | Heart of England

Map 2

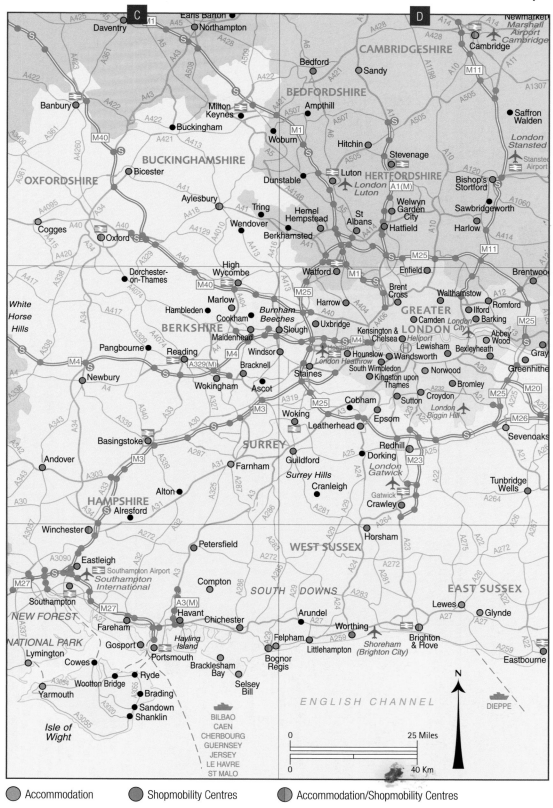

C D

Daventry • Earls Barton
Northampton •

A425 A45

M1 A5 A43 A428 A428 A14 A14 Newmarket
Marshall
Airport
Cambridge
Cambridge •

A422 A43 A508 A509 A422 A421 A10 A1198 M11 A1307

Banbury • Milton
Keynes
Buckingham • Bedford • Sandy •

A422 A422 A507 A507 A505 A505 A120 A1060 Saffron
Walden •

BEDFORDSHIRE CAMBRIDGESHIRE

M40 Bicester • Woburn •
M1 Hitchin • Stevenage
London
Stansted Stansted
Airport

OXFORDSHIRE BUCKINGHAMSHIRE Dunstable Luton
London
Luton A1(M) Bishop's
Stortford

Aylesbury • Tring • Hemel
Hempstead St
Albans Welwyn
Garden
City Sawbridgeworth •

Cogges • Wendover • Berkhamsted Hatfield Harlow • M11

Oxford • High
Wycombe Watford • Brent
Cross Enfield • Brentwood •

Dorchester-
on-Thames • M25 M1
M25 Walthamstow •
Romford • A12

White
Horse
Hills Marlow • Burnham
Beeches Harrow • Camden
GREATER
LONDON Ilford •
Barking • M25

BERKSHIRE Hambleden • Cookham • Slough Uxbridge • Kensington &
Chelsea Heliport Lewisham Abbey
Wood

Maidenhead • London
City Gray •

Pangbourne • Reading Windsor • London Heathrow Hounslow • Wandsworth Bexleyheath • Greenhithe

Newbury • Wokingham • Bracknell Staines • South Wimbledon
Kingston upon
Thames Norwood • Bromley • M20

Ascot Woking Cobham Sutton Croydon M25 M25
M3 Leatherhead Epsom London
Biggin Hill Sevenoaks •

Basingstoke • SURREY Redhill M26

Andover • Farnham • Guildford London
Gatwick Dorking M23 Tunbridge
Wells •

Alton • Surrey Hills Cranleigh • Gatwick Crawley A25

HAMPSHIRE Alresford • Horsham •

Winchester • Petersfield • WEST SUSSEX EAST SUSSEX

Eastleigh Compton • SOUTH DOWNS Lewes • Glynde •

Southampton Airport
Southampton
International Havant
Chichester Arundel • Worthing Brighton
& Hove

Southampton M27 Fareham Felpham Shoreham
(Brighton City) Eastbourne •

NEW FOREST Lymington Gosport Hayling
Island Bognor
Regis Littlehampton

NATIONAL PARK Cowes • Portsmouth Bracklesham
Bay ENGLISH CHANNEL DIEPPE

Wootton Bridge Ryde • Selsey
Bill

Yarmouth • Brading •
Sandown
Shanklin BILBAO
CAEN
CHERBOURG
GUERNSEY
JERSEY
LE HAVRE
ST MALO

Isle of
Wight N

0 25 Miles

0 40 Km

⬤ Accommodation   ⬤ Shopmobility Centres   ⬤ Accommodation/Shopmobility Centres

Map 3

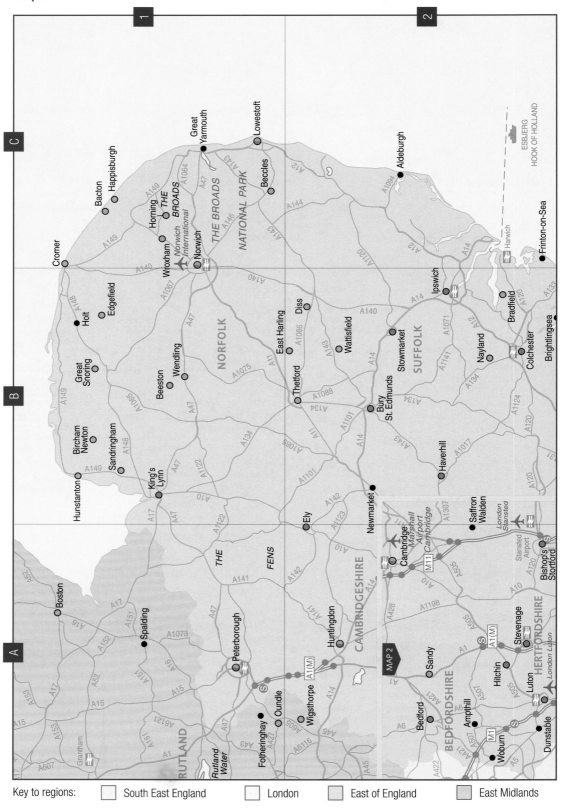

Key to regions: ☐ South East England ☐ London ☐ East of England ☐ East Midlands

Map 3

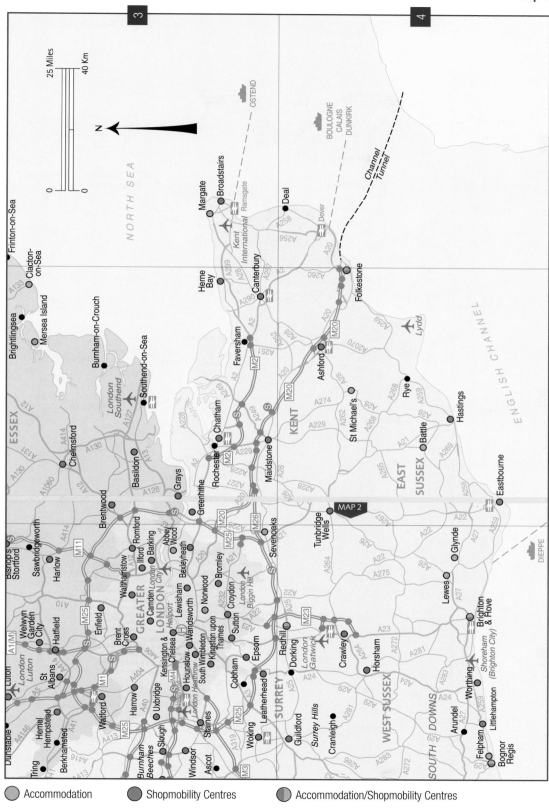

Accommodation Shopmobility Centres Accommodation/Shopmobility Centres

Map 4

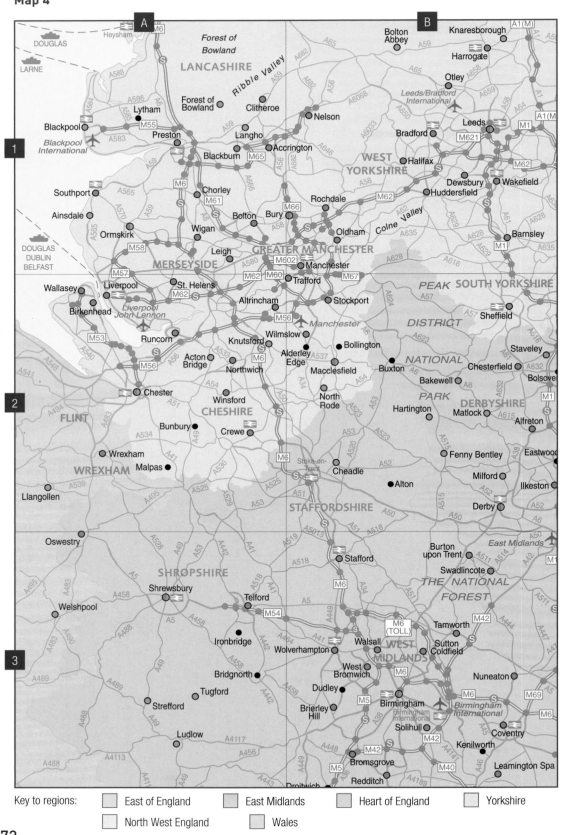

Key to regions: East of England · East Midlands · Heart of England · Yorkshire · North West England · Wales

Map 4

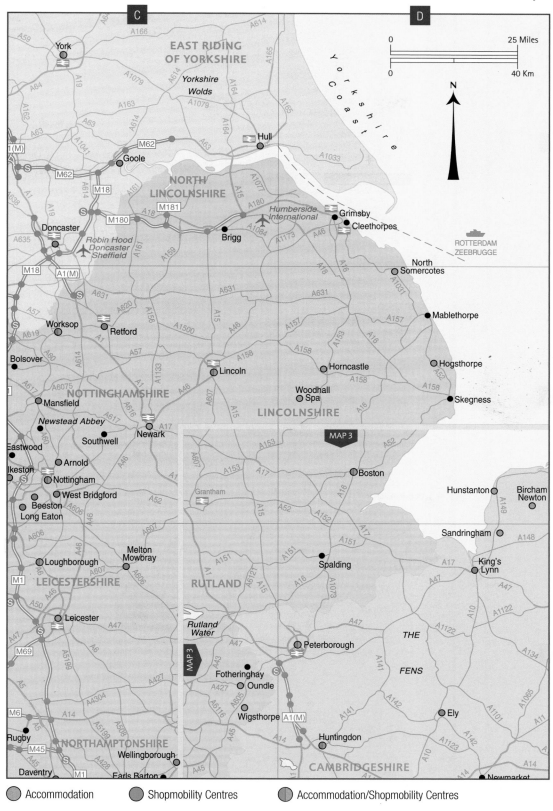

Accommodation   Shopmobility Centres   Accommodation/Shopmobility Centres

Map 5

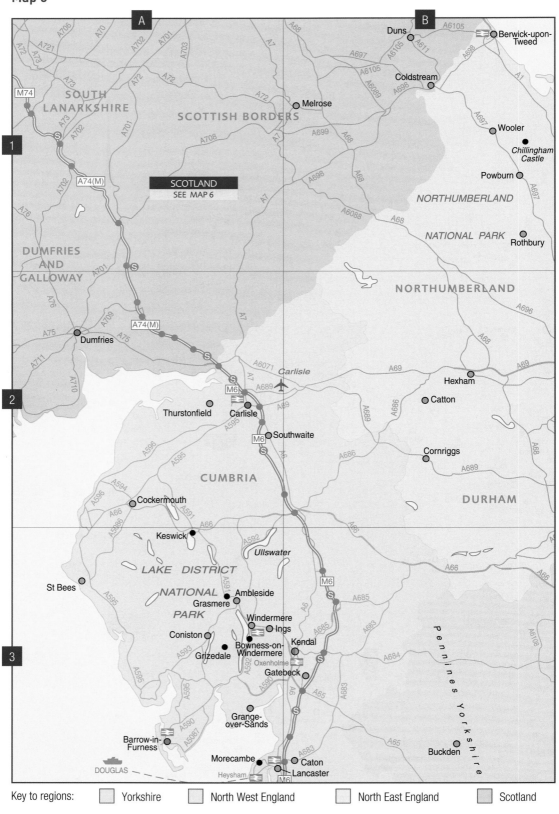

Key to regions: Yorkshire   North West England   North East England   Scotland

Map 5

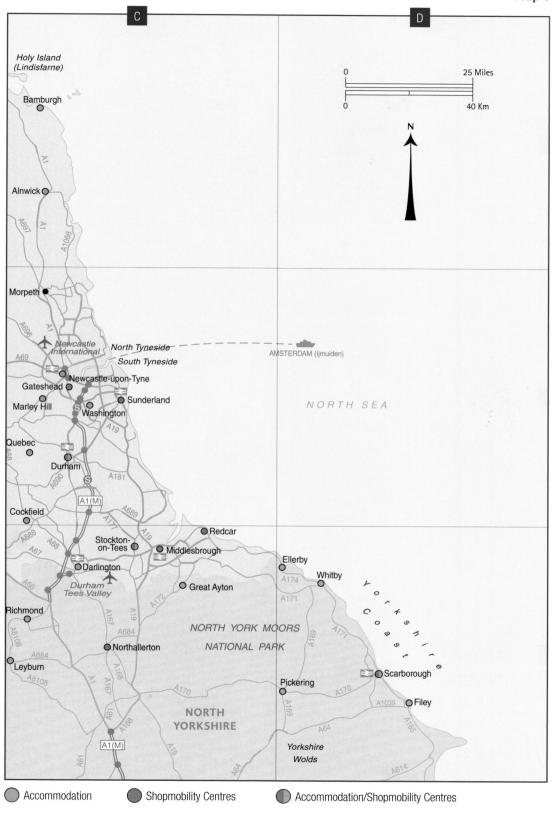

Holy Island
(Lindisfarne)

Bamburgh

Alnwick

0   25 Miles

0   40 Km

N

Morpeth

Newcastle
International

North Tyneside

South Tyneside

AMSTERDAM (Ijmuiden)

Newcastle-upon-Tyne

Gateshead

Sunderland

Marley Hill

Washington

N O R T H   S E A

Quebec

Durham

Cockfield

A1(M)

Stockton-
on-Tees

Redcar

Middlesbrough

Ellerby

Whitby

Darlington

Durham
Tees Valley

Great Ayton

Richmond

NORTH YORK MOORS

NATIONAL PARK

Scarborough

Northallerton

Leyburn

Pickering

Filey

NORTH
YORKSHIRE

Yorkshire
Wolds

○ Accommodation   ● Shopmobility Centres   ◐ Accommodation/Shopmobility Centres

Map 6

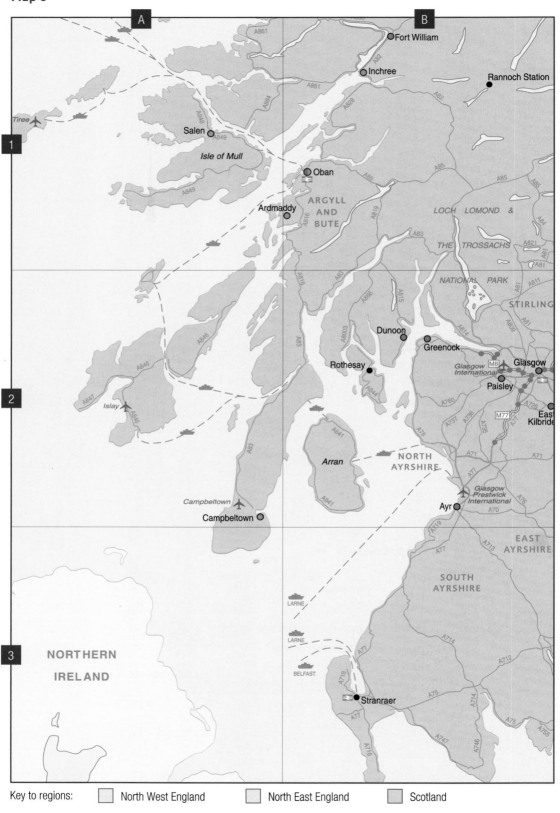

Key to regions: North West England   North East England   Scotland

Map 6

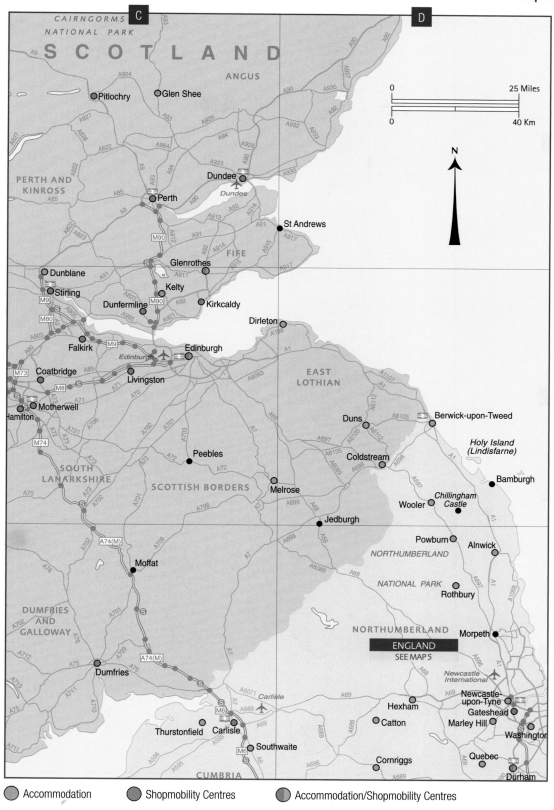

Accommodation Shopmobility Centres Accommodation/Shopmobility Centres

Map 7

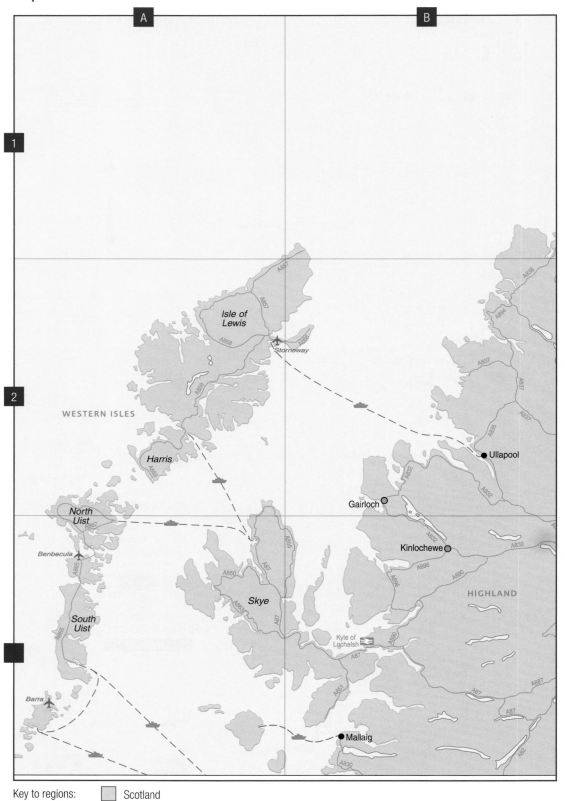

A

B

1

2

Isle of
Lewis

Stornoway

WESTERN ISLES

Harris

North
Uist

Benbecula

South
Uist

Barra

Skye

Kyle of
Lochalsh

Mallaig

Ullapool

Gairloch

Kinlochewe

HIGHLAND

Key to regions: Scotland

Map 7

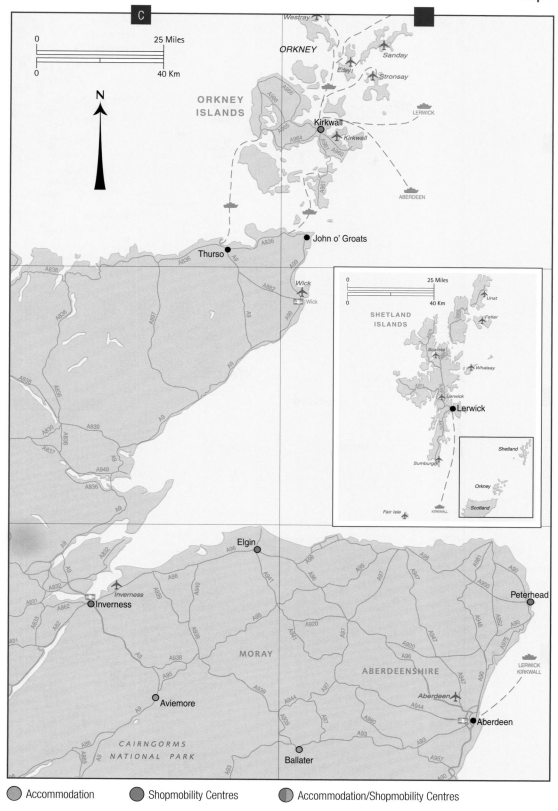

C

0 — 25 Miles
0 — 40 Km

N

ORKNEY

Westray

ORKNEY ISLANDS

Sanday

Eday

Stronsay

A966

A965

A964

Kirkwall

Kirkwall

LERWICK

A961 A960

A963

ABERDEEN

A836 John o' Groats

Thurso A9

A99

A838

Wick

A882

A9

Wick

A897

A9

A836

A838

A836

A839 A839

A836

A837

A949

A836

A9

SHETLAND ISLANDS

0 — 25 Miles
0 — 40 Km

Unst

Fetlar

Scatsta

Whalsay

A971

Lerwick

Lerwick

Shetland

Sumburgh

Orkney

Fair Isle

KIRKWALL

Scotland

A9

A832

Elgin

A96

A98

A95

A97

A98

A981

A90

A96

A96 A940

A941

A96

A947

A950

A9

Peterhead

A832 *Inverness*

A939

A920

A941

A97

A946

A952

A90

A862 Inverness

A831

A82

A95

A920

A947

A975

A833

A938

A939

A941

A920

A953

A9

MORAY

ABERDEENSHIRE

A947

LERWICK
KIRKWALL

A95

A9

Aviemore

A944

A97

Aberdeen

A944

A831

A96

A93

A960

Aberdeen

CAIRNGORMS
NATIONAL PARK

A93

A957

A889

A9

A93

Ballater

A90

● Accommodation   ● Shopmobility Centres   ◐ Accommodation/Shopmobility Centres

Map 8

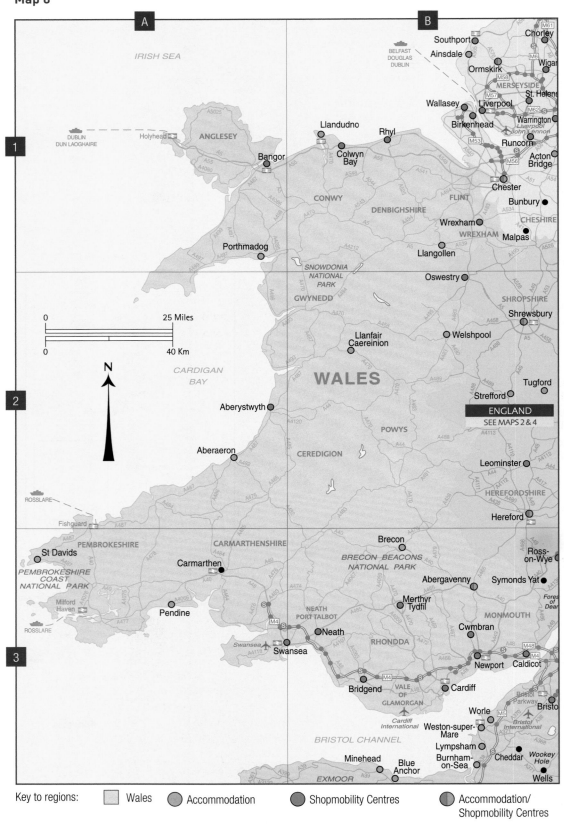

Key to regions: ▢ Wales ● Accommodation ● Shopmobility Centres ◐ Accommodation/ Shopmobility Centres

National Accessible Scheme index

Establishments listed here have a detailed entry in this guide

381

🐾 Mobility level 1 cont.

🦽 Mobility level 1 cont.

🦽 Mobility level 2

Mobility level 2 cont.

Mobility level 3 Independent

♿ Mobility level 3 Independent cont.

♿ Mobility level 3 Assisted

♿ Hearing impairment level 1

Index of Display Adverts

Index by place name

A

P continued

Q

R

S

T

U

V

W

W continued

Y

Index by property name

C continued

G continued

H

H continued

I

J

K

L

M

N

N continued

O

P

Q

R

S

S continued

T

U

V

W

Y

Z

Published by: Tourism for All UK
c/o Vitalise, Shap Road Industrial Estate,
Kendal LA9 6NT in partnership with
RADAR and Shopmobility UK

Chief Executive: Jenifer Littman

Chairman: Sir William Lawrence

**Compilation, design, editorial, production
and advertisement sales:** Heritage House Group,
Ketteringham Hall, Wymondham, Norfolk NR18 9RS
t 01603 813319

Publisher: Kate Kaegler

Publishing Manager: Sarah Phillips

Production Controller: Deborah Coulter

Group Director: Kelvin Ladbrook

Cover Photo: Supplied by Jubilee Sailing Trust
www.jst.org.uk **Design:** Jamieson Eley

Design & Prepress: PDQ Digital media Solutions Ltd

Printing: Burlington Press

Maps: Based on digital data © ESR Cartography

Photography credits: © Crown Copyright;
Alan Richards; Allan McPhail; ATOC; Bill Robinson;
Britain on View; British Tourist Authority; Daniel Bosworth;
David Williams; Duncan Phillips; Giles Park;
Historic Royal Palaces; Intercontinental Hotels; June Hoyle;
Jonathan Cosh/Visualeye; National Express/PAGE ONE;
Northwest Regional Development Agency;
NTPL/Hugh Palmer; NTPL/John B Taylor;
NTPL/Mike Fear; NTPL/Rob Judges; Pawel Libera;
photolibrary.com; Photofusion; Robin Smithett; Rob Wheal;
Simon Finlay; Stage Group; The Royal Yacht Britannia;
Transport for London; Visit London;
Visit Scotland/Scotish Viewpoint; Visit Wales; Vitalise;
www.freeimages.co.uk

© Tourism for All 2011

ISBN 978-0-85101-482-1

An OpenBritain guide.

OPENBRITAIN.NET